'*Chinese Male Homosexualities* is an original study of what happens when the translation of global gayness "fails". What we get are politically astute insights developed in dialogue between Kong and the Chinese gay men he came to know . . . in Hong Kong, London and mainland China. Resolutely anti-essentialist about both gay identity and Chinese culture, Kong convincingly argues that contradictions lie at the heart of queer struggles for rights, community and intimacy . . . a must read.'

– Professor Lisa Rofel, University of California, Santa Cruz, US

'There is no book out there like this one. Navigating between European ideals of liberal recognition and Confucian notions of filial obligation, between neoliberal markets and residues of (post)colonial regulation, between cosmopolitan consumerism and alternative socialist imaginaries, Kong's ethnography of Chinese gay men in Hong Kong, London, and the PRC is exhilarating and inimitable.'

– Professor David L. Eng, University of Pennsylvania, US

'*Chinese Male Homosexualities* is that rare and joyous thing: an intellectually substantial book that is also a good read. Individual interviewees' stories bring the intellectual arguments to life.'

– Professor Chris Berry, Goldsmiths College, University of London, UK

'This is a stunning empirical study of sexual worlds that are rarely associated with China, and a highly creative synthesis of the sociology of sexuality and queer theory. A powerful book that will be of interest to China scholars as well as sexuality researchers.'

– Arlene Stein, Rutgers University, US

Routledge Contemporary China Series

Nationalism, Democracy and National Integration in China
Leong Liew and Wang Shaoguang

Hong Kong's Tortuous Democratization
A Comparative Analysis
Ming Sing

China's Business Reforms
Institutional challenges in a globalised economy
Edited by Russell Smyth and Cherrie Zhu

Challenges for China's Development
An enterprise perspective
Edited by David H. Brown and Alasdair MacBean

New Crime in China
Public order and human rights
Ron Keith and Zhiqiu Lin

Non-Governmental Organizations in Contemporary China
Paving the way to civil society?
Qiusha Ma

Globalization and the Chinese City
Fulong Wu

The Politics of China's Accession to the World Trade Organization
The dragon goes global
Hui Feng

Narrating China
Jia pingwa and his fictional world
Yiyan Wang

Sex, Science and Morality in China
Joanne McMillan

Politics in China Since 1949
Legitimizing authoritarian rule
Robert Weatherley

International Human Resource Management in Chinese Multinationals
Jie Shen and Vincent Edwards

Unemployment in China
Economy, human resources and labour markets
Edited by Grace Lee and Malcolm Warner

China and Africa
Engagement and compromise
Ian Taylor

Gender and Education in China
Gender discourses and women's schooling in the early twentieth century
Paul J. Bailey

SARS
Reception and interpretation in three chinese cities
Edited by Deborah Davis and Helen Siu

Human Security and the Chinese State
Historical transformations and the modern quest for sovereignty
Robert E. Bedeski

Gender and Work in Urban China
Women workers of the unlucky generation
Liu Jieyu

China's State Enterprise Reform
From Marx to the market
John Hassard, Jackie Sheehan, Meixiang Zhou, Jane Terpstra-Tong and Jonathan Morris

Cultural Heritage Management in China
Preserving the cities of the Pearl River Delta
Edited by Hilary du Cros and Yok-shiu F. Lee

Paying for Progress
Public finance, human welfare and inequality in China
Edited by Vivienne Shue and Christine Wong

China's Foreign Trade Policy
The new constituencies
Edited by Ka Zeng

Hong Kong, China
Learning to belong to a nation
Gordon Mathews, Tai-lok Lui, and Eric Kit-wai Ma

China Turns to Multilateralism
Foreign policy and regional security
Edited by Guoguang Wu and Helen Lansdowne

Tourism and Tibetan Culture in Transition
A place called Shangrila
Åshild Kolås

China's Emerging Cities
The making of new urbanism
Edited by Fulong Wu

China–U.S. Relations Transformed
Perceptions and strategic interactions
Edited by Suisheng Zhao

The Chinese Party-State in the 21st Century
Adaptation and the reinvention of legitimacy
Edited by André Laliberté and Marc Lanteigne

Political Change in Macao
Sonny Shiu-Hing Lo

China's Energy Geopolitics
The Shanghai Cooperation Organization and Central Asia
Thrassy N. Marketos

Regime Legitimacy in Contemporary China
Institutional change and stability
Edited by Thomas Heberer and Gunter Schubert

U.S.–China Relations
China policy on Capitol Hill
Tao Xie

Chinese Kinship
Contemporary anthropological perspectives
Edited by Susanne Brandtstädter and Gonçalo D. Santos

Politics and Government in Hong Kong
Crisis under Chinese sovereignty
Edited by Ming Sing

Rethinking Chinese Popular Culture
Cannibalizations of the canon
Edited by Carlos Rojas and Eileen Cheng-yin Chow

Institutional Balancing in the Asia Pacific
Economic interdependence and China's rise
Kai He

Rent Seeking in China
Edited by Tak-Wing Ngo and Yongping Wu

China, Xinjiang and Central Asia
History, transition and crossborder interaction into the 21st century
Edited by Colin Mackerras and Michael Clarke

Intellectual Property Rights in China
Politics of piracy, trade and protection
Gordon Cheung

Developing China
Land, politics and social conditions
George C.S. Lin

State and Society Responses to Social Welfare Needs in China
Serving the people
Edited by Jonathan Schwartz and Shawn Shieh

Gay and Lesbian Subculture in Urban China
Loretta Wing Wah Ho

The Politics of Heritage Tourism in China
A view from Lijiang
Xiaobo Su and Peggy Teo

Suicide and Justice
A Chinese perspective
Wu Fei

Management Training and Development in China
Educating managers in a globalized economy
Edited by Malcolm Warner and Keith Goodall

Patron-Client Politics and Elections in Hong Kong
Bruce Kam-kwan Kwong

Chinese Family Business and the Equal Inheritance System
Unravelling the myth
Victor Zheng

Reconciling State, Market and Civil Society in China
The long march towards prosperity
Paolo Urio

Innovation in China
The Chinese software industry
Shang-Ling Jui

Mobility, Migration and the Chinese Scientific Research System
Koen Jonkers

Chinese Film Stars
Edited by Mary Farquhar and Yingjin Zhang

Chinese Male Homosexualities
Memba, tongzhi and golden boy
Travis S.K. Kong

Industrialisation and Rural Livelihoods in China
Agricultural processing in Sichuan
Susanne Lingohr-Wolf

Chinese Male Homosexualities

Memba, tongzhi and golden boy

Travis S. K. Kong

Routledge
Taylor & Francis Group
LONDON AND NEW YORK

First published 2011
by Routledge
2 Park Square, Milton Park, Abingdon, Oxon, OX14 4RN

Simultaneously published in the USA and Canada
by Routledge
270 Madison Avenue, New York, NY 10016

Routledge is an imprint of the Taylor & Francis Group, an informa business

Typeset in Times New Roman by
Florence Production Ltd, Stoodleigh, Devon
Cover design by K. Chan
Printed and bound in Great Britain by
CPI Antony Rowe, Chippenham, Wiltshire

British Library Cataloguing in Publication Data
A catalogue record for this book is available from the British Library

Library of Congress Cataloging in Publication Data
Kong, Travis.
Chinese male homosexualities: memba, tongzhi and golden boy/
Travis S.K. Kong.
p. cm. – (Routledge contemporary China series ; 52)
Includes bibliographical references and index.
(ebook) 1. Gay men – China – Identity. 2. Homosexuality – China.
I. Title.
HQ76.2.C5K66 2010
306.76′620951 – dc22 2009051976

ISBN: 978-0-415-45189-5 (hbk)
ISBN: 978-0-203-84920-0 (ebk)

For James Bell and JC

Contents

Illustrations

Foreword

Hybridic sexualities and the search for global intimate citizenship: introduction to Travis Kong's *Chinese Male Homosexualities*

Ken Plummer
(Emeritus Professor of Sociology, University of Essex)

> There are many ways to become, to be, to act, to feel sexual. There is no one human sexuality, but rather a wide variety of sexualities.
> (John Gagnon, *Human Sexualities*, 1977, Preface)

> We may all be sexual citizens, but we are not *equal* sexual citizens.
> (David Bell and Jon Binnie, *The Sexual Citizen*, 2000)

Human sexualities are – everywhere and always – symbolic, multiple and changing. The starting point of any study these days has to include a deep recognition of the multiplicities and varieties of human sexualities. From ancient texts to modern, it is not possible to travel far in the worlds of desire without encountering the documentation of massive human difference. From the *Kama Sutra* or the *Decameron* to Freud's polymorphous desire and Kinsey's continuum, the mobilities and flux of human sexual variety is a known core feature of human social life. There are multiplicities of sexual meanings, behaviours, identities, cultures and politics: and all are routinely in contradiction and tension with each other. In a sense, this tensionful flow is precisely what drives human life on. Any voice that speaks of a unified essence these days just cannot be taken very seriously.

Given human sexual diversity, all societies proceed to channel and regulate human sexualities – through various laws, customs and habits. The vast world of desire is always placed under certain restrictions. The when, where, why, what and how of sexualities help provide scripts, discourses and rules which channel these complexities into patterns. As a consequence most social orders function with notions of good (or insider) sexualities, and bad (or outsider/transgressive) sexualities. They are mutually reinforcing: boundaries mark out the good and the bad. But there is a lot of range, even here, with both the varieties allowed and the conventions established.

All this may be universal. But in the contemporary world, these basic processes – of diversity and control – have become embroiled with the wider process of globalization and glocalization. The diversities and sexual organization of one culture now enter other cultures through a host of processes (including mediatization, digitalization, migration, tourism and travel, consumption, global cities, etc.) to create sexual hybridization and a kind of sexual diaspora.

For some this has signalled the clash of sexual civilizations and sexual cultures (borrowing from the thesis of Huntington); for others this has meant a worrying sense that we may all turn out the same – the standardization, homogenization, even McDonaldization, of sexual life across the globe. But for others, myself included, we find that the pluralities of the past unfold into the new pluralities of the future. The sexual has always meant plurality, and now this pluralization is becoming increasingly visible and global, and is taking new forms. Borrowing Jan Nederveen Pieterse's delightful terms (in his *Globalization and Culture*), we could talk about the arrival of a 'global sexual melange'. We might go even further and talk about *the balkanization of sexualities* (where a dominant group (say the mainstream gay culture) splits and splinters into myriad other ones) and *the creolization of sexualities* (when a core group (say sex workers) is shaped by multiple influences from outside). The widest general process is what might be called the hybridization of sexualities, and with it comes a new politics of hybridity.

Hybridity in Chinese life

Travis Kong's inspirational book adds another elegant documentation to this ever-emerging mosaic of multiple global sexualities and their challenging diversities at the start of the twenty-first century. There is much to learn from it. The study aims to show 'the complexity of globalization in the kaleidoscopic life of Chinese male homosexualities – in Hong Kong, London and China' (p. 8). We are immediately in three different lands, with their wildly different histories. At the heart of this book are the case studies of what might conventionally be called 'gay men' in the cities of Hong Kong, London, Guangdong, Shanghai and Beijing. The men are all in some sense 'Chinese' and 'gay' but in these very terms lie definitional problems of the mysterious essence. At various times we enter the worlds of the diasporic and feminized 'golden boys' in London, the cosmopolitan and conspicuously consuming 'memba' in Hong Kong, and the urban and civilized 'tongzhi' and transient and stigmatized 'money boys' in China. These new worlds have meant 'the creation of different hybridized gay identities' (p. 194). Same-sex sexualities are never cut from the same cloth. A homosexual is not a homosexual is not a homosexual. We have to learn to live with (and love) the varieties, the differences, the hybridic.

Kong's study finds three broad clusters of Chinese men in *search of meaning* in their sexual lives, in worlds of rapid social change, post-colonialism, globalization – and confusion. It tells of emerging new *sexual stories* in which we find new *sexually imagined communities*. It is a study too of *the plurality, multiplicities and differences of sexualities* in the contemporary world – a move right away from any sense that there is one true Chinese sexual way, or indeed *any* one true sexual way anywhere. Shaped as they may be by familistic Confucian ideals from the past, there is now a flurrying of *new sexual identities* under construction and this book suggests a patchwork of such differences, as new identities generate *the hybridization of sexualities*. Here too *sexualities are always on the move* – across time and space we find *sexscapes*, *sexual flows* and *sexual mobilities*. These men transform their lives as they move to spaces full of new possibilities, as they move from the cities of the East to the cities of the West – from communism to capitalism, from rural to global city, from colonialism to post-colonialism. Kong plays well with the idea of trans: here are transnationals, transformations, translations and ultimately transgressions – drawing from Aihwa Ong's term transnationality but extending it. Here we have entered the world of *transexualities* ('trans' literally means 'across', 'beyond', 'over' or 'to the opposite side' – from the Latin). Here are *trans global sexualities* at work.

There is more. This is a study also of *sexualities as body projects*, as the men of this study work on their different 'Chinese bodies' to make them acceptable to self and others – displaying them, sexing them and reading the bodies of others. Yet as Kong remarks, Western body styles have 'had profound impact upon the Chinese gay male body' (p. 207). We also enter the worlds of *queer*: *queer identities*, *queer politics* and *queer global culture*. There is a *politics of sexualities* in which we find emergent *social sexual movements* and new-world debates on *sexual citizenship*, *intimate citizenship* and *cultural citizenship*, and the *new sexual rights* that are coming to be attached to the diversities of *sexual lifestyles*. Kong seeks to understand how his men become sexual citizens in these localities. We also see the working of the markets – as China opens its doors to capitalism and Hong Kong continues its long love-affair with this economic form. Each suggests new pathways of *sexual commodification* and neo-liberal *sexual individualisms*: for Hong Kong memba, consumer citizenship links gay identity with leisure and lifestyle; but it is there in discos in China too. Within all this we also find *generational sexual differences*. As Kong shows, our differences are also always generational: the Maoist period stressed social class for an older generation and was collective; but more recently a newer generation has become more individualistic (pp. 169–70) from socialist citizenship to market citizenship, as he puts it (via Keane) (p. 169) – 'a process of gay self-fashioning as a form of DIY citizenship' (p. 172).

Diasporic sexualities, reflexive understanding

There is, then, much to savour in Travis Kong's book. It is a study of hybridic sexualities and their refashioning across the globe. In this, his book joins a newly emerging field of study, in Latin America and in Asia, which looks at the shifting internal and external borders of the sexualities of nations and countries. There has been a recent flourishing of new work by new scholars who reject the presumptions of much Western theorization about queer and gay. The 2005 Asian Queer Studies Conference was emblematic of this when it brought together in Bangkok some 600 academics and activists. It marked a turning point for all this challenging new work. What we are charting here are hybridic and cosmopolitan sexualities in their lived political contexts. Often, as here, this research produces ethnographic work of the complexities and subtleties of grounded lives in specific locations, which is always much more messy, contradictory and ambiguous than wider theories or dogmatic positions allow for.

Often they connect – as with Kong's work – to deep personal struggles mirrored in their academic work. Here are the voices of many Chinese gay men for sure – but with the complete empathy of its researcher who has been there in his own life. Kong writes in a personal and engaging style – he brings an unstuffy (if still 'academic') way of reflecting on his own life as he connects with his subjects: he is not distant and far away, but very engaged: his own life deeply reflects those of many he has studied. Born in Hong Kong of strong but poor family, he makes the trips to England as a student, and explores his own heavily stigmatized Chinese homosexuality. This is not divorced academia poncing around. Kong writes from what he calls a 'transnational queer biography' and nicely muddles his text by its also being 'in part an analysis of my own life'. More and more of this kind of reflexivity is being demanded in the new social sciences. The old distances of fake and spurious objectivity are, hopefully if slowly, on the way out.

Sexual cosmopolitanism

I think here of a growing number of other influential studies this book joins: Richard Parker's *Beneath the Equator* (1999), Don Kulick's *Travesti* (1998), Martin Manalansan's *Global Divas* (2003), as well as Mark Padilla's *Caribbean Pleasure Industry* (2007) and Tom Boellstorff's *The Gay Archipelago* (2005). Studies such as these have led me to a growing awareness of what we might call sexual cosmopolitanism. For the moment I define this as an awareness of, and a willingness to live with, human sexual variety. The history of cosmopolitanism is a long, complex one showing the enormous variety of meanings that have been given the term. In its widest sense it has been defined as 'citizens of the cosmos'. For the Ghanian-American Kwame Anthony Appiah in his book *Cosmopolitanism: Ethics in a World of Strangers* (2006) it is a 'universal concern and respect for legitimate difference'. We could go on: Robert J. Holton's recent study *Cosmopolitanisms* (2009) has catalogued over 200 meanings. It is clear though that it is neither globalization nor multiculturalism. Nor does it mean to suggest, as it is often made to, a kind of sophistication, even superior lifestyle (usually associated with metropolitan living) – an elitist cosmopolitanism. Indeed, Kong suggests this may be the allure for some of his 'rural' Chinese gay men who are attracted to the bright lights of the city, and indeed make the change from unsophisticated gay to queer sophisticate within their work as they meet new experiences and see new classes (p. 179).

For simplicity here, we might just think of the political, cultural and personal dimensions of cosmopolitanism. *Cultural sexual cosmopolitanism* reveals the wide array of meanings and practices of human sexualities that forms the ways of life of multiple modernities – the vast array of sexual cultures, including gay, lesbian and queer ones. *Political sexual cosmopolitanism* takes us into debates about sexual rights and governance – of global intimate citizenship and ways of loving and living with differences in our lives. And *personal cosmopolitanism*, which suggests, following on from Ulrich Beck's influential study *The Cosmopolitan Vision* (2004 German; 2006 English), the ability – an attitude – to sense and empathize with a range of different positions in the world, many of which will be contested, and to seek out some common ways of living around them, and moving on.

The enemies of sexual cosmopolitanism are those who espouse *sexual fundamentalisms*. By this I mean those who (a) reject pluralism, (b) promote conservative and traditional beliefs in an absolute way, often critiquing all aspects of modernity and (c) usually refer to a time-honoured (often sacred) text which is given a strict and single interpretation. Kong also shows examples of a backlash of some Protestant- and Catholic-based NGOs that are actively and openly against non-normative genders and sexualities in Hong Kong. Just as we have seen the rise of sexual cosmopolitanism in recent decades, so we have also seen the continuing journey of sexual fundamentalism. This tension is a long historical one and it is not likely to go away or be easily resolved. It may be a feature of social life that needs dealing with in each generation.

Global intimate citizenship: universals in a world of differences

One recent pathway into all these tensions is the idea of intimate citizenship, which highlights the doings of gender, eroticism, relationships, reproduction, feelings and identities; and our most intimate desires, pleasures and ways of being in the world. It links all this to rights, duties and governance. There are spheres where people have rights and duties in their personal lives, where they can flourish with the best kind of intimate lives available to them, and where they can agree to disagree about what this is – respecting the diversities and differences of others. There is absolutely no way this can ever imply one model, one pattern, one way: it is a loose term which comes to designate a field of stories, an array of tellings, out of which new lives, new communities and new politics are emerging – exactly as Kong describes here. It suggests and helps to sustain public discourses on the personal life.

The struggles over such rights now take place not only in local arenas but also in global ones. They are part of universalizing strategies in what has now become the search for a global standard of human rights and a global citizenry. We see it embodied in the work of many NGOs and the work of the United Nations. Kant's famous principle – the peoples of the earth have entered into a universal community – has now been developed to the point where a violation of rights in one part of the world is starting perhaps to be felt everywhere. Cosmopolitanism above all else sees us as universally part of the same world but as incorrigibly different. *People everywhere are different and there is much to be learnt from these differences. But at the same time, 'humankind' is one.*

Ultimately, I think the book can be seen as a series of case studies in the making of intimate citizenship. In his three locales, Kong is concerned with the struggles to create a decent life and a valuable identity in sexual worlds that are very different. Case studies run through the book – the political struggle for sexual rights in the new Asian lesbian and gay movements; the paradoxes of seeking rights to be consumers in a capitalist-based pink economy and a neo-liberal world that marginalizes those who don't fit; and the growth of lesbian and gay marriage, and civil partnerships across the world. His three locales all provide radically different contexts for these concerns – coming as they do from vastly different histories of capitalism, family life and human rights. This is why the movement across these borders makes for such a fascinating book.

Kong is concerned with both 'rights' and advanced capitalism – and the debates of the contemporary neo-liberal world realities as they take major inroads to China, flourish in Hong Kong and are alive (if increasingly sick) in London. China itself has moved from 'socialist citizenship' into a new 'market citizenship'. And this has brought rapid changes and uncertainties. In London, we have a well-established gay and queer culture that is confronted by the new migrants: connecting to their families, advancing their careers and becoming 'overseas brides'. The neo-Confucian Asian families are so pre-eminent in cultural life and shape all this. In Hong Kong we find 'Sexing Hong Kong citizenship' (p. 46). Throughout there is a continuing problem of inclusion and exclusion. Here we find Asian familism, old colonial citizens with few rights, and capitalist cultures turned communist back to capitalist gliding round the globe, touching the most hip of Western queer cultures and life in the Big Cities, generating rights debates and ultimately adding to the global sexual melange. These are exciting times. The State of course plays a major role in all this – and Kong sees it as both 'an enabling and a limiting institution' (p. 203). In all three spaces, it now gives some support – even rights – to some kinds of homosexualities while still controlling, regulating and policing 'the others' at its borders. In this sense, the state creates the idea of the normal homosexual and the bad homosexual. Not all the new developments are for the good (he seems very critical of the tendencies towards objectification and marketization in the gay world).

Kong struggles to clarify many of the tensions that all this brings. He is concerned with the emergence of a sociology of sexuality that takes seriously the significance of categorizations and identities, and the problems this brings. He is concerned with the challenge of postmodern thinking in a range of fields – the postcolonial, the new space theorists and of course the lessons of the queer theorists. And he is concerned with the constant struggles between difference and sameness, the unique and the general, the cosmopolitan and the fundamentalist. In all this he attempts to bridge human rights and intimate citizenship with sociology and queer theory, the personal with the political, the local with the global.

A pluralistic universe

Over a hundred years ago, the leading American philosopher William James made his arguments for the world we live in as being a 'pluralistic one' – as have many others before and since. The challenge for all is to somehow live together with all this difference. And it is not an easy way. Too often we fall pray to unitary doctrines of sameness, and fundamentalist statements of the one and only way. Of course, living with too much plurality can push lives into chaos, and guides through this labyrinth are needed. But the recognition of pluralities has long seemed to me to be a requirement for living. As this book so clearly shows, we are the dialogic animal who dwells in difference, and we should never forget it.

Acknowledgements

This book is a culmination of years of study of the identities, intimacy and sexuality of Chinese gay men, and of even more years of trying to live as one.

I have accumulated many debts in the course of writing this book. My first thanks must go to my PhD supervisor, Prof. Ken Plummer. During my PhD candidacy and the various other stages of my career, Ken always gave me his kindest support, warmest encouragement and best advice. It is he who taught me that sociology should stem from understanding precarious human social life. It is also he who showed me how to live as a gay man with pride and integrity.

I am very grateful to the support from three previous academic departments to which I have been affiliated: the Department of Sociology, University of Essex (special thanks to Brenda Corti, Mary Girling and Diane Streeting); the Department of Applied Social Sciences, the Hong Kong Polytechnic University (my greatest gratitude to Prof. Diana Mak for her continual warm and generous support); and the Department of Sociology, University of Macau. I am also grateful to my present department – the Department of Sociology, The University of Hong Kong – for granting me time to finish this book. Special thanks go to the department head, Prof. Karen Joe Laidler.

I am deeply thankful to Carol Lai, who introduced Routledge's editor Peter Sowden to me. Many thanks go to Peter for his generous support for this publication and to John Thorne for his patience in polishing my English, as well as in providing me with critical and inspiring comments on a tight schedule. Needless to say, all imperfections and errors remain my sole responsibility.

There is no way I can thank all the people who have helped me to finish this book. I would like to thank, first of all, two of my teachers/friends – Dr Denny Ho and Dr Arlene Stein – who taught me in my early days and stimulated my interest in sociology. Without their encouragement, I would not have had the courage to begin my academic career.

My memory often lingers on those days in the 1990s when I studied in England, and especially on those days when I was doing my PhD; this was the most difficult period in my life, when I was travelling back and forth between Hong Kong and England, struggling with a tight study schedule and with financial difficulty, as well as living seemingly endless days of loneliness.

That's why I am particularly grateful to the friends whom I met through the University of Essex – Nirmal Puwar (I always miss you!), Sanjay Sharma, Klesse Christian, Lindsey Moon, Don Mahoney and Matthew Waites. They made my apparently unbearable days in the UK bearable through wonderful times of debating post-whatever-ism, sharing our longing for love, and struggling with all the vicissitudes of life. I am also thankful to Rob Stone (my MA and PhD internal examiner); Jeffrey Weeks (my PhD external examiner); and Julia O'Connell Davidson, who inspired me to study prostitution.

In the course of writing this book I have been very lucky to know the following individuals, to whom I am intellectually indebted, as they have inspired me and/or provided me with useful references and contacts: Natalia Chan, Pheng Cheah, Chen Kuan-hsing, Sealing Cheng, John Cho, Ding Naifei, John Erni, James Farrer, Josephine Ho, Hans Huang, Peter Jackson, Lucetta Kam, Jeroen de Kloet, Ben Ku, Russell Leong, Helen Leung, Lim Song-hwee, Dennis Lin, Liu Shih-diing, Kam Louie, Padilla Mak, Gina Marchetti, Meaghan Morris, Ning Yin-bin, Pan Siuming, Elspeth Probyn, Janet Salaff, Mirana Szeto, Denise Tang, Tang See-kam, Daniel Tsang, Day Wong, William Wong, Yan Hairong, Yau Ching and Audrey Yue. Thanks also to my students, who helped me in the final stage of proofreading: Cheuky Chu, Amory Hui, Alex Li, Collin Li, Eva Li and Vanessa Tsoi.

I owe a particular debt to the following individuals who read draft chapters of this book and gave me extremely generous, inspiring and useful feedback: Børge Bakken, Chris Berry, Jan Currie, David Eng, Elaine Jeffreys, Lam Wai-man, Maggy Lee, Ken Plummer, Lisa Rofel, Arlene Stein, and two of my dearest colleagues/friends, Ho Sik-ying and Karen Joe Laidler.

Different friends at different points of my life have given me their precious love, meticulous support, and timely encouragement, even though they may not have noticed doing so. They have contributed not only to the creation of this book, but also to the conditions that made it possible. I am deeply thankful to them: Amanda Antell, the Chan family, Bruce Chan, K. Chan, Cheng Kin-man, Nancy Cheung, Connie Choi, Annie Fan and Henry Wong, Freeman Huen, Eva Hung, Hung Keung, Simon Ip, Teresa Kwong, Lisa Lam, Jenny Lee, Bobo Lee, Ken Leung, Mak Wai-kwong, Mak On-kei, Fion Ng, Ah Pad, Ellen Pau, Doris Poon, Poon Pokit, Johan Schnaus, Sikay Tang, Werner Valentin, Benson Wong, Wong kin-wai and Karen, Gloria Yeung, Kamy Yeung, Raymond Yeung, Kendy Yim and Gordon Young.

Very special thanks go to these men in my life: DY, who taught me that life, like theatre, is full of possibilities; Michi Schnaus, who gave me the most remarkable and memorable times when we were both in London; Francisco Morral, who kept me sane by offering his sweet smile, precious love and warmest support despite my constant immature discharges of anger, frustration and sadness to him; James Bell, who shows me the charm of insanity and provides the ideal resort in Perth where I can rest and recharge; and JC, who grounds me with concrete vicissitudes of life and delivers his best takeaway to me.

I have received the warmest kind of support and care from my family. I was born into a working-class Chinese family. Without their love and material support, I can hardly imagine how I would have been able to start my academic career. I am especially grateful to my three sisters. They are 'working daughters', in Janet Salaff's term, which describes young women in the 1970s in Hong Kong who sacrificed themselves by giving up secondary education and who ended up in factories to benefit the family economy. As a son, I was the beneficiary of a patriarchal family ideology, and was able to continue my education and remain free to pursue what I wanted to do in my life. I always feel indebted to them, and feel even guiltier whenever they say they do not mind. However, I deeply regret that most of them cannot yet read my work. I hope I will translate this book into Chinese for them, even though they may not agree with the arguments I put forward in the book.

Finally, I am grateful to the following individuals and organizations who have provided referrals: Chung To, Steven Ku, Rager Shen and Jacky Zheng (Chi Heng Foundation); Kenneth Cheung (Hong Kong Rainbow); Leo Yiu (Midnight Blue); Elaine Lam and Yim Yuet-lin (Zi Teng). Last, but definitely not least, I am very grateful to all of my respondents whose voices appear in these pages, who gave up their time for me and got little in return. I can only hope that I have done justice to their stories.

The author would like to thank the following for permission to reprint material in this book:

Raymond Yeung for permission to reprint Figures 1.3–1.4 (*Cut Sleeve Boys*, dir. Raymond Yeung, 2006); Leo Yiu for permission to reprint Figures 1.5–1.6 (Destination, Leo Yiu, 2009); and Nutong Xueshe for permission to reprint Figures 2.4–2.6 (In/Out: Hong Kong Tongzhi Art, Nutong Xueshe, 2007).

Hong Kong University Press for kind permission to reprint as Chapter 7 in this book ('Sex and work in a queer time and place'), a revised version of 'Outcast bodies: money, sex and desire of money boys in Mainland China', published in Yau Ching (ed.), *As Normal as Possible: Negotiating Sexualities in Hong Kong and China*, HKU Press (Queer Asia Series) 2010.

Koninklijke Brill NV for kind permission to reprint an earlier version of one section of Chapter 4 ('Memba making family') which was published as 'Where is my Brokeback Mountain?' in *Social Transformations in Chinese Societies* (2009b, 4: 135–59).

Abbreviations

CCP	Chinese Communist Party
HKLGFF	Hong Kong Lesbian and Gay Film and Video Festival
IDAHO	International Day Against Homophobia
LGBTQ	Lesbian, gay, bisexual, transgendered and queer
LRCHK	Law Reform Committee of Hong Kong
MB	Money boy
MSM	Men who have sex with men
NGO	Non-governmental organization
PRC	People's Republic of China
RTHK	Radio Television Hong Kong
SAR	Special Administrative Region
SIU	Special Investigation Unit

Note on romanization

All non-English terms are Chinese unless otherwise stated. I italicize all of them throughout this book – except tongzhi and memba in headings and after their appearances with full explanations in the Introduction, because of their frequent use. I include the Chinese characters in their first appearance in each chapter. I do not use English plural markers (e.g., tongzhi instead of tongzhis).

The romanization of Chinese characters follows the *pinyin* system, which is now widely used in mainland China and in most recent academic writings in other languages. I use http://humanum.arts.cuhk.edu.hk/Lexis/Lindict/, an online version of Lin (1972). Cantonese romanization is used for terms specific to Hong Kong, as Cantonese is the most common language in Hong Kong and is different from Mandarin (*Putonghua*), the official dialectic used in mainland China. Whenever Cantonese romanization is used, it will be specified (e.g., *tungzi* (Cant.)). I use http://humanum.arts.cuhk.edu.hk/Lexis/Canton/, an online version of Wong (1980).

Introduction

Bodies that travel

Let's travel to three locales.

13 December 2008 ***3 p.m., Causeway Bay, Hong Kong***

Today was the first Hong Kong Pride Parade. It began in the busiest area of Hong Kong, Causeway Bay. The theme was 'Celebrate Love'. The declaration of the parade was: 'We are *tongzhi* (同志): We are gays, lesbians, bisexuals, transgendered, cross-dressers, transsexuals, sex workers, SM role players; we practise sexual diversity'.

Expecting only 500 participants, the rather constant number that have appeared for the past four years at the International Day Against Homophobia (IDAHO) events held in Hong Kong, the organizers were very happy when around 1,000 participants – *tongzhi* or *tongzhi*-friendly participants – turned up, walked from Causeway Bay, along Hennessy Road, and ended up in Southorn Playground, Wanchai, where performances, dances and shows were staged.[1]

I went to Causeway Bay with my friends and marched under the sun and the clear blue sky. A queer friend from Taiwan said to me, 'It's nice to territorialize public straight space on a lovely Sunday afternoon!' I totally agreed with her, but my very best *memba* (Cant.: the local parlance used exclusively for self-identification among Hong Kong gay men) friend, a few days ago when I invited him to join the march, had said,

> Oh, I'm sorry, I can't make it. You know, I am not your type of people, I can't join you. It's too 'out' to go to the street! What if my family sees me in the crowd, from the television or newspaper? I'd better go shopping, Christmas is coming, I don't want to miss the final big sale!

To a certain extent, I agreed with my *memba* friend's attitude: Why should people with non-normative genders and sexualities have to 'come out' in the first place? To what extent does sexual identity relate to politics?

Hong Kong is a Chinese society that experienced more than 150 years of British colonialism before 1997, when it was handed back to China. It is now

Figure 1.1 Hong Kong Pride Parade in 2008 (author's photograph).

Figure 1.2 Performance in Southorn Playground, Wanchai after the Hong Kong Pride Parade in 2008 (author's photograph).

governed by a Special Administrative Region (SAR) government. With this specific colonial and post-colonial history, Hong Kong people have always been considered only 'partial' citizens, in terms of enjoying various civil, social and political rights.[2] If Hong Kong citizens are only partial citizens, how can we understand Hong Kong *tongzhi* who fight for their rights as 'sexual citizens'? With the colonial history and present post-colonial environment of Hong Kong, what kind of citizenship do Hong Kong *tongzhi* define and realize?

From the few *tongzhi* organizations that existed before the 1991 decriminalization of homosexuality – made a serious crime by the colonial government in 1842 – there has been a mushrooming of *tongzhi* organizations, as well as a flourishing of *tongzhi* commercial and consumption venues since the 1990s. Although the pride parade and the IDAHO events have been held, most *tongzhi* in Hong Kong are not passionate about political activism.[3] Discussing fighting for equal opportunities based on sexual orientation, bargaining for same-sex marriage, coming out to families and the public, fashioning a sexual citizenship, etc., apparently are not the major agendas inside the community.

Why is this the case? Why are queer identities in Hong Kong constituted more by conspicuous consumption rather than by political activism? What kind of queer energy can be produced if political channels are blocked? Why do Hong Kong *tongzhi* tend to negotiate an identity that seems to be confined within familial heteronormativity by the deployment of 'family biopolitics'.[4] To what extent have colonial and post-colonial governance and other social, economic, political and cultural factors contributed to the development of Hong Kong's *tongzhi* movement, and what (sexual) spaces can be created, imagined and practised?

23 July 2007 — *Monday 7 p.m., Jeff's house, London, UK*

I am sitting on the balcony of my friend/informant Jeff's penthouse in London. Born in Hong Kong, Jeff moved to settle in London at the age of nine, in the early 1980s, as a result of his family's strategy of social and economic advancement. We are discussing the films of our friend, the director Raymond Yeung, which Jeff has been involved in making.

Raymond's first feature film, *Yellow Fever* (1998), tells the story of a Chinese gay man, Monty, who has lived in London for many years. Monty desperately seeks a 'white knight', until one day he is confronted and tempted by his new 'yellow' neighbour, Jai Ming. Raymond's latest film, *Cut Sleeve Boys* (2006), tells the story of two Chinese British gay men who search for self-acceptance and love in London. One character, Ash, is an effeminate gay man who can only face his straight-acting ex-army boyfriend by wearing lady dresses. The other character, Mel, is a circuit muscle man who fits right into British gay culture but rejects his provincial white boyfriend, who runs away from Wales to London to live with him.

Raymond was the director of the Hong Kong Lesbian and Gay Film and Video Festival (HKLGFF) for three years (2000–2003). He admitted that he always had difficulty finding queer films made by Asians and, even if he found them, they were usually overwhelmingly concerned with the issues of coming out, family pressure or racial discrimination. He wanted to write a romantic comedy about modern gay Asian lives. *Cut Sleeve Boys* is a story of a new generation of British Chinese gay men who have no problem assimilating in London. Indeed, as Raymond says in the director's note, 'They have become the city itself – confident, successful, and sophisticated, with the power to choose. They are a new generation of British Chinese who dare to and can have it all.'

Why and what have made Hong Kong gay men migrate to Western countries such as Britain in the first place? Migration is always a complex act, which is triggered by many factors, such as poverty, social mobility, political uncertainty and even sexuality, and migration can be made individually or with family. Apart from the reasons of social and economic advancement, Hong Kong people, especially middle-class people and professionals, have been migrating to other countries (e.g., the UK, the US, Canada and Australia) from the 1980s and early 1990s, as a reaction to the political anxiety of the 1997 issue, the year when Hong Kong had to return to China.[5] In a series of highly visible migration tides, hidden invisible queer migration has occurred. If lesbians and gay men are only 'partial' citizens in British society, what about these migrant Chinese gay men, who constitute both a 'racial' and a sexual minority, and who live between British and Chinese cultures, and within a British-dominated gay subculture? In what ways is a 'native dreaming' for the West translated into an 'imagined and desired whiteness' (Frantz Fanon, *passim*; Manalansan 1993: 68), resulting in what we commonly call the 'potato queen' (i.e., an Asian gay man who is predominantly interested in Caucasian men); or in Raymond's

Figure 1.3 Mel with two men in a London club (from *Cut Sleeve Boys*, dir. Raymond Yeung, 2006).

Figure 1.4 Ash hugged by his ex-army boyfriend (from *Cut Sleeve Boys*, dir. Raymond Yeung, 2006).

re-appropriated traditional Chinese euphemism for the male homosexual, the 'cut sleeve boy'; or in what I have coined the 'golden boy', a young virgin boy who is innocent, infantile, feminized or even androgynous under the Western gay gaze (Kong 2000: Ch. 6, 2002: 31–39)? How many of such men can act like Ash or Mel – affluent middle-class Asian gay men who have no problems at all about assimilating into the mainstream white society and can be, as Raymond says, 'confident, successful, and sophisticated, with the power to choose'?

23 October 2004 *Saturday 11:00 p.m., Beijing, China*

Situated across from a busy main road, Destination is a new and trendy gay bar in Beijing. Even though gay bars in China have often been raided by the police, Destination still attracts hundreds of fashionable young men wearing fine designer-label clothing, form-fitting T-shirts and denim jeans that outline their genitals and buttocks. Without much knowledge about the queer subtext of what they are wearing, these young men apparently are keen to reject the labels of 'mental patient' and 'hooligan', the two dominant categories in which men with same-sex desire have been placed for at least the past four decades. They are proud to call themselves 'gay' or *tongzhi*, and very keen to embrace and consume the global gay look one can easily find in London, New York and Paris. Although living under the pressure to get married (or, indeed, already married), they have successfully manoeuvred between the straight and the gay worlds.

Initiated by the then General Secretary of the Communist Party of China, Deng Xiaoping, in 1978, many reforms (e.g., agricultural decollectivization,

Figure 1.5 Destination (2009, photo provided by Leo Yiu).

the creation of a market economy, the enhancement of social mobility, modernization and internationalization) have changed China's economic, political, social and cultural landscapes over the past few decades.[6] In what ways have all these changes, usually crystallized as 'opening up' (*kaifang* 開放) – which on the one hand resulted in an apparent lessening of state monitoring of private life and created a new social environment for young people in general, and gay men in particular, to engage in sexual and romantic interactions; but on the other, still rules out particularities of certain sexual behaviours and practices – affected *tongzhi*? What are the freedoms and pleasures, as well as dangers and dominations, created in these newly emerged social (and sexual) spaces?[7]

One of my young informants – Ah Bei, who was born in Xi'an and is now settled in Guangdong – said to me, 'I am a *tongzhi* . . . I am out to my family, at university and now at work . . . for me, being a *tongzhi* means culture, enrichment, plurality and passion . . . but my family still wants me to get married.'

In China, people – particularly those who live in rural areas – are still expected to get married and bear children. Literature repeatedly pinpoints that the family has been the major obstacle for gay men and lesbians to come out.[8]

Why is this the case? How can Chinese gay men live such familial hetero-normativity of 'family biopolitics'? However, the gay person has slowly been transformed from a mental patient or hooligan persona to a representative of a kind of 'new humanity' (Rofel 2007: 1) in the twenty-first century, allowing him/her to tap into individuality, difference, sophistication, liberation and modernity. How much does this transformation relate to the market economy, cosmopolitanism and neo-liberalism of globalizing China?

Male prostitution constitutes a major component in the gay scene in China (Jeffreys 2007; Rofel 2010). Bluntly labelled 'money boys', men who sell sex usually bear three stigmatized identities: sex worker, homosexual and rural–urban migrant (Kong 2005a, 2008, 2010). As rural migrants, they have always been considered outsiders in the cities, due to their rural *hukou*, the household registration system that restricts mobility in China. Inside the gay world, they are discriminated against, due to their rural status and their commercial exchanges for love. They move in and between big cities in greater China (e.g., Beijing, Shanghai, Shenzhen, Hong Kong, Macau, etc.) and/or other countries (e.g., Thailand, Malaysia, Singapore) in search of basic survival, economic opportunities, better living conditions, social mobility, love and sex. But is this rural–urban migration their only option? As queer transient labour, what is the 'bare life' (c.f. Agamben 1995)[9] of the money boy who wanders cities for love, work and, perhaps, liberation?

Figure 1.6 Destination (2009, photo provided by Leo Yiu).

Transnational study of Chinese male homosexuality and citizenship

Modern male masculinities and homosexualities have emerged in contemporary Chinese societies, in parallel with the fast pace of globalization, de-colonization and neo-liberalism. The result has been the development of the hybridized gay male identities 'gay (*gei* 基 Cant.)', '*memba*/member', '*tungzi* (同志 Cant.)/*tongzhi*', 'golden boy', 'money boy', etc., as well as of various queer communities and 'scenes' (Kong 2000, 2002, 2004; Ho 1997: Ch. 4 and 5; Ho and Tsang 2004a). How might we understand Chinese male homosexualities within the constellation of global gay culture? Globalization usually refers to a series of social, cultural, economic, technological and political changes involving an intense flow of goods, capital, data, ideas, images and people across borders, that constitute a complex interplay – integration, interdependence, conflict, chaos – among nations throughout the whole world.[10] To what extent does such an 'intensification of global interconnectedness' (Inda and Rosaldo 2002: 2) shape and influence the most intimate aspects of one's life? In terms of Chinese male homosexuality, to what extent does the intense flow of queer images, ideas, bodies, desires, capital, commodities, etc. shape the contours of Chinese queer space, or 'homoscapes' (Parker 1999: 218–21)?[11] How are such large-scale processes of global flow experienced, mediated, embodied, articulated, appropriated and interpreted by Chinese gay men who live in specific localities?

This book is about Chinese gay men[12] and aims to capture the complexity of globalization in the kaleidoscopic life of Chinese male homosexualities – in Hong Kong, London and China (major sites: Beijing, Shanghai, Guangdong) – with a thesis of citizenship and globalization. It documents how Chinese men realize same-sex desire, perform gay identity, organize same-sex encounters, form relationships, fashion queer spaces for their own use, fight against social discrimination and domination – in short, how they become (sexual) citizens in these localities. It tracks the numerous queer flows – of capital, bodies, ideas, images, commodities – that traverse the globe, and explores the lived experiences of Chinese gay men.

Globalization is an uneven and spatially differential process that reproduces asymmetrical patterns of inequalities and exclusions.[13] Scholars such as Ulf Hannerz, Aihwa Ong, Inderpal Grewal and Caren Kaplan[14] suggest that a 'transnational', rather than a globalization, study can address more accurately the asymmetries of the globalization process.

Building from these scholars' works, I use the term 'transnational' in four specific ways. First, I use *transnational* to mean, not only movement in space between nations, but also that between cities and regions. This book is thus a study of Chinese male homosexualities across borders, and discusses various Chinese gay male bodies, identities and practices that travel back and forth between different spaces, such as those of Hong Kong, London and different cities and areas within mainland China, such as Beijing, Shanghai, Guangdong, etc.

Second, the 'trans' of transnationality involves *transformation*. This book aims to examine the macro level of political–economic transformations that structure the lives of most Chinese gay men in the different localities. These involve, for example, the laws governing same-sex activities in all locales; the 1997 issue and (post-)colonial administration of gay male bodies in Hong Kong; immigration laws and recent legal reforms regarding same-sex partnerships which facilitate/inhibit the flow of Chinese migrant gay men to Britain; and the market reform and the 'retreat' of the state on private matters that have generated various sexual spaces in China since the later 1970s. The book also aims at an understanding of how the actors mediate these transformations by creating different publics and 'counterpublics',[15] and an articulation of various cultural and social meanings embedded in identity, desire and practices concerning love, intimacy and sexuality. It is through these dual processes of 'governmentality' – in the Foucauldian sense of both the 'being-made' and the 'self-making' of subjects (e.g., identity/citizenship) (Foucault 1982, 1988, 1991) – that the sexual politics of Chinese gay men are made.

In this work, the 'trans' also implies *translation*. As Erni (2003) has argued, many of us 'have dreamt of de-westernizing theoretical protocols instructed by western thinkers' (p. 381). But how can this critical dialogue be possible if global academia as a whole is 'a series of hierarchical centers of knowledge-power' (p. 382)? How is it possible 'to translate the translation' (p. 384), that is, to translate between Chinese cultural meanings and those supplied by globalized, hierarchic academia? Instead of 'faithfully' doing the translation work, which I doubt can really bring out 'authentic' and 'original' meanings, I am more interested in the situation of things being lost in translation (de Kloet 2008: 200–206; Leung 2007: 1–6, 2008,[16] Ho and Tsang 2007[17]). When translations 'fail' – when Chinese queer identities and politics do not follow the same path as those of the West, when human rights and notions of sexual citizenship seem to be understood differently in the Chinese context, when sexual identity does not necessarily prescribe an individualistic notion of identity, when sexual identity does not necessarily contradict heterosexual marriage, etc. – what we gain from these moments of misfit between global gayness and gayness in the Chinese context are some insights – queer insights – that force us to face the neglected voices of the local and challenge the imagined Western queer 'origin' in the study of homosexuality.

Finally, 'trans' implies *transgression*. This book aims to transgress disciplinary boundaries, and to allow us to create possible trans-regional, comparative and multi-sited studies that enrich our understanding of non-normative genders and sexualities. In another sense, this book is also about certain Chinese gay men whose stories can be seen as *transgressions* of moral, social and sexual norms and cultures that lie within the metaculture of heteronormativity and even those within the homonormativity of the gay world. It is hoped that the book will thus tell us something about the politics that we can imagine.

* * *

This book situates in the current debates on sexual citizenship (e.g., Evans 1993; Weeks 1998; Richardson 1998, 2000, 2001, 2004, 2005; Bell and Binnie 2000; Plummer 2001, 2003; Phelan 2001; Seidman 2005). It draws attention to three discussions: (1) the emergence of lesbian and gay movements, particularly the new rights-based assimilation politics since the 1990s, centred on the question of whether the fight for the expansion of equal rights challenges the heterosexual assumption of citizenship discourse or whether the inclusion of gay men and lesbians in the mainstream demands that they support and reinforce the heterosexualization of queer life; (2) the emergence of substantial queer consumption venues, centred on the question of whether the pink economy articulates sexual rights and facilitates cultural belongings or whether it constructs a cosmopolitan and class-based consumer citizenship that marginalizes those who fail to attain; and (3) the emergence of gay and lesbian couples and families, centred on the question of whether such newly emerged forms of intimacy challenge familial heteronormativity and create alternatives to intimate relationships and family lives or whether they endorse a particular heterosexual relationship (e.g., monogamy) and conform to a heterosexual way of life. I also examine the recent debate on the relationship between neo-liberal governance and sexuality (e.g., Cooper 1995, 2002; Richardson 2005) and the emergence of global queer identity, and its influence on non-Western queer formation (e.g., Altman 1995, 1996a, b, 1997, 2001) and its discontents (Manalansan 2003: 5–9; Rofel 2007: 89–94).

Guided by these questions, this book includes three case studies of the process of making sexual citizenship, in three Chinese locales (Hong Kong, London, and Guangdong). In this transnational study, we can grasp the complexity of 'situated' knowledge about citizenship and Chinese male homosexuality, and link 'political economies with manifestations of sexual, racial, and gender hierarchies that are at once local and global' (Rofel 2007: 2).

I hope this book will be seen as a contribution to a new sociology of homosexuality – one that incorporates insights from sociology and queer theory, with a transnational turn to 'new queer studies' (e.g., Manalansan 2003: 5–9; Cruz-Malave and Manalansan 2002: 1–10; Eng *et al.* 2005; Wilson 2006; Johnson *et al.* 2000).[18]

Three traffics – the outline of the book

Chapter 1, 'Study of Chinese male homosexualities', lays the groundwork for my cumulative argument. I will first delineate my theoretical matrix, which engages sociology with queer theory and other disciplines (e.g., cultural anthropology, post-colonial studies, cultural studies), situating my study within new queer Asia studies and within the present debate on globalization. I will then spell out my power-resistance paradigm and explain the central theme of the book – the making and remaking of sexual citizenship among Chinese gay men – in Hong Kong, London and China.

Globalization is an uneven process that reproduces spatially uneven development, and the flow of capital, commodities, people, images, and ideas is never equal among locations. The rest of the book is thus structured according to three transnational traffics,[19] which allow three concrete critiques for three specific socio-political circumstances.

Part I Hong Kong

My starting point is Hong Kong. The stories and narratives I am going to tell demonstrate the interplay of sexuality and colonial history, state governance, family biopolitics, the market and the spatial constraints of Hong Kong. In contrast to the subjects in Western literature, which tends to assume that heterosexuals are citizens with full access to various political, civil, and social rights, Hong Kong people have been only 'partial' citizens, in terms of access to various rights, under the colonial and post-colonial administrations. It is with this specific historical background that we can understand the sexual politics of Hong Kong *tongzhi*. I will argue that queer energy within political channels has been blocked, and has been diverted to the creation of three major sexual spaces confined within the parameters of 'scattered hegemonies' (Grewal and Kaplan 1994: 7),[20] such as those of colonial and post-colonial governance, familial heteronormativity and spatial constraints. These three spaces are: a vibrant queer cultural world that has successfully countered the traditional pathological personification of homosexuality but is subject to neo-liberal governance, censorship, commercial considerations and a backlash from conservative force, mainly from some Protestant Christian- and Catholic-based non-governmental organizations (NGOs) (Chapter 2); a substantial queer infrastructure of consumption venues that links gay identity to consumer citizenship but is subject to homonormativity (e.g., cult gay masculinity) and market economy (Chapter 3); and personal space for creating intimate relationships that is yet subject to family biopolitics and familial heteronormativity (Chapter 4). It is in relation to these three spaces that we can understand how Hong Kong gay men make and remake sexual citizenship.

Part II London

My next stop is London. In Chapter 5 I look at how Hong Kong members of queer diasporas live in London, the capital of its former colonizer. I argue that there are (at least) three types of migrant gay men: those brought to the UK as 'brides' by their Western gay boyfriends; those brought according to their families advancement strategies; and those who go with deliberate strategies for their own personal advancement. Some of these migrants succeed in gaining residency in the UK, including those who get residency through their same-sex relationship under the Civil Partnership Act 2004. Informed by queer diasporic studies (e.g., Leong 1996; Eng and Hom 1998; Eng 2001; Manalansan 2003), this chapter looks at how Chinese migrant gay men live as Chinese-British citizens, at the intersection of 'race', the sexuality of British society, Chinese culture, and the British-dominated gay community. It is thus a story of queer migration.

Part III China (Guangdong, Beijing, Shanghai)

My third stop is China. Chapter 6 tells the stories and narratives of Chinese gay men who now reside in Guangdong, and examines how *tongzhi* identity is subject to global capitalism, state socialism, market economy and familial patriarchy. I track down the emergence of gay identity in the 1990s and the trajectory of changing sexual cultures embedded in the family, work unit (*danwei* 單位), popular culture and the state during the transition from the Maoist period to the reform era. The coming-to-term of new gay identity has slowly shifted from the medical and deviant discourse of homosexuality and has tapped into a new cultural and urban citizenship that emphasizes 'quality' (*suzhi* 素質), individuality, difference and modernity.

While Chapter 6 delineates the Chinese *tongzhi*'s claims to cultural and urban citizenship, Chapter 7 discusses those men who have extreme difficulty in making these claims. This involves the 'bare life' of the 'money boy' – the queer transient labourer who lives in Beijing or Shanghai and is subject to the interlocking effects of three stigmatized identities: that of rural-to-urban migrant, that of men who sell sex, and that of a man who has sex with other men.

Archive of queer feelings, subcultures and lives of Chinese gay men

This work is informed by my academic study of Chinese male homosexualities over the past 20 years in three major sites. Hong Kong is the place where I was born and brought up and eventually came out as a gay man in the early 1990s. It is the primary site at which I have been researching gay male identities and sexualities since 1996, and engaging in queer activism and queer pedagogy since 2000. Over the years when I lived and studied in the UK in the 1990s, I tried to live openly as a gay man, and I immersed myself into the London gay scene. This is the site where I found intricate complicated relationships between race and sexuality, and where I devoted myself to queer diasporic studies. London is a place to and from which I have made frequent trips since returning to Hong Kong in 2000. I started to explore and investigate mainland Chinese masculinities and sexualities since 2004, and I have especially drawn attention to the narratives of rural-to-urban male migrants who sell sex. In this regard, I myself can be seen as having a transnational queer biography. The analysis in this book is thus part of an analysis of my own life, and the research on gay sexuality and intimacy that I have conducted since the 1990s is thus intertwined with my own story, which feeds back into the narrative.

In-depth interviews, with a life history approach, have formed the backbone of my research. In 1997–98 I interviewed 34 Chinese gay men, in Hong Kong and in London. I followed this up by interviewing one-third of them again in 2007–8, when I also interviewed another 26 Chinese gay men (11 in Hong Kong and 15 in Guangdong), for a total of 60 life histories. Most of my interviewees were found through personal contacts and referrals from *tongzhi* organizations, and then through the snowball method. I tried to interview people with as diverse backgrounds as possible (in terms of age, education, marital status, family status, occupation, etc.) in order to reflect the diversity of the population (see the Appendix for the profile of interviewees). In addition, between 2004–5, I interviewed 30 other Chinese men who have sex with other men in exchange for money, in Beijing (n = 14) and Shanghai (n = 16), and their stories appear in the final chapter (Chapter 7).

The stories told in this book are sexual stories (Plummer 1995), with specific timings and generations, bound up with historical moment and place. These transnational and generational tales are told with laughter, joy, happiness and pride, as well as with tears, anger, remorse, shame and guilt. They are powerful, at least for me, as they reveal emerging narratives which have not been heard before, or which have only been told in a very negative way – as 'perverted', 'bizarre', 'promiscuous', 'bad', 'immoral', etc. These queer narratives, as shown elsewhere, are 'dynamic, political, and constantly contested' (Plummer 2008: xiii), as they are 'counter stories', that challenge and direct our thinking about male identities, masculinities and sexualities and start to break down the claims of grand theories about queer lives. The participants knew that their stories would be told publicly, and might have not only the effect of expanding their life-space (c.f. Ho 2006: 564) but might also contribute to a new public space where old and new scripts about personal lives might be juxtaposed, competed, challenged, redefined, and negotiated.

What I am trying to do in this book is thus to document and archive certain Chinese gay men who share a marginalized sexual identity as homosexuals (being 'gay', 'queer', '*tongzhi*', '*memba*', 'golden boy', 'money boy', etc.) as well as how they feel, experience and realize same-sex desire; how they create new space; how they make sense of their lives; how they become sexual citizens, etc. The book can thus be seen as an archive of Chinese gay men's lives, subcultures and feelings in Hong Kong and elsewhere. As argued by Halberstam (2005), an archive of queer lives, subcultures and even feelings is not simply a repository but is also 'a theory of cultural relevance, a construction of collective memory, and a complex record of queer activity' (pp.169–70).[21] It is through such a documentation of Chinese gay men's lives, subcultures and feelings that I would like to contribute to the archive of queer studies of non-Western non-normative genders and sexualities.

Terms of discussion

Terminology is problematic, as every term has its exclusionary effect, or, in a Foucauldian sense, its disciplinary effect. For example: the term 'homosexual' traditionally carries a medical inclination that has been protested by lesbian and gay scholars; 'lesbian and gay', all too often, has the tendency to imply, specifically, only white middle-class lesbian and gay experiences, and has been challenged by queer theorists; 'queer' is now widely used as an umbrella term for non-normative gender and sexual identities, but the term has not been embraced by some 'lesbian and gay' scholars, especially those of earlier generations, as the term had a very negative connotation in the past (Medhurst and Munt 1997: xi–xvii).

The term '*tongzhi*' has been used widely to signify non-normative genders and sexualities in the Chinese context, and functions similarly to the English term 'queer'. In contrast with the term 'homosexual' (*tongxinglianzhe* 同性戀者 in Mandarin, *tungsinglyunze* 同性戀者 in Cantonese), which has a clinical connotation, *tongzhi*, like 'gay and lesbian' or 'queer', is used for self-identification.

'Tongzhi', literally, means 'common will', and is usually translated as 'comrade'. It was originally used by the father of the modern Chinese nation, Sun Yixian (孫逸仙 – Sun Yat-sen in Cant.), who encouraged Chinese people to fight against the Qing imperialist regime in the early twentieth century. His saying, 'The revolution has not been successful; comrades should fight for it until the end' became a famous slogan of the revolution in both the Republican and People's Republic of China (PRC) eras. It was appropriated as a synonym for lesbian, gay, bisexual, transgendered and queer ('LGBTQ') in Hong Kong, after the First Gay and Lesbian Film Festival, held in 1991, was referred to as the Tongzhi Film Festival by playwright Edward Lam. The queer connotation of the term became very popular in both the gay and straight communities in Hong Kong and Taiwan, and later in the gay community in China. Another term, *ku'er* (酷兒), literally meaning 'cool child', is a local mutation of 'queer' used in Taiwan, but it has never been popularized in Hong Kong or in China.

The term 'tongzhi' is *pinyin* romanization of Putonghua (Mandarin Chinese). In Cantonese the term is pronounced *tungzi* – the two terms bear no difference in meaning. Since 'tongzhi' has been used almost exclusively in both academic writings and in popular culture in Hong Kong, I use 'tongzhi' throughout this book, including in the Hong Kong context, in order to avoid confusion, but one should bear in mind that, in daily conversation, Hong Kong Cantonese pronounce it *tungzi* rather than 'tongzhi'.

Another term that needs explanation is 'memba'. It is a local parlance used exclusively by Hong Kong gay men for self-identification. Strictly speaking, 'memba' is not a Cantonese romanization, as it is a combination of English and Chinese, a typical example of what we call 'Chinglish'. It is a Cantonese derivative of the English term 'member'.

I choose to employ the terms 'homosexuality', 'lesbian and gay men', 'queer' and 'tongzhi' rather interchangeably in order to draw out and suspend the theoretical discrepancies and political tensions among them, such as the heterogeneity of non-normative genders and sexualities (e.g., different connotations in 'homosexual', 'lesbian and gay man' and 'queer') and the 'misfit' of the appropriation of Western theory for the Chinese context (e.g., the tension between 'queer' and 'tongzhi') (c.f. Leung 2008: 1–6). The title 'Chinese male homosexualities' signifies the diverse meanings, practices and identities of Chinese gay male same-sex sexualities.

Finally, throughout the book, the terms 'West' and 'Western' principally signify the political, economic, social and cultural practices and hegemonies of countries originated from Western Europe, as well as their allied hegemonic circulations of power in countries such as those of Northern America, Australia and New Zealand. The terms 'Asians' and 'Orientals' are used interchangeably to refer to people from Southeast and East Asia, rather than from South Asia or the Middle East as used by Edward Said in *Orientalism*.[22]

1 Study of Chinese male homosexualities

There is a Third World in every First World and vice versa.
(Trinh T. Minh-ha, *Of Other Peoples*)

So, I think my problem and 'our' problem is how to have *simultaneously* an account of radical historical contingency for all knowledge claims and knowing subjects, a critical practice for recognizing our own 'semiotic technologies' for making meanings, *and* a no-nonsense commitment to faithful accounts of a 'real' world, one that can be partially shared and friendly to earth-wide projects of finite freedom, adequate material abundance, modest meaning in suffering, and limited happiness.
(Donna Haraway, *Simians, Cyborgs, and Women*)

In this chapter, I will first delineate the theoretical ideas that have enabled me to carry out a transnational study of non-Western non-normative genders and sexualities. I draw principally from the sociology of homosexuality and queer theory, but also from feminist scholars of the 'politics of difference', cultural anthropology, post-colonial studies and cultural studies. Building upon previous work on Chinese homosexualities by myself and others, I situate my work within the recently emerged Asian queer studies, itself within the global/transnational study of sexualities.

Second, I will propose a pluralist model for a power-resistance paradigm, stemming from the post-structuralist conception of identity. In this paradigm, identity consists of a dual process of 'subject-ification', a Foucauldian concept of both 'self-making' and 'being-made' under the 'art of governmentality' of 'scattered hegemonies' at various levels: systematic, community and personal – in which power is manifested, produced, negotiated, and resisted through schemes of discipline, control, administration and surveillance. The recent sexual citizenship debate illustrates this paradigm and provides the main site for my analysis of Chinese sexual citizenship, using Chinese gay men as an example, in three different locales – namely, Hong Kong, London and China (major sites: Guangdong, Beijing, Shanghai).

Whose gaze? Who's gay?[1]

Genealogy is itself a will to power. Instead of offering a 'better' knowledge-regime, Foucault (1977, 1984a, 1984b) uses genealogy to decentre the whole Western form of universal knowledge, by laying down alternative and subjugated knowledges and thereby opening up other regimes of the truth-game – the other; other worlds, other peoples, other identities; other cultures and other languages (Hall 1991: 12).

In a similar vein, Abbas and Erni (2005: 1–12) argue that the current moment of cultural studies is that of the 'post-colonial predicament', in which cultural studies scholars from around the world challenge the broad hegemony of Western modernity and knowledge. They suggest taking cultural studies 'to internationalize the field a little further' in order to facilitate 'the visibility, transportability, and translation of works produced outside North America, Europe, and Australia' (p. 2).

To paraphrase Abbas and Erni: what I propose to do in the following section is to internationalize queer studies a little further. However, I am not adding Chinese homosexuality to a total study of *world* homosexuality, nor am I recovering a local and authentic origin for the study of Chinese homosexuality. Instead, I am writing a brief alternative genealogy of the study of homosexuality that is aware of some neglected voices and is critical of the constructed singular origin (read: Western) of the study of homosexuality. This brief history enables me to understand contemporary Chinese homosexualities on a transnational scale.

Sociology of homosexuality: essentialism and social constructionism

Let's start from the West. From the 1900s to the 1950s, the study of sexuality was heavily dominated by sexology, psychoanalysis and psychiatry. Scholars of these disciplines held what we now call an essentialist notion of sexuality, according to which sex was basically viewed as an overpowering biological force and instinctual drive; and considered sexual identities to be the cognitive realization of a genetic predisposition (Epstein 1987: 11; Weeks 1985: 8, 2003: 7).[2]

Parallel to the rise of the gay and lesbian movement in the 1960s, the sociology of homosexuality slowly emerged from the sociology of deviance,[3] with notions of social stigma and subcultures for understanding the homosexual underworld (e.g., Plummer 1975: Part 3), and employing the 'sexual scripts' perspective to understand the social meanings of being (homo)sexual (Gagnon and Simon 1974: 19–26; Ch. 5). This paved the way for a new sociology of homosexuality that theorized and problematized the notion of 'homosexual' and sought to explain the nature, origin, social meaning and changing forms of modern homosexual identities and cultures. This is now known as the essentialist–constructionist controversy. Briefly put, while essentialists believed that homosexuality, as a universal phenomenon, existed across time and space and had its own continuous and coherent history, social constructionists emphasized the idea that sexuality and sexual identities were socially mediated historical constructions that belonged less to biology and more to the world of culture and meaning (Epstein 1987: 11).[4]

The sociology of homosexuality came into full force in the 1980s. It not only problematized the notion of 'homosexual', but also challenged the 'heterosexist assumptions' in virtually all social institutions. It turned to the societal reactions towards homosexuality (e.g., homophobia) and documented various levels of discrimination, ranging from personal boycotts and street violence to social and cultural exclusions and legal and political punishment. Two approaches can be seen in this period. First was the sketching of the socio-historical conditions – for example, gay subcultures, professionalization of medicine and the rise of industrial capitalism – that gave rise to the 'making' of a homosexuality identity.[5] The second approach focused on the 'micro-interactionist' process that explored the concept of homosexual identity in terms of a coming-out process: identity confusion > identity comparison > identity tolerance > identity acceptance > identity pride > identity synthesis. This rather teleological tendency of the 'coming out model' (Cass 1979, 1984)[6] in turn informed the notion of identity politics and involved 'a struggle for identity, a development of sexual communities, and the growth of political movements' (Weeks 1985: 195).

Queer theory – a critique of hetero–homo symbolic configuration

As Fuss (1989: 108–9) rightly points out, the sociology of homosexuality, manifested as social constructionism, has the theoretical capacity to explore the variations among and within sexual subcultures by rejecting the view of homosexuality as an eternal and culturally uniform condition. A constructionist view of homosexual identity thus opens the door to studies of the production of all sexual identities. 'Homosexuality', 'heterosexuality', 'bisexuality' and other sexual identities are all seen as 'classifications' – historically contingent categories – rather than as transhistorical phenomena. Thus constructionism allows us to study the 'making' of a gay subject, a lesbian subject or even a heterosexual subject in different historical or ethnic contexts. Constructionists finally led us out of the realm of ontology (what the homosexual is) and into the realm of social and discursive formations (how the homosexual identity is produced).

The constructionist position, however, has a major problem. Seidman (1993) argues that, while constructionists have uncovered an ethnocentric bias in gay and lesbian scholarship that universalizes present-centred, culture-bound perspectives, they have not applied the same critical awareness to their own discourse.

> If categories of same-sex intimacies are marked by the sociocultural context of their origin, is not the same true of our categories of analysis?

> And, if representations are embedded in broad national environments, are they not likewise stamped by the more particular social traits of their producers, for example, their class, race, ethnicity, nationality, age or gender?
>
> (Seidman 1993: 128)

Seidman (1996: 9–13) argues that one possible solution to this predicament might be to adopt a post-structuralist strategy. Post-structuralists claim that there has been an epistemic shift – from the humanist standpoint of an individual subject creating himself or herself to the standpoint of a 'structural' order, and from the resisting gay subject to the analysis of the homo/hetero code and its pervasive structuring of modes of thoughts, knowledge and culture, the themes of which are both sexual and non-sexual.

The 'Foucauldian Deluge' (Plummer 1998: 608–9) heralded a distinctive discursive or post-structuralist turn to the study of homosexuality in the 1980s.[7] Foucault not only challenged the essentialist view of sex (in this regard, his work is aligned with social constructionism), but contested the very knowledge of sexuality itself, the 'science of sexuality', that conceptualized our multifarious erotic experiences as a coherent, organized, hetero/homo sexual being. Foucault (1980) conceived of the rise of modern society that consists of a modern state with other social institutions and various disciplines ('demography, biology, medicine, psychiatry, psychology, ethics, pedagogy, and political criticism' (p. 33)), in which sexuality is centred as the major system of social control of bio-power (pp. 139–57). 'A psychiatrization of perverse pleasure' was one of the strategies to transform same-sex desire ('the sodomite') to same-sex identity ('the homosexual').[8]

Foucault's 'deconstructivist turn' has been largely employed in 'queer theory', which is post-structuralism/postmodernism applied to sexualities and genders.[9] The contributions of canonical queer academic theory (e.g., Eve Sedgwick 1990; Diana Fuss 1989; Judith Butler 1990; Teresa de Lauretis 1991; and anthologies Diana Fuss 1991 and Michael Warner 1993), according to Seidman (1995: 123–31), are twofold. First, queer theory criticizes the closure of the ethnic modelling of homosexuality by rethinking identity as a category containing conflicting and multiple meanings that interlocks with other categories such as those of gender, race and class. This multiplicity renders identity permanently open, hybrid and fluid, which in turn facilitates coalition-building based on a politics of difference.[10] Second, queer theory criticizes homosexual theory as merely a theory of a social minority, and opens up the idea that 'homosexual' theory can be seen as a general social theory and critique. Mainstream sociology of homosexuality views homosexuality as the property of an individual or group. This property, or identity, is explained either as being natural (the essentialist position, which claims that there is 'some "essence" within homosexuals that makes them homosexual – some gay "core" of their being, or their psyche, or their genetic make-up' (Epstein 1987: 11, emphasis original), or social being (the constructionist position, which claims that '"homosexual," "gay," and "lesbian" are just labels, created by cultures and applied to the self' (p. 11, emphasis original)). Queer theorists argue that both of these approaches have favoured a view of homosexuality as the condition of a social minority. Queer theory, however, treats the heterosexual/homosexual binary as a master framework for constructing the self, sexual knowledge and social institutions. This binary sex system, or power/knowledge regime, creates rigid psychological and social boundaries that inevitably give rise to systems of dominance and hierarchical organization.

Queer theory contests the unified notion of homosexual identity, that is the 'very telos of Western homosexual politics' (Seidman 1996: 11), and addresses a problem that seems to be neglected by sociologists, namely, the social functioning of the heterosexual/homosexual binary. Since the focal terrain of critique for queer theorists is the Western symbolic configuration, they tend to ignore the 'lived experiences' of gays and lesbians (and hence the whole idea of empirical fieldwork) and devote themselves mainly to literary criticism (Plummer 1998: 609–11).

Sociology/queer theory

The sociology of homosexuality is still a major force in shaping current political debates about homosexuality and lesbian and gay politics, but some of the most innovative work in lesbian and gay studies has occurred in the humanities. Sociology has much to learn from queer theory, as queer theory has from sociology. Instead of dismissing one or another, I join other scholars who take into account the merits of each approach. These scholars, while putting articles together in anthologies, have a clear awareness of the dynamics between sociology and queer theory. The anthologies include: Seidman's *Queer Theory/Sociology* (1996), Medhurst and Munt's *Lesbian and Gay Studies: A Critical Introduction* (1997), Richardson and Seidman's *Handbook of Lesbian and Gay Studies* (2002), and Corber and Valocchi's *Queer Studies: An Interdisciplinary Reader* (2003). The present work is attentive to the dynamics of institutional and structural order in the formation of the sexual self, but preserves the critical spirit of queer theory that is sensitive to the textualization of queer experiences.

The advances of both sociology and canonical queer theory in understanding Western queer cultures and communities, however, offer very little to an understanding of non-Western homosexuality. The complex intertwining relationship between culture and sexuality outside the Western world has only been seriously examined in studies in cultural anthropology and post-colonialism and the later studies of the globalization of sexuality, and in new queer studies.

Studies of non-Western, non-normative genders and sexualities

Anthropology and post-colonialism

Anthropologists have the tradition of studying 'other' cultures (with the earliest studies based mainly on travel reports from missionaries, traders and seamen), and anthropological texts and ethnographic materials provide some discussion of non-Western sexuality. Early key scholars (e.g., Malinowski 1922; Mead 1952) touched upon the issues of gender and sexuality in people living in Melanesia. Later scholars who carried out gender and sexuality studies have tended to charge former scholars with being Eurocentric, pointing to the fact that they exoticized/eroticized the 'other' and over-emphasized the 'differences' of non-Western sexual cultures as sexual 'excess', 'promiscuity', largely ritualized or visible homosexuality, and transgenderism. They have also pointed out that the sex/gender systems in non-Western countries seem to be different from the systems found in European and Anglo-Western countries, in that terms such as male/female, man/woman or masculine/feminine may not be so easily distinguished in non-Western countries and are believed to be modern inventions heavily influenced by Western biological and medical discourses.[11]

Another major force in examining the intertwining relationship of race and sexuality is post-colonial theory (Williams and Chrisman 1993; Mongia 1996)[12] and diasporic studies. Chow (1998: 2–5) summarizes four major forms of post-colonial critiques. The first is that of the Western representations of non-Western cultures, pioneered by Edward Said's notion of Orientialism (1978). The second is that of Gayatri Chakravorty Spivak's (1988) 'Can the subaltern speak?' – the ultimate silent female subaltern, who always lives under the multifarious hierarchical discriminations of race, class and gender. The third is conducted through analysis of minority discourse, with an emphasis on voices of subordinated 'others' (e.g., Gilles Deleuze, Felix Guattari, David Lloyd). The final critique is that provided in the celebration of hybridity, advanced by Homi Bhabha and others.[13]

As noted by Chow (1998: 2–5), although post-colonialism has shared a lot with post-structuralism's sense of subversiveness and radicalism, the very nature of its investigation of the European 'otherness' in fact forces post-structuralist theory to confront the issue of race – 'the history of racial and cultural imperialism that lies at the "foundations" of the theoretical dislocation of the sign' (p. 5). In this sense, post-colonialism challenges post-structuralist theory's own position as the 'other' of Europe, as it is also the 'other' within the European tradition.

Drawing heavily upon the legacies of post-structuralism, queer theory and post-colonialism, post-colonial queer theorists argue that post-colonial sexual identities are not merely the additive experiences of 'race', gender, class and sexuality; nor do they include simply another variation of the Western homoerotic experience. Rather, they are seen as the result of multifarious and contradictory forms of oppression within specific institutional arenas. Sexual identity should therefore be understood in terms of this 'politics of difference' in order to avoid suppressing the multiple ways of experiencing homosexual desires.[14] Taken together, I share with cultural anthropology and post-colonial studies the understanding of modern sexual cultures in Asia as part of Asian cultures and modernity. We should take into account factors such as colonial histories (if any), traditions and religions, the growing affluence of most Asian countries, and the (de)colonialization strategies of the states. All these factors play crucial roles in shaping ideas about gender, sex and sexuality, and possible forms of sexual expression (e.g., on dating, romance, premarital sex, virginity, abortion, divorce, birth control, homosexuality, pornography, prostitution) under the whole process of globalization and decolonization. We should also pay attention to how the emergence of new sexual identities, cultures and communities simultaneously shape and reshape the social life of a particular country, and even the global processes of change (Kong 2006a).[15]

Studies of Chinese homosexualities

Writings about homosexuality in Hong Kong emerged in the late 1970s. This may be partly due to the slow emergence of the homosexual subculture as a social phenomenon, and partly due to the responses to the colonial government's legal reform of decriminalizing male homosexual acts, which resulted from a series of police scandals (e.g., Lethbridge 1976; Hong Kong Government 1983; Samshasha 1997 [1984], 1989; see Chapter 2).

Samshasha's works are exemplary of this period. Drawn from extensive historical materials such as official court records, medical manuals and many other textual and visual evidences, Samshasha's (1984) Chinese-language book *History of Homosexuality in China* tracks the hidden history of 'same-sex love' in China from the Zhou Dynasty (11th century BC to 221 BC) to the 1980s. In response to the decriminalization of homosexuality debate and the homophobic social environment, Samshasha's work was timely. It not only pointed out that ancient China had a long and celebrated tradition of 'same-sex love', but also countered the dominant thought, and one of the key debates at the time of publication, which was that homosexuality was a disease/sin brought from the West, as homosexuality had been first criminalized in Hong Kong only when the British came to rule in 1842.[16] He concluded that homosexuality existed in Chinese history but that homophobia was imported from the West, and appealed to anti-colonial sentiments and patriotic cultural pride. He later changed his argument, in the second edition in 1997, and conceded that homophobia did exist in Chinese culture, but that it functioned more 'implicitly'.[17] With his burning desire to unfold a hidden history of Chinese homoerotic tradition, Samshasha's works painted a picture of Chinese homosexuality as a distinctive culture, that was ready to 'come out' and was determined to 'find its own path'. This implicit essentialist conception of homosexuality partly fused into later studies and also into the local gay and lesbian movements.

Since the 1990s, studies from social science perspectives (mainly in sociology and political philosophy) have overwhelmingly focused on identity formation and its relation to issues such as coming out and social discrimination, as well as gay and lesbian politics and movement, and these include my previous works (Kong 2000, 2002, 2004). These studies have primarily employed qualitative research methods such as in-depth interview, life history, participant observation and/or virtual ethnography as the methods of inquiry.

The transition from homosexuality-as-same-sex-experience in ancient China to homosexuality-as-an-identity (be it 'homosexual', 'gay' or 'tongzhi') in contemporary times involves a question of construction. Fused with social constructionist and later post-structuralist thrusts, studies have been devoted to the 'making of the homosexual/gay/lesbian/tongzhi identity' in contemporary Hong Kong, with its unique (post-)colonialism, tourism, capitalism, Westernization and neo-Confucianism (Ho 1995, 1997; Chou 2000; Kong 2000). The self-identities of gay men and lesbians, and especially the issues of coming out and forming relationships, have been examined – in particular, the conceptualization of gay and lesbian identity as tongzhi identity (Chou 2000); the interracial relationships between Hong Kong gay men and their Western partners (Ho 1997; Ho and Tsang 2000; Kong 2002) and/or Chinese partners (Kong 2002); gay men and parent families (Ho 1999), and gay men and lesbians 'doing' families (Kong 2009b; Wong 2006); and gender performance in lesbian identity (Kam 2003, 2008; Lai 2004; Tong 2008). Personal identity has also been discussed in relation to broader gay and lesbian movements in the post-colonial context (Ho 1997; Ho and Tsang 2004a) – in particular, in Chou's (2000) advocacy of Chinese tongzhi politics, my discussion of gay men's 'politics of the weak' in both straight and gay worlds (Kong 2004), Tang's (2008) formulation of lesbians' appropriation of urban spaces, my (Kong 2004) and Lau's (2004) critiques of the gay community, and Wong's (2007) discussion of the IDAHO anti-discrimination movement.

Another major force in queer studies is from the humanities. Through analysing literal and visual texts (mainly films, but also novels and other cultural texts), scholars have produced many queer texts to intervene in Western and local discourses of gender and sexuality. With their intense engagements with queer theory, cultural studies and gender studies, they have decentred the multifarious interlocking of binaries such as global/local, masculine/feminine, heterosexual/homosexual and many more, at various nexuses such as those with colonialism, nationalism, sexism and racism in contemporary Hong Kong post-colonial culture. Most of the time they implicitly make a parallel analysis of queer culture and politics (manifested through various cinematic or other literal representations of genders and sexualities), on the one hand; and Hong Kong's post-colonial experiences (crystallized, by and large, in Hong Kong cultural identity, in a broader cultural studies debate), on the other. Notable examples are Yau's (2005) and Leung's (2008) analyses of queer culture in post-colonial Hong Kong; Szeto's

(2004) writing of the meanings of radicalism in Chinese societies; Mak's (2000) formulation of bisexuality out of her 'queer discomfort' with queer and tongzhi discourses; Li's (2003) discussion of gender and sexual performance and ambivalence in Chinese operas; and Chan's (2005) 'indulgence' with late queer icon Leslie Cheung.[18]

The dominant paradigm of the study of homosexuality in mainland China is still that of medical science, and the focal point is usually on risky male homosexual behaviour in relation to HIV/AIDS (e.g., Liu *et al.* 2006; Wu *et al.* 2004; Zhang *et al.* 2000; Wong *et al.* 2006; Wong and Kong 2007). In social sciences, studies have focused overwhelmingly on gay identity, especially on how to reconcile gay identity within the family and marriage institutions, the work unit (*danwei* 單位), and society, mainly using interview and life story research methods – e.g., Ruan and Tsai 1988; Li 1998; Gil 2002; Tong 2005; Sun *et al.* 2006; Jones 2005, 2007; and Wei 2007. Rofel's (2007: Ch. 3 and Ch. 5) discussion of contemporary gay and lesbian identities reveals an insightful critique of the newly emerging gay identity under the reign of cosmopolitanism and nascent consumerism.

In the humanities, studies have largely focused on the changing conception of same-sex desires and love under the rigorous processes of modernization, Westernization and globalization through historical analysis and literacy criticism. These studies are particularly sensitive to the global/local and Western/Chinese binaries and offer critical views for understanding Chinese genders and sexualities. These include, for example, Louie's (2002) groundbreaking work of theorizing Chinese masculinity in terms of *wen* (文) and *wu* (武) through Chinese literature; Song's (2004) discussion of the 'fragile scholar' and Wu's (2004) discussion of homoerotic sensibilities in Chinese literature in pre-modern or late imperial China; Kang's (2009) discussion of the relationship between male homosexuality and nationalism from 1900 to 1950 through translated sexological writings, tabloid newspapers, literary works and Peking operas; Sang's (2003) articulation of the neglected female same-sex desire from the late imperial period to the Republican era through literary writings by or about women-preferring women; and Lim's (2006) meticulous critique of the monolithic notions of both 'Chineseness' and 'homosexuality' through representation of male homosexuality in contemporary Chinese cinema in Hong Kong, Taiwan and China.

Globalization study of sexuality and new queer Asia studies

Since the 1990s, globalization has become a buzzword in academia. In sociology, the discussion of globalization can be traced back to the earlier discourses of social change, such as those of modernization theories (e.g., Walt Rostow, Talcott Parsons) and the Marxist dependency and underdevelopment theories (e.g., Immanuel Wallerstein, André Gunder Frank). Recent studies of globalization are interdisciplinary or trans-disciplinary, and call for attention to theoretical traditions and perspectives as widely diverse as Marxism,

Weberianism, functionalism, postmodernism, critical and feminist theory, cultural studies, international studies, post-colonial studies, literature and so on (Robinson 2007, accessed online on 8 August 2008); and even point to a new paradigm shift in social sciences, that of a 'new mobilities' paradigm that emphasizes mobility and fluidity of social processes and movements of people, capital, information and images (Sheller and Urry 2006; Urry 2007). However, as noted by Plummer (2001: 248), 'Although globalisation is well recognised and much discussed, very few studies ever talk about the connections of this process to the intimate life.'

Works on globalization of sexuality that critically examine the interplay among the apparently distinctive spheres of the political, economic, social and cultural (e.g., Binnie 2004; Altman 2001; Farr 2007; Padilla *et al.* 2007; Herdt and Howe 2007: Part 5) are slowly emerging. They can be *broadly* classified according to three distinctive but interrelated domains: (1) the relationship between sexuality and political globalization, particularly the emergence of global sexual/intimate citizenship and its various human rights claims, along the line of the critique of global, neo-liberal and transnational governances (e.g., Bell and Binnie 2000: Ch. 7; Binnie 2004: Ch. 2; Plummer 2003: Ch. 8; Weeks 2007: Ch. 8); (2) the relationship between sexuality and economic globalization, particularly the emergence of global pink economy and its construction of global, consuming sexual identities, cultures and communities, along the line of the critique of cosmopolitanism and the commodification and gentrification of urban queer space (e.g., Hennessy 2000: Ch.4; Bell and Binnie 2000: Ch. 6; Binnie 2004: Ch. 4; Binnie and Skeggs 2004); and (3) the relationship between sexuality and cultural globalization, particularly the emergence of so-called global gay culture and identity, exemplified by Dennis Altman's 'global queering' (1995, 1996a, 1996b, 1997, 2001), along the line of a critique of cultural imperialism (e.g., Manalansan 2003: 5–9; Boellstorff 2005: 25–30; Rofel 2007: 89–94).

Many scholars point out that globalization is an uneven process that reproduces spatial inequalities and differential patterns of exclusion. For example, in her conceptualization of space and place in terms of social relations, Massey (1994) emphasizes that we have to go beyond viewing globalization as merely a process of speeded-up or instantaneous communication and constant global flows, and acknowledge 'the spatial reorganization of social relations, where those social relations are full of power and meaning, and where social groups are very differentially placed in relation to this reorganization' (p. 121, Ch.6). Arguing mainly from the African context, Ferguson (2006) underlines globalization as 'a matter of highly selective and spatially encapsulated forms of global connection combined with widespread disconnection and exclusion' (p. 14). Trouillot (2003) uses the term 'globalitarism' to refer to the dominant ideology that 'aims to propose the teleology of the market as the new master narrative of Western modernity' (p. 48), which has been silencing the tremendous increase of inequalities both within and across boundaries. Trouillot (2001: 129) argues that globalization has led to global polarization, and that the global map has increasingly become full of 'black holes'. Globalization should thus be seen as 'at once a matter of selectively dense interconnections and extensive disconnection and adjection' (Inda and Rosaldo 2008: 33). This is why Hannerz (1996: 6), Ong (1999: 4–8) and Grewal and Kaplan (1994: 1–33), call for a transnational instead of a globalization study, as the term 'transnational' can address the asymmetries of the globalization process.

When applied to sexuality, transnational sexualities are attentive to 'connections and flows that traverse a variety of locations, including not only those of class, gender and ethnicity, but also of urban, rural and other geographies' (Farr 2007, accessed online on 8 August 2008). 'Transnational sexualities' highlights the instabilities of binary terms such as dominator/dominated, centre/periphery, colonizer/colonized, tradition/modernity, global/local, etc., and cross-cuts the binaries by recognizing that 'particular genders and sexualities are shaped by a large number of processes implicated in globalization, including capitalism, diasporic movements, political economies of state, and the disjunctive flow of meanings produced across these sites' (Blackwood 2005: 221). As a whole, 'transnational sexualities' addresses questions of 'globalization, race, political economy, immigration, migration, and geopolitics' (Grewal and Kaplan 2001: 666); conceptualizes the complex terrain of sexual politics that is 'at once national, regional, local, even "cross-cultural" and hybrid' (p. 663); and examines 'multiple, fluid structures of domination' or 'scattered hegemonies' (Grewal and Kaplan 1994: 1–33) that structure new patterns of inequalities and contemporary resistance in traversal spaces.

It is with such a background that studies of non-Western non-normative sexualities and genders have slowly emerged as forming a distinctive discipline within globalization and transnational studies of sexuality which can be seen as new queer studies (Manalansan 2003: 5–9; Cruz-Malave and Manalansan 2002: 1–10; Eng *et al.* 2005).[19]

In Asia, Wilson (2006) notes two major approaches that have emerged as what can be called 'new Asian queer studies'. One is that of American queer diasporic studies (e.g., Eng 2001; Manalansan 2003; articles collected in Leong 1996; Eng and Hom 1998). This body of work acknowledges the global dominance of Western powers but 'emphasises the significance of culture, history, race, capitalism and geography for sexuality' (Wilson 2006, accessed online on 8 August 2008) by identifying multiple trajectories for queer love, sex and politics in non-Western contexts. However, while such an approach focuses on members of diasporas who have migrated to, or have been born in, Western societies, another approach – what Wilson (2006) refers to as 'queer regionalism, queer Asianism or queer pan-Asianism, Asian queer cultural studies or queering Asia' (accessed online), all of which may be called 'critical regional Asian queer studies' (Johnson *et al.* 2000) – conceptualizes queer life in the complex modernities of the non-West, Third World and global south, as the centres of transnational queer analysis. As argued by Wilson (2006),

'. . . these analyses highlight power relations *within* Asia, stressing internal hierarchies and inequalities alongside those of the greater world system' (accessed online). Works that can be regarded as taking this approach include, for example, Erni and Spires 2001; Boellstorff 2005; Gopinath 2005; Blackwood 2005; Rofel 2007; articles edited in Jackson and Cook (1999), Berry *et al.* (2003), Wieringa *et al.* (2007), Martin *et al.* (2008) and the special issue of *China Information* 2008, 22 (2), edited by Jeroen de Kloet. This approach resonates with the editors, Chu Wei-cheng and Fran Martin, of a recent queer issue of *Inter-Asia Cultural Studies* (2007: 8(4)), whose aim is to provide space for 'the abundant heteroglossia of "local" theorizations that inevitably come along with the queer struggles carried out at specific locations' (483, emphasis original).

Study of Chinese male homosexualities

To sum up, the sociology of homosexuality enables me to view sexuality and sexual identities as socially mediated, historical constructions, and helps me to grasp the interplay between concrete living queer experiences and social institutional orders, and with even larger global (queer) processes. I am committed to spelling out the institutional regulation of Chinese male homosexuality – particularly by the state, the market, the queer community, and the family – that has had, and continues to have, a major impact on how same-sex desires among Chinese gay men are realized, organized and experienced.

I also gain insight from queer theory, which not only enables me to challenge the assumed stable notion of sexual identity that unifies anatomical sex with gender and desire, but also acknowledges the disciplinary effect of the binary opposition of heterosexuality/homosexuality as a master framework for constructing the self, sexual knowledge, social institutions, and the modern regime of sexuality. Queer theory thus helps me to criticize the disciplinary effect of being gay as a white middle-class gay male experience; to question the coming-out model as a privileged political act; and to challenge identity politics as the only sexual politics. This opens up a perspective that enables me to see how the heterosexual/homosexual binary is mediated by a complexity of interlocking factors, including race, gender, region and nation.

Although the sociology of homosexuality and queer theory are my principal theoretical tools, I owe much insight to cultural anthropology, post-colonial studies, cultural studies and the recent globalization and transnational studies of sexuality, which offer a more nuanced understanding of the complex relationship between sexuality and racial identification; and with other 'scattered hegemonies' such as colonialism, nationalism and cosmopolitanism; in non-Western contexts on a globalizing, but unequal and asymmetrical, transnational scale.

Building upon the previous work done in the study of Chinese homosexualities in Hong Kong and in China, I wish to contribute my study to new queer Asian studies by examining the interplay between individual biography, local social institutions and broader global/transnational processes through the data from extensive fieldwork (interviews, life stories, ethnography) on Chinese gay men in three different locales: Hong Kong, London and China (major sites: Guangdong, Beijing and Shanghai). In the following, I spell out my theoretical framework for understanding self-identity and the making of sexual citizenship among Chinese gay men.

The power-resistance paradigm

My theoretical framework is drawn from a post-structuralist conception of a power-resistance paradigm, based on a 'politics of difference' about identity within the matrix of domination and mapped onto a transnational time/space geography of sexuality.

This theoretical framework rests on a politics of difference about identity, which I share with the post-structuralist critique of a unified notion of identity that includes deconstructionism (e.g., Derrida 1976; Mouffe 1995; Hall 1996a, 1996b),[20] queer theory (e.g., Fuss 1989: Ch.6, Seidman 1995), and Black feminist thought on intersectionality (e.g., Crenshaw 1989; Collins 1991, 1998; hooks 1981; Anthias and Yuval-Davis 1983, 1992).[21] Briefly put, every identity has a history, and one's identity cannot be separated from one's racial and ethnic identification; sexual, national or class positions; age; and even one's physical fitness and place of origin. 'Gay' and 'lesbian', as identities, cannot be considered apart from these other identity-components or categories of difference; there is no separate, independent 'gay' or 'lesbian' experience that can be marked off (Seidman 1995). Generalized categories of 'gay' and 'lesbian' are not useful, as there are only gay men and lesbians, who simultaneously occupy particular positions according to race and ethnicity, class, sex, gender, age group, physical embodiment, national social position, place of origin, etc. (Fuss 1989: Ch.6; Mouffe 1995).[22] We, or our identities, thus *embody*, through various forms and meanings, a vast and rambling multiple positioning and re-positioning of the self (Hall 1996a).[23]

A matrix of identities gives rise to a matrix of oppression: in terms of gender, men over women; in terms of sexuality, heterosexuals over homosexuals, bisexuals or transgendered; in terms of class position, ruling or middle class over working class; in terms of education, higher education over low or no education; in terms of race and ethnicity, white over non-white, or Han-Chinese over other ethnic minorities; in terms of age, adults over children or the elderly; in terms of physical body, able-bodied over disabled; in terms of space, urban over rural; in terms of work, 'decent' work over 'dirty' work, such as sex work.

This politics of difference rejects the essentialist notion of identity. For example, a Chinese middle-class gay man living in the UK may be penalized by heterosexuality and racism but privileged by the class structure, at a given time. Identities are always multiple and involve identity-components and categories of difference which intersect or combine with one another, in multiple and sometimes contradictory ways. They are thus necessarily unstable, as subjects cannot be totally fixed or determined. Identity is constructed by a 'constant movement of overdetermination and displacement' (Mouffe 1995: 318).

As suggested by Black feminist thought (e.g., Collins 1998, 1991: Ch. 2), the politics of difference rejects an additive model of oppression that treats systems of oppression (e.g., race, gender and class) as separate, and instead points to a matrix of oppression that highlights the intersections and interconnectedness, or the 'intersectionality' of how interlocking systems of oppression structure experiences in any given socio-historical context. Thus an individual may be the oppressor or the oppressed, or simultaneously oppressor and oppressed, depending on the context at a given time. This oppression comes from the multiplicity of intersections of difference, rather than from a single source.[24]

These matrices of identities and oppression fit into a post-structuralist power-resistance paradigm which depicts identity construction as itself a part of the disciplinary and regulatory structures that frame the self, body, desires, actions and social relations. Foucault's (1982) formulation of the relationship between the subject and power represents the best illustration. Foucault argues that power not only produces and reproduces itself in structural control – of law, sovereignty and prohibition – but also circulates and consolidates through the perpetuation of ideology and the internalization of norms. It is through such a dual process of 'subject-ification' that we are 'being-made' and 'self-making' as *subjects*.[25]

Following Foucault's thought, we can argue that power is realized through various fine capillaries that constitute individuals as subjects under different knowledge/power regimes, on three main levels: the systemic level of social institutions such as the state, the market, schools, churches, the media, etc.; the community level of the cultural context created by race, class, gender and sexuality; and the individual level of personal biography (c.f. Collins 1991: 225–30, 1998: 235–40).

In terms of sexuality, heteronormativity (or 'compulsory heterosexuality', 'heterosexual matrix', 'heterosexism')[26] is usually identified as the major form of oppression. Berlant and Warner define heteronormativity as

> more than ideology, or prejudice, or phobia against gays and lesbians; it is produced in almost every aspect of the forms and arrangements of social life: nationality, the state, and the law; commerce; medicine; and education; as well as in the conventions and affects of narrativity, romance, and other protected spaces of culture.
>
> (Berlant and Warner 1998: 554–55)

Heteronormativity manifests itself in structural control at the systemic level, mediated at the community level and internalized at the personal level.[27]

A rigid sex hierarchy (Rubin 1993)[28] is installed via laws, media, education, family, religion, etc., which provide sites for the production of a 'good' sexuality. This gendered sex hierarchy produces the binary opposition heterosexuality/homosexuality. Such a definition correlates with other pairings such as good sex/bad sex, normal/perverted, healthy/unhealthy, moral/immoral, public/secret, and so forth, which in turn structure our modes of thought, knowledge and culture. It is through the disciplining surveillant gazes at different levels that sexual minorities are constituted and internalized as 'bad', 'perverted' or 'immoral' citizens. So heteronormativity, in company with other oppression systems (or knowledge-power regimes, in the Foucauldian sense) such as patriarchy, sexism, racism, hegemonic masculinity, nationalism, etc., ally to form 'scattered hegemonies' (Grewal and Kaplan 1994: 7) that construct our identities, desires and practices in a traversal space.

However, no matter how explicit political leanings, sexualities, or agendas might be, the social construction of sexuality has never been fully installed, as it is constantly being subverted by practices. As Foucault (1980) argued, '(W)here there is power, there is resistance, and yet, or rather consequently, this resistance is never in a position of exteriority in relation to power' (p. 95). In other words, power comes from both above and below, so it cannot be overthrown, but only resisted or reversed. If Foucault is right, 'power is tolerable only on condition that it mask a substantial part of itself. Its success is proportional to its ability to hide its own mechanisms' (p. 86). Ideology is the winning and securing of hegemony over time. As Hall (1977) suggested, 'It is crucial to the concept that hegemony is not a "given" and permanent state of affairs, but has to be actively won and *secured*; it can also be lost' (p. 333, emphasis original).

Looking from this angle, the sites of domination are indeed the potential sites of resistance. Resistance usually takes two major forms. On the one hand, resistance can be overt and directly confront dominant cultural values, usually taking the form of visible political action by a collective of politically charged individuals. Lesbians and gay men can employ different strategies in order to speak against a specific enemy (e.g., the government), or to change the situation (e.g., the law), or to create a new field (e.g., reclaim a queer-intolerant space and make it queer-tolerant). Thus the whole lesbian and gay movement emphasizes the notion of community building, personal identity and lifestyles, crystallized in identity politics since the 1970s and the later-emerged rights-based assimilation movement since the 1990s.

On the other hand, resistance can also be covert and indirect. In *The Practice of Everyday Life*, de Certeau (1984) articulates the importance of 'tactics' in his discussion of the micro-politics of everyday life (e.g., talking, reading, shopping, cooking, etc.), in terms of resistance to the norm. Tactics are ways of making use of the 'already-made' cultural system to achieve one's own desires by introducing alternative meanings to the dominant cultural system. Tactics are an art of the weak. These tactical 'ways of operating': 'victories of the "weak" over the "strong" . . . clever tricks, knowing how to get away with things, "hunter's cunning," maneuvers, polymorphic simulations, joyful discoveries, poetic as well as warlike' (p. xix), do not in any sense constitute an open and confrontational approach for dealing with the powerful, but consist of more subtle activities that continuously upset social and cultural norms. In his ethnographic study of Malaysian peasants, Scott (1985) argues that there are many hidden and invisible 'everyday forms of resistance' that can be seen as 'weapons of the weak', which serve as 'hidden scripts' or 'offstage discourses of the powerless'. This 'politics does not look like politics', and so it is often neglected in the social scientific discussion of the modes of politics.[29]

In terms of sexuality, the tactical way of acting thus constitutes another form of resistance to sexual norms, and is often employed by those who have no privileged position to overtly challenge societal dominations over sexuality. For example, Chauncey (1994) discusses the significance of urban gay culture in New York in the first half of the twentieth century, which might have contributed to the conditions that made gay liberation possible. In response to the government's zoning policy of restricting 'counterpublic'[30] sexual culture, Berlant and Warner (1998: 558–64) argue that the fleeting, ephemeral and 'sleazy' public sexual cultures (e.g., tearooms, streets, bars, sex clubs, parks, boutiques, porn shops) have the potential to nurture a critical mass which might transform the area into one publicly accessible sexual place.[31]

These everyday practices of micro-resistance, even when carried out by politically unconscious subjects, are merely ways to put up with the daily injustice of life while holding onto a sense of dignity. But the subversive potential of these practices of micro-resistance cannot be underestimated, as they might weaken 'the power of the powerful' in a silent way that could serve as an off-stage rehearsal for open assault. As Duncombe (2002: 7) reminds us: 'The first act of politics is simply to act.'

The spectrum of political engagement, or what Duncombe (2002: 5–8) calls 'scales of resistance', varies according to the agents or subjects (the degree of their political self-consciousness and appropriation of culture), the social unit engaged (society, subculture or individual), and the results (revolution, rebellion or mere survival). The scale and scope of resistance also depends collectively on the political, social and cultural circumstances in each country or city. It is thus important, especially through the sociology of homosexuality, to address the institutional regulation of sexuality – by the state, the market, the media, the family, and by other social institutions – that has had, and continues to have, a major impact on how sexuality is organized and experienced (Corber and Valocchi 2003: 10–12).

On the individual level, the scale and scope of resistance depends on the position of the subject, according to his/her biography, education, age, class and even degree of physical fitness. Extending Bourdieu's (1986) notion of class as consisting of various capital movements through social space,[32] I use the term 'embodied capital' to refer to the possession of economic, social, cultural and symbolic capital by lesbians and gay men. The amount of civil, political and social rights lesbian and gay men obtain shapes their overall political bargaining power in society, and the overall form and balance of that power as well. The amount of economic capital (e.g., income and property) they possess determines their basic 'creditability' within an essentially manipulative system. The cultural capital they acquire (e.g., a physically fit body, an 'appropriate' consumption lifestyle, a standard language or a 'respectable' educational background) and the kinds of groups, people and locations they affiliate with (their social capital) greatly affect their physical and social admittance. The extent to which they acquire these various forms of capital determines how they define citizenship, identity, gayness, masculinity, taste, beauty, desirability, respectability and so forth; as well as their positions in overall straight and queer social spaces.

The debate over sexual citizenship

> We may all be sexual citizens, but we are not *equal* sexual citizens.
> (David Bell and Jon Binnie, *The Sexual Citizen*, 2000)

The recent discussion of sexual citizenship illustrates the dynamics of this theoretical framework. The notion of citizenship has long been neglected in the social sciences but has recently become a significant concept for understanding the complicated interplay between the state and the individual in the increasingly global world.

The debate over citizenship can be seen broadly as taking place among and within three broad traditions: liberalism, communitarianism and republicanism (e.g., Janoski 1998: 6–8; Isin and Wood 1999: 7–9). The first presents the classic 'rights and duties' model, as exemplified in T. H. Marshall's (1950) notion of citizenship as involving three clusters of citizen rights – civil, political and social – centred on justice under the law, for political participation and basic human welfare.[33] This model focuses on reciprocal sets of rights and obligations, such as the right to the enjoyment of civil, political, social rights and the obligation to pay taxes, obey laws, etc. The second tradition, sometimes called the 'town hall' model (Plummer 2003: 51), emphasizes volunteerism and civic virtues in civic culture, thus prescribing an active concept of citizenship as meaning participation in civil society. Janoski (1998: 7) identifies scholars proposing this model, from Alexis de Tocqueville, in the early 1800s, to Emile Durkheim in the early 1900s, to Robert Bellah *et al.* and others in the 1990s. The third model, the civic republican tradition, attempts to protect against both state abuses and the greed of the market. Relevant scholars, as identified by Janoski (1998: 7–8), range from Karl Marx in the nineteenth century to Antonio Gramsci in the early 1900s and to Jürgen Habermas and others more recently, who have been concerned with complex democracies and social movements and with improving democratic communication. Thus the debate over citizenship has been about rights and obligations, about status and membership, about practice and participation, and about identity and belonging (Delanty 2007: 16–17).

Early modern discussion of citizenship usually rested on the assumption of a unified notion of the citizen, and was implicitly drawn with the middle-class white heterosexual married man as prototype. A proliferation of new cultural and social identities and subsequent politics of difference have criticized this limited and inclusive notion of citizenship, with arguments over who is to be included and who excluded from the definition of citizenship, along the lines of class, race and ethnicity, gender, sexuality, religion, etc. Marshall's model of citizenship, for example, has frequently been charged with failure to accommodate categories of difference, and of patterning inequalities and exclusions of 'other' groups, such as the underclass, racial minorities, women, lesbians and gay men, migrants, and many others. This has laid bare, first, the racial dimensions of the model (e.g., Anthias and Yuval-Davis 1992: 30–32); second, its gendered nature (e.g., Walby 1994); and finally, the sexual aspect of the concept; concerning which I gain insights from the sexual citizenship literature (e.g., Evans 1993; Weeks 1998; Richardson 1998, 2000, 2001, 2004, 2005; Plummer 2001, 2003; Bell and Binnie 2000; Phelan 2001; and Seidman 2005).

The present discussion of sexual citizenship thus joins in the debate over citizenship by challenging the model of 'ideal' sexual citizenship, as implicitly assumed in the current discourse on citizenship. The ideal citizen is usually seen as 'an individual whose sexual behavior conforms to traditional gender norms, who links sex to intimacy, love, monogamy and preferably marriage, and who restricts sex to private acts that exhibit romantic or caring qualities' (Seidman 2005: 237). As argued by Weeks (1998: 38), a new discussion of citizenship thus should embrace a multiplicity of interlocking strands that reveal the dense interconnections of race, class, gender and sexuality.

Arguing from the situation of lesbians and gay men in Britain in the late 1990s, Diane Richardson (1998) offers a strong critique of Marshall's definition of citizenship, which prescribes the civil, political and social rights of an 'ideal' citizen. She argues that lesbians and gay men are only 'partial' citizens, as they lack certain civil rights, such as the right to marry or the right to serve in the military. Their political rights are limited, as there are only a few 'out' MPs or MPs concerned with lesbian and gay issues. They are also restrained from full access to social welfare, through restrictions such as those in employment, housing, education and parenting. As a result, they, like women and racial and ethnic minorities, have been excluded from full access to the public realm, and ultimately from the nation and nationality, which are assumed to be reserved for males, whites and heterosexuals. They are also excluded from the private sphere, as the right of privacy is primarily a right of legally married heterosexuals. Thus sexual citizenship is extremely circumscribed and privatized, and the limited grant of certain rights (e.g., decriminalization, age of consent) works largely within the parameters of a 'heterosexist public/private divide' (p. 89).[34]

By advocating different versions of citizenship (e.g., feminist citizenship, sexual citizenship, intimate citizenship, erotic citizenship), feminists and queer scholars hope to expand the definition of citizenship to include a wider range of sexual practices, personal identities and intimate relationships. An example of this is Evans' (1993) first conceptualization of sexual citizenship as a form of consumer citizenship through the interplay between the state and the market, involving 'partial private, and primarily leisure and lifestyle membership' (p. 64), and also Richardson's (2000) comprehensive theorization of sexual citizenship in terms of three rights – conduct-based rights ('rights to various forms of sexual practice in personal relationships'), identity-based rights ('rights through self definition and the development of individual identities') and relationship-based rights ('rights within social institutions: public validation of various forms of sexual relations') (pp. 107–8). Bell and Binnie (2000) claim that 'everyone is a sexual citizen', and we need to see 'citizenship as a sexualized project' (p. 142). As Phelan (2001) says,

> The question, then, is not 'queer or not', or 'how to make citizenship queer', but how to queer citizenship – how to continue the subversion of a category that is nonetheless both crucial and beneficial for millions of people around the world.
>
> (Phelan, 2001: 140–41)

Three major avenues of struggle for sexual citizenship are documented, discussed and debated in the literature: the equal rights assimilation movement, the emergence of queer communities and the fight for same-sex marriage. These three struggles can be understood within the power-resistance paradigm, as they are struggles within areas of domination.

Since the 1990s, the lesbian and gay movement has focused on equal rights-based assimilationist politics. Within this normalization discourse, lesbians and gay men are represented as oppressed minorities who ask for inclusion in mainstream society, and who deserve rights and responsibilities equal to those of heterosexuals. This politics of assimilation is highlighted by Sullivan (1995), who argues that most gay men and lesbians are 'virtually normal' and want simply to be fully integrated into society: '. . . gay citizens vote for their own government, pay for it with their own taxes, and have an equal right to participate in it in the same manner as any other citizen. Their unequal treatment by their own state is a fundamental abrogation of fundamental rights' (p. 216) (see also Bawer 1993).[35]

This 'integrationist' argument, however, has been challenged, as it highlights 'normalization' to straight culture but downplays the subversiveness of queer culture (e.g., Bell and Binnie 2000: 44–48; Richardson 2004: 395–400; Seidman 2005: 233–38; Warner 1999: Ch. 3). By making an interesting contrast and comparison between Andrew Sullivan and Judith Butler, Warner (1999) argues that lesbians and gay men, for Sullivan (1995), are virtually normal but 'deluded into pathological queerness by the leagued forces of immature theorists, wounded self-esteem, and the prohibition on marrying' (p. 142); while for Butler (1993), all straight and gay people are virtually queer but are normalized for a coherent identity. It is this possibility of queerness, subversion and resistance that is inevitable to the formation of 'normal' subjects that should be emphasized. As Berlant and Warner (1998) remind us, making a queer world, or queer counterpublics, 'has required the development of kinds of intimacy that bear no necessary relation to domestic space, to kinship, to the couple form, to property, or to the nation' (p. 558). We tend to ignore those mobile, fragile and ephemeral 'scenes' that constitute queer subcultures. This is not just about gay men queering public toilets, streets, parks, shopping malls, etc., but also about mobile arenas such as 'drag, youth culture, music, dance, parades, flaunting, and cruising' (p. 561). These scenes or actions are often trivialized as 'lifestyle', but they apparently serve as examples of practices of micro-resistance. No matter how fleeting and ephemeral, their subversive potential cannot be underestimated.

The net result of the assimilationist or integrationist movement is the creation of 'good', 'normal' homosexual citizens, who are 'expected to be gender conventional, link sex to love and a marriage-like relationship, defend family values, personify economic individualism, and display national pride' (Seidman 2002: 133); and 'bad', 'perverted' and 'dangerous' queers who are not asking for inclusion in the mainstream, nor are they making any rights claims by participating in official civil society or even bordering it to perform as 'good' citizens who follow conventional heterosexual sexual and intimate practices (Warner 1999: Ch. 2; Dangerous Bedfellows 1996[36]). While making sexual (say, lesbian and gay) identities known and public, or even allowing them to find a 'proper' home in the mainstream, is one option, the creation of alternative 'counterpublics' and a 'hanging there', without asking for compromise or inclusion in the mainstream, is another. As Plummer (2003) addresses this dilemma, 'How can someone be "queer and radical" and yet be a "good citizen"?' (p. 64).

The first question is thus: *To what extent is the fight for equal rights for lesbians and gay men merely a matter of asking for inclusion into the mainstream by replicating the heterosexualized term of 'good citizen', and to what extent can the notion of sexual citizenship offer a subversive challenge to the heterosexualization of human life and bring about real transformation in society?*

The second debate is about the emergence of a consumer citizenship among gay men and lesbians under the flourishing of pink economy. The most salient and visible queer movement can be seen from the successful 'territorialization' of queer spaces through the establishment of various commercial and consumption venues (Evans 1993: Ch. 4; Bell and Binnie 2000: Ch. 6; Bell 1995; Hennessy 1995). This substantial queer infrastructure, confined by the logic of pink economy, has numerous effects. It helps to nurture a notion of queer cultural citizenship that has successfully shifted from the traditional image of 'citizen-pervert' to that of 'good consumer citizen' who supports and adheres to dominant cultural norms and values. Such citizens are thus model consumer-citizens (e.g., happy gay couples as the perfect DINKs – Dual Income No Kids) and builders of stable communities (Bell and Binnie 2000: 97). This development has also given rise to the vibrant and evident queer leisure spaces, which provide significant sites for identity formation, cultural belonging and social networking. However, this queer citizenship is cosmopolitan-oriented, commercially driven and conspicuously consumed; it is class-based, gender-based and race-based, and thus serves as a new site of power rather than as a site of resistance.

So the second question is: *To what extent do pink economy and the emergence of commercialized queer space facilitate the articulation of sexual rights and end discrimination against sexual minorities; and to what extent do they privilege certain gay and lesbian consumption patterns that marginalize other queer bodies along the lines of class, gender, race, age, body type, place of origin, etc.?*

The third space of sexual citizenship is centred in the private sphere, and especially involves coming-out politics and the recent discussion of same-sex marriage. Coming out is seen as a privileged political act, and same-sex marriage as a tool for attacking the very core notion of heteronormativity, by making a claim to something that lesbians and gay men lack. However, coming out is usually a political move marked by socio-economic status and cultural underpinnings (Seidman 1998; Seidman *et al.* 1999). Drawing insight from Butler's (1993: 226–30) critique of identity politics (usually crystallized in coming out),[37] Bell and Binnie (2000: 103–4) argue that it is important to ask for whom being out is an available and affordable option before declaring it a universally necessary condition for sexual citizenship. Moreover, same-sex marriage tends to privilege a particular form of heterosexual relationship – namely, marital-style sexual coupledom in a domestic setting – as the yardstick for measuring all relationships and the basis for love, care, support and any rights-claims entitlement – and to subsequently marginalize 'alternative intimacies' such as non-monogamy, polyamory, public sex, and many others.[38]

So the third question is: *To what extent do a coming-out model and same-sex marriage promote sexual citizenship; and to what extent do they privilege an 'out' person as 'politically correct' and consider a closeted person as 'unauthentic', and privilege a coupledom model that marginalizes 'alternative intimacies' widely practised in queer communities, especially among gay men?*

Two recent challenges concerning citizenship should be taken into account: the ideological ascendency of neo-liberalism as a new form of governance, and the challenge of globalization and transnational development that results in a hegemonic ideal of global queer identity or citizenship.

Neo-liberalism is usually seen as an economic ideology that is advanced through certain policies (e.g., deregulation, privatization, loosening restrictions on capital or trade movement), mostly of Western states and international financial institutions such as the International Monetary Fund and the World

Bank. These policies attempt 'to "roll back" the state and the role of government, and leave decisions about allocation, production and distribution in the economy to the global market, thereby excluding or limiting measures that restrict or redistribute the wealth of individuals' (Hudson and Slaughter 2007: 4–5).

Instead of seeing neo-liberalism as simply a political philosophy or economic ideology, I agree with scholars (e.g., Nikolas Rose, Wendy Brown, Aihwa Ong, Lisa Rofel) who view neo-liberalism as a new mode for governing citizens, according to Foucault's notion of governmentality. For example, Rose (1996) argues that what he calls 'advanced' liberalism is a dominant mode of governance in the UK and other advanced liberal-democratic countries. The neo-liberal rules marketize expertise knowledge through budget discipline, accountability and audit system; privatize government activities, ranging from public utilities such as water, gas, electricity to civil services, prisons and police, 'at a distance', thus bringing an end of welfare; and devise new technologies for constituting individual citizens as active citizens seeking to 'enterprise themselves'. As a result, the ideal of the 'social state' gives way to the 'enabling state' (Rofel 2007: 16), in which neo-liberal policies of 'shrinking' the state go hand in hand with remaking the citizen-subject – not the citizen with claims on the state, but a self-enterprising one who is an entrepreneur of himself or herself (Ong 2007: 14).

In terms of sexuality, recent studies examine the tension between the process of neo-liberal governance and sexual citizenship (Cooper 1995, 2002; Richardson 2005). For example, Richardson (2005) argues that the neo-liberal techniques of governance have shifted from a 'policing of the self' to promoting a desire for normativity and respectability. In the past, lesbians and gay men were portrayed as mad, bad or sad individuals with potential subversive power to challenge social norms and values, and thus there was a need for external regulation and control. The newly emerging self-regulated neo-liberal sexual subjects have internalized new norms for being responsible and respectable good citizens: They choose stable cohabiting relationships. Such 'good' sexual citizens serve to demarcate a new boundary with bad and dangerous sexualities and citizens, and make a safe lifestyle of 'low risk' to society. The question is that, although neo-liberal governance goes hand in hand with the politics of normalization and incorporates lesbians and gay men as socially valued members of society, at what cost does it do so?

The fourth question is thus: *To what extent are we constituted 'good' sexual citizens under the state's neo-liberal regulation of sexuality, and to what extent can we end state regulation of adult intimate relationships and personal lifestyles?*

Another challenge concerning citizenship is that of globalization and transnational development. As pointed out by many scholars, Marshall's notion of citizenship rests on the assumption that the boundary-fixed nation-state controls the citizenry of an imagined political identity, granting them various rights. However, globalization and transnational developments have opened

Part I

Hong Kong

Introduction

From colonial citizenship to enterprising citizenship

Hong Kong has been transformed from a colonial city under British administration (1842–1997) to 'Asia's world city' under SAR governance (1997–). A very brief sketch of the history of the change of citizenship in Hong Kong will serve as a backdrop for later discussion of sexual citizenship in Hong Kong.

Ku and Pun (2004: 2) point out that what is distinctive about this megalopolis is its political identity as a quasi-city state that has changed form. In the past, Hong Kong people were either British subjects/nationals, or refugees/immigrants. Today, most of the people regard themselves as 'permanent residents' of Hong Kong and citizens of the People's Republic of China. Hong Kong people rarely refer to themselves as *gongmin* (公民 'citizens'), implying a sense of civic identity. Instead they merely use the term *shimin* (市民 'city people'), or people of the city.[1]

From 1842 to 1997, Hong Kong was a British colony. The colonial government promoted 'law and order' as the ideology of governance and constructed colonial subjects with minimal civil, political and social rights.[2] As argued by So (2004: 236–38), at least up to the first half of the twentieth century, Hong Kong people had no voting rights[3] and no power to select their own government, and laws such as the Societies Ordinance restricted certain organizations, activities and publications that criticized the colonial state. As for social rights, the colonial state promoted a laissez-faire economic philosophy and maintained a hands-off policy with regard to employment, housing, health care, pensions, and other social welfare for Hong Kong people. Hong Kong people were merely residents – neither citizens nor subjects of either the United Kingdom or China. As a result, Hong Kong residents enjoyed minimal civil, political and social rights – a situation which can be regarded as mere 'colonial citizenship', and showed little loyalty to the British colonial regime. This mutual exclusiveness between the polity and society is best characterized by Lau's (1982) 'minimally integrated socio-political regime.'[4]

The relationship between the colonial government and its ruling subjects has changed significantly since 1949, the year the Communist Party took power in China, when thousands and thousands of refugees/immigrants began to flee to Hong Kong from mainland China. The colonial government employed various means to de-nationalize, depoliticize and 'civilize' (modernize), in order to produce new urban–civic subjects. The colonial government deployed 'de-nationalizing' policies to consolidate its control over Hong Kong after 1949, delinking Hong Kong from the Chinese economy, suppressing communist infiltration in Hong Kong, while it continued to privilege English, rather than Chinese, as the dominant and official language (So 2004: 237–38). Ho (2004) argues that the colonial government depoliticized Hong Kong society through two means: by refraining from interfering in Hong Kong-Chinese society so as not to provoke the people; and by advocating economic laissez-faire to justify its rule. Thus the colonial government blocked major access to political rights (e.g., political freedom and participation), prioritized economic development and granted those civil rights that related exclusively to market rights, and promoted social welfare as only a residual concept, emphasizing that Hong Kong people should seek help from their families, voluntary agencies or the market for their welfare needs, rather than from the government.

A significant change in colonial governance and citizenship occurred in the 1970s, after riots in 1966 and 1967. In order to reclaim its legitimacy, the government, still restricting political rights, granted certain social rights through various programmes and policies, such as a massive public housing plan to accommodate over half of all Hong Kong residents, labour laws to protect workers' lives according to international labour standards, increased welfare expenditure to help the socially disadvantaged, the implementation of nine years of free education and expansion of the number of places in higher education (So 2004: 239). Around the same time the government engaged in a 'civilizing' project to promote a new cultural citizenship. As argued by Turner and Ngan (1995) in the edited book *Hong Kong Sixties*, the colonial government helped promote a new design for Hong Kong identity/citizenship, as '[S]eparation from China demanded new self-images of the Hong Kong body, moulded by Western ideas of time, health and efficiency, and western ideals of posture, fashion and physique' (p. 38). In the same book, Turner (1995) argued that the various campaigns and slogans of 'community building' – such as 'Fight crime', 'Clean Hong Kong', 'Hong Kong for Hong Kong people', 'Be loyal to Hong Kong', and 'We are a family living under one roof' – of the 1970s by no means served to empower social citizenship, but merely served as a way to nurture a sense of local belonging and to encourage a new identity – modern, cosmopolitan, and Westernized – with the ethos of economic rationality.[5]

Not until the 1980s did the colonial government start to grant certain political rights to Hong Kong people, through a process of democratization in preparation for the handover of sovereignty (So 2004: 239–40; Lo 2001:

132–39). The 1989 June Fourth Incident[6] is believed to have been a turning point that triggered the colonial government to grant more civic and political rights to Hong Kong people. The Bill of Rights was enacted in 1991; the Equal Opportunity Commission was established in 1996; and, under the last Governor, Chris Patten, the government broadened the franchise arrangements governing the Legislative Council's (LegCo) functional consistencies, reduced the voting age for Hong Kong people from 21 to 18 and issued pledges to monitor the performance of government departments. However, this resulted in only a semi-democratic status for Hong Kong people, who, today, still cannot directly elect the Chief Executive. While half of the seats (30) in the Legislative Council are filled by direct election according to geographical constituency, the other half (30) are still filled indirectly via functional constituency elections.

Hong Kong entered a new era in 1997, when it became a Special Administrative Region (SAR) of China. So (2004: 241–43) considers that the SAR government wants to promote a new mode of citizenship, different from that of colonial times. However, the SAR is caught in a dilemma of 'nationalization' and 'localization': on the one hand, the SAR government wants to keep a distance from mainland China and so does not push too much any re-nationalization project in Hong Kong, which would reduce Hong Kong to a status similar to that of other cities such as Guangzhou. On the other hand, the SAR state cannot promote a strong sense of local identity, which might be read as a threat to the PRC and a strategy promoting practical independence, such as that of Taiwan at present.

The perceived solution has thus been to transform Hong Kong as a global city within the grandiose framework of 'one country, two systems' (Ku and Pun 2004: 2; c.f. Ku 2002; So 2004: 241–43). Underlying this hegemonic state project is the enterprising individual – the ideal citizen–subject, who relies on self-enterprise and self-help. Although Hong Kong has never been a welfare state, both the colonial government and the SAR government have always employed neo-liberal language. As argued by Ku and Pun (2004: 7), there are striking similarities between the 'civic, urban, economistic, and self-reliant subject' under colonial rule and the 'enterprising individual' of neo-liberal ideology since the 1980s. In this neo-liberal discourse of 'enterprising citizenship and competitive economy', issues of civil, political and social rights can be sidestepped, and rights can even be cut back, such as through Public Order Ordinance and Article 23 of the Basic Law.[7] It is also because of this neo-liberal drive for global competitiveness that the SAR is concerned about its 'population quality', in terms of talents and value-added human resources, which, Sautman (2004) argues, creates a hierarchy of citizens: 'citizen' of Chinese elite tycoons, 'denizen' of expatriate British and Japanese, and 'margizen' of Filipino and Indonesian domestic helpers and Nepalese and Pakistani workers.[8]

To sum up: Hong Kong people have never been granted full access to political, civil and social rights. The fight for direct election of the Chief

Executive and the demand for universal suffrage have been major agendas in democratic campaigns since 1997. Although Hong Kong people enjoy certain civil and social rights, these rights are conditional, granted according to categories such as race and ethnicity, age, class, sexual orientation, etc., that deprive minorities such as the immigrant Chinese (especially lower-class Chinese migrant women), South Asians workers, and elderly and sexual minorities. Moreover, rights can be 'cut back', in accordance with various political and economic crises.

The development of citizenship in Hong Kong has thus always been circumscribed by the parameters of economic ideologies (e.g., laissez-faire, neo-liberalism). Any citizenship-rights claims are subsumed under the paramount concern for economic prosperity, which is believed to develop best in a 'harmonious' political and social environment. Hong Kong people have tended to accept their political impotence, to believe in open society, and to rely on the idea of competitive individualism to solve problems. Hong Kong citizens are thus constructed as law-abiding and self-enterprising subjects, and can be characterized as politically aloof, economically inclined, individually competent, hardworking, flexible and pragmatic.

This constructed ideal citizen is gendered, racialized and sexualized. The image is more or less that of a middle-class, local-born, heterosexual Chinese man, who not only is successful in material accumulation, with his owned flat and car, but also successful in building a nuclear family with wife and kids.

The politics of de-politicizing culture

Hong Kong has long been described as an apolitical society, due to colonial administration and neo-Confucian teachings that stress harmony. Is being 'apolitical' a characteristic of Hong Kong (or, for that matter, Chinese) people, and is being 'political' a particular characteristic of Western people? What are meant by 'political' and 'radical', and what is 'subversion'? What ends and purposes do these terms imply?

Although Hong Kong people may not be particularly interested in, and may even be alienated from, organized and institutional politics, they are indeed practically involved, if not passionately interested in, the 'political' sphere of life. In order to understand more clearly the 'political' of Hong Kong people, we have to shift from institutional political spheres to other spheres, such as the market economy, the civil society, the media, popular culture, and the private realm of family and marriage, which are also involved in 'politics'.

Chiu and Lui (2000: 1–19) have argued that social movements and collective actions within civil society have long been present in Hong Kong political history, though their significance has often been overlooked and their impacts have often been underestimated. Especially since the 1960s, post-war local-born generations have expressed frustrations and discontents with the government (e.g., with government corruption), poor living standards and conditions of public housing, and the persistence of poverty in affluent Hong Kong. Student activism and grass-roots protests, manifested as strikes, protests and other collective actions, have challenged colonial government policies, social injustice and discriminations, in issues ranging from those of labour, housing, environment and even gender. The 1989 June Fourth Incident and the July 1 March in 2003[9] can be seen as examples of the continuation of such activist social participation.

Lam (2004) also challenges the common myth that Hong Kong society is apolitical and that Hong Kong people are politically indifferent. She argues that, although lawful political participation, channelled by and on behalf of the government, may be limited (especially before 1997), numerous social groups and organizations and the media are active outside the traditional channels of political influence, have demonstrated considerable capacity to organize and mobilize protests of discontent and have put forward their demands to the government.

Abbas (1992) accounts for Hong Kong's situation by pointing to its 'compensatory' economism and 'infamous' coloniality. Hong Kong people's economic success is interpreted as a result of its lack of political autonomy and self-determination.

> One of the effects of a very efficient colonial administration is that it provides almost no outlet for political idealism (until perhaps quite recently); as a result, most of the energy is directed towards the economic sphere . . . If you cannot choose your political leaders, you can at least choose your own clothes. We find therefore not an atmosphere of doom and gloom, but the most paradoxical phenomenon of *doom* and *boom*: the more frustrated or blocked the aspirations to 'democracy' are, the more the market blooms.
>
> (Abbas 1992: 5; emphasis original)

In other words, since governance in Hong Kong provides few outlets for political aspirations and idealism, people's energy has been directed towards economic pursuit and consumption, as well as towards cultural production and consumption of popular culture. Abbas' witty argument echoes the well-established literature in which the emergence of the cultural identity of *hoeng gong jan* (**香港人** Cant.: 'Hong Kong people'), has been discussed since the 1960s.[10]

The level and scope of political participation and mobilization, however, has been dramatically changed, enhanced and transformed since 2003, the year when an estimated half a million Hong Kong people marched on 1 July to voice out their political, economic, social and cultural dissatisfaction. These dissatisfactions about the government - poor governance, slow democratic development, structural budgetary deficit, several social inequalities; in accompany with the wide use of mass media (especially the internet) and the rise of various social, cultural and political groups for mobilizations which all seem to have contributed to the changes of the political landscape in Hong Kong in recent years (Sing 2009).[11]

Finally, Ho (2004) points out how (post-)colonial governance has emphasized the family as a self-regulating and self-reliance mechanism which successfully turns people away from government and to their families for support, welfare needs and resources, while effectively undermining the development of social citizenship and community. Family is thus considered as a 'morally right form of self-organization' (p. 33). This argument debunks the myth of the over-emphasis on family as stemming from Hong Kong people's respect for Confucian tradition and opens up a new perspective for viewing the family as a tool of self-governance. That Hong Kong people pivot their lives in the private sphere may not be due to their adherence to tradition (especially to the so-called 'family values' of the Confucian tradition, which are echoed by the promotion of 'family values' by conservative Christianity in the United States), but may be an effect of the nature of state governance. Ong (1993, 1996, 1999) makes a similar point that the Hong Kong family is the effect of state discipline on the refugee/immigrant families of post-war Hong Kong.[12]

Sexing Hong Kong citizenship

In such a socio-political environment, what kind of sexual citizenship are Hong Kong tongzhi making or remaking? How does the government shape the contours of 'sexual' movements in Hong Kong? What has been done by tongzhi and tongzhi organizations?

In the following three chapters, three spaces of sexual citizenship in Hong Kong will be examined, with particular focus on Hong Kong memba. The first can be seen in the tongzhi movement. First, subject to colonial and post-colonial governance, the tongzhi movement has tended to confine itself to assimilationist politics in fighting for sexual rights. While it gains support from both the gay and straight worlds, it apparently creates a class of 'good homosexual citizen' at the expense of 'dangerous citizen-pervert'. Not until the launch of IDAHO events did a more reflexive sexual politics begin to emerge. Second, the blockage of political channels has led to the production of a vibrant queer cultural world that has successfully transformed the 'homosexual' from a pathologically deviant subject to a cosmopolitan citizen, although he is still subject to neo-liberal governance, censorship, commercial funding and sponsorship, and is constantly challenged by anti-gay (mainly religious) NGOs.

The second sexual space is a vibrant and obvious queer commercial one, which provides a significant cultural arena contributing to queer consumer citizenship and is governed by pink commerce and homonormativity or 'cult gay masculinity', through which many Hong Kong memba are placed in a subordinate position.

The third space of sexual citizenship is the private sphere of family, love and marriage. Although subject to familial heteronormativity, Hong Kong memba struggle for a personal space of gay identity within the parameters of family biopolitics. Although they are not particularly interested in discussing the possibility of same-sex marriage, they passionately engage in various 'intimate projects' that seek alternatives to heterosexualized definitions of family, marriage and love.

2 Queers are ready!?

Sexual citizenship and the tongzhi movement

> The Tongzhi Movement (同志運動) is stagnant, hardly moving at all in the political arena. Thus, the Tongzhi Movement (同志運動) has become merely tongzhi activities (同志活動). Still at a very preliminary stage, we talk about a liberation movement for sexual rights, with the tongzhi community as a subaltern group that needs political struggle to re-dispose and re-inscribe its own rights.
>
> (Anson Mak and Mary Ann King, 'Hong Kong's tongzhi movement: through the eyes of queer sisters', 1997)

> Queers are ready (we are ready),
> Rainbow is ahead of us
> Queers are ready (we are ready)
> We are determined to be united,
> We are devoted bearing the same faith.
> Queers are ready.
>
> (Theme song, International Day Against Homophobia, Hong Kong, 2008)

In 1997, Anson Mak and Mary Ann King wrote an article on the Hong Kong Tongzhi Movement and argued that tongzhi groups at that time were not concerned about equal rights but were focused on organizing social activities and parties that rendered their endeavour merely a matter of tongzhi activities, not a movement. Since 2005, the International Day Against Homophobia (IDAHO) has been organized annually in Hong Kong, and the first Gay Pride Parade was held on 13 December 2008. But does this mean that local tongzhi activities have finally transformed into a tongzhi movement? What constitutes a movement? If it is a political movement, why are there always so few tongzhi participants? One of the organizers of IDAHO said at the first IDAHO event, 'We've made history, or herstory!' – but what kind of history are we making? Who is the 'we' in this history? What spaces for sexual identity have been established and can be imagined in this, Asia's world city? What are the limitations of these spaces, their boundaries, and their margins?

In this chapter I will examine the complicated relationship between sexuality, citizenship and government regulation, using Hong Kong's tongzhi movement as an example. I will first outline the changes in laws governing homosexuality in Hong Kong (especially the decriminalization of homosexuality in 1990) and argue that tongzhi in Hong Kong have always been considered outsiders in the discourse of citizenship. The early tongzhi movement tended to resemble the government's rhetoric of 'social harmony' and 'economic primacy', and its propaganda against any 'radical' democratic movement. It promoted a harmonious and non-confrontational politics driven by the notion of assimilation and normalization, and this tended to suppress radical and confrontational queer politics.

A 'third way' for queer politics, between those of assimilation and radicalism, has been slowly emerging recently. However, most tongzhi in Hong Kong are not interested in formal politics. I will argue that this 'apolitical' nature of Hong Kong tongzhi, as reflected in the low priority given to fighting for institutional same-sex rights, is only one side of the story. It is the contribution of tongzhi to cultural production in the media and popular culture that provides a major space for disrupting the hegemonic heterosexist norm, and has subsequently transformed the tongzhi from a perverted personage to a cosmopolitan and transnational cultural subject. Although more diverse representations of tongzhi in the cultural sphere have brought about a certain claim for cultural citizenship, I will argue that queer visibility, both in the mainstream and alternative media, is still subject to neo-liberal regulation and control, which in turn confine it within 'the institutionalization of heteronormative forms of social and cultural life' (Richardson 2001: 163).

Decriminalization of homosexuality

Consistent with the colonial government's overarching ideology of 'law and order', Hong Kong closely followed English law (Liang 1987),[1] including laws governing homosexual conduct (Lethbridge 1976), during the whole colonial period (1842–1997).

It is generally argued that male homosexuality was quite tolerated in ancient and imperial China (Van Gulik 1961; Chou 1971: 90–93; Bullough 1976: 300–310; Ruan and Tsai 1987; Ruan 1991: 107–20; Ruan 1997: 57–59; Samshasha 1997; Hinsch 1990). The laws concerning homosexuality in the Qing Dynasty (AD 1644–1911) were mostly preoccupied with male homosexual rape, especially that of minors (Samshasha 1997: 245–46; Hinsch 1990: 139–46; Sommer 1997; Ng 1987; Lethbridge 1976: 310–17; see also Chapter 6). However, the colonial government made buggery[2] a crime in Hong Kong in 1842, and Hong Kong thereafter was to follow English law – for example, the death penalty for buggery was abolished in 1861 in England, and Hong Kong followed suit in 1865; the Criminal Law Amendment Act of 1885, dealing with acts of 'gross indecency' between males,[3] was made into law in Hong Kong in 1901.

Yet the colonial government made no effort to put the Sexual Offence Act of 1967, which decriminalized male homosexual conduct in private in the UK, into law in Hong Kong. Lethbridge (1976: 306–10) argues that this may be due to three factors: 1) homosexuality was not even perceived as a social problem by the population, and thus the government had no reason to change the law, as such a move might have been considered too radical and liberal; 2) homosexuals in Hong Kong, especially Chinese homosexuals, were extremely discreet under British rule, which can be seen from the very low number of reported arrests; and 3) the few more 'visible' homosexuals were usually Europeans and it had become police practice, supported by the government, not to prosecute them.[4]

The public debate about homosexuality came to the surface when the Scottish police inspector John MacLennan was charged with acts of gross indecency and then found dead in his apartment in 1980.[5] The case is meticulously discussed in Ho (1997: Ch.1). Briefly put, his death was alleged to have been a murder and a police cover up, which raised media attention to challenge the justice and integrity of the colonial government. The colonial government responded by appointing a judicial committee (Commission of Inquiry) to investigate the case and another committee (the Law Reform Commission of Hong Kong, or LRCHK) to review laws governing homosexual conduct. The Commission of Inquiry, in 1981, concluded that the case was one of suicide, while the LRCHK published a report in 1983 recommending that sexual conduct in private between males over the age of 21 should not be prohibited by law (Hong Kong Government (Law Reform Commission of Hong Kong) 1983, 1988). This recommendation stirred up a lot of heated debate about homosexuality in society in the 1980s. This decriminalization-of-homosexuality debate involved many interesting issues, such as whether homosexuality was scientifically proven to be normal, whether homosexuality was a 'Western' disease, and whether homosexual activity was a human right. The recommendation was finally implemented by the Crimes (Amendment) Ordinance in 1991. This final move seems to have been made as a response to the issue of the prospective return of Hong Kong to PRC rule in 1997, in reference to the effects of the Bill of Rights, and out of an urge to speed up legal and democratic reforms in the aftermath of the 1989 June Fourth Incident (Ho 1997: 75–79; Chan 2007: 39).

Decriminalization, however, did not mean legalization: the colonial government only agreed to decriminalize male homosexual acts under certain conditions (e.g., two men aged 21 or above, and sex 'in private'). The colonial government had no interest in endorsing gay rights or even in recognizing a gay lifestyle. Sir David Ford, then Chief Secretary, summarized the debate in the Legislative Council as follows:

> A vote in favour simply signifies recognition that personal moral codes may differ and can co-exist in a society. Nor does a vote in favour signify a state of approval, it signifies only recognition of an individual's rights

> to personal choice in his private sexual matters. A vote in favour does not signify personal acceptance of the rightness or wrongness of such act, but only suggests whether such acts committed between consenting adults and in private merit the mobilisation of the full machinery of law enforcement.
> (Daily Information Bulletin, Government Information Service 7-11-1990; quoted in Ho 1997: 84).

The decriminalization act had numerous effects in the 1990s: It not only protected gay men who engaged in certain private sexual acts but also triggered off the mushrooming of local tongzhi groups and the establishment of various venues of entertainment (e.g., clubs, bars, saunas, karaokes, etc.), which subsequently led to the development of queer subculture (see Chapter 3 for the development of a commercial queer scene). Moreover, the ten years of debate transformed homosexual conduct from a legal issue to a social one, and involved the creation of the 'homosexual' as a distinct social type. Subsequently, the decriminalization led to the emergence of homosexual identity in Hong Kong (Ho 1997: Ch. 4; Ho and Tsang 2004a). However, parallel with this development was the creation of two types of homosexuals – the 'decent' homosexuals who met and had sex with other adult males 'in private', and the 'reprehensible' minority who indulged in public acts and/or with partners under the age of 21. It is the latter type that remained under surveillance, and such individuals were controlled and disciplined, as evidenced by reports of cases of arrest since the 1990s (Ho and Tsang 2004a: 671). As argued by Richardson (2001: 157) in the British context, this private/public division tended to stipulate that homosexual relationships should be carried out 'in private' and confined gay and lesbian (or tongzhi in my case) rights as 'private individual rights' rather than as 'human rights'. Moreover, as Mort (1980) and Evans (1993: Ch.2–5) argue, British law reform tended to equate sexuality with morality and to consider sexual matters to be private and personal, thus creating a type of homosexual subject which was individualistic and pleasure-seeking, and nurturing a gay subculture with an apolitical character.[6] Hong Kong tended to confirm their observations.

Laws concerning homosexuality have not changed much since 1991. In the 1994–95 legislative session a straight ex-LegCo member, Anna Wu, put forward a bill (the Equal Opportunity Bill) containing provisions outlawing discrimination against sex, family status, disability, race, ethnicity, sexual orientation, etc., but it appears that the bill was considered too comprehensive and thus inappropriate by other legislators, and so was strategically postponed (Chan 2007: 44–45). The Government eventually established three ordnances outlawing discrimination – one based on sex (i.e., involving marital status, pregnancy and sexual harassment), another on disability and the third on family status. The first two were passed in 1995 and the third in 1997.[7] More recently, in October 2008, the Government enacted anti-discrimination laws applying to race and ethnicity, but no bill to prohibit discrimination according to sexual orientation has yet been enacted. A significant challenge to the present law arose in 2005 when a 20-year-old young man, William Leung, filed for judicial review and charged that the unequal age of consent for homosexuals (21) and heterosexuals (16) was unconstitutional, as it violated the Basic Law and the Bill of Rights. After judicial reviews, the High Court judged the differential ages of consent as unconstitutional, in August 2005. Although the Government made an appeal, the Court of Appeal confirmed the High Court's decision in September 2006 (Chan 2008).

Compared to gay men in other Asian countries where male homosexual conduct is still considered a criminal offence (e.g., Singapore, Malaysia), Hong Kong gay men tend to enjoy more political freedom. However, the overall legal, political and social situation of gay men as well as other tongzhi in Hong Kong is still far from satisfactory (The Hong Kong Christian Institute *et al.* 2006). Tongzhi have always been considered social outsiders. Although tongzhi have the political right to vote, their capacity to exercise political power is limited. There are no 'out' tongzhi government officials or elected politicians, and there has only been one 'out' candidate in any election (Cheung Kam-hung, in the district elections of 2003, who failed to be elected), although a few politicians have been concerned about the case of sexual minorities in relation to ideas of human rights and equal opportunities (e.g., ex-LegCo members Christine Loh, Lau Chin-shek, and Dr Fernando Cheung Chiu-hung; and present LegCo members Emily Lau, Cyd Ho, Chan Yuen-han; and members of the newly-formed (2007) League of Social Democrats such as Leung Kwok-hung, Wong Yuk-man and Chan Wai-yip). As noted by Richardson (1998: 88) in her discussion of UK politics, being 'out' is usually seen as a positive disadvantage, if not a disqualifier, for political office.

In terms of civil rights, there is no legislation against discrimination on the grounds of sexual orientation. Same-sex partners are not entitled to the right to marry, or the right to adopt children, the right to inherit if a partner dies intestate and so on. Age of consent was only equalized in 2005. For example, same-sex partners cannot apply for public housing and other housing benefits that heterosexual married couples can apply for. They run the risk of being dismissed or passed over for promotion once their sexual orientation is revealed. In churches of some denominations, tongzhi Christians repeatedly receive messages against homosexuality; some have even come under pressure to receive aversive therapy or conversion counselling, have been asked temporarily to stop coming to church, or have even been barred from regular Sunday services. Although different sexual orientations have been included in the Guidelines for Sex Education in schools, whether this topic is taught depends on individual schools and teachers. Schools can be places where severe and brutal abuse and bullying of lesbians and gay men take place (Hong Kong Government 1996: 4–8; Kong 2000: Ch. 4; The Hong Kong Christian Institute *et al.* 2006: 86–134).

In such an adverse environment, why cannot we see a strong resistance against societal injustice regarding sexuality?

Desiring the normal? Tongzhi politics and post-coloniality

Assimilationist politics

National political and cultural characteristics play crucial roles in the creation of modern queer identities and in the development of national queer movements. Western queer politics has changed from a separationist politics to an assimilationist politics under neo-liberal regimes since the 1990s (e.g., Bell and Binnie 2000: Ch. 2; Richardson 2004; Warner 1999; Seidman 2005), while the tongzhi movement in Hong Kong has always employed an assimilationist politics.

From 1842 to 1990, tongzhi in Hong Kong were highly discreet. Even in the debate on decriminalization of homosexuality, the pro-decriminalization alliances consisted mainly of straight people rather than tongzhi. The battle was thus not between homosexuals and heterosexuals, but involved alliances according to gender, class, age, religious background, etc. (Ho 1997: 82–92). After homosexuality was decriminalized in Hong Kong in 1991, tongzhi organizations began to flourish. These early tongzhi organizations were mainly self-help, service-oriented and community-based in nature. The inward-oriented style of identity-building seemed to be a major concern, and non-confrontational tongzhi politics seemed to be the main strategy. For example, the Ten Percent Club and Horizons both offered regular social gatherings, recreational activities and tea dances. Horizons and Satsanga provided counselling services. The Hong Kong Blessed Minority Christian Fellowship and Isvara both encouraged the spiritual development of tongzhi. The 1997 Tongzhi Forum and XX Group focused on cultural and media issues. Freeman and the Joint University Queer Union claimed to organize non-political activities.

These groups' main sites of struggle seemed not to be on legal or political terrain, and the groups seldom organized large-scale collective action to strive for legal protection against criminalization; nor did they demand gay rights or engage in any confrontational political actions. What these gay 'activists' tried to do was to promote members' participation in their organizations. Their aims were not to change the law but simply to educate other tongzhi and to develop a tongzhi community in which people could be more positive about being gay, or tongzhi, so as to identify themselves within a wider 'we' group (Ho 1997: 204–26; Kong 2000: 260–67).

This non-confrontational politics is best illustrated by the Chinese Tongzhi Conference organized in 1996, which sent out a press release called 'Manifesto of the 1996 Chinese Tongzhi Conference' on 8 Dec 1996:

> **6. Confrontational Politics in the West Should Not Be Imposed upon Chinese Societies.**
>
> The les-bi-gay movement in many Western societies is largely built upon the notion of individualism, confrontational politics, and the discourse of

> individual rights. Certain characteristics of confrontational politics, such as through coming out and mass protests and parades may not be the best way of achieving tongzhi liberation in the family-centred, community oriented Chinese societies which stresses [sic] the importance of social harmony. In formulating the tongzhi movement strategy, we should take the specific socio-economic and cultural environment of each society into consideration.
>
> **7. We Should Respect Each Other Regardless of Sexual Orientation.**
>
> We are a group of Chinese tongzhi unashamed and proud of who we are. While we do not deny our sexual orientation, we do not advertise the sexual aspect of our life. If the society can deal with this issue without prejudice, everyone [sic], tongzhi or otherwise, need not highlight her or his sexuality. People should respect each other as an individual [sic] regardless of sexual orientation and other social differences. With this goal in mind, together we can build a better society.

The rhetoric of the tongzhi movement has not only essentialized Western and Chinese cultures and overlooked the complicated relationships between the two, but has also resembled the rhetoric of the government in the face of the democratic movement. The colonial Hong Kong government had always used the notion of 'respect local culture' to depoliticize Hong Kong society through the minimally integrated socio-political regime (Lau 1982; Ho 2004; Law 1998). The SAR government has since emphasized the notion of 'Chinese' values such as 'harmony' and 'moderation' in its propaganda against any radical democratic approach (Lau 2002; Lam 2005; Ngo 2000).

As argued by Wong (2004), the local tongzhi movement has advanced a 'desexualized politics of respectable citizens', which normalizes the *difference* between homosexuals and heterosexuals: 'those who identify as gay or lesbians in our community in Hong Kong are not pathological people, but productive and contributing members of society' (Hong Kong Gay Coalition 1996: C59; quoted in Wong 2004: 207).

> Gay men and lesbians do not differ at all from heterosexuals in their value systems. We all value loving families, long-term partners, the success of the Hong Kong economy, the work ethic, and good dim sum. Attempts to conceptualize gay men and lesbians as morally deficient, evil, or as destructive to the family are all biased.
>
> (Hong Kong Gay Coalition 1996: C74; quoted in Wong 2004: 207)

The movement has tried to dissociate homosexuality and pathology, downplay the 'sexual' aspects of gay and lesbian identity, and draw similarities between heterosexuals and homosexuals by highlighting how good tongzhi are. In this assimilationist politics, tongzhi have been seen as good citizens ('productive and contributing members of society'), identified with the same 'core' values promoted by the Hong Kong government (e.g., 'loving families, long-term partners, the success of the Hong Kong economy, the work ethic, and good dim sum'). This assimilationist politics shows striking similarity to Western assimilationist politics. The 'normal tongzhi' is more or less the same as the normal lesbians and gay men depicted in the assimilationist movement in the United States promoted by Sullivan (1995) and Bawer (1993). The 'normal' gay is one who is expected to be gender conventional, who links sex to love, enjoys a marriage-like relationship, defends family values, personifies economic individualism, and displays national pride (Seidman 2002: 133).

Although the tongzhi movement has aimed at inclusion in the mainstream, it nevertheless has overlooked its internal logic of exclusion. There has been a long history of internal schism inside the tongzhi community, notably promoted by lesbians and other queer women who have felt excluded and dismissed (Mak and King 1997). The announcement to the media that no women would be involved in the 1998 Tongzhi Conference, by a gay organizer of the conference, triggered anger and frustration that subsequently led many lesbians to move out of male-dominated tongzhi groups and to set up women-exclusive organizations (Tang 2008: Ch.6).[8]

Radical queer politics

However, parallel with local democratic politics in the post-1997 era, Hong Kong tongzhi politics have recently become more aggressive and more actively concerned with the rights of sexual minorities. For example, The Ten Percent Club, Horizons and the Hong Kong Blessed Minority Christian Fellowship have recently started to become involved with gay rights (equal opportunities). Queer Sisters has associated itself as part of a larger social democratic movement concerning women's issues and human rights. New groups have been established with equal rights as one of their major agendas – e.g., Civil Rights for Sexual Diversities, F' Union, Women's Coalition of Hong Kong SAR, and Nutong Xueshe (女同學社).

Set up in 1998, Rainbow of Hong Kong is a tongzhi group that strives for equal opportunities, but the group uses a somewhat radical and confrontational approach to advance its political ends. In 2001, members of the group Rainbow Action protested that the Hong Kong Red Cross's blood donation guidelines discriminated against male homosexuals.[9] They scuffled with security guards and police at a World Red Cross Day ceremony held in Telford Plaza in Kowloon. Some waived a large banner from the first floor and threw anti-discrimination leaflets down to the public gallery. In 2002, two gay members married two lesbian members in order to use the loophole of the legal marital status to apply for public housing. They sought inclusion by declaring their belief in mainstream values about monogamy and intimacy, even though they practised open relationships in real life. They presented themselves as respectable citizens who paid taxes (although, in fact, they belonged to a low-income group exempted from tax payment).[10] In the same year, in support of a BDSM couple who had organized a BDSM party that was raided by the police and were subsequently charged,[11] Rainbow members dressed in SM outfits and tied themselves to the main gate of the Central Police Station. They were later charged by the police. In 2003, they condemned Hong Kong's then Roman Catholic Bishop, Joseph Zen, for publishing two articles in a church newsletter arguing against same-sex marriage. They struggled with church officials, went to the front and held a kiss-in, and shouted slogans at worshippers during a mass at the Hong Kong Catholic Cathedral of the Immaculate Conception.

All of these actions were widely condemned by the straight population, who charged the group with being 'disrespectful to society' – as well as by most tongzhi organizations, who believed that the group has 'brought shame to the tongzhi community'. Some tongzhi organizations drew a line between themselves, as 'good' homosexuals, and the group, who were 'dangerous freaks'. Their anger and frustrations seemed to stem from the fact that they disliked the founder (along with other active members) of the group, who openly declared that he was a bisexual, a freelance sex worker, a BDSM practitioner, and into open relationships. While most tongzhi tried hard to get into the 'charmed circle' of Rubin's (1993) notion of sex hierarchy (see Chapter 1 note 28), members from Rainbow Action 'shamelessly' enjoyed the dangerous pleasure of testing 'the outer limits' in order to advance a radical sexual politics. They were thus the 'bad boyz', 'dangerous queers' or 'dissent sexual citizens' who do not ask for inclusion into the mainstream nor make any claims of performing as good citizens. They exemplify the other side of what it may mean to be 'gay' – to be outsiders, 'to be transgressive, to be radical, to be a threat, to be a queer' (Plummer 2003: 42).

The third way?

There is a well-established literature debating the pros and cons of assimilationist or normalization politics in the West (e.g., Bell and Binnie 2000: Ch. 2; Richardson 2004; Warner 1999; Seidman 2005). Which kind of tongzhi politics is the most appropriate for Hong Kong seems to be a major issue for Hong Kong tongzhi activists. Tongzhi movement strategy should be formulated in the specific socio-economic and cultural contexts, and to take post-coloniality seriously. If it is important to realize the potential threat that confrontational politics may bring to society, it is equally important to recognize the potential harm of living under the trope of 'social harmony'. If the discourse of individual rights in coming-out politics should not be privileged, the discourse of family-centred community that may serve as a new closet mechanism should also be challenged. If it is right to fight for the rights that tongzhi are deprived of in the discourse of sexual citizenship, it is also important to ask what costs (such as in the creation of 'good' and 'bad' homosexuals and the internal schisms along the lines of gender, class, etc.) we have to pay for assimilationist and normalization politics. To stress that homosexuals and heterosexuals are the *same* has the positive effect of de-stigmatizing homosexuals, especially within the confines of 'good citizenship'; however, it is precisely the *difference* between homosexuals and heterosexuals, usually promoted by radical queers, that brings forth the subversive potential of the outsider who radically challenges heteronormativity and other social injustices.

Figure 2.1 The first IDAHO in 2005 (author's photograph).

The IDAHO parade carries messages of both anti-homophobia and the celebration of different sexualities. The first IDAHO event was held in 2005, for two reasons: (1) to commemorate the date when the World Health Organization lifted homosexuality from its classified list of diseases in 1990; and (2) to respond to the attacks from the religious right in opposition to equal protection for all.[12]

Figure 2.2 Die-in action in 2007 IDAHO (author's photograph).

Figure 2.3 2009 IDAHO. Marching to Central Government Office (author's photograph).

After four years, the IDAHO committee now consists of 16 queer and queer-friendly NGOs,[13] whose campaigns have focused on discrimination based on sexual orientation (e.g., 'Turn Fear to Love' (2005), 'Stand up against prejudice' (2006) and 'Legislation is the best education' (2007)) and on gender (e.g., 'Gender diversity, no discrimination' (2008)). The number of participants has remained quite constant over the years, at around 500. The event has been quite structured, with openings by different individuals and NGOs, declarations, a 'die-in' action,[14] chanting and marches.

As noted by Tang (2008), IDAHO is 'an anti-homophobia march but at the same time, it is so rare to see a group of lesbians, gays, bisexual and transgender people and their allies together in public' (p. 194). Similarly to Mouffe's (1995) radical democratic politics, IDAHO promotes not so much a politics organized exclusively around a particular identity (in this case, a sexual identity), but rather a coalition politics organized around specific issues, struggles, goals, and broadly demarcated principles (e.g., equal opportunity, discrimination against homophobia) that bring together queer and non-queer parties with different interests. This is reflected in the organizers and supporting partners, which run from tongzhi NGOs to tongzhi-friendly NGOs such as women's groups (e.g., The Association for the Advancement of Feminism), sex worker groups (e.g., Zi Teng, Action For Reach Out, Midnight

Blue), human rights groups (e.g., Amnesty International Hong Kong Section), groups that concern a broader social movement (e.g., Social Movement Resource Centre (SMRC Autonomous 8A)) and religious groups (e.g., Hong Kong Christian Institute); and to private companies and businesses (e.g., Durex, Ziz Skincares for Men, gay bars such as Propaganda and Works, transnational Asian gay online fridae.com, gay online radio gayradio.com and gay magazine *Dim Sum*). Participants have included politicians in different years (e.g., Dr. Fernando Cheung Chiu-hung, Emily Lau, Leung Kwok-hung, Wong Yuk-man) and queer representatives from mainland China (e.g., from Beijing, Chengdu, Guangzhou, Shenzhen) and Taiwan.

In 2008 the theme song was 'Queers Are Ready' – a 'queer' cultural jamming of the pro-democratic movement's appropriating, in their fight for universal suffrage, of the Beijing Olympics theme song 'We Are Ready'. Participants chanted some provocative slogans, such as 'We are indecent, we are queer', 'We are obscene, we are proud', and 'Perversion is normal, morality is pretentious'. The rally, on the one hand, sought inclusion and equal rights to individual freedom, democracy and justice; on the other, to upset heteronormativity by showing its hegemony and instability.[15]

The organizers of the first Gay Pride Parade, on 13 December 2008, expecting only 500 participants, were very happy when around 1,000 participants – tongzhi and non-tongzhi, and people from China and Taiwan – turned up, and walked from Causeway Bay down to Wan Chai. The walk attracted a lot of media reporting.

I went to all the IDAHO events and the Gay Pride Parade. I knew many participants, a substantial number of whom were not tongzhi. The number of participants, however, was far from satisfactory. If only 1 per cent of the almost 7 million Hong Kong population is queer, there should have been around 70,000. If only 1 per cent of this queer population had joined the event, there would still have been at least 700 participants. Yet more than 700 participants attend a gay club on a Saturday night. Where were they?

Queer cultural citizenship: from perversion to queer as folk

The lack of interest tongzhi have shown in institutional politics is only one side of the story. While they are not interested in fighting for equal rights (no matter whether political, civil or social), they are passionate about economic consumption and cultural representation. They are keen to be different, to claim a non-stigmatized identity and to embrace a new lifestyle – i.e., they are concerned with the cultural aspect of citizenship in terms of 'the right to symbolic presence and visibility (vs marginalisation); the right to dignifying representation (vs stigmatisation); and the right to propagation of identity and maintenance of lifestyles (vs assimilation)' (Pakulski 1997: 80).

The shift from an institutional politics to a cultural politics may be accounted for by two factors: a colonial administration that provided almost no outlets for political idealism, and the fact that Hong Kong people either seek non-traditional channels to mobilize their discontents (Lam 2004) or to direct themselves towards economic consumption or cultural production (Abbas 1992).

The family is a tool of governance (Ho 2004; Ong 1993, 1996, 1999). It not only becomes a self-regulating and self-reliance mechanism that turns people away from the government for support, welfare needs and resources, but also serves as a powerful closet mechanism that prevents any visible and public manifestation of homosexual love. Coming out is thus largely considered a shame brought upon the family, which should be avoided – especially, any act that may easily be gossiped via family and kinship networks, which are mediated by the high density of Hong Kong and its intense flow of information (Kong 2002; see Chapter 4).

Therefore, it is through the representation and participation of tongzhi at various cultural sites and in economic consumption (see Chapter 3) that we can see how tongzhi have appropriated a sense of cultural citizenship that has subsequently transformed the homosexuality from a perverted form of personhood to that of a cosmopolitan cultural subject. It is with this understanding that we can see the sexual politics of Hong Kong tongzhi. And it is from this perspective that we can appreciate the allegedly 'apolitical' nature of most tongzhi groups of the past. Although legislative change was not their central political interest, they nevertheless actively challenged the dominant social codes through cultural representations and exposed the power of heteronormativity by showing the lives of tongzhi. Similarly to Scott's (1985) Malaysian peasants, these tongzhi groups participated in an invisible and hidden movement that was normally difficult to notice. As argued by Ho and Tsang (2004a: 688), 'these discursive practices should not be eliminated from the discourse analysis of political participation even though it may be difficult to determine their social significance and effectiveness.'

Cornel West (1987) considers the academy and 'literate subcultures of art, culture, and politics' as two main venues through which Black intellectuals in America formulate cultural politics to challenge societal discriminations and injustices. In Hong Kong, civil education and the academy do not serve this purpose.

Under both the colonial and the SAR governments, civil education has long been criticized for nurturing an ideology of competitive individualism and a belief in the open society. The education system has been producing 'economic man', but not critically thinking beings. It emphasizes memorization and the system of massive 'do-or-die' examinations (Lee 1994, Yee 1989[16]). The results of this are 'passive' and 'unresponsive' students and technocrats who conform to the ideal for business and administrative bureaucracies. As Lee (1994) argues, the academy seems not to be the ideal place for an intellectual culture in Hong Kong, as 'the educational system (from kindergarten to university) is, if not anti-intellectual, ineffective in promoting intellectual life due to its rigid curricula, the discouragement of individuality and the inherently problematic medium of education' (p. 15). Ho and Tsang (2004b: 704–5) point out that the public sex education that started in the 1950s had a dominant agenda of fertility control and contraception, as it was predominately carried out by the government-subvented Family Planning Association of Hong Kong. Throughout the years, from the first memorandum on sex education topics in 1971 to the 1997 revised guidelines, the Education Department has shown a strong bias towards moral indoctrination and has confined the consideration of human sexuality either to biology, sexual anatomy and physiology, or to emotional well-being and interpersonal and familial relationships, without touching upon sensitive issues such as homosexuality, pornography, prostitution, etc. Students instead had to turn to mass media (newspaper, magazines) for information about sex (see also Ng 1998; Ng and Ma 2004: 491–92).

Moreover, the academy is not the ideal place for an ideological battle over tongzhi issues. Currie *et al.* (2006) convincingly argue that academic freedom in Hong Kong has long reflected political and ideological factors, as can be seen in the limited extent to which academics criticized the colonial government before 1997 and the SAR and Chinese governments since 1997. They point out that a newly emerged restriction of academic freedom has seemingly arisen. Stemming from economic pressure derived from neoliberal governance, the Hong Kong universities are moving towards deregulation, which can be seen in the streamlining of their governance, the delinkage of academic salaries from civil service pay, and the reduction of substantiation and tenured positions and corresponding increase in contract staff. Under the pressure of cutbacks in higher education funding and a gearing towards more governance and management, Hong Kong universities have been more extreme than Anglo-American universities in assessing academic staff in terms of a 'performativity' culture (Research Assessment Exercise) that emphasizes productive output in terms of publications in international journals and of grants. As they worry, the real threat to academic freedom is that academics will give up writing for local publications and push the system towards academic conformity. Under such pressure, 'sensitive' and 'controversial' issues are even harder to voice.

The formal channels – civil education and the academy – are therefore neither those through which to nurture a tongzhi movement nor those for waging an ideological battle. The cultural space – media and popular culture – thus becomes the major space for the production of texts and practices that disrupt the hegemonic heteronormativity.

There is a well-established literature that delineates the emergence of local consciousness and cultural identity in popular culture under the colonial governance (e.g., Lui 1997, 2007; Ng 2001; Wong 1998; Mathews 1997; Abbas 1997; Leung 2004). In terms of cultural politics, visibility is a key issue for social inclusion and exclusion and the development of possible ways of resistance (Richardson 2001: 157). In the intersection between sexuality and culture, it is important to understand how tongzhi have been represented and framed in various cultural sites, such as in film, theatre, music, dance, literature, etc.

The age of shame

As I have argued elsewhere (Kong 2005b), before the 1980s, homosexuality was only hinted at, or was pathologized, in popular culture. For example, queer ambivalence took two major forms, according to the *wen-wu* (文-武) tradition,[17] in films in the past. First, homosexual love could only be celebrated when male or female actors cross-dressed, with masculine and feminine gender roles sustained by the tradition of transgenderism and the *wen* ideal of Chinese masculinity (e.g., Cantonese opera and melodramas in the 1960s). Second, a space for male homosocial/homosexual eroticism could only be imagined in martial arts films where the *wu* ideal of Chinese masculinity and male bonding was emphasized (e.g., Bruce Lee's and Zheng Che's films in the 1970s). If the male homosexual was directly represented, he was always ridiculed as a 'sissy' or was mocked as a kind of sexual pervert, or was a victim. The homosexual character in *Sex for Sale* (dir. Chang Tseng-chai, 1972) seems to have been the first directly depicted male homosexual in Hong Kong cinema (Maike 2000: 59–63; c.f. Yau 2005: 167–75). The film follows a similar plot to that of *Midnight Cowboy* (dir. John Schlesinger, 1969), which presents the life of a straight male prostitute: the main actor has a homosexual friend who kills himself at the end of the movie after showing his secret love for him. In television, the popular soap drama *A House is Not a Home* (TVB, 1977) portrays the main actress's younger brother as a 'sissy' gay man. Although the role of the young man was only a minor one in the drama series, it seems to have been the major representation of a local gay man in television in the 1970s.

Forbidden love

Changes occurred in the 1980s as a result of four major phenomena. First, the death of Inspector John MacLennan in 1980 triggered the controversy over discrimination towards homosexuality. The controversy lasted for ten years. Different parties included the government, moral defenders (especially, Christian fundamentalists and evangelists), social workers, teachers, lawyers, academics, cultural workers, politicians and so on, both pro- and anti-gay, who debated what homosexuality was – whether it was in-born or not, whether it was normal or not, whether it came from the West or stemmed from Chinese tradition, and whether it was a matter of human rights. In this debate, a deviant social behaviour was transformed into the social identity of 'homosexual' (Ho 1997: 111–51; Ho and Tsang 2004a).

Second, a transnational network of lesbians and gay men led to the emergence of informal gay subcultures. Samshasha was an important figure in the development of the HK tongzhi movement.[18] Samshasha studied in the United States in the 1970s and said he had been re-educated in the golden age of gay liberation in the States. As an Asian representative of Third World Gay and Lesbian Delegates, he visited the White House in 1979 to discuss the human rights of Asian gay people. He came back to Hong Kong in the early 1980s and discovered that Hong Kong people were impoverished with respect to their knowledge of homosexuality and that the society was very homophobic. He could not believe that Hong Kong had no support groups for gays and lesbians, and no commercialized gay scene. He thought the gay development of Hong Kong lagged behind that of the States by about 20 years. He then drafted a 'Chinese Gay's Statement', wrote articles in the middle-class lifestyle *City Magazine* and started publishing and distributing a newsletter called *Pink Triangle Magazine.* A lot of people who later became active in the movement came out to him. An informal gay subculture was thus formed. It is believed that this social network triggered the formation of the underground gay organization Ten Percent Club in 1986. Since homosexuality was still illegal at that time, gay activities took place largely underground.

The rise of the cultural collective Zuni Icosahedron in the 1980s was the third important cultural phenomenon that nurtured queer development in Hong Kong. Danny Yung is the chief founder of Zuni Icosahedron. He returned to Hong Kong in the mid 1970s after living in the United States for more than ten years. As an active member of the Asian American community movement in the States, he had come to identify himself as a 'marginal being': 'to be marginal is apparently to enjoy all the advantages of being free to engage in discourse and critiques, to observe and to create' (Yung 1997b: 29). In order to achieve these goals in his artistic pursuits, Yung started to write conceptual comics, then experimental films, videos and finally theatre, through which he was drawn deeper into the 'marginal' artistic community of Hong Kong. The whole experience inspired him to set up Zuni Icosahedron, an experimental dance and theatre group. 'Dialogue' and 'collective creativity' have been two integral elements in his artistic creation. Through different collaborative works, Yung and other 'marginal beings' (e.g., Edward Lam, Mathias Woo) have critically examined the relationship between the margin and the system and explored the conflict between arts and the establishment.

Although Yung's major concern seemed to be the overall cultural development of Hong Kong, his pluralistic and liberal artistic direction enabled him to draw upon a large pool of artists. These artists, to a certain extent, expressed their dissatisfactions with different facets of the existing colonial society and created their own visions and imaginations of social ideals. In a way that reflected Mouffe's (1995) radical democratic politics, this artist collective fashioned a politics that was not necessarily centred on any particular identity, sexual or otherwise, but rather was organized around the broader democratic goals of developing a liberal and open society. Under these main principles, a joyous celebration of homosexual love and a subversive critique of heterosexism were conjoined in a critique of colonial society.

Last but not least was the commodification of identity (and the male body), a development originating in the West that has spread through the process of globalization and has been driven by the commodity logic of capitalism since the 1980s. From the 1980s onwards the naked male body has been increasingly displayed and sexualized in Western popular culture. The classic examples of glorification of the naked male body in the TV commercials in the 1980s are models James Mardle slipping into a bath with his Levi's jeans and Nick Kamen stripping off his jeans in a launderette (Mort 1988a: 201–2). This narcissistic new image of men is more about how they (especially their bodies) look different for themselves and to other men, giving room for homosexual identification. Advertisers have started to deploy a market strategy of using 'polysemic' images of pop stars and fashion models in order to attract both queer and heterosexual consumers – images that the latter do not notice as appealing to queers, or that do so without offending heterosexuals (Clarke 1993).[19] This allows the spectator the possibility of multiple sexual identifications, including homosexual identification. As Evans and Gamman (1995: 32) wrote, this 'gave readers "permission" to be promiscuous with images, and . . . permitted images to function ambiguously, and thereby to speak to a range of different subject positions'.

In contrast to Western aesthetics of the male body, the Chinese male body has always been desexualized. In mainstream popular culture in Hong Kong, the naked male body was seldom exposed. When a stripped man appeared, it was usually in a comedy (Maike 1993a: 79–80). However, the commercialization of the male body has been occurring in Hong Kong since the 1990s, and it is now not uncommon to see TV commercials, films and other forms of popular culture that feature the naked male body, with strong homoerotic undertones (Kong 2006b).

Queer as folk

Since the 1990s, there has been an increasing queer visibility in popular culture and the mainstream media.[20] On the one hand, popular culture has been saturated with homophobic ideology and gay men have been stigmatized as deviants, campy sexual perverts, victims or villains. Gay men are usually portrayed as having come from dysfunctional or abusive families. They are often represented as 'hysterical men' (the logic of 'a woman trapped in a man's body'); alleged to be 'fashion victims', and almost always over-dressed, middle class and well educated; and hang around in highly Westernized places such as Lan Kwai Fong.[21] Popular culture enjoys this virulent voyeurism and administers a heteronormative form of discipline in the framing of its homophobic reports and stories. Gay sex is the focal point of 'examination', in this voyeurism. Anal sex, group sex or public sex in the gay lifestyle is always exaggerated, and gay men are alleged to be promiscuous and thus responsible for the spread of AIDS. By placing heterosexuals and homosexuals in two antagonistic and oppositional positions, popular culture successfully stigmatizes the latter as the deviant type (c.f. Chou 1995: Ch. 8–10; Chou and Chiu 1995: 198–204).

On the other hand, living with a lack of political rights in the formal political structures, some locally born members of young generations have channelled their political sensibilities into cultural productions (Au Yeung 2006).[22] Some of them are queer or queer-friendly, and are gradually coming to occupy strategic positions in the mass media, offering subversive critiques of heterosexual culture. This may even suggest that queer culture is being celebrated. Using their own expertise and strategic positions in society, queer or queer-friendly cultural artists occupy a place in popular culture, but at the same time maintain queer perspectives by negotiating, subverting, exposing, and opposing homophobic and heterosexist definitions, images and terms of analysis that mark them off from the dominant culture of heterosexuality.

For example, in mainstream media, the late movie star Leslie Cheung's 'delicate sensitivity' fashioned a new sensibility of masculinity that is considered an 'icon of transgression' (Chan 2005), through his cross-dressing and manifestation of long-lasting love for his 'very good friend' at public events.[23] Pop-music star Anthony Wong, with his socially and politically charged songs and his sometimes-outrageous and provocative looks, is the very image of a queer icon. His 'descendant' might be Denise Ho (a.k.a. HOCC), who often appears in distinctive androgynous costumes in public events (e.g., in a red warrior's costume and a beard in concerts). She 'came out' casually in a public TV game show in July 2009 and her songs have heavy undertones of male same-sex eroticism (e.g., 'Rolls-Royce') and lesbianism (e.g., 'Rosemary', 'Goodbye. Rosemary'). As a publicly 'out' gay director, Stanley Kwan's *Yang ± Yin: Gender in Chinese Cinema* (dir. Stanley Kwan, 1996) – sort of a Hong Kong version of *Celluloid Closet* (dir. Rob Epstein and Jeffrey Friedman, 1995, based on the book with the same name by Vito Russo, 1981) – shows clips of some 45 Chinese films from the past that have touched on issues of gender and sexuality, intertwines these clips with his personal interpretations of these films from a gay perspective, and even includes a recorded conversation with his mother about his own homosexuality at the end of the film.

Using theatre and writings as his major weapons, Edward Lam confronts the straight world by using bold expressions in his speech and writing (e.g., in his plays, such as *How to Love a Man Who Doesn't Love Me* (1989), *Scenes from Men's Changing Room* (1991), *Once a Princess, Always a Princess* (1995); and *Water Margins* (2006); and in his books, such as *Too Many Men Too Little Time* (1996) and *27.01.97–30.09.97* (1997)). Likewise, using mainly photography, and later books (e.g., *The Map of Burning Desire*, 2001) and films (e.g., *The Accident*, 1999; *The Night Corridor*, 2003), as his media of expression, Julian Lee Chi-chiu normalizes the ideas of homosexuality, BDSM, dragging, etc., under the umbrella of 'radical' and 'liberal' sexual and gender practices. Maike has established his own unique style of gay writing through his highly camp but brilliant analysis of gay films, as well as by his witty but subversive 'queer reading', 'twisting' and 'reading against the grain' of straight films (e.g., *Fake Sexual Bible*, 1993a; *Photocopies*, 1993b; *The Male Boundary*, 1994; *Sex Text*, 2000; *Single-minded, Double-entendre*, 2003; and *Spellbound*, 2005). Wong Chi-lung and Leung Cho-yiu have produced very popular theatre pieces about new-generation gay men (e.g., *Best Memories in My Life*, 2003; *Queer Show*, 2004, 2006, 2008; *Mr. Snow White and Mr. Cinderella*, 2008). Meanwhile, Yau Ching has been doing a large amount of feminist and queer writing in literary criticism (e.g., Yau 2005), and her movie, *Let's Love Hong Kong* (2005), is the first lesbian feature length independent film. Finally, as the most-acclaimed video artist in Hong Kong, Ellen Pau has had her video, *Songs of the Goddess* (1993), screened at many festivals overseas as a major lesbian representative of independent video in Hong Kong.

Collections of soft local gay stories are surfacing (e.g., *Coming Out Stories of Hong Kong Tongzhi* (Chou *et al.* 1995); *Stories of Hong Kong Tongzhi* (Chou 1996b); *Suddenly Single* and *Almost Perfect* (Yip 2003, 2004)). Free gay papers have been published for a few years now, such as *G Magazine* (until 2007) and *Dim Sum*, and gay soft-pornographic books can be bought at newspaper kiosks. Due to advancements in electronics, a new local virtual space was created in the 1990s and has become extremely popular. Gay websites and chat lines are numerous (e.g., www.gayhk.com; www.fridae.com; www.tt1069.com). The internet is a new way for queers (especially young queers and those who live in homophobic Asian societies) to identify one another through sexuality, language and values (Berry *et al.* 2003: 1).

Other more independent and ephemeral forms of 'queer self-inscription' are in the making. Leung (2008: Ch. 5) calls these the 'do-it-yourself' queer projects. She uses examples from short films shown at the Hong Kong Lesbian and Gay Film Festival (HKLGFF); stories from Kam Lucetta's edited anthology *Lunar Desire: Her Same-sex Love, In Her Own Words* (2001); narratives told in the Women's Coalition of Hong Kong's oral history project (*In The Tracks of Their Love: Oral History of Women Who Could Fall in Love with Women in Hong Kong* (2004); and the internet radio programme *What the Hell Kind of Tongzhi Movement?* (2005), hosted by queer activists Connie, Ah Lik, Wai Wai and Siu Cho on the independent radio station People's Radio Hong Kong. On a voluntary basis, driven by community rather than commercial or academic needs, and receptive to audience feedback, these queer cultural producers set themselves apart from formal channels of representation such as those of academia and mainstream media and culture, and create a new and often neglected space for archiving queer subcultural lives.

The various – negative and positive – representations of gay men and lesbians are significant for the fight for the rights of cultural citizenship, as they suggest 'real' and 'diverse' representations of sexual minorities in their real lives. The rather traditional portrayal of the tongzhi as a perverted sad personage has slowly been replaced by a new cultural cosmopolitan subject with diverse names, such as 'gay/*gei*' (基 Cant.), 'gay/*gei lo*' (基佬 Cant.), '*tungzi*' (同志 Cant.), 'memba' (Cant.), 'brokeback', '*jat zai*' (1仔 Cant.), '*ling zai*' (零仔 Cant.) and '*gamgong Barbie*' (金剛芭比 Cant.) for gay men; and 'lesi', 'pure', 'TB' and 'TBG' for lesbians. The image of the new cultural gay male subject oscillates between the extremes of that of a closeted gay man and that of an out, loud and beautiful memba, who is a campy, bitchy type. He may be a very 'straight' gay man, probably with a well-built gym body, who is an educated, cosmopolitan lifestyle expert and a woman's best friend.[24]

But no matter how he is represented, this new cultural subject has increasingly become a transnational one, due to circulation along the Asian queer circuit of desires, parties and cultures in the global queering process.

In Hong Kong, tongzhi, as a self-fashioned notion of cultural citizenship, has a heavy undertone of middle-class or bourgeois individualism that is intricately related to conspicuous consumption. This notion of queer citizenship creates a hierarchy of queer citizens that privileges certain bodies but disadvantages others along the lines of class, gender performance, age, race and ethnicity, and so forth. This hegemony of the newly emerged queer cultural citizenship inside the gay community will be examined in the next chapter. In the rest of this chapter I will examine queer visibility in relation to new forms of social governance associated with neoliberalism.

Queer citizenship and neoliberal governance

The rather vibrant queer subcultures have been subsumed under neoliberal regulations, especially those dependent on government funding and commercial sponsorships, and the backlash from Protestant Christian and Catholic NGOs. First of all, Hong Kong has always exercised a strict code of censorship, implemented by the statutory Broadcasting Authority of the government. Programmes are readily censored when they contain materials which are considered 'sensitive' or 'controversial', especially when they contain issues that involve sexuality (e.g., homosexuality, obscenity or pornography) or politics that may 'dampen the relationship among neighbouring countries' (i.e., the Hong Kong–China–Taiwan political relationship) (Hong Kong Cultural Policy Studies 1995).

Second, the government has always been criticized for its lack of long-term vision in regard to cultural development in general and arts development in particular. This problem can be traced back to colonial times – the colonial government advanced the notion that the best cultural policy was to have no cultural policy, beginning in the late 1970s, and thus made little effort to nurture the cultural identity of Hong Kong people (Yung 1997a; Ooi 1997; Chan 2008[25]). The government, however, tended to favour the notion of high arts, and to equate professionalism with excellence. It thus either privileged a Western cultural and language orientation or a national Chinese traditional culture – always taking an international or national, rather than a local and/or experimental, perspective.

Since the 1990s, the Home Affairs Bureau and Arts Development Council (a statutory body set up by the government in 1995), as well as private businesses, have increasingly sponsored cultural and arts activities, but it has been through this financial support that a new level of 'accountability' has become evident for queer organizations who need subsidies.[26]

Third, as noted by Ho (2008), East Asia's new liberal states, although they have claimed respect for diversity, sometimes work closely with the pastoral power of Protestant Christian- or Catholic-based NGOs for a 'reign of civility and respectability' that regulates sexual acts, identities, information and exchanges. There has been a strong backlash opposing the tongzhi movement in Hong Kong from religious (mainly Protestant Christian- and Catholic-based NGOs) groups. The IDAHO event was in fact triggered by an anti-gay Christian front, the Hong Kong Alliance for Family (see note 12)

It is thus that we can see a new governance of queer visibility in Hong Kong. Three examples are worthy of note. First, the Broadcasting Authority issued a serious warning to Radio Television Hong Kong (RTHK), a government radio/television channel, after receiving complaints from Christians concerning 'Gay Lover', a July 2006 episode of the long running and highly acclaimed RTHK documentary programme *Hong Kong Connection*. The Broadcasting Authority charged that the episode was 'unsuitable for family viewing' because the documentary featured a gay man and a lesbian couple and a discussion of the possibility of same-sex marriage; and that it was 'too positive' about homosexuality and tended to be 'promoting an acceptance of gay marriage'. The documentary was said to present only a 'partial' view of this 'controversial' issue, without giving enough 'pro-and-con arguments'.[27] Three of the interviewees, including Siu Cho, a post-graduate student at a local university, took the case to court and eventually won the legal battle in 2008. In an open thank-you letter to their supporters sent by email on 12 May 2008, the three litigants summarized the whole court case by saying:

> . . . Although Hartmann's judgment is very encouraging and made a timely redress of injustice, we are saddened by the very fact that the sexual minority needs to safeguard our very fundamental human rights in a cost- and time-consuming legal battle. The government simply failed to properly do its job to stick itself [sic] to the principle of equality but became complicit in discrimination and hatre [sic]. We are convinced that it is high time the government enacted an anti-sexual orientation discrimination law, as a means of long overdue legal protection and public education.
>
> What Hartmann stroke [sic] down is not only the discriminatory decision by the Broadcasting Authority, but also the whole set of the homophobic assumptions (i.e., homosexuality is *always* controversial, representation of the gay and lesbian people's life without opposing views is *always* a promotion of it). Discrimination and hatre [sic] in their various and subtle forms will not immediately end because of this victory. (emphasis original)

The case not only shows that Hong Kong tongzhi are still culturally and socially discriminated against, but also demonstrates the profound effect of the highly subjective censorship law on freedom of speech, which is easily influenced by conservative force, especially those of antigay religious groups.

Second, Nutong Xueshe is a newly formed tongzhi organization that works for the betterment of tongzhi through educational, cultural and media projects. The group organized a series of creative workshops in 2006 and the artwork produced during the workshops went on a public exhibition tour, starting from the Hong Kong Cultural Centre, in 2007. The exhibition, entitled 'In/Out: Hong Kong Tongzhi Art', was organized around different themes, in response to various anti-gay/backlash actions by religious, social and political forces. The government, as one of the funding bodies, urged the organizer to submit all their artworks to the Obscene Article Tribunal for classification. The organizer did so under the threat that the government might withdraw all funding if there were any complaints about the exhibition. After the examination, it was strongly advised that some of the works be removed from the exhibition.[28] Although Nutong Xueshe held a press conference, in which I was one of the guest speakers, to launch the exhibition and accused the government of having ambivalent censorship guidelines, they had to remove some artworks from the public exhibition (Nutong Xueshe 2007). The event not only involved the infringement of freedom of speech but also cast a doubt for the organizers as to whether they would have difficulties in receiving funding from the government in future proposal applications. As Chasin (2000) points out, in the US context, 'among gay-related causes, the smaller, more local, more grassroots organizations, and those working for radical social change' (p. 202) are usually least favoured by corporate and donor funders. As a result, 'market-related funding mechanisms – while providing increased visibility for the larger

Figure 2.4 Organizers from Nutong Xueshe put on the warning sign in the exhibition 'In/Out: Hong Kong Tongzhi Creative Workshop and Exhibition' at Hong Kong Cultural Centre (23–29 Jan 2007) (courtesy of Nutong Xueshe).

Figure 2.5 One of the 'problematic' artworks: 'Victim of my soul', by Ele. 'In/Out: Hong Kong Tongzhi Creative Workshop and Exhibition' (courtesy of Nutong Xueshe).

national service-oriented organizations – can contribute to the invisibility and/or the de-resourcing of less mainstream organizations' (p. 202).

Finally, the HKLGFF, first held in 1989, evolved from an event sponsored by the independent non-profit Hong Kong Arts Centre that emphasized educational documentaries and art-house cinema. In the pre-internet era, HKLGFF served the important function of showing many queer films that the Hong Kong population would not be able to watch in any other venues, as well as provided a chance for tongzhi to get together socially. The event had a significant symbolic meaning for the development of 'queer space' in Hong Kong in the 1990s. However, working within a tight funding constraint, the festival has always been charged with being a cultural product for consumption and an upper-middle-class event, typified by its screening of subcultural, avant-garde and alternative genres with no Chinese subtitles. Tang (2008: 238–42) points out that the festival has become increasingly commercial since Fortissimo Films became an official sponsor in 2000. Being both the co-chairman of Fortissimo Films and chairman of HKLGFF, the late Wouter Barendrecht successfully brought internationally renowned queer films to Hong Kong audiences and constructed the festival as 'a foreign import, an expatriate hobby

Figure 2.6 One of the 'problematic' artworks: 'Thou shalt love thy neighbor as thyself', by Siu Cho. In/Out: Hong Kong Tongzhi Creative Workshop and Exhibition (courtesy of Nutong Xueshe).

and a middle-class gay male event' (p. 240). The festival has been caught in the dilemmas of balancing mainstream commercial blockbusters with alternative, independent, experimental films; and of over-representing Western middle-class gay films and under-representing local, lesbian and transgendered films.

Conclusion

National political and cultural characteristics have played a crucial role in the development of national lesbian and gay movements. Under both colonial and post-colonial governments, Hong Kong tongzhi groups have not only exhibited a non-institutional character in (queer) politics but have also tended to buy into the language of the power structure. There has always been a gap between personal identity and community politics in Hong Kong. Hong Kong tongzhi organizations' primary concern has been with identity-formation rather than with political and legal platforms. The tongzhi movement has been dominated by rights-based assimilationist rhetoric, which has tended to suppress a more radical and transgressive politics. The urgent agenda for activists is to find a 'proper' way that is sensitive to the political and cultural environment in Hong Kong. A new way of queer politics has slowly emerged since 2005, when IDAHO was first staged.

With the blockage of formal political channels, the queer energy of tongzhi has tended to transform itself to cultural energy. Although governance in Hong Kong limits the nurturing of critical mass through civil education and academia, a more vibrant queer cultural world has been emerging, which is evident in the various forms of media and popular culture in civil society. It is this cultural development that has successfully countered the traditional pathological deviant personage of homosexuality with a cosmopolitan queer cultural subject. However, the queer cultural world is not an autonomous sphere of queer inscription. It too is subject to various constraints. Popular culture has shown a dual, contradictory nature on the issue of homosexuality. On the one hand, a homophobic ideology saturates tabloid newspapers, in which tongzhi are negatively framed and represented. On the other hand, there is a new trend of homophilia, which appears more often in independent and non-profit making cultural productions. Cultural workers, queer performers and queer NGOs are struggling for basic survival within the parameters of neoliberal governance, censorship and commercial consideration, and are constantly being challenged by anti-gay Christian NGOs. They struggle for visibility, and challenge what is meant by the 'normal' way of life and heterosexist terms of reference in everyday life. In so doing, they weaken the power of the powerful (c.f., de Certeau 1984; Scott 1985). It is this bottom-up cultural movement that can bring about a social force for change that may 'lead to the diffusion of political sites, proliferation of political spaces, expansion of range of strategies of contestation and widening the arenas for democratic movement' (Ho and Tsang 2004a: 689).

3 Memba only

Consumer citizenship and cult gay masculinity

> Male homosexual citizenship is predicated on the conjunction of individual consenting adult freedoms including, indeed particularly, those of a consumer market, and the reinforced stigma of immorality which bans this citizen from the 'moral community' and polices him into privacy. As gay men claimed their leisure and lifestyle market, the market claimed them, colonised and exploited gay sexuality. The potency of the modern homosexual male's 'virilisation' is as much economic as it is sexual, allowed to exercise his rights as consumer but denied 'equal' rights elsewhere, and on the whole he doesn't seem to mind.
>
> (David Evans, *Sexual Citizenship*, 1993)

19 May 2007 ***Saturday, 11 p.m., Sheung Wan***

Rice Bar[1] is a gay bar situated in a back street in Sheung Wan, an aging, mainly residential area next to the vibrant and cosmopolitan areas of Central and Soho. I went there with a friend. When we arrived, my friend sighed as usual, 'Too many men, too little time!' The bar was jam-packed, and more than 30 young men were standing around outside the bar. The scene resembled one from a Hong Kong-style gangster movie, in which triad members from different 'gangs' had gathered, ready to fight. A closer look, however, revealed a very different picture. It was more like a fashion show. You could easily find a guy with a Louis Vuitton handbag, a pair of Gucci sunglasses, an Abercrombie & Fitch T-shirt, a Versace belt, a pair of Levis denim jeans, and a pair of Prada shoes. Or find another one with the same labels but different combinations, say, a Gucci handbag, a Prada belt or a pair of Versace shoes. Here, you name a label, you see the label. With a perfect haircut, they all dressed in fine designer-label clothing and accessories, conspicuously and shamelessly showing off their bodies. Their V-shaped, well-trained torsos radiated, not aggression and violence, but erotic energy and sexual appeal, to any man passing by.

After 2 a.m., some of the men rushed to Propaganda (PP), a gay disco in Hong Kong. Despite its infamously bad music and unbelievably high prices, PP still attracts at least a thousand gay men on any Saturday night. They are keen to take off their shirts and expose their hard-trained gym bodies, down alcohol, enjoy the techno music, and flex their muscles in a glamorous atmosphere. At around 4 a.m., some were still making 'confessions on a dance floor' while others were keen to take off – ready to go to other, smaller rave and druggy parties. The night was young!

Perhaps the most successful realization of sexual citizenship for tongzhi in Hong Kong is consumer citizenship, manifested in the emergence of various

Figure 3.1 The crowd in front of Rice Bar (2004, author's photograph).

consuming queer spaces, such as the bars, clubs, saunas, boutiques, cafés, etc., which seem to be passionately endorsed by many. These are facilitated by the free market economy embedded in neoliberal government policies. If such 'pink economy' consumption is so central for the articulation of gay sexual rights, we must consider its extent, limits, and the myths in the discourse involved.

This chapter continues the discussion of sexual citizenship in Hong Kong through an examination of a newly emerged queer cultural citizenship that links sexual identity, conspicuous consumerism and post-colonial space as part of the global queer culture. After a brief introduction of how such citizenship is increasingly defined in terms of consumption, I turn to the situation in Hong Kong, focusing on how consumption contributes to the development of sexual identity in general and to the emergence of commercial spaces for open lesbian and gay existence in particular. I will argue that the apparently successful 'territorialization' of queer spaces and pink economy has helped nurture a notion of queer cultural citizenship which has successfully shifted the traditional image of 'citizen-pervert' to that of 'good consumer citizen' and has provided a significant and positive cultural sense of belonging for tongzhi for identity formation, cultural and sexual exchange, and networking. This queer citizenship, with its close association with consumption, has distinctive features: it is cosmopolitan in outlook, commercially driven,

Figure 3.2 The crowd in front of Rice Bar (2004, author's photograph).

conspicuously consumed on the body, led by specific style ideas and defined through distinctive body types. It defines and gives meaning to personal identity, lifestyle, and even influences the logic of desire. This queer citizenship may be a derivative of a 'global queer identity' (Altman 1995, 1996a, 1996b, 1997, 2001), but it serves less to promote cultural uniformity and identification than it does to divide, as it demarcates those who can fully access this ideal and those who cannot along lines of class, age, gender, sexuality, race and body type. Using the Hong Kong memba as example, I will argue how tongzhi manifest this notion of queer citizenship and adopt a 'flexible gay citizenship'[2] by conforming to, resisting, or even redefining the dominant terms of reference; and use their embodied cultural capital to manoeuvre among different sites of power and domination and to create their own sense of gay citizenship.

Consumption, identity and sexual citizenship

There is a well-established literature examining the nature of contemporary consumption.[3] For example, Campbell (1987), following Weber's thesis on Protestant ethics and the spirit of capitalism, traces 'elective affinity' from the Romantic Movement in eighteenth- and nineteenth-century Europe to the spirit of modern consumption. Campbell argues that, while the Protestant ethic fostered ascetic and puritanical values that focused on hard work and opposed the pursuit of pleasure, Romantic ethics nurtured an emotional and sensual way of life in which people were increasingly more aware of personal pleasure. Modern consumption has gradually grown from the mere satisfaction of biologically driven needs to a socially, culturally and symbolically mediated process for the construction of social identities, especially those of the middle class (Bocock 1992: 122–28). However, not everyone welcomes this process. For example, Marcuse (1964: 4–9) criticizes the exploitative nature of modern consumption, as modern consumer capitalist interests have superimposed 'false needs', especially through the mass media and advertising – 'the prevailing needs to relax, to have fun, to behave and consume in accordance with the advertisements, to love and hate what others love and hate' (p. 5) and the effect of this upon individuals who have no control. Bourdieu's (1984) critique of taste in French society offers a sophisticated analysis in which consumption is conceptualized as a way to differentiate among groups through the appropriation of various capitals – economic, social and cultural – that might cut across social classes. Moving beyond true/false needs or social class, Baudrillard (1988) postulates that all consumption is always, in part, a consumption of a symbolic sign system: '. . . what is consumed are not objects but the relation itself – signified and absent, included and excluded at the same time – it is *the idea of the relation* that is consumed in the series of objects which manifests it' (p. 22, emphasis original). Bocock (1992: 149–51) argues that Baudrillard has shifted the role of desire in theorizing consumption. Rather than being constructed as an attractive woman or a handsome man, one is induced to desire what one wants to be through purchasing commodities. This is articulated succinctly in a famous contemporary poster – 'I shop, therefore I am'.

Modern consumption exhibits two distinctive features: conspicuous consumption and individualization. First, consumption is a 'badge' of social and sexual identification – one has to be *seen* to consume, rather than simply to consume. Such consumption thus demonstrates its sexual and erotic appeal to oneself and others and is used as a way to express one's selfhood, for example, masculinity (Mort 1988a, 1988b). Second, the site of consumption has moved from the traditional family to the individual, whose specific lifestyle

> connotes individuality, self-expression, and a stylistic self-consciousness. One's body, clothes, speech, leisure pastimes, eating and drinking preferences, home, car, choice of holidays, etc. are to be regarded as indicators of the individuality of taste and sense of style of the owner/consumer.
>
> (Featherstone 1987: 55)

Not only traditional housewives, but also new consumer groups such as young people, 'metrosexuals' and gay men and lesbians, have increasingly become the targets of the market. Modern consumption, manifested in the blatant form of conspicuous consumption on the body, links to the whole process of individualization concerns about identity, personal choice and style.

Moreover, as Fiske (1989: Ch. 2) argued from the 'politics of the weak' tradition (e.g., de Certeau 1984; Scott 1985), shopping can never be a radical subversive act, as it can never change the system of a capitalist–consumerist economy. However, if money is power in capitalism, then voluntary buying is an empowering moment for those who are subordinate within the economic system. This is because any single act of buying means multiple acts of rejection of those commodities not bought. The exercise of choice and the selection in shopping thus constitute, not merely 'buying into' the system, but also exercising power, control and cultural autonomy by the subordinates, who make their own cultural uses of this power.

It is this 'politics of consumption' that links consumerism and economic power with identity politics, and so leads to the debate over who can exercise what kind of consumer rights to claim a cultural identity that awards the status of 'cultural citizenship' within the market economy (Pakulski 1997; Turner 2001: 18–22). Thus Evans (1993), in the first conceptualization of sexual citizenship in literature, discusses a notion of consumer citizenship that links up gay identity with leisure and lifestyle membership: 'As consumers we are unique individuals with needs, identities and lifestyles which we express through our purchase of appropriate commodities' (p. 45).

It is well known that sexual minorities, especially gay men, are obsessed with consumption, and are ideal consumers for market targeting. But why is this the case? In addition to the general pattern of increasing global consumption in our everyday lives, the fact that many lesbians and gay men enjoy going shopping so much can be seen as being due to an effort to counteract the lack of power in other social arenas – specifically in the realm of social rights – among gay men and lesbians. Binnie (1995) shows that many young lesbians and gay men in 1990s Britain cared less about laws and legislations (e.g., age of consent) than about the 'freedom to consume music, dance, spectacle and sex' (p. 190). Queer consumerism is a powerful assertion of queer economic power, and it becomes the *major* assertion of queer power when society still limits many of the civic, political and social rights among gay men and lesbians.

Despite the neoliberal techniques of governance, lesbians and gay men have successfully transformed themselves – from sad, bad or mad social outcasts with potential subversive power to challenge social norms and values, to responsible and respectable consumer-citizens who are the supporters of dominant ideas and norms. They are now lifestyle experts, and so we need the queer eye for fashion, food and wine, grooming, interior design and culture (the 'Fab Five') to inform the allegedly boring, shabby and non-sensitive straight guy, just as shown in the US TV series *Queer Eye for the Straight Guy* (see p. 237 note 24). As the perfect DINKs, with high purchasing power and little liability, middle-class and upper-middle-class lesbians and gay men are the builders of stable communities, and adhere to most dominant heterosexual values and ideas (e.g., Bell and Binnie 2000: Ch. 6; Richardson 2001: 161–63).

However, this notion of sexual citizenship has been criticized as privileging the consumption of certain lifestyles. This universal and attractive appeal of citizen membership depends heavily on economic ability to exercise the right to consume in the first place, and thus inevitably excludes some – especially economically weaker groups such as women, the working class, the youth, new migrants, etc. – from full citizenship (e.g., Evans 1993: Ch. 4; Binnie 1995; Bell and Binnie 2000: Ch. 6; Richardson 2001: 161–63; Hennessy 1995: 159–77). As Richardson (1998: 95) succinctly says:

> Lesbians and gay men may be free to consume but only within certain spatial and cultural boundaries. The boundaries of citizenship as consumerism are the limits to where, when and how we can consume lesbian and gay 'lifestyles'; the boundaries of (heterosexual) tolerance and of 'public spaces' in which consumer communities can exercise their right to consume. (Emphasis original)

As Binnie (1995: 187) reminds us, pink businesses, after all, do business rather than charity. The debate is whether this new 'pink economy' can empower lesbians and gay men for the fight for social rights and entitlements, or whether this 'pink economy' merely serves as another form of capitalist colonialization and exploitation of queer sexuality.

What of the situation in Hong Kong? In the following, I will briefly discuss the emergence of queer consumer citizenship through the development of the commercial queer scenes in Hong Kong since the 1990s that have accompanied the shift in the image of gay men and lesbians from that of perverted citizens to that of decent citizens (discussed in Chapter 2). I will then discuss how this newly emerging queer citizenship – a derivative of the global queer citizenship, serves not for cultural identification or uniformity but acts as a dividing line that privileges certain gay citizens along the line of class, gender, age, race and ethnicity, etc. – can be seen as involving a hegemonic cult of gay masculinity (c.f., Connell's (1995) hierarchy of masculinities). Following Foucault's (1982, 1988, 1991) concept of the 'being-made' and 'self-making' of governed identity and the 'techniques of the self', I will then discuss the strategies that Hong Kong gay men employ in dealing with this complex web of domination and in creating their own version of citizenship.

Life inside – two stories in Hong Kong

Before the 1990s there were very few commercial venues in Hong Kong that catered to queer clientele. Notable exemptions were the gay bar *Dateline* in Central, the gay disco *Disco Disco* (*D.D.*) on Hong Kong Island and the gay bar *Wally Matilda*, later called *Wally Matt*, located in Tsim Sha Tsui, on the Kowloon side. Under the British laws that criminalized homosexuality and the general colonial culture of obedience, Hong Kong tongzhi were conformist in most senses and were strongly pro-establishment. Although *D.D.* and *Dateline* both closed down in the late 1980s, the commercial queer scene in Hong Kong expanded in the early 1990s with the development of a sufficiently large queer market, allowing an increasing number of queer-oriented businesses to be established.

This proliferation of queer visibility can be accounted for by three factors. The first is the general affluence of the society beginning in the 1980s and the accompanying popularity of a Western-modern style of consumption culture of drinking, dancing and clubbing.[4] The second is the decriminalization of homosexuality in 1990, which not only protected tongzhi (mainly memba) in legal terms but also led to the mushrooming of queer organizations and the establishment of different entertainment venues for them, such as nightclubs, saunas, karaokes, etc.[5] These two developments provided meeting places for the constitution of queer identities and 'communities'. The third factor is the scarcity of physical space, which translates into extraordinarily high prices for land use under the housing policy of the government, consequently restricting most Hong Kong tongzhi (especially the young, single and economically deprived) to living in their family homes. This shared residence not only creates pressure for them to come out to their families, which is always hard for them (see Chapter 4), but also affects their lifestyles, encouraging them to hang around more in public space. As they have difficulty inviting queer friends home, the bars, clubs, karaokes, shopping malls and cinemas become the places for social gathering (e.g., for partying). Travelling to nearby mainland China, Taiwan, Japan and Thailand has also become a common practice during holidays, or even weekends, for those who can afford to do so. Hong Kong queer bodies are thus not homebodies, but rather public, consuming and travelling transnational bodies.

Since the 1990s there has been a massive growth in the number of sites for queer consumption, including bars, clubs, cafés and saunas. These venues may be quite short lived, reflecting the strong competition among pink businesses. They are mainly located in shopping areas in Central, Wan Chai and Causeway Bay on Hong Kong Island, and in Tsim Sha Tsui, Jordon, Yau Ma Tei and Mongkok on the Kowloon side.[6] In addition, druggy parties used to be organized in large warehouses, convention centres or theatres, usually before or during big holidays, but these have now moved to Shenzhen due to the zero tolerance drug policy of the Hong Kong government.[7] There is also an increasing trend of small-scale home drug parties (5–10 persons) (Kong *et al.* 2009).

Commercial queer spaces not only serve as meeting places where lesbian and gay men can freely express their sexuality and create certain social and even political bonds among themselves, but also change the perception of lesbians and gay men, as it is in them that Hong Kong gay men can be seen as no longer citizen-perverts, but good citizens with decent occupations and excellent taste in fashion and lifestyle, as well as non-threatening male subjects who are 'women's best friends' (see Chapter 2).

However, we must ask whether it is easy to survive in such extravagant queer spaces and live up to this ideal of glamorous citizenship. When I interviewed Calvin in 1997 he was 32 years old, medium-sized and a professional in a medical field. He dressed conservatively and was very straight-acting. His conversational style was rational and articulate, reflecting his professional training. After his first gay romance was discovered by his family and he was forced to leave his boyfriend, at the age of 15, he was 'silent' about his sexuality to his family and in his workplace (see Chapter 4). During his school days in the 1980s, however, he had had some good friends, and they used to hang out together. Their friendship continued after their secondary education. When they all started to work, in their early twenties, Calvin asked them one day, if they had to choose between a man and a woman, who they would choose. The question sparked off a heated discussion, in which they came out to each other. He and his friends then went through many different stages of coming out to the gay world during the 1980s:

> I think we are quite conservative. After that 'collective coming out' session, we didn't go out to any gay venues but rather subscribed to gay magazines or videos from overseas. We chipped in to rent a P.O. Box together. After we got tapes, we would go to each other's homes to view them. Later, some of us went to *Dateline*, but I didn't. Rather, I looked up the classified section of *Hong Kong Magazine*. I think I was quite reserved. Usually I responded to some classified advertisements rather than putting my own advertisement. So I started to talk to other gay men . . . well, I met up with some guys but, at that time, I was very choosy and I

wanted the perfect guy, you know, like any one of the models in those magazines and tapes. I didn't find anyone very interesting, really.

After a period of time we all thought that we should open ourselves up more. So we went to the gym. Unfortunately I didn't find anyone interesting there either . . . I went to the gym for a couple of years. I did a stupid thing. I mistakenly assumed a guy was gay. He shouted at me and scolded me in the gym. I was very shocked and hurt. I stopped going after that, and the gym period died out.

Afterwards, I started to go clubbing. I saw a lot of very trendy and good-looking guys. They were very up-town and very 'in'. They were quite different from those guys I met at the gym. But I guess you should have good communication and social skills if you go clubbing. I don't know how to talk to strangers. Then I found that no one seemed to be interested in me. However, I don't like dancing and I have problems with my ears. I can't talk in such a loud environment.

So, some of my friends suggested that we might try saunas. For me it is very easy to accept the fact that you can have sex with a person without any emotional attachment. But the overall experience was not promising. I remember that the first time I went to a sauna I was 'confronted' by many different types of gay men. They were very . . . well, I always thought that all gay men should be young, good-looking, middle class, a bit camp, but above all they should be the 'good boy' type – I don't know why, maybe I didn't have any references before. My original conception of gay men came from the books or magazines that I had read, and also from discussions between my friends and myself. Anyway, in saunas, I saw that some of them looked like construction workers, some of them smoked all the time, some swore all the time, some were really ugly or very fat, and some were very old. So in saunas, I saw all sorts of gay men. Then I suddenly saw my future. I would get older and might still be hanging out in these places.

I was quite pissed off by going to saunas. Saunas are solely for sex and the people there are very pragmatic. I was bluntly refused by some guys and those experiences hurt me very much. I felt very sad, but sometimes I could find some good fellows. I think I am addicted. If I am going out with a guy, I stop going there. But if I am dumped, I will go there again. In fact, I met my present partner in a sauna and we have been together for a year.

The 'coming out session' had happened when Calvin was 24, in the mid 1980s. During that time debates about the decriminalization of homosexuality and subsequent public discussions about the issue had surfaced, but the overall societal atmosphere was still one of extreme homophobia. Moreover, there were only a few social or commercial gay venues. With these limitations, both real and imagined, Calvin and his friends sought resources overseas by subscribing to gay publications, or by responding to personal advertisements in the English language, highly Westernized local leisure *Hong Kong Magazine*. Westernized gay images and lifestyles structured their aesthetic values and defined their 'objects of desire'. Thus, Calvin looked for a perfect man such as 'any one of those models in those magazines and tapes', and was 'shocked' to see 'all sorts of gay men' when he first went to a local sauna.

Calvin and his friends then went to gyms, which are a common place for 'gay peeping'. However, the risk of 'queering' a straight place is that one might easily find the wrong object of desire. After Calvin mistakenly assumed a man in a gym was gay and was bluntly rebuked, he entered the gay world more directly. However, the overall experiences were not very satisfying. The scene was characterized by wild and glamorous all-night extravaganzas, which Calvin was expected to participate in. Thus he ended up going to saunas for sex and perhaps even for love. However, even the mere engagement in sex in this context required him to have a specific type of physique – it is the gym-type body that is glorified.

Calvin and his friends, like many gay men, wanted to explore their secret sexuality after they came out to each other and to their close friends. However, they found that the commercial gay world, like society at large, was not easy to live in. Rather than a totality, the commercial gay world should be seen as consisting of fragmented and segmented sites, in which domination and subordination still exist.

Community, like identity and citizenship, has a dual nature, entailing both the articulation of commonality and consensus and also implying exclusion and difference. That is, a community is based on the notion of collective inclusion, with an implicit understanding of who is and who is not to be admitted. The 'admission ticket' to the commercial queer world seems to depend on unspoken ideas of queer citizenship embedded in these sites, and a distinctive possession of economic, cultural, social or symbolic capital (c.f., Bourdieu 1986, 1984, 1989).

I knew Ivan through some friends in the arts circle. In 1998, he was 22 and had just graduated from a local university, where he had studied humanities and had been into art and theatre. He had grown up almost ten years later than Calvin. Unlike Calvin, he was out to his family and friends and was working in a gay-friendly organization where he was out to everyone at the workplace. Calvin and Ivan seem to represent the gay men of two different decades. However, although times have changed, some features of the queer world may not have. Ivan said,

> The gay scene is very middle class. It seems that it requires everyone to have the same identity, the same sort of lifestyle, the same conditions for consumption. Some guys spend a lot of time getting into this circle. . . . Well, this may not be a problem for them or for me. But I think the gay world should have something more. If the gay scene is defined by the middle class, then working-class gay people are made invisible. Disabled

> people are also made invisible. Lesbians, I think, are totally invisible. So, what is going wrong? . . . I don't know how to solve this problem but I think that society always tells us that, if you live comfortably, don't make any noise, and if you are happy, don't be concerned about any social issues. So I guess the overall atmosphere is problematic, which is why the gay world in general is problematic.

Ivan was very critical of the queer world in the late 1990s and was the only one of my interviewees who related the problems of the queer world to some general problems of the larger social environment. He is right to point out that the commercial queer scene in Hong Kong, as in post-colonial capitalist society generally, is stratified along the lines of gender, class, race, age and body.

Generally speaking, the commercial queer scene is largely male-dominated, highly class-specific, youth-oriented, camp-phobic and fashion conscious, and has always been coloured by a substantial Western input. This cluster of distinctions defines gay citizenship, and members are required to conform. Like the compulsory heterosexuality, or heteronormativity, that operates in straight society, social discrimination arises through a hegemonic cult of gay masculinity within the gay commercial world.

To understand this scene, first of all, D'Emilio (1983) may be right in pointing out that the development of capitalism, and thus the growth of gay sites of consumption, has made possible the emergence of a lesbian and gay identity and subculture. The logic of late capitalism requires a high level of consumption to sustain pink businesses, and the commercialized gay scene thus involves patterns of class difference. As the economy has boomed in Hong Kong over the past few decades, the Hong Kong gay subculture has grown spectacularly, particularly since the 1990s; and so capitalism has been endemic to this growth. However, the average monthly salary of a fresh university graduate is HK$7,000–8,000 (equivalent to about 500 pounds), but a bottle of beer costs HK$50 or more in a pub or club, and the fee for admission to a club is HK$150 or more; and so potential members of the subculture had better have some money in their pockets.

The gay bars and clubs in Hong Kong are roughly divided according to class difference: bars on the Kowloon side cater to working-class or 'unpretentious' gays with various body shapes; while bars on Hong Kong Island attract predominately middle-class, hip, cool and 'in' young male professionals with 'standard' gym trained bodies.

Second, the queer world is a man's world. The visibly queer spaces, especially the sites of consumption, are mainly occupied by gay men. This might reflect the relatively economically deprived status of women (especially lesbians), but it also reveals the preoccupation of gay men with same-sex hedonism. Although this study does not investigate the life histories of Hong Kong lesbians, other studies suggest that they feel excluded from the queer world. As one lesbian said in an interview, 'Most of us have got used to having nothing.' Another remarked, 'We have no status, no say, no nothing, we are not even seen as human beings. In the straight world, at least you are a woman, but in the gay world, you are nothing' (Turner 1994: 17). 'Lesi' places, as compared with gay places, seem to be more 'invisible' – lesbians may 'queer' some straight bars, hang out in gay bars or in a few lesbian-identified bars and cafés clustered largely in Causeway Bay and Happy Valley.[8] Hong Kong, like other major cities, has a clear but disproportional gay and lesbian split, in terms of entertainment venues.

Third, Hong Kong's architecture exemplifies Western forms because of the territory's colonial history and the impact of globalization, and this is true of the venues in the Hong Kong queer world. The interior designs and atmosphere of most bars and clubs strongly exhibit Euro/American styles and rhetoric. These venues are not deliberately created to attract Westerners: some venues, such as the bars *Why Not*, *Wally Matt* and *Rainbow Pub* and saunas such as *Galaxy*, *ABC* and *Double* cater mainly to local gay men. However, the idea of the English or the 'West' has connotations of symbolic value that are usually associated with ideas of sophistication, modernity, wealth, education, culture and sexual liberality.[9] It is quite common for two Chinese gay men, who speak Cantonese perfectly, to speak in English in certain bars in Central. These premises are reputed to provide better service to Westerners or Westernized Chinese. It is thus interesting to see how space, sexuality and race are intricately intertwined. There is always an internal rivalry between Hong Kong and Kowloon bar-goers. While the former find the latter too local, provincial and working class, with little taste in fashion, grooming and culture, the latter complain that the former are 'arrogant', 'middle class' and pretending to be '*gwailo/gweilo*' (**鬼佬** Cant.: 'Caucasian man'. See below). Bars in Central have more Western and overseas Chinese clientele, while bars in Kowloon have more local Chinese. The racial hierarchy replicates the spatial hierarchy of the city.

Gay citizenship as hegemonic cult of gay masculinity

Aged 36 in the second interview in 2007, Jeff migrated to the UK in the 1980s but had lived for a couple of years in Hong Kong in the 1990s and had now resided in London. He said to me once when he was in Hong Kong:

> A lot of Hong Kong gay men try to be something. They try too hard to be something – you know, the best dressed, the best face, the best body, the best whatever, really . . . that's why they tend to be aggressive or even look down on you . . . perhaps, in fact, if they could be more comfortable and relaxed the whole situation would be much better!

Jeff, from a rich family and an architect, embodies all the essential capital to be a 'perfect' gay citizen – he is good-looking, young, rich, fashion-conscious, cosmopolitan, with a decent job, and possessing a hard gym-trained body.

Yet even he has found the Hong Kong gay world difficult to live with. So what is really going on here?

Connell (1995) defines hegemonic masculinity as 'the configuration of gender practice which embodies the currently accepted answer to the problem of the legitimacy of patriarchy' (p. 77). It not only guarantees the subordination of women in society but also defines other masculine styles as inadequate or inferior. Connell identifies four types of men whose masculinities are 'under pressure': young working-class men without regular jobs, who fail to be traditional breadwinners; gay men, who show sexual interests in other men and thus contradict the basic definition of masculinity as heterosexual; men who are involved in the environmental movement and so live and work with feminists in settings where gender hierarchy has lost its legitimacy; and men in middle-class occupations who rely on technological knowledge without the social authority provided by capital and the older professions.

These situations create a hierarchy of masculinities privileging certain men and stigmatizing others. Hegemonic masculinity is a culturally and historically specific ideal, changing over time, that men support but may not embody, and it seems to create rigid psychological and social boundaries that inevitably give rise to systems of dominance and hierarchical organization.[10]

Likewise, the self-fashioned notion of queer citizenship has a heavy undertone of middle-class or bourgeois individualism and is intricately related to conspicuous consumption. Functioning like hegemonic masculinity, this notion of queer citizenship, what may be called 'hegemonic cult of gay masculinity', creates a hierarchy of queer citizens that privileges certain bodies and disadvantages others along the lines of class, gender performance, age, race and ethnicity, and many more. In the following, I expand on my earlier recognition of the dualities of the sexual body (Kong 2004) to discuss the body politics of Hong Kong memba in the gay community.

Straight-acting body versus effeminate body

As Connell (1995) argued, '(T)he choice of a man as sexual object is not just the choice of a body-with-penis, it is the choice of embodied masculinity. The cultural meanings of masculinity are, generally, part of the package' (p. 156). The most 'desirable' gay man in the Hong Kong gay scene seems to be one who is smart, bright, well built, manly, straight-acting, macho, career-minded and emotionally in control. These attributes are all very typical cultural definitions of being a man. That is why nearly all of my informants have had the experience of being in love with a straight man. The idea of the physical perfection of the masculine-and-muscular look seems to dominate the whole gay scene, and the gym culture has swept over the whole gay globe. A 'masculinization of the gay man' (e.g., 'butch shift', 'macho' style) has occurred, in which 'strong' masculinity has been claimed, asserted, or re-appropriated by gay men. This macho look seems to focus entirely on the body, glorifying the athletic male body.[11]

Although a few informants showed distress at 'Muscle Mary', or in local parlance *gamgong Barbie* (金剛芭比 Cant.) (i.e., well-built, usually gym-trained, masculine bodies, but may display feminine mannerisms), they tended to accept the macho build as an aesthetic ideal. Quite a lot of my informants were hostile to gay men who are feminine in appearance and in mannerism. Comments such as these are common across all ages: 'If I met a boy who is very camp, very dependent, I would definitely be turned off' (David, 43, self-employed catering businessman, interviewed in 1997); 'I am looking for a man, not a woman.' (Frank, 35, unemployed in 1997; and at 46, insurance sales, 2008); 'If you are a man, you should behave like a man. If you are a woman, you should behave like a woman. Please behave like a human being!' (Robert, 20, student, interviewed in 1997).

Camp or feminized memba have always been laughed at, ridiculed and even bullied in both the straight and gay worlds. Moreover, Hong Kong memba stick to a rather rigid role division of 'top' and 'bottom', or in the local parlance, 1 and 0. The 1/0 division reflects not just sexual practices (1 being inserter and 0 insertee) but also personality (1 being active and independent and 0 being passive and dependent) (Lau 2004).[12]

My respondents, like many memba, did not seem to consider anything beyond these existing gender and sexual orders. They were not only hostile to hyper-feminine men but also disliked people who were bisexuals, transvestites, transsexuals or sadomasochists, as they found them 'weird, perverted and abnormal.' They were rigid in role-playing and privileged the top over the bottom, as the latter is closely associated with femininity. In order to be popular in the gay world, Hong Kong memba are expected to have manly mannerisms together with homosexual desires – that is, to act like straight men but to desire their own gender.

The young body versus the aging body

As I have observed elsewhere (Kong 2004), youthfulness and beauty (defined mainly as the athletic body) are the most prominent assets of 'embodied cultural capital' that one can possess for gay citizenship. This is reflected in the constant portrayal, in the Hong Kong gay press, of models who are young (probably in their early twenties), trendily dressed, healthy-looking, and possessing gym-trained bodies.

Eric's experiences illustrate the significant role age plays in the gay world. Eric was 59 in 2008, a medical professional and an artist. He is a very spiritual man, into Catholic mysticism. When I first met him in 1997, I was inspired by his wisdom and listened to his bittersweet life at his clinic. He told me that he was unlucky. When he was young, in the late 1970s, the gay space was severely limited and he did not hang out at all, but lived in total secrecy. The times changed and many gay spaces opened up but he still did not go out, as he could not fit in these new spaces. He told me the other side of the glamorous gay nightlife.

> I think the whole world is like this, very youth-oriented. If you have youthfulness, you have the world. Everything is fun, everything is good. But if you have passed your youth you will find out that the world is not so interesting and is less fun. And you have to accept the fact that you can't have the best and you must realize your limitations. I am now 48 and not 38, or you are now 28 and not 18. The gay scene is so youth-oriented that you can't get into it. If you can't get into it, what space is left for you?

He had a photographic exhibition in 1997 which focused on ageing memba, who, to him, were the '1 per cent of the 10 per cent'. By documenting their passions and desires, Eric revealed the character of their lives – an altogether different culture that was 'more part of a fast-fading heritage that has run out of its own prosperity'. Eric seldom goes out, and immerses himself in his couple life, profession and artwork.

Gwailo body versus Chinese body

Before the 1990s, the presence of Caucasian men, locally called 'Westerners' (*saijan* 西人 Cant.) or 'foreign devils' (*gwailo/gweilo* Cant.),[13] including expatriates, tourists and businessmen from Britain and other parts of the world, was substantial in the queer scene and even dominated it. Respondents who were born before the 1980s all spoke positively about Caucasian men.

> I prefer *gwailo* . . . when I was at school, my English wasn't so good. I thought I could learn something from *gwailo* that I couldn't learn from my family, school or friends . . . I was very lucky as I met a lot of *gwailo* who were very, very nice to me. I was very happy . . . and I learnt a lot . . . and I quite like Western romance. [What is Western romance?] Well, Chinese romance is more reserved. A lot of things you don't talk about . . . but Western romance is different, it's more direct and passionate . . .
>
> (Alan, 36, dancer, interviewed in 1997)

> They (*gwailo*) are more beautiful and are nicer. And you can see many different types. You can only see one type of Hong Kong gay man – campy and bitchy!
>
> (Jonathan, 33, student, interviewed in 1998)

> I find *gwailo* very attractive – you know, those facial features, perfect tits and butts, bulbous biceps – but I never fancy going out with any one of them.
>
> (Aron, 33, para-medical profession, interviewed in 1997)

Caucasian men – the economic and socially privileged positions that these *gwailo* (Cant.) attained in Hong Kong, the cultural and symbolic implication of sophistication and modernity (especially through the expression of the alleged 'Western romance') that they carried, the physical (the allegedly 'masculine' and 'athletic') figure that they embodied – were attractive to Hong Kong memba, especially to those who were young or economically deprived. It was not uncommon to see the pairing of an older, richer and more 'manly' Caucasian man with a younger, slimmer and more effeminate Chinese gay man with a lower-class background (Kong 2002). By using their sexual contacts with (usually older) Caucasian men, these Chinese gay men, sometimes called 'potato queens', were able to win entry into the Western world. The will to hook up with Caucasian men in order to seek social mobility was intensified by the spatial constraints, the pattern of family residence and the issue of decolonization, and has led to a major stream of queer migrants to Western countries (see Chapter 5).

However, *caufui* (溱魁 Cant.: 'going out with a *gwailo*'),[14] and the appeal of Caucasian men and their colonial advantages over Chinese gay men, have gradually declined since the 1990s, parallel with the shifting of the sovereignty of Hong Kong from Britain to mainland China (Ho and Tsang 2000).[15] I was surprised to hear that the majority of those in the young generations do not normally find Caucasian men appealing. When I asked Christopher, who had just turned 18 in 2008, about what kinds of men he fancied, he ruled out Caucasian men immediately, '*Gwailo*? No way, I can't even communicate with him . . . talking in English is already a problem, how can you expect him to understand you?! . . . I can only accept gay men from Hong Kong.' If the '*gwailo*-potato queen' pairing signified the replication of racism and colonialism within the structure of desire during the colonial time, then who is the new star and who is the new subordinate in the transnational hierarchy of queer citizenship in post-colonial Hong Kong? Caucasian men have lost the supreme position they once had, yet they still occupy a certain 'market niche' in the globalized, English-language-dominated world, but they are now facing real competitors with the rise of an affluent middle class and the production of well educated, bilingual, transnational, cosmopolitan professional local Hong Kong gay men. Such men are now admired as the new stars.

These new gay citizens, however, produce the new marginal groups: the gay men from mainland China and elsewhere, who constitute ethnic minorities in Hong Kong (e.g., South and Southeast Asians). There is an ongoing discussion in Hong Kong about how new Chinese or other ethnic migrants have been excluded, marginalized and stigmatized as 'margizens' in Hong Kong.[16] Likewise, discrimination against gay Chinese migrants inside the gay circle is quite obvious. As Christopher continued his ethnic priorities for dating, he said:

> I don't like those who come from mainland China . . . I don't like to speak Mandarin. [How about those who can speak Cantonese from the mainland?] Even if they speak Cantonese, it's Chinese Cantonese, not Hong Kong Cantonese . . . it's so *noeng* (娘 Cant.: 'out of fashion'), they

> are still not developed . . . well, even though China is developing, they still lag behind . . . I just find them very provincial!

The able body versus the disabled body

Tony was 21 in 1998. He was good-looking, but had difficulty in speaking, listening and walking. When I first met him I could see from his handsome face his burning desire to tell me about his tragic life. Our conversations have always been through writing. Of course, he has had extreme difficulty in finding a boyfriend. I was introduced to him through his ex-boyfriend – another informant, Edward, who was 25 in 1998, tall and slim, a fresh graduate from Australia. They met at the well-known gay beach, Middle Bay, but their relationship only lasted for about two months. Edward describes their relationship:

> I met Tony in Middle Bay . . . Then I discovered that he was deaf and dumb, and he also had a problem with walking. We sort of went out together for two months. We 'talked' through writing. Then I thought it wasn't so nice anymore. . . . One day, I called him and he said that he didn't have as much confidence as me, as I could talk. I then said that I couldn't help it. It is not my problem, is it?

Tony usually went to beaches or public toilets to find sexual partners; he seldom went to bars or clubs. He was very keen to find a boyfriend but his physical disabilities prevent him from finding one. He attempted suicide but failed, and the case was reported in the press. He constantly thought about suicide. I have lost contact with him. Whenever I think of him, I think of Spivak's (1988) seminal paper, 'Can the subaltern speak?' Does Tony represent the ultimate gay 'subaltern', who lives in the negligible margin, in complete silence?

The remaking of gay citizenship

As discussed in Chapter 1, identity cannot be separated from one's 'categories of difference', such as one's racial, ethnic, sexual, national or class position, one's age or even one's state of physical fitness. Through various forms and meanings, our identities embody a multiple positioning and repositioning of the self. However, embodied identities are not merely the additive experiences of these 'categories of difference'; rather, they are the results of multifarious and contradictory sets of oppression within specific institutional arenas.

It is in this 'politics of difference' that the possibility for sexual politics of Hong Kong memba lies. Hong Kong memba who live up to the hegemonic queer citizen ideals may benefit from their embodied cultural capital in their daily interactions; conversely, the hyper-feminine body, the elderly body, the skinny body, the disabled body, the poor body and many others are all regarded as subordinate gay variants – as 'failed' bodies or second class citizens. However, the negative characterizations of these attributes should not be treated as fixed, as there are many ways of reacting to the hegemonic ideal.

The first of these ways is through conforming. When I first met George in 1997, he was 24, very skinny and feminine in appearance and mannerism. He told me he had always been verbally abused in both the straight and gay worlds. Then one day I saw him in a social gathering. I was shocked, as he had shaved off his hair and grown a beard, and was wearing a sweater that showed off his tanned, gym-trained body. His new 'butch and macho look' had brought him back into the circle of admiration and he seemed to enjoy very much his newly acquired, embodied capital. He reminds me of a very 'manly'-acting memba friend who said to me once, 'I could be very camp, sissy, and dramatic and all that, but I hated the associated stigma and insults, so from day one, I decided to act straight.'

Similarly, Matthew was tall and slim, and a fashion designer. He always dyed his hair different colors. When I first met him ten years ago he was 38 and 'blonde', and I thought he was only 28. Of course, he was flattered by my incorrect guess. He dressed very well and worked out frequently. Through vigorous exercise, and/or expensive grooming and facial products, these men have been able to produce young-appearing bodies and hide their ages. Moreover, Matthew was Eurasian and could speak perfectly in both English and Cantonese. He insisted on speaking English in bars and clubs, as he believed he would receive better service.

These men seem to conform to Butler's (1990) formulation of identity as consisting of a string of performances made coherent through repetition: 'Gender is the repeated stylization of the body, a set of repeated acts within a highly rigid regulatory frame that congeal over time to produce the appearance of substance, of a natural sort of being' (p. 33). Their skills as performers and the success of their performances depend very much on how well they act out the 'scripts' of hegemonic cult gay masculinity and gay citizenship. Acting butch, acting straight, acting young and even acting 'Western' apparently serve as major components of conformity that may grant you an appealing identity within the gay world.

However, reaction to the hegemonic ideal does not always mean accommodating oneself to it – some react by resisting or by withdrawal. Ivan, for example, was an effeminate gay man. Contrary to George's conformism, Ivan has tried to redefine masculinity by using his 'femininity', without equating it with powerlessness. By appearing in drag in his art performance, he had used 'femininity' as a weapon to challenge the rigid gender order, to upset the very notion of masculinity. A lot of 'ex-potato queens' have questioned the 'phallus is white' as the only logic of desire, and have started dating local Chinese men. Respondents such as Eric tended to immerse themselves in work rather than to conform to the hegemonic masculine ideal, to find a way of life in withdrawal from gay public spaces.

The hegemonic queer citizen ideal dominates Hong Kong gay bars and clubs, yet 'subordinate' queer bodies can still find themselves certain hidden, but usually more transient, places. The set up of *Rainbow Pub* (2000–2006) was a sign of this, as it opened up a new space for gay men who did not conform to the super-macho body type (although the bar maintained a strict policy of not allowing women to come in). *Rainbow Pub* gained the reputation of attracting 'bears' and their admirers. Every Saturday more than a hundred large-frame memba would dance in a commercial building in Jordon on the Kowloon side, which offered a spectacular view of Hong Kong Island. Unfortunately, the bar was shut down. However, there are a few saunas that specifically target 'bears' as their clientele.

The sixth-floor toilet in the massive shopping mall of Langham Place in Mongkok was a hot spot in the summer of 2008 when a bunch of secondary school boys hung around there. These secondary school gay boys, with limited consuming power to hang out at bars, clubs or even saunas, cruised in a shopping mall and used the technology of Bluetooth for communication.[17] However, once a public space becomes a place for sexual excitement, it inevitably entails a risk of criminality: the space of surveillance = space of desire = space for manoeuvre, and the moment of resistance is actually the very moment of government (Woodhead 1995: 238–9). This toilet became a famous 'cottage' that attracted a lot of gay men. However, after a few months, there were many complaints. In order to resume heterosexual public order, the shopping mall management exerted its power and control by installing a surveillance TV camera, on that floor only. What remains is now a camera installed at the top corner of the ceiling in the corridor, and the 'cottage' has reverted to a simple public toilet. I have no idea where the secondary school gay boys have gone.

Finding a gay space for love and consumption is not easy in Hong Kong, but finding a new space outside Hong Kong has become an option. Due to the close proximity of Hong Kong and mainland China, sex tourism to mainland China, especially since 1997, has become a new way for Hong Kong gay men to find sexual gratification. There has been a mushrooming of gay bars, clubs and saunas since the 1990s in Shenzhen (www.utopia-asia.com/shensaun.htm), the closest China city to Hong Kong, and one of the main clients are Hong Kong gay men.

Stuart was 35 in 1998, a construction worker from a working-class background who had worked at many manual jobs. He had a 'masculine' body. Fed up with the high level of consumption in the Hong Kong gay scene, he went to Shenzhen to find cheaper gay entertainment, although he knew that he was running the risk of being blackmailed by money boys, robbed by thugs or caught by the police.[18] Stuart 'kept' a mainland Chinese straight boy for a few years – the relationship was mainly economic. Others with higher incomes, such as Eric and Matthew, go to other Asian countries (e.g., Thailand, Singapore, Taiwan, Japan) for their enjoyment. Such gay sex tourism within Asia not only reflects the political economies of different Asian cities but also brings strong linkages in rhetoric, lifestyle and culture that may foster a transnational gay identity (Altman 2001; Bollestorff 2007a: Ch. 6; Martin *et al.* 2008: 1–27).

Conclusion

Communities that revolve around bars and discos, and the 'ghetto' are particularly significant in queer culture, because these serve as markers in contemporary queer history and contribute to contemporary urban queer identity. The neo-liberal economy helps to nurture a queer citizenship that has successfully transformed the old image of gay men and lesbians as perverted citizens to an image of respectable cosmopolitan consumer citizens.

Following the queer critique, which emphasizes the heterogeneous and hierarchical nature of queer space and identity,[19] I have argued that these 'sites of desire' are in fact also 'sites of power and domination', but are more invisibly so. In Hong Kong, a well-developed and visible queer world is evident and a more positive notion of queer citizenship has materialized – yet it is a male-dominated, class-distinctive, camp-phobic, youth-oriented, Western-style and cosmopolitan one. By analysing Manchester's gay village, Binnie and Skeggs (2004) urge us to rethink the matter of access and knowledge in queer space: 'who can use, consume and be consumed in such a gay space?' (p. 39) Their analysis suggests that there are cosmopolitan winners and losers, and that gender, race and class have always intervened in the commodification of gay space:

> The cosmopolitan is produced through consuming difference, but only certain differences. The gay man is frequently positioned as necessary for that consumption as a signifier of difference, but this consumption of difference is only available to those who can (and want to) access different cultures.
>
> (Binnie and Skeggs, 2004: 52)

Living under the influence of this dominant ideal, Hong Kong memba tend to conform to a hegemonic embodied Western-derived cosmopolitan masculinity, in which the 'ideal' male citizen is one who is physically fit, straight-acting, macho, non-feminine and economically secure; and the popular 'ideal' gay male citizen is one who acts straight, is young, and is physically fit. The hegemonic masculinity of the straight world is virtually the same as that of the gay world, and determines the objects of desire of Hong Kong memba, setting forth the possibilities and limits of their forming relationships.

Power is not unified, and neither is gay identity. To paraphrase Ong's (1999) description of Hong Kong businessmen who hold multiple passports and shuttle among cities around the world for better family advancement, I have suggested that Hong Kong memba are caught within the disciplinary hegemonic cult of gay masculinity and the practice of conspicuous pink consumption. They seek flexible positions among the myriad possibilities (and problems) of global queer citizenship. They negotiate – conform, resist or redefine – a flexible and pragmatic gay identity that is sensitive to different institutional arenas, in order to find love and intimacy. Making use of their own embodied capital, they struggle and live under different forms of domination inside the gay world, governed by commercially driven notions of hegemonic gay masculinity. Some succeed, some fail, some still whirl in the middle. A man's world is tough, and a gay man's world is even tougher!

4 All about family

Intimate citizenship and family biopolitics

> . . . modern heterosexuality is supposed to refer to relations of intimacy and identification with other persons, and sex acts are supposed to be the most intimate communication of them all. The sex act shielded by the zone of privacy is the affectional nimbus that heterosexual culture protects and from which it abstracts its model of ethics, but this utopia of social belonging is also supported and extended by acts less commonly recognized as part of sexual culture: paying taxes, being disgusted, philandering, bequeathing, celebrating a holiday, investing for the future, teaching, disposing of a corpse, carrying wallet photos, buying economy size, being nepotistic, running for president, divorcing, or owning anything 'His' or 'Hers'.
>
> (Lauren Berlant and Michael Warner, 'Sex in public', 1998)

> Perhaps it would be better to ask oneself, 'What relations, through homosexuality, can be established, invented, multiplied and modulated?' The problem is not to discover in oneself the truth of sex but rather to use sexuality henceforth to arrive at a multiplicity of relationships. . . . To be 'gay', I think, is not to identify with the psychological traits and the visible masks of the homosexual, but to try to define and develop a way of life.
>
> (Michel Foucault, 'Friendship as a way of life', 1996)

In the discourse of modern citizenship, the model for the citizen usually rests on the assumption of a dominant scripting of a long-term monogamous heterosexual pairing, legitimatized in the marriage institution and manifesting the best form, that of the nuclear family – a married heterosexual couple and their unmarried heterosexual children – which then forms the basic unit of society.

Such a discourse, that renders the family and the marriage institution the necessary sites of intimacy, seems to be central in UK politics (e.g., Richardson 1998: 91; Bell and Binnie 2000: 53–61; Weeks *et al.* 2004), as well as in that of the US (e.g., Berlant and Warner 1998: 548–50; Meeks and Stein 2006). Familial heteronormativity, as the major component of such family ideology, is produced through the state apparatus – such as that of welfare, taxation, education, etc. – which goes beyond the sexual and romantic realms and penetrates into the various activities of our everyday lives, as succinctly depicted by the long list in the above quote by Berlant and Warner (1998: 555).

So what is the position of queers in this family picture? What if the family discovers that one of its members is gay, lesbian, bisexual or just a little bit queer? What is the space for these queer kids? And if to be 'gay', as Foucault (1996) suggests, 'is not to identify with the psychological traits and the visible masks of the homosexual' (p. 310), what kind of new 'way of life' can we define, imagine and practice?

With the backdrop of the socio-political, cultural and commercial queer development in Hong Kong in the previous two chapters, this chapter discusses how Hong Kong gay men, through coming-out practices and through forming intimate relationships with other men, challenge the heterosexist assumptions of citizenship within the realms of family and intimacy. I will argue that family ideology goes hand in hand with governance in Hong Kong. Borrowing the idea of 'family biopolitics' from Aiwha Ong (see below), I will argue that family biopolitics is an effect of state discipline, which affects family practices and ideologies that regulate healthy, productive and heterosexual bodies. Familial heteronormativity, one product of such biopolitics, is produced via the family institution, characterized by 'utilitarian familism' (Lau 1978, 1982: Ch. 3–4), or the 'harmonious family' in the SAR regime, and the marriage institution and couple relationship, crystallized in the notion of monogamy.

In the first half of the chapter, I will discuss how Hong Kong gay men, or memba, live as gay sons within heterosexual families, and the ways in which they challenge the disciplinary codes of familial heteronormativity. The focal point will be their coming-out practices. I will then focus on the ways in which they form intimate relationships and their own families, and consider how they deconstruct family and the ideology of the intimate long-term monogamous couple relationship. In both of these ways, memba negotiate the dual process of 'being-made' and 'self-making' to claim a citizenship of intimacy that enables them to experiment with a new 'way of life' in the hegemonic socio-cultural environment of heteronormative citizenship.

Biopolitics of the Hong Kong family

Family studies in Hong Kong began with a functionalist framework based on how traditional Chinese patriarchal extended families had changed under the vigorous processes of modernization and Westernization. The focal point was how the Chinese family had adopted and been modified under the imperatives of the greater industrialization of Hong Kong, and how this resulted in different forms of family, such as the stem family, the nuclear family, the isolated conjugal family (Wong 1972, 1975) and the modified extended family (Lee 1987; Podmore and Chaney 1974). The ideological orientation of these studies was that of a utilitarianistic familism (Lau 1978, 1982: Ch. 3–4).[1]

By materializing the conventional sinological characterization of the Chinese notion of filial piety, Lau (1982) explains the allegedly apolitical but blatantly economic characteristics of the post-war Chinese immigrants/refugees. Despite being inward-looking and materialistic, like the ideal economic man, these immigrants/refugees were not individualistic, but were rather preoccupied by attachment to family values. The Chinese family takes the form of 'utilitarianistic familism', as defined by Lau (1982) as:

> the normative and behavioural tendency of an individual to place his familial interests above the interests of society and of other individuals and groups, and to structure his relationships with other individuals and groups in such a manner that the furtherance of his familial interests is the overriding concern. Moreover, among the familial interests, material interests take priority over non-material interests.
>
> (Lau, 1992: 72)

Utilitarianistic considerations loom large in relations between family members, emphasizing the norm of mutual assistance in economic exchange, family ownership of property and economic cooperation. These considerations usually extend to those who occupy peripheral status – i.e., those in wider family groupings that consist of relatives and fictive kin, who form a fluid collection of people (*jatgaajan* 一家人 Cant.: 'all in the family').

In his grand design to explain the colonial miracle, Lau (1982) proposed what he called the 'minimally-integrated socio-political system' of post-war Hong Kong society, in which polity and society were seen as mutually exclusive. The colonial government was alleged to have no intention to intervene much with the population, as the Chinese people, oriented towards utilitarianistic familism, were allegedly busy with family issues rather than with politics, and seeking help from family and relatives rather than making demands on the government. With such a 'perfect match', carefully played up by each party through 'boundary politics', Lau (1982) offered a functionalist framework to explain the colonial miracle of relative political stability and economic prosperity.

> the Chinese society can be considered as an inward-looking, self-contained and atomistic society with apolitical orientations and low potentials for political mobilization. Such a society is a perfect complement to the 'secluded' bureaucratic polity, and their [sic] coexistence as well as mutual avoidance provides a clue to the explanation of political stability in Hong Kong.
>
> (Lau, 1982: 68)

Instead of a perfect natural match, however, scholars (e.g., Law 1998; Ho 2004) have argued that colonial governance had skilfully picked up Chinese filial piety and utilitarian intentions to manage colonialism. Ho (2004) argues that one of the colonial government strategies used to depoliticize Hong Kong society was to block major access to political rights, to prioritize economic development and only grant those civil rights that related exclusively to market rights, and to restrict social welfare as a residual concept, with the underlying principle of charity and benevolence. Hong Kong people were to seek help from their families, voluntary agencies or the market, rather than from the government, to satisfy their welfare needs. In other words, utilitarianistic familism is not a cause, but is rather an effect, of 'managerial colonialism' (Law 1998),[2] and it undermines the development of social citizenship and civil community.

The new SAR government continues this tradition and has promoted the family as a core value in Hong Kong society, and as an essential part of 'Chinese culture'. In the 2001 Policy Address, the first Chief Executive, Tung Chee-hwa, said, 'Our society has always recognised the importance of the family. Harmonious families are a source of comfort and care for individuals; nothing can fully replace this relationship' (paragraph 110). In the 2005–6 Policy Address, the second and present Chief Executive, Donald Tsang Yam-kuen, made this more explicit: 'Cherishing the family is a core value of our community. Family harmony is the foundation of social harmony' (paragraph 45).

So what kind of family is the government referring to? Donald Tsang, in his 2006–7 Policy Address, provides the answer.

> The nuclear family, comprising a married couple and their unmarried children, is the most common type of family unit in Hong Kong. That said, married couples in general still maintain close and mutually supportive relationships with their parents and siblings, that is, among their extended families . . . Mutual care and support between two generations and among married siblings is a virtue long practised by Chinese families that should be encouraged and promoted.
>
> (Tsang, 2006–7, paragraph 39)

Committed to this goal, the government set up a Family Council in late 2007, headed by the Chief Secretary for Administration, to discuss in detail the core family values and harmonious relationships among family members, and how to encourage the community to participate in promoting these values and relationships.

Borrowing the idea of 'biopolitics' from Foucault's (1982, 1988, 1991) explanation of modern governance of the population, Ong (1993: 753–62, 1996: 748–49, 1999: 117–19) proposes what she calls 'family biopolitics' to understand the rational and normative practices that regulate 'healthy, productive and successful bodies' within the Chinese family, and calls 'family governmentality' into deployment in economic activities for economic well-being. Like Law (1998) and Ho (2004), Ong argues that 'utilitarianistic familism' is not inherent in Chinese culture, but rather is the effect of state discipline on the refugee/immigrant families of post-war Hong Kong. Under the British rule and in the competitive conditions of laissez-faire capitalism, Hong Kong families of all classes developed extraordinary discipline for hard work, fierce competition and tight control over family members, in order to improve family livelihood and wealth. Family biopolitics thus constitutes the subject's sense of moral wealth, which is 'based on endurance and diligence in income-making activities, compliance with parental wishes, and the making of sacrifices and the deferral of gratification, especially on the part of women and children' (Ong 1999: 118).

If family biopolitics is a series of family practices and ideologies that regulates economic, productive and successful Chinese bodies, it also entails a code of practice that disciplines healthy, reproductive and heterosexual bodies. Familial heternormativity, as part of 'family governmentality', can be seen as the deployment of family biopolitics to produce the subject's sense of moral worth, and requires the children, especially sons, to comply with parental wishes to get married and bear children in order to continue the family blood, and to do nothing to harm family status and reputation.

Families with gay sons

What is the life of a gay son, born under such a disciplinary code of biopolitics of the Chinese heterosexual family, like? Calvin[3] was born in the late 1960s, into the second Hong Kong post-war baby boom generation. He comes from a conventional middle class family, with parents and three siblings. When I interviewed him in 1997, he said:

> I was brought up in a traditional family – dad, mum, and four brothers and sisters, including myself, the youngest . . . I know my family loves me and I do love them . . . they give me total freedom to do whatever I want . . . and at that time, I was very young, in secondary school, I thought that when I liked something, my family would like it too, maybe because I had a good relationship with them, and I was so in love with my first love and was so happy . . . we had those love notes and I just dropped them everywhere . . . but when my family found out, they were very angry, we had a big big fight . . . they then gave me a strict choice: either I stayed at home or else I lived with him. Come on, I was in Form 5, how could I move out to live with my boyfriend? . . . there was actually no choice at all!
>
> . . . for my siblings, they thought being gay wasn't normal . . . but for my dad and mum, they thought it was related to whether I was a good son or not . . . being gay, for them, meant that I was a bad son!. . . . I thought over and over again, and decided that I should maintain a good relationship with my family. I didn't want to hurt them, I wanted us to live more peacefully . . . so after that incident, we never talked about it.
>
> . . . and then I moved out nine years later, after I got a job . . . it has become much easier since I moved out . . . but even now, I know their

> expectation, they still want me to have a healthy lifestyle, i.e., to marry a woman and have a family . . . sometimes when I am unhappy, I can feel their sadness. They don't know how to comfort me and I don't want to disclose too much about myself . . . they care about me and they want me to be happy . . . but we just don't talk about it anymore . . .

Like Calvin, Jonathon is part of the second post-war baby generation. He was 33 in 1997 when we first met in the UK. He was working for an art company and lived with his family, which consisted of his parents, two sisters and one younger brother. He studied arts and got a scholarship, with which he could stay in the UK for a year. He had no pressure from his family concerning his career choice, but he had always had the big problem of telling his family about his sexual orientation. When I interviewed him in 1997, he said,

> First of all, they [his family] will be under pressure if I tell them. I don't want to give them pressure . . . In traditional Chinese culture, they would be unhappy and would mind if you didn't marry, but I don't think it is necessary. If you tell them that you are gay, you will create lots of problems, and you can't solve them. So, leave them alone . . . [Why would your family be under pressure?] Your relatives will ask your parents why you don't marry . . . I can't find an answer for them . . . I am close to all of my family members. They care about me and they admire me. But they don't know why I study so hard. Even though we are close, we can't really talk at that level. I won't let them know. I don't know how to explain it to them. I don't know how to express myself. It's like giving birth. A woman tells you that giving birth is really painful, but how could I know? How could I understand her pain?

Calvin and Jonathon represent the most common type of Hong Kong gay men born in the 1960s and 1970s, who constitute the bulk of my respondents (see the Appendix). Their parents are first or second generation immigrants/refugees, who came to Hong Kong from mainland China during the 1940s–1950s. They had grown up in families with siblings, with a conventional division of labour and a conventional power structure in place. That is, they had employed fathers who had gone out to work, and who claimed authority within the family; and domestic mothers who, although they might have worked part time, were responsible for child care and managing the family's emotional life, especially the emotional lives of the children. This 'distant father/seductive mother' family form was dominant in the post-war period in Hong Kong.

These gay men's parents, especially their fathers – like those described by Lui (2007: 15–25) for the first generation of Hong Kong people[4] – were hardworking, pragmatic and law-abiding, putting family as the top priority and granting freedom to their children to pursue careers without much intervention. They were, typically, emotionally reserved, tending to show affection through material rewards rather than through talking, sharing or playing with the kids. Moreover, some of these gay men's sisters (e.g., Jonathon) were the 'working daughters' (Salaff 1976) who sacrificed themselves by giving up secondary or higher education and ended up working in factories to benefit the family economy, as part of the 'modified centripetal family' (Salaff 1981).[5] As a whole, such a family was an affectivity-charged patriarchal social unit that used, not intimate or affectionate expression, but rather material satisfaction to structure the interpersonal relationships within the family, favouring sons over daughters (Kong 1993).

However, it is one thing for this seemingly harmonious, economics-driven, patriarchal Chinese family to favour sons over daughters and to open up a space of freedom for the son's development; but it is quite another thing if they discover that their son is gay. These men grew up at a time when homosexuality was still a criminal offence, and was perceived as a social problem. There was hardly any positive discussion of homosexuality and hardly any gay subculture for support (see Chapters 2 and 3).

Calvin and Jonathon revealed most of the anxieties commonly felt by my respondents under the family biopolitics that regulated their homosexual desires and disciplined them to be docile heterosexual sons. They feared the disciplinary Chinese values such as filial piety, which defined a good son as one who was obedient ('being gay, for them, meant I was a bad son'). They were vulnerable to the overwhelming power of marriage and the regulatory obligation for a son to continue the family's blood ('they would be unhappy and would mind if you didn't marry'). They were afraid of the idea of shamefulness that their being gay would bring upon their families, due to the face issue.[6] ('Your relatives will ask your parents why you don't marry . . . I can't find an answer . . .'). And they did not know how to defend themselves against the prejudicial view that being gay is abnormal, perverse and deviant ('for my siblings, they thought being gay wasn't normal'). Although they tended to enjoy freedom to choose which subjects to study and which jobs to accept, they had to live under the family biopolitics that defines a good son in terms of familial heteronormativity.

What of the new generation? I interviewed ten gay men who were born after 1980. Born in the 1980s, Bowie was 23 in 2008 and was studying at a university in Hong Kong. He lives with his parents, one younger sister and a Filipina domestic helper. His parents are of the second post-war baby generation, and are both working. When he was studying in secondary school, he said, he lived under great pressure, as his parents had a lot of expectations for his studies. He was sent to Australia to obtain a degree, and he explored gay life there. However, due to a financial problem in his family, he was forced to come back and to continue studying for his degree in Hong Kong.

> They sent me to study in Australia . . . I was under great pressure facing the Form 5 examination. I did it quite badly . . . they gave me a lot of pressure. I told my parents that they didn't know how to be good parents.

> And they told me once that 'No one taught us how to be good parents, you have to accept this'. But I don't think so, I think you should learn to be a good parent . . . well, they are both young, in their forties . . . and then when I was in Australia, my mum called me and wanted to chat with me . . . we hadn't talked for quite a while. She said 'What have you been up to?' I then . . . I then told her, 'Don't you think that we are quite distant?' . . . she admitted it, and asked me why, and then I told her, 'I have problem in love, but I dare not tell you . . .' She later told me that she cried for a whole week.

Bowie was living with his family when I interviewed him. He said he was very unhappy to come back to Hong Kong, as he seemed to have great difficulty living as a gay person in Hong Kong.

Christopher had just turned 18 in 2008. He was a Form 6 student who was now preparing for public examination. He lived with his parents and one younger sister. His parents are both running businesses and have a high expectation of him to obtain a bachelor degree.

> I find it very hard to study, I have great pressure. I am very serious about studying, I want to get into a university . . . but I find it really hard to catch up with the syllabus . . . this is also my parents' expectation . . . maybe they did not go to university, that's why they are so keen that I should get into one. . . . They think that examination is everything, I shouldn't do any other things . . . They would call me endlessly, just checking if I am studying . . . and my mum is smart. I don't know why, every time I lied to her about where I was, she knew it . . .
>
> Even though I know studying is the most important thing, I won't be just studying . . . I met a guy . . . we had only been together for a week . . . through the internet and we took some photos together, kissing, hugging and stuff . . . I saved them in the family computer. I used to save gay porno . . . my dad would query if he found the sizes of some files were too large. I lied to him and said they were music files. I got away with this lie many times and he didn't find out . . . but this time I saved the file at the wrong location and he was smart enough to find the photos . . . I was so scared, as they were very angry. I said I liked boys, but maybe I would like girls later . . . you know the excuse . . . but still, they were shocked, sad, and cried . . . my parents are both very young, in their thirties, and they are quite open-minded in other things, but they said they could not accept this . . . and they said the society cannot accept it either . . .

After the coming out, Christopher thought that he should tell everyone. He wrote in *xanga* (a blogging community) about his sexuality, and most of his friends, classmates and even church people (he is Christian) knew that he was gay.

Bowie and Christopher represent the young cohort born in the 1980s and 1990s. Their parents are of the post-war baby generations, for whom society

> between my parents and me, and it is not essential to read anything under the surface, and it is not necessary to have a meeting to talk to them face to face. I believe that some messages can be communicated in a more subtle way. In fact, what the parents of gays want to see is basically the fact that their children are doing well in the society, they have a business or a job, they are doing what a decent being should be doing, they have family responsibility and they take care of them when they are old. If you have done all these things, your parents tend to stop asking what you do behind closed doors. It is a kind of mutual respect. Since I decided to start my gay life ten years ago, I have been educating my parents bit by bit, by saying that not everyone needs to get married . . . what you really want to see is a good son who will take care of you. I guess they should be pleased, as I see them nearly every day and they don't need to worry about their financial problems . . . I am not getting away from the coming out problem; rather I am looking at the problem and finding the best way of handling it.

David hid everything under the table, and outwardly conformed to traditional Chinese values, but he also tried actively to educate his parents to accept his gayness. He resisted marriage without directly confronting Chinese values, and tried to be a good Chinese son, but with a queer difference.

Since talking about sexuality seems to be a taboo in the family, these respondents hide their sexual orientations and avoid talking about them. They claim, and perhaps think, that they are being honest to everyone, while keeping everything under the table. These peaceful tactics do not explicitly challenge the hegemonic family values, but they are subversive in the sense that they challenge marriage without involving any direct confrontation. What gay men who employ them worry about is how long their families will accept such avoidance and such tactics. They hope that their families will come to know in an unspoken way, and acknowledge their sexuality with hidden consent. What they want to maintain is not an 'out, loud, and proud' gay self, but a good relationship with their family members.

The third way of responding to familial heternormativity is to confront it. Norman's coming-out experience was quite drastic. When I interviewed him in 1997, he was studying in Form 5, and a classmate who was gay and fancied him kept phoning him. His aunt, who discovered this, reported to his father:

> . . . he [his father] knows how to make you tell the truth. He asked me in a very nice way if I was gay. It seemed that being gay didn't bother him. He seldom talked to me in such a nice way. But after I admitted it, he changed his face completely. He said 'I won't give you any money anymore and please leave this house.' He talked in a very unusual, quiet and calm way. 'Do you know how other relatives will think of me if they know you are like that? . . . If I'd known before, I would have killed you at birth.'

Norman was very frightened and upset. He then found a job to earn his living, borrowed some money from one of his relatives to pay his tuition fees, and stayed with a friend.

Coming out is an act that violates the notion of compulsory heterosexuality and the conventional institution of marriage. The act of coming out certainly upsets the family, usually resulting in rejection and isolation of the son and guilt feelings, depression or anger on the parents' side, as exemplified in Norman's case and others (e.g., Ho 1999). Of my respondents, only a few had come out to their families, and those who had come out had only done so to certain family members, usually their sisters (if any), then their mothers and brothers (if any). The father seems to be the most difficult person to come out to.

Coming out, however, does not always end up in drama. Jason was only 20 years old in 2008. He came from a poor single-parent family and lived with his mother and a brother. At the time when he had just split up with his boyfriend, he was unhappy, and when his mother did something wrong, he just 'exploded' and came out to his mother:

> After I split up with my ex, and it was the time for public examination, I was so out of control, and I had a big fight with my mum. My ex gave me a painting for my birthday and I stuck it on the wall of my bedroom but my mum tore it off. I was so angry, I then broke three of her fishing rods, one of her electric pianos and the front door of the house. I acted like a Godzilla!!! I then packed my stuff and stayed with my grandmum . . . I didn't talk to her [his mother] for three months . . . and then one day I wrote her an email. I told her that I was a memba and the painting was from my ex-boyfriend and I also told her what had happened between me and my ex . . . She then wrote me back, and said, 'Do you think that I don't know about you? I am your mother . . . when I was young, I fell in love with a girl, but nothing happened . . . I am still in my thirties, I still don't know what will happen next to me, so you don't have to be so sure which road you would like to take now. Anyway, I won't mind if you take this road. The most important thing is that you should be happy!

Two weeks after that email, Jason moved back home. He still kept the email, and showed it to me. But since then he has been very close to his mother – as he said, he could talk to her about everything. Coming out, thus, is not always leaving home, as Calvin and Norman did; it can also be about reconciliation within the family institution.

To be out or not to be out?

As the cornerstone building block of society, the family has traditionally been seen as the antithesis of homosexuality. Lesbian and gay studies in the West from the 1950s to the 1970s focused overwhelmingly on identity and coming-out issues and usually offered a strong critique of the family, which was supposed to be hostile to homosexuality (Weeks *et al.* 2004: 341–43; Stacey 2003: 145–51).

Adopting Foucault's (1980) view on Western sexuality and power, Boellstorff (2005) argues that the subjectivity of Western gay and lesbian selves originates in the 'confessional model', in which 'sexuality is a core element of self-identity that must be confessed and integrated into all domains of life' (p. 209). The self's authenticity depends on one's coming out, as a form of self-development – first coming out to oneself, then to one's parents and friends, then in the workplace and to the world.

This 'homosexual identity formation' model (e.g., Plummer 1975: 131–52; Troiden 1979, 1988: 41–58; Cass 1979, 1984) has been the foundation of the identity politics in the West (e.g., Plummer 1995: Ch. 6; Weeks 1985: Ch. 8). On the personal level, coming out is a common practice for asserting one's gayness. The act becomes both a signifier of liberation and a political act of resistance against the supremacy of heterosexual domination (e.g., as with the slogan 'Out of the closet and into the streets!'). Not to come out – to remain in the closet – is usually seen as a negative and inauthentic way of being oneself. And coming out usually involves leaving home as a sign of liberation of sexual identity and a separation from the parental family, which is supposed to be hostile to homosexuality. On a collective level, fighting against discrimination is a major concern of gay men and lesbians, in order to reclaim their legal, political, economic, social and cultural status once their sexual preferences have been disclosed. This notion of identity politics – as a struggle for identity, as a development of sexual communities, and as a growth of political movement (Weeks 1985) – has been criticized, especially by queer theorists, for privileging the act of coming out, essentializing identity, and neglecting the social and economic conditions of coming out as a necessary condition of sexual citizenship (e.g., Butler 1993: 226–30). Some of them even argue the decline of the social significance of the closet (Seidman *et al.* 1999, Seidman 2002[8]). However, the coming-out model is still the dominant model for asserting one's gayness and for judging 'good' and 'bad' sexual citizens.

In his analysis of East Asian films and videos, Berry (2001) argues that there are two dominant forms of representation of gay identity in East Asian societies. The first one 'appears as a problem within the networks of kinship obligations that constitute the family and bind the individual onto it' (p. 213). The second one appears 'as something lived in marginal spaces' (p. 213), as if 'out' gay men and lesbians were orphans.[9] This seems to be the model that holds true in the case of Hong Kong.

Coming out is never an easy task for queers, and it involves a lot of serious thought and calculation in relation to the overall societal environment – in relation to laws governing homosexuality, media and cultural discussions, and to the availability of queer subculture. However, in Hong Kong, the family, as a tool of state governance, not only becomes a self-regulating and self-reliance mechanism that turns people away from the government for support, welfare needs and resources; but also serves as a powerful closet mechanism.

Moreover, the scarcity of physical space translates into extraordinarily high land prices, and this, backed up by state regulations for housing allocation, contributes to the pattern of familial residence (Kong 2000: 129–30). This may be the reason the family is always regarded as the encompassing disciplinary mechanism for Hong Kong tongzhi.[10]

Coming out can be a political act that challenges the notion of compulsory heterosexuality. However, the very idea of individuality and its implicit economic and material assumptions sometimes clash with the notion of the relational self embedded in the biopolitics of Chinese families. Seidman *et al.* (1999), for the US context, argue that closet practices should be seen as 'a strategy of accommodation and resistance which both reproduces and contests aspects of a society organized around normative heterosexuality' (p. 10). That is, closet practices should not be seen as merely negative and repressive, and as preserving the power of heterosexism by fashioning a self-loathing homosexual. Rather, closet practices might also be seen as productive, as they not only avoid the risks of unintended exposure, but also create a protected social space that permits individuals to fashion gay selves and to navigate paths between the straight and gay worlds.

My respondents negotiated gay identities, in relation to the familial heteronormativity prescribed by family biopolitics, in various ways and to different degrees, ranging from total closeting to total coming out to the family. Most tended to accommodate to hegemonic family values through such tactics as getting married, lying, being ambiguous, using the 'no-time-no-money' formula, keeping silent or redefining what is meant by a good son. Most resisted marriage and compulsory heterosexuality without direct confrontation. Even those who came out to their families tried very hard to maintain good relationships with family members. However, no matter which tactics they employed, they acted within the parameters of family biopolitics. I agree with Wong (2007): that coming out in Chinese society usually does not imply leaving home; on the contrary, coming out more often means coming home. Resolving the tension between sexual identity and family relations continues to be a major issue for Hong Kong tongzhi. As rightly pointed out by Berry (2001), the Asian queer problem for the family is not so much about sexual behaviour itself, but is 'an exclusive sexual orientation whose development into an exclusive sexual and social identity in turn interferes with the ability to perform one's role in the family' (p. 215). The real opposition is sometimes not so much between homosexuality and heterosexuality, but 'between those who are willing and able to play traditional family roles and those who are not' (p. 219).

Memba making family[11]

How do we understand Hong Kong tongzhi who form intimate relationships and even form their own families? Same-sex marriage has no legal status, and debate about it is still at an early stage. None of my Hong Kong respondents had married same-sex partners.[12] In the remainder of this chapter, I will discuss how Hong Kong memba form intimate relationships under the heterosexual monogamy model that defines courting, falling in love, getting married and forming families. It is through their making of intimate relationships that we will be able to see how they deconstruct the family ideology and create alternatives for intimate citizenship. First of all, however, we must understand what 'gay' means to them and what their idea of family is.

Family we choose

Jeff came from a rich family and was an architect. He was 26 in 1997, a closeted young gay man who was almost totally ignorant of the gay subculture. However, as he said, he was a fast-learning baby. He had now transformed from an upper-middle-class closeted gay man to an 'out and loud' queer with an in-your-face attitude, who was politically liberal, sexually adventurous and fashion conscious. He was now settled in England, but had lived back and forth between Hong Kong and London in the 1990s. When I re-interviewed him in 2007, he said:

> If I were straight, I would do what other straight people normally do – you know, get married, have children, etc, etc . . . but if I were straight . . . I wouldn't have to open to a lot of things that I've seen or experienced . . . that's what it is to be gay . . . I would probably become a doctor, I wouldn't have gone to do art . . . I wouldn't have been exposed myself to so many different things . . . the club scene, the drug scene, the gay scene . . . and I think if I were straight, I would be much more narrow-minded . . . self-thinking, independent-thinking . . . I think this is the difference.

Jeff might have exaggerated the difference between straight and gay lives a bit. However, when asked what being gay meant to them, most of my respondents, like Jeff, reported that 'being gay', in addition to the widely experienced social discrimination and marginalization, meant 'liberation', 'freedom', 'pleasure' (in particular, 'sexual pleasure'), 'opportunity', etc. In their accounts they frequently drew on heterosexual, and especially married, life for comparison, charging it with being boring, mundane and mindless – even though some preferred this stable life, as seen in Wing Gor's and Christopher's narratives. The difference seems to come from the fact that they had had to invent, from A to Z, relationships that were still formless (Foucault 1996: 309).[13] New narratives and new 'sexual stories' (Plummer 1995) are thus in the making.

Even though most of them did not have their own families, they certainly had their own visions of what family was about. As Jeff said:

> My family . . . since my dad passed away, now it's just my two brothers and my mother, really, that's my family, . . . and Klaus [his latest

> boyfriend], he is certainly part of my family . . . and Thompson [his ex-boyfriend] . . . and I have a circle of contacts, I have a circle of close friends . . . and friends are also part of my family. You are always part of my family!

Many informants tended to expand the definition of family to include a range of people such as their lovers and ex-lovers, members of families of origin and groups of close friends. Not unlike the 'commune' ideal in the US among 1960s hippies, this 'friend-as-family model' (Weeks *et al.* 2001: Ch. 3), or 'families we choose' model (Weston 1991: Ch. 5), is very prominent in queer life. This is especially the case for those who are non-heterosexual as friends provide emotional, social and even material support, as well as an affirmation of identity and belonging.[14]

As Altman (1982: 190) points out, 'what many gay lives miss in terms of permanent relationships is more than compensated for by friendship networks, which often become de facto families.'

The monogamy model

A profound transformation of personal lives – in relation to family, marriage, other interpersonal relationships, and sexuality – has taken place in late modern societies, influenced as they are by the rapid advance of globalization and the ramifications of individualization. This has resulted in a variety of patterns of (re-)organized intimacy that successfully dissociate sex, love and the marriage institution – e.g., single-hood, cohabitation, voluntary childlessness, the step families, single-parenthood, 'open marriages', multi-adult households, gay and lesbian couples, etc. (Weeks 2003: 100).[15] In all of these patterns, one significant new factor is that the couple relationship has replaced marriage and family as the major site of intimacy in many modern societies. Jamieson (2004) argues that, from the 1950s to the 1990s, at least in the industrialized West, the emphasis shifted from the married domestic heterosexual couple to 'a range of forms of emotionally intense dyadic relationships between two equal adults' (p. 39), be they married, cohabiting or living separately, with or without children, heterosexual or homosexual, etc. However, the result of this development has not been the end of marriage or family but the emergence of marriage-like arrangements (e.g., cohabitation, serial monogamy, same-sex marriage) and neo-conventional family types (e.g., step family, single-parent family, and the childless and fewer-children family).

Central to the couple relationship is the notion of monogamy. Although the idea was criticized by feminists in the 1970s as sexual exclusivity, the institutionalization of coupledom and the presumed ownership of another individual (Jackson and Scott 2004: 152), monogamy, or non-monogamy but with secret affairs (rather than non-secret non-monogamy), are still norms for a couple relationship (Jamieson 2004: 35–38). Hence, adultery and 'affairs' are still regarded as major marital or relationship problems and as legitimate reasons for divorce or the break-up of a relationship, as these appear as breaches of the marriage contract, breaches of trust between couples and breaches of implicit rules of erotic ethics. As noted by Weeks (2003: 99), in Britain and other Western countries, serial monogamy (not promiscuity), rather than lifelong marriage, has become the norm.

Giddens' (1991, 1992) notion of a 'pure relationship' tries to capture the nature of the modern intimate relationship. A pure relationship is 'a relationship of sexual and emotional equality' (Giddens 1992: 2) between individuals, in which 'trust can be mobilised only by a process of mutual disclosure' (Giddens 1991: 6). A pure relationship may not last forever, as it depends on mutual satisfaction. It is through 'the acceptance on the part of each partner, "until further notice", that each gains sufficient benefit from the relation to make its continuance worthwhile' (Giddens 1992: 63, emphasis original). A pure relationship refers to 'confluent love', which is not necessarily heterosexual or non-exclusive (i.e., not necessarily monogamous). However, although the concept of a pure relationship does try to accommodate the practice and idea of non-monogamy, Giddens puts certain limits to the non-exclusionary possibilities of couple arrangements.[16] Non-monogamous relationships (from secret affairs to open relationships including, for example, threesomes and swing couples) may be practised, but 'living as a couple' remains the ideal domestic state for most adults (Jamieson 2004: 35).

Debates have centred on how 'quasi' forms of couple relationship are regarded as 'derivative' or 'secondary' to this ideal (e.g., Heaphy *et al.* 2004; Stacey 2003). Arguing from the cultural imagination of the family in Western gay literature, Woods (1998: 345) ascertains that lesbians and gay men are indeed 'inventing new configurations of relationship which might be called alternative families or alternatives to the family'.[17]

Lesbians and gay men have tended to move from a politics of identity in the 1970s to a politics of relationship and partnership rights in the 1990s and beyond, and the focal point has been on the debate over same-sex marriage. While some argue for the right to marry out of a politics of recognition and the notion of equality, others worry that an extension of marital rights to lesbians and gay men would expand state control over citizens' private lives, privilege the monogamous couple form, close off other possibilities, and reinforce the binary between marital and non-marital intimacy.[18]

Discussions have been engaged in concerning the emerging patterns of intimate relationships among lesbians and gay men in different Western societies.[19] One key issue is the difference between heterosexual and non-heterosexual relationships, with the cornerstone of the couple relationship, crystallized in the notion of monogamy, under attack. Although non-heterosexual relationships are not necessarily non-monogamous, same-sex couples are unlikely to take monogamy for granted. This is why Giddens (1992) argues that 'monogamy has to be "reworked" in the context of commitment and trust' (p. 146, emphasis original) and frequently refers to lesbian and gay men having more open and equal relationships, thus serving as good examples of pure relationship. Without much baggage of traditional gender expectations and heterosexual guidelines and scripts (e.g., monogamy), it is said that lesbian and gay men are 'condemned to freedom' in reconstructing relationships on their own terms.

Memba love stories – monogamy and beyond

> Between tricks and lovers and exes and friends and fuckbuddies and bar friends and bar friends' tricks and tricks' bar friends and gay pals and companions 'in the life', queers have an astonishing range of intimacies.
>
> (Michael Warner, *The Trouble with Normal*, 1999)

Tsang (1987) pointed out that the ideal prototype of intimacy in Hong Kong tends to be lifelong and heterosexual, with monogamous marriage as the actualization of romantic love and the precondition for sex. Any deviations from this – such as premarital and extra-marital sexual intercourse, sex without love, masturbation, reading pornography and homosexuality – are all considered problematic.[20]

I agree with Tsang (1987): that this dominant ideal of intimacy comes from neither Judaeo-Christian nor Chinese traditions, but is a hybridized product of late Christian culture, the Western courtly tradition of love, and neo-Confucian teachings. In late Christian culture, love represents a summation of Christian virtues, such as the enhancement of kindness and righteousness and the discouragement of jealousy and resentment. In the Western courtly tradition, love ennobles and disciplines the self and thus becomes the central symbol of the individual's quest for identity, integrity and fulfilment (Swidler 1980: 121–25). In neo-Confucian teachings, love is desexualized, confined according to familial obligations and conditioned by sexual asceticism. In all three traditions, love is infused with moral meaning. The lifelong, heterosexual and monogamous notion of love is privileged, and serves as a yardstick with which to measure any form of love.

The only legal marital form in Hong Kong is a specifically Western form of monogamous marriage. Polygamy and arranged marriage have hardly been practised in Hong Kong since the 1970s. Hong Kong has tended to follow Western trends in the transformation of the sphere of intimacy. For example, there has been a trend of increasing premarital sex among secondary school students and out-of-school teens (Ng and Ma 2004: 493), while the median age for first marriage for men has increased from 27.0 in 1981 to 30.8 in 2003 and to 31.2 in 2007; the ages for women have increased from 23.9 to 27.8 to 28.3, respectively. This may be associated with the rise of cohabitation. Meanwhile, divorces have increased from 354 cases in 1972, to 2,062 in 1981, to 13,425 in 2001 and to 18,403 in 2007; single-parent families have increased from 34,538 in 1991, to 58,460 in 2001, to 72,326 in 2006; and remarriages[21] have increased from 1,891 in 1981, to 3,333 in 1986, to 5,896 in 1996 and to 15,060 in 2007 (Census and Statistics Department, HKSAR: Women and Men in Hong Kong: Key Statistics 2008; Lam *et al.* 2005).

As specific social, economic and political changes in Hong Kong have occurred, new family and quasi-family types have emerged, including those of cohabiting couples, step families, single-parent families, 'astronaut families' (i.e., with family members shuttling between two countries) (Ong 1999) with kids returned from abroad (Salaff *et al.* 2009), cross-border Hong Kong-mainland families (Leung and Lee 2005; So 2003), quasi-polygamous families (married Hong Kong men with mistresses in China – *baau yi naai* (包二奶 Cant.: 'to keep a second wife') (Tam 2005; So 2003), new-arrival immigrant Chinese families (Pun and Wu 2004), and probably many more (e.g., Mulvey 2005).

With this background, I ask: How do Hong Kong memba form intimate relationships under the hegemonic heterosexist presumption of cultural citizenship? What alternative 'way of life' can be practised?

I first interviewed Aron in 1997 before he migrated to Canada in 1999. At that time, he was 33 years old, a medical professional, and had been living with a man (Steve) for four years, but their relationship was then on the rocks:

> I don't like to fool around with love. I can't accept the idea that you can hang out every weekend and then bring different guys back home. It may be very difficult to find someone whom you can live with forever, but at least you should try . . . So if I go out with a bloke, at least in the beginning, I can't accept that he goes cruising . . . I never tried one-night stands or any casual sex.

Martin turned 37 in 2007, by which time he was a media curator living in London who travels around the world. When I first interviewed him in 1998, he was a student in London with a boyfriend in Germany. He was very wild in terms of sexual adventures. Having sex with many men seemed to be a daily routine for him. As he said in 1998:

> So every day I just go to school, I am alone, I go clubbing every day. Well, actually I go clubbing three or four times a week, other times I go cottaging.[22] Well, I quite like it. You don't need to love them just for sex, and you have a lot of experiences. It's so natural . . . it's such a man's kind of thing.

Most gay men I interviewed seemed to be torn between the two scripts illustrated above. On the one hand is the romantic script of finding Mr Right – a more 'feminine-inclined' discourse that prescribes an ideal trajectory of a relationship through courting, dating, falling in love, lifelong commitment and sexual exclusivity. This is the script commonly found in mainstream popular heterosexual love stories (Illouz 1997[23]). However, this script runs against another script – the script of sexual adventure. This is the script for seeking excitement – a more 'male-centred' discourse that emphasizes a spontaneous and explosive male sex drive, sex as fun, and pleasure without commitment. This is the one that is largely endorsed and facilitated by the gay culture (c.f. Adam 2006; Mutchler 2000[24]).

Mutchler (2000) argues that, although heterosexuals and lesbians also experience gendered sexualities, the uniqueness of gay men's sexuality is due to the men's dual positions as *males* (in the sense that they share with many heterosexual men the view of sex as an irresistible and impulsive drive, according to the 'biological or hydraulic' model); and as *gay* men, who have unique sexual outlets within gay culture (e.g., 'dark rooms', public toilets). What I am interested in is how the respondents, especially those who are in relationships, live out different alternatives, governed by these two scripts, under various social constraints.

1+1 = 2: monogamous ideal

Before Aron migrated to Canada in 1999, he split up with Steve, who he had been going out with for four years. When he looked back at that relationship, he said:

> Oh! It's too long. Four years. It seemed to be too long. Many things had happened . . . Honestly speaking, how can you only love one person in your whole life? But I thought that as I was going out with him, I shouldn't allow myself to love others . . . You know, at first, I thought that we were the perfect match but then I discovered that we weren't . . . I used to be very healthy. I mean, I like hiking, camping, having picnics, all of those sorts of thing, but he didn't . . . But more than that, we had different agendas in our lives . . . at that time, there was a tide of migration, which I thought was an opportunity. I thought living elsewhere would be a good chance for me to experience many different things . . . Steve seemed to have obstructed my own development. It may be unfair to say that, but I think that our relationship couldn't go any further . . . I then found out that he fancied another guy. I wasn't angry . . . if it had happened two years previously, I would have definitely gone mad . . . in fact, before I left Hong Kong, we still lived and slept together. Isn't it weird? . . . so if I go out with a bloke, at least in the beginning, I can't accept that he goes cruising. After some time, if the attraction has gone, I don't know . . . maybe it is all right to hang out.

The romantic or Mr Right script, or love myth (Swidler 1980[25]), involves the attempt to define one's self by the free choice of a partner. The prerequisite for such self-definition of identity is faithfulness. Faithfulness to one's own choices becomes faithfulness to one's self, and the ability to make a commitment and 'stick to it' is seen as a measure of the successful formation of one's identity (Swidler 1980: 128). Although having no socially binding forces such as marriage to centre on, Aron is very serious about having a committed relationship. He believes it to be quite impossible to love only one person in his life, but he is willing to 'stick' to the choice he has made. He prefers to choose only once, 'after which commitment closes off alternative choices and alternative identities' (p. 128). He is faithful to the unwritten contract sanctioning the ideal of committed love. The sexual relationship seems to be a significant tool for measuring the 'faithfulness' of his commitment.

What goes wrong with the monogamous relationship? It could be a 'natural' progression, a loss of passion ('if the attraction has gone'), a dissatisfaction with certain aspects of the partner ('I used to be very healthy . . . but he didn't (sic)') or personal growth and development ('Steve seemed to obstruct my own development'). Such difficulties may drive gay men to consider searching for another 'right' person, or to desire sexual experimentation ('maybe it's all right to hang out') (c.f. Yip 1997: 295[26]). Modern moral ideals of the self tend to emphasize self-actualization and the continuing demands for growth and change in adulthood. A good relationship may not be defined by how much a person can commit to a relationship, but rather by how much one can learn about oneself from a relationship. Continuing self-exploration, rather than a crystallized identity, structures the notion of modern love.

Although monogamy was reported as an ideal aspiration, most respondents acknowledged the gap between practice and the ideal, and tended to treat it not as a given or a restrictive rule but as an active choice that should be accomplished (Adam 2006: 11; c.f., Mutchler 2000, Heaphy *et al.* 2004). If this ideal cannot be realized, what other possibilities can be imagined and created?

Unlike the model of monogamy, which usually demands emotional and sexual exclusivity, non-monogamy can take three different forms: emotionally exclusive but sexually non-exclusive; emotionally non-exclusive but sexually exclusive; and both emotionally and sexually non-exclusive. None of my informants, and none reported elsewhere (Yip 1997[27]), were employing the 'emotionally non-exclusive but sexually exclusive' model. The other two models will be discussed here: One is what I call the '2 + many' model – that is, having an emotionally monogamous relationship but engaging in casual sex as well. The other is the '2+ 1' model – that is, developing another 'quality', but secondary, relationship (c.f. Adam 2006[28]).

2 + many: emotionally monogamous but engaging in casual sex

Few respondents who were in relationships referred to themselves as practising an 'open relationship', even though they may have had numerous casual sexual encounters. For them, open relationship means 'no relationship', as 'a relationship is a commitment' and open relationships mean 'fooling around and having different boyfriends every weekend'. And what constitutes a relationship is the 'quality' of a relationship, not the duration. As Joey, a 22-year-old university student, said in 2008:

> My definition of a boyfriend is whether you put *gamcing* (感情 Cant.: 'emotion, love, affection') in it. You have been experiencing sadness, happiness, etc. – it's not just about sex . . . and it's nothing to deal with the duration. It could be just a day or a week.

Such accounts of non-monogamous practices seem to involve a compromise between the Mr Right script and the sexual adventure script: commit to a primary loving relationship with a man but seek sexual gratification with other men. Non-monogamy is interpreted as a distinction between sex and love – to be more precise, between sex with the partner, which is regarded as 'sex-with-love', which should take place with a 'significant other' and should be exclusive; and sex with casual partners, which is seen as 'sex-as-fun' and thus can be performed with many different 'anonymous' men.[29]

When I first interviewed Calvin in 1997, he was going out with a man. He was very committed to his boyfriend. He liked to take care of his boyfriend and treated him like a 'princess'. But he would go to saunas for casual sex secretly:

> I think I basically believe in monogamy but I can have sex with others. If I just wanted sex, I wouldn't talk to him [the casual partner] much. I'd be very committed to having sex but I would also let him know that this would be the only time. I don't like the idea of a part-time lover . . . I would say quite clearly that this was the first and also the last time.

Peter was 26 when I interviewed him in 1997. He had been living with a man and his family for a couple of years. He sometimes had other affairs but he regarded these affairs as simply fun. However, he mainly kept them secret – a typical 'don't ask, don't tell' policy:

> [Our relationship is] very stable. I think we are like a straight couple. We live together and we share everything . . . Well, sometimes I will go out for fun. I won't tell him that I do it but I hope that he doesn't do it. As far as I know, he doesn't. But he found out I did once . . . We had a fight when he found out that I had sex with others, but we are still together. I don't think either of us wants to split up . . . Maybe that's because we live together. We are happy. My family can accept him and his family can accept me as well . . . I like staying at home and playing TV games or having a pet. He accepts it. So when I have a day off, I usually stay at home and we just play TV games. We are both happy with this way of life.

Matthew was 38 and single when I interviewed him in 1998. He had been living with his boyfriend for eight years. He said he talked explicitly with his boyfriend about the rules. He could not accept that either he or his boyfriend could have casual relationships if they were both in Hong Kong:

> I told him . . . If you are away from Hong Kong, no matter whether you are on holiday or at work, you can do whatever you want to do. I don't care. But if you are in Hong Kong, please don't do anything . . . If you have an affair, you have given him a chance. You shouldn't give anyone any chances at all . . . that's because Hong Kong is so small, and the gay world is so small. Everyone knows everyone. The one you sleep with may be my friend's friend. It's so easy. Then I will feel very embarrassed, very awful . . . Basically, if you have a relationship, I don't think you can totally open up your relationship. Don't be too outrageous.

Martin seems to be an extreme case of experimentation with sex and love. When I first met him, ten years ago, he was very proud of having a loving relationship with his German boyfriend, whom he said he was deeply in love with. They eventually got legally married as same-sex partners in Germany in 2002. When they were together, they liked to go cruising together. They frequently visited 'cottages', parks, dark rooms and saunas. They enjoyed open group sex very much. They developed different strategies for cruising. Cruising together was actually one way of enhancing their relationship. However, they had their own rules. For example, they could not cruise separately; if they did, they could not stay till dawn. When I re-interviewed him in 2007, he had separated from his German boyfriend, but he was still into this mode of relationship with other men.[30]

These accounts illustrate tactics that most respondents employ to deal with their non-monogamous practices, which range from total secrecy to total disclosure, with implicit or explicit rules. Calvin conceals the information about his casual encounters in a highly discreet way but sets the rule of 'no second date' for himself. Peter values very much his family life with his partner, practices the 'don't ask, don't tell' policy, and treats casual acquaintances as recreational fun that one should not take too seriously. Matthew chooses to talk it over by establishing explicit ground rules (e.g., 'if you are in Hong Kong, please don't do anything'). Finally, Martin and his boyfriend follow the rules of 'doing together' and 'don't sleep till dawn'. These non-monogamous practices could be criticized as forms of selfish sexual gratification, but they seem to be the ways in which my respondents protect their primary relationships.

2 + 1: 'quality' secondary relationship

James was 22 when I first interviewed him in 1998. At that time, he was single. He enjoyed cottaging and clubbing, and was then studying at a university in Hong Kong. I interviewed him again in 2008, when he was working as a freelancer and had been living with his present boyfriend for five years (2003–8). In 2008, he talked about his previous romances in retrospect. He had been with a man whom he regarded as the second boyfriend of his life, and their relationship had lasted for three years (2000–2003). During this period with his second boyfriend he also had another relationship, for almost two years:

> At that time . . . I didn't live with my second boyfriend . . . I then met a man, a married man . . . he is Chinese but migrated elsewhere, but came back to Hong Kong quite frequently . . . we saw each other quite often . . . almost once or twice a week. Sometimes I would stay in his place . . . so it was very frequent . . . but of course I wouldn't see him during the weekends . . . as I had to be with my boyfriend . . . I thought I told him at the very first beginning that I had a boyfriend already but he didn't seem to understand . . . we were together for almost two years . . . then one day in ICQ he found out I did have a boyfriend . . . he was very upset and ended the relationship. . . .
>
> . . . the difference between these two men [i.e., his second boyfriend and the married man], hmm . . . I treated my boyfriend as boyfriend because we did what lovers would do, like dining out, watching movies, shopping – and he had met most of my friends . . . and more importantly he had met my family . . . and we spent time at major festivals . . . [with] the married man, we did less of that sort of thing . . . more into sex . . . but still we did develop something more than sex . . . but it's hard to tell . . . well, I never told my boyfriend about this . . . by the way, when I was with him and the married man, I also had some few acquaintances . . . but they were more fleeting . . . maybe seeing them once or twice a month.

What distinguishes James's non-monogamous practices from those of the previous respondents is the development of a secondary and 'quality' relationship. James marked off this second man (the married man) from other, more fleeting and casual, sexual acquaintances. What he had with the married man was something more than sex, something difficult to tell – there was something special about that relationship which was much more than other casual sexual encounters. Although he placed the married man in a special position, where no one else could be a substitute, not even his 'official' boyfriend at that time, his relationship with his 'official' boyfriend was, in this sense, of the same nature. He had no intention to substitute the married man for his 'official' boyfriend, who was more public and socially important (' . . . he had met most of my friends . . . and . . . family') and with whom he shared other more important 'quality' time (e.g., festival times, birthdays, weekends, etc.). As a result, he regarded his relationship with the married man as secondary.

While James kept his affairs secret, other respondents chose to disclose their other relationships. The third party is usually regarded as secondary in importance, and the two relationships are normally distinguished by 'love' and 'fun', respectively. However, without any institutional binding forces (e.g., marriage, parents, children), relationships can easily slip from one type to another – from primary to secondary, or vice versa.

Discussion and conclusion

As the previous chapter suggests, Hong Kong tongzhi's resistance to the hegemonic heterosexualized notion of cultural citizenship lies not in their fight for equal rights or legal recognition, but in their claiming of a cultural citizenship that expresses pride, dignity and difference in popular culture. This chapter continues this discussion, but focuses on the private lives of Hong Kong gay men, or memba.

Coming out is not easy for lesbians and gay men, as it involves serious considerations of the socio-political environment of a society, which may include laws governing homosexuality, the public discussion and tolerance/intolerance of homosexuality, the availability of queer subculture and even the access to physical space. In addition to these factors, Hong Kong memba seem to face a bigger challenge, as the coming-out issue is always related to the family institution. This is because the family has been made significant for fulfilling various social and welfare needs, which might otherwise be provided by the government. Family biopolitics, in assisting state governance, not only regulates the well-being of economic production, but also disciplines reproductive heterosexual subjects. It is through this family biopolitics of creating cultural citizenship through a dual process of 'making' and 'being-made' – that we can understand more fully the sexual politics of Hong Kong memba.

Hong Kong memba negotiate suitable gay identities through various strategies – ranging from outright disclosure to secret closeting, from leaving home to coming home, from 'out, loud and in-your-face' attitudes to tactical 'ways of operating' (de Certeau (1984))[31] – in order to create sexual spaces within the parameters of the family biopolitics.

Hong Kong memba are not interested in discussing same-sex marriage – rather, they are passionate to create new scripts for couple relationships. It is widely claimed that heteronormative culture has numerous adverse effects on gay lives, yet it is also argued that the lack of institutional support and cultural guidelines may have some unintended positive consequences (Heaphy *et al.* 2004: 169).[32] Without much pressure from any presumed script governing intimacy, Hong Kong memba, like other gay men and lesbians elsewhere, are relatively free to create new scripts that might set them apart from the heterosexual hegemony of 'doing' courtship, marriage, intimacy and family practices. Their narratives challenge the traditional definition of family according to biological links and nuptial arrangements. They broaden the definition by including not just 'families of origin', but also 'families of choice' – the latter consisting of their boyfriends and chosen friends. Their intense investment in 'friendship' and their flexible separation of sex and love can be seen as a form of gay politics. This is because this 'family we choose' or 'friends-as-family' blurs the 'boundaries between (non-erotic) friendship and (erotic) partnership, which effectively open(s) up space for a notion of family bridging the erotic and the non-erotic, bringing lovers together with friends'

(Bell and Binnie 2000: 137). New space is thus created through the innovation of various forms of personal relationship that separate love, sex, family and marriage, so that the meanings of 'lover', 'friend', 'partner', and 'family', among others, can be redefined (Foucault 1996; Nardi 1999; Bech 1997: 141–48). It is precisely the lack of social scripts and the new space of freedom that might be created in homosexual culture that renders gay friendship/relationship political. As Bell and Binnie (2000: 134) remind us, a call for a 'sexual politics of friendship' is thus in turn a call for the remaking of sexual citizenship.

The heterosexist hegemonic ideal of intimate citizenship privileges the monogamy model in structuring the couple relationship. Juggling between the romantic and sexual adventure scripts, Hong Kong memba have 'ventured out' – either together or separately, openly or in secret, with explicit or implicit rules – to have different forms of relationship, ranging from fleeting casual sexual encounters to 'quality' but secondary relationships. They have experimented with different ways of 'doing' intimacy, and challenge what is traditionally viewed as the cornerstone of couple commitment: sexual exclusivity. They subvert the monogamous ideal by separating emotional and sexual fidelity. Although the memba I interviewed did not challenge the notion of coupledom, they are in fact creating alternative lifestyles[33] and sexual and intimate relationships that go beyond the culture of 'compulsory monogamy'.

Part II

London

5 Queer diaspora

Hong Kong migrant gay men in London

> *Home bodies, homelands, homosexuals* . . . This litany begins at home. Through words and ideas we seek ourselves, as we seek others.
>
> . . .
>
> *Where is home?* Home is just around the corner or may originate in communities halfway around the world. We were born colored. Somewhere between brown, yellow, black, and red relative to the light and sea, the continent, and your angle of vision.
>
> . . .
>
> *Whose body?* Lesbian, gay, or straight. Bisexual or transgendered. HIV positive or negative. . . . activists or academics who articulate the body politic. Queer or just *qurious*.
>
> (Russell Leong, *Asian American Sexualities*, 1996)

Originally a radio show and later a TV series, *Little Britain* has attained huge success in the British entertainment industry since its first release in 2003. It is a British TV comedy featuring different characters from all walks of life in Britain, exaggeratedly parodied by creators and actors David Walliams and Matt Lucas. One of the famous characters, Daffyd Thomas, played by the 'out' gay creator and actor Matt Lucas, is a provincial young gay man living in a tiny Welsh village who chooses to believe that he is 'the only gay in the village'. The 'only gay song', ending with 'because I am gay . . . A big fat gay! A proper gay! The only gay!', sung by Daffyd, was the climax of the live charity show *Comic Relief* in 2007. I was surprised by the outrageous, bold and blunt lyrics of the song, sung by Matt Lucas. For me, it was more than his excellent and funny performance of the gay character Daffyd; it was also a declaration of his own personal life, screamed out on the stage: 'I am gay, a big fat gay'.

I was hoping that one day we would have such an 'out' gay character and/or actor/actress in the entertainment industry in Hong Kong or in mainland China. My mind was moving fast, as I travelled across continents and arrived in Great Britain. I was thinking about my respondents in London. They had moved to the UK in the 1980s and 1990s and now were residents there. What made them leave Hong Kong? How did they experience, as Chinese men, life in the ex-colonizer's land? In what ways would their sexuality play a part in their minority status in the UK? Were they proud and ready to say that 'I am gay, a Chinese British gay'? Is a Chinese British gay a 'proper gay'? Where was their home? I was, like Leong, *qurious*!

If citizenship is a dual process of 'self-making' and 'being-made' within the webs of power that are linked to the nation-state and civil society (Ong 1996: 737; Foucault 1982, 1988, 1991), I wonder in what ways Chinese in Britain play out the 'new ethnicity' (Hall 1996c).[1] What kind of citizens are they making, or being made into? If British gays and lesbians are 'partial' citizens in terms of their less-than-full access to various rights, do gays and lesbians of colour – Chinese migrant gay men in my case – encounter more problems in the interlocking of race and sexuality in British society at large, as well as inside the gay community?

In this chapter, I will discuss three types of Hong Kong migrant gay men who went to Britain in the 1980s and 1990s. Comprising a racial and sexual minority, they tend to suffer from various forms of subordination from the white and heterosexual society at large, as well as in the sexualized gay community in particular. Although they live under the dominant imagery of the sexual stereotype of the 'golden boy' in the gay racial hierarchy, Hong Kong gay migrant men struggle and find ways to realize a new notion of gay citizenship as British Chinese gay men, performing with competing scripts of self-formation within the complex web of domination.

Chinese as an ethnic minority in Britain

In contrast with the case in Northern America and Australasia, Chinese in Britain are few in number, comprising only 0.4 per cent (n = 247, 403) of the total population (N = 58, 789,194) and 5.3 per cent of the non-white ethnic population (n = 4,635,296) in the 2001 census (www.statistics.gov.uk, accessed online 26 Nov 2008). As the result of a careful and conscious effort of the state in its immigration policies, this relatively small-sized ethnic group is often neglected in academic studies – in both the acclaimed British studies on race and ethnicity, which concentrate on Asian or Asian British, and Black or Black British, the two largest non-white populations in the UK,[2] and also in 'overseas-Chinese' studies, which are overwhelmingly concentrated on the experiences of Chinese in the Chinese diaspora and/or on native-born new generations in Northern America and Australasia.[3]

As literature reveals,[4] the Chinese have come to Britain in different waves, subject to heavy socio-economic and political factors and to the state's immigration policies and practices. The earliest records of Chinese in Britain are those of poor, ill-educated young seamen, primarily from the southern part of Guangzhou, China, as a result of the growth of Britain's maritime trade with Asia (e.g., the British East India Company) in the eighteenth and nineteenth centuries. These Chinese seamen received little attention, existing alongside the early image of the 'Chinaman', which was then characterized by the racist rhetoric of a 'Yellow Peril', and which oscillated between that of an opium smoker and that of the evil Chinese criminal infamously portrayed in Sax Rohmer's popular Fu Manchu novels and short stories (e.g., Parker 1998: 67–74; Baker 1994: 291–93).

The Chinese community before the Second World War in Britain consisted mainly of a diminishing group of seamen and their wives, scattered in small settlements in port cities, who sustained an enclave economy of laundries, restaurants and grocery stores. They were not looking for long-term settlement. They were not treated well, and they left little trace of their lives.

Three factors frequently mentioned in the literature contributing to the significant population growth of Chinese in Britain in the 1950s and early 1960s, which today accounts for the majority of the Chinese population in Britain, were: (1) the British Nationality Acts of 1914 and 1948, which guaranteed freedom of access to the UK for Commonwealth citizens; (2) the demand for exotic foods, including Greek, Indian and Italian as well as Chinese, which triggered an ethnic catering trade in the post-war period in Britain; and (3) the disruption of the lives of villagers in the New Territories of Hong Kong due to the fierce competition for jobs with the tides of refugees coming from the Mainland (Skeldon 1994a: 25–26; Baker 1994: 293–303; Parker 1998: 74–78).

However, this migration pattern changed dramatically in the early 1960s. The introduction of the Commonwealth Immigration Act of 1962 and legislation in subsequent years not only restricted the numbers of Commonwealth workers entering Britain, but also channelled them into catering, via an employment voucher system. A second wave of immigrants is thus characterized in the literature as consisting of chain migration and employment concentration in the catering industry. By the late 1960s the Chinese population in Britain constituted the following main groups: the newly arrived migrant catering labourers, originating largely in the New Territories, Hong Kong, many of whom spoke Hakka; students and professionals from former British colonies Hong Kong, Singapore and Malaysia; and refugees from Vietnam; and these were added to the remaining population of earlier seafarers and laundry owners and their descendants (Parker 1998: 76–78; Baker 1994: 303–5). The dominant image of Chinese in Britain today is thus still that of 'restaurateur', due to the high concentration of Chinese in the catering business.

As pointed out by Skeldon (1994a), it is not Britain, but Canada, the United States, Australia and New Zealand that have become the main settler destinations for Hong Kong people since the 1960s, partly because of the increasing restrictions on migration and the decline in demand for Hong Kong Chinese catering workers in Britain, and partly coinciding with the end of major restrictions on non-European immigration into the latter countries since the 1960s.[5]

In response to the general fear concerning the transfer of sovereignty in Hong Kong in 1997, the British government offered a right-of-abode scheme to a very limited quota of the Hong Kong population. It was believed that the scheme would alleviate the political anxiety that Hong Kong people bore in facing the political uncertainty of the handover, and that it would also prevent a (potentially) huge immigration tide rushing to Britain. The surprisingly low number of applications for this scheme before the deadline showed that the orientation of Hong Kong people was much more towards North America and Australasia than towards Europe (Skeldon 1994a: 35–37).

In the contemporary discourse of race, Chinese in Britain are seen as successful and 'upward mobile' (Cheng 1996), and this is attributed to the 'traditional virtues of thrift, hard work, filial piety, and *guanxi*' (Lee *et al.* 2002: 608). Due to the strength of kinship networks and relationships (*guanxi* 關係), they are seen as the 'the least assimilated' ethnic minority, reluctant to change their way of life to suit British social expectations (Tam 1998[6]). Chinese in Britain have tended to share similar images with those in North America in contemporary times. They are the 'model minority' (Kibria 2002: Ch. 5). As Ong (1998: 151) states, '[I]mages of Oriental docility, diligence, self-sufficiency, and productivity underpin contemporary notions that the Asian minority embodies the human capital desirable in good citizens, in contrast to those who make claims on the welfare program.'

As argued by Rassool (1999: 23–24), racial discourse in Britain has historically been focused on the image of immigrant = alien = problem to be managed through immigration control and through social welfare intervention programmes. Benton and Gomez (2008: Ch. 6) document the racism that Chinese have experienced throughout their existence in Britain. For example, back in the early days, Chinese seafarers were fiercely exploited by their British merchant marine employers, usually with state approval and support. They were seen as constituting a threat of economic competition with working-class whites, and tended to produce a moral panic as a result of media accounts, as an ethnic threat, with problems of drugs, gangs and violence. Racial attacks and riots occurred. The Chinese in the post-war era, however, have tended to suffer less racist abuse and discrimination than the earlier settlers. As argued by Benson and Gomez (2008: 19), this is because of Chinese immigrant concentration in small self-employed businesses, which can be seen as a strategy to overcome language barriers, racial discrimination and other disadvantages experienced in Britain. This strategy in turn made it difficult for them to enter the labour market and compete with native British. This self-sustained tendency can be seen as conforming nicely to the government's (especially the Thatcher Government's) strategy of promoting small enterprise as a way to deal with racism.

Although the spectacular success of Chinese students in British education and of Chinese males' success in the higher end of the employment structure outside the catering industry has led to the achievement of the status of 'model minority', research in the 1990s showed that educated Chinese were still vulnerable to several types of discrimination, ranging from the fact that they needed better qualifications than their white colleagues to get the same job to the facts that they received less pay, were more likely to be denied promotion to senior management (i.e., the glass ceiling effect), and were more likely to become unemployed (Benton and Gomez 2008: 314–18; Pang 1996, 1999).

Nowadays, Chinese in Britain are still under-represented in British society. There is no Chinese-British MP in the British political system (Khong 2008). In the mass media they are largely absent, or appear as certain stereotypes, such as Kung Fu master, triad gangster, restaurant waiter/waitress in Chinatown or hardworking professional.

Gay men and lesbians as 'partial' citizens in Britain

Gay men and lesbians have long been treated as only partial citizens in terms of accessing rights in British society. A well-established literature has documented the fight against discrimination by gay men and lesbians (e.g., Plummer 1999; Weeks 1990; Healey and Mason 1994). Examples of this battle are numerous, and include the struggle to abolish laws prohibiting homosexual behaviour in both public and private spaces; the challenging of unequal treatment and discrimination in all spheres of life, ranging from the educational system to the workplace to the household; and the attacks on the core values of heterosexist society, such as the demand for same-sex marriage, and for gay and lesbian parenting and adoption. Using action strategies such as mass demonstrations, consciousness-raising groups, sit-ins and lobbying, the aim of gay and lesbian politics is to build a cohesive and visible political and sexualized community.

In terms of legal reform, the recent major developments in Britain were the Sexual Offences Act 1967 (drafted in the spirit of the Wolfenden Report in 1957), which decriminalized certain sexual acts between men in private in 1967; the Sexual Offences (Amendment) Act 2000, which equalized the age of consent between heterosexuals and homosexuals in 2000; the repeal of Section 28 of the Local Government Act 1988, which had prohibited the promotion of homosexuality as 'pretended family relationship', in 2003; and the Civil Partnership Act 2004, which allowed same-sex couples to obtain an official partnership status, with which they could enjoy most of the rights enjoyed by heterosexual married couples in 2004 (e.g., www.stonewall.org.uk, accessed online 26 Nov 2008).[7]

Achievements of the gay and lesbian struggle can be seen in, at least, the following developments (e.g., www.stonewall.org.uk, accessed online 26 Nov 2008; Plummer 1999, 2003: 78–80): (1) the setting-up of various political groups that strive for legal and social reforms (e.g., the Gay Liberation Front in the 1970s, and Stonewall and Outrage since the late 1980s) and the increasing numbers of 'out' MPs in Parliament; (2) the growth of social groups for counselling, help lines, HIV/AIDS and drug support; (3) the rise of thousands of lifestyle groups for different ages, ethnic groups, sports, sexual tastes, and other interests; (4) the diverse representations of gay men and lesbians in the mass media (e.g., in TV series such as *Out on Tuesday*

(1989–90), *Gaytime TV* (1995–99), *Queer as Folk* (1999–2000), *Clapham Junction* (2007); films such as *Victim* (1961), *My Beautiful Laundrette* (1986), *Beautiful Thing* (1996); gay papers such as *Gay Times*, *Attitude*, *QX*, *Pink Paper;* etc.); (5) the massive growth of the gay, or pink, economy, involving cafés, bars, clubs, saunas, boutiques, beauty salons, and rally events and marches, sponsored by major businesses; and (6) the opening up of lesbian and gay studies and publications in most universities – what Escoffier (1998: Ch. 4) calls the *Ivory Closet of Lesbian and Gay Studies*.

However, we should be cautious about this apparently successful 'territorialization' of queer space. Klesse (2007: Ch.1) gives a plausible account of how UK legal practices construct heterosexist terms of citizenship by banishing queer identities, sexualities and relationships from the public sphere (c.f. Cooper 1995, 2002: Ch. 6; Stychin 2003: Ch. 2).[8] Although the Sexual Offences Act 1967 decriminalized certain sexual acts between men in private, it also created two types of homosexuals – the 'decent' homosexuals who met and had sex with other adult males over the age of 21 'in private'; and the 'reprehensible' minority who continued to indulge in public acts, or with under-aged partners, who should be controlled.[9] As argued by Bell and Binnie (2000: 53–61) and Stychin (2003: Ch. 2), although the New Labour Government recognizes the values of lesbian and gay relationships, the heterosexual family values are still upheld by the government, despite the recent legal reforms.

As a reflection of the society at large, the gay community in London is disproportionately white, middle class and British. However, it is also multi-ethnic and multicultural, although ethnic minorities have always been under-represented. The commercial gay scene can be a site for identification, for love and romance and for social and sexual networking, but it can also be 'a market economy based on sexual commodification' (Keogh *et al.* 2004a: 12). Sexual stereotyping is common for different groups, such as Black and Irish (Keogh *et al.* 2004b),[10] as well as for Asians and Chinese.

The hegemonic gay citizen is constructed as a middle-class, well-educated, adult British man with a masculine body (see Chapter 3, note 11). Under this construct, Black Caribbean men and Chinese men seem to serve as two ends of the pole of sexual stereotyping in the racial hierarchy: the former are perceived as 'hyper-masculine' and 'hypersexed' (e.g., active, domineering, strong, large), the latter as 'hyper-feminine' and 'undersexed' (e.g., passive, friendly, smooth, small). As Fung (1996) argues for the North American context, '(S)ince the whites fall squarely in the middle, the position of perfect balance, there is no need for analysis, and they remain free of scrutiny' (p.179; see also Fung 1995).

When golden boys meet white men . . .

In the UK where Chinese remain an ethnic minority group, popular stereotypes of the character and physique prevail into the millennium. In particular, the Chinese male bodies, hard or soft – whether their owners are opium smokers or yellow perils, Kung Fu masters or talented professionals, Chinamen or nerds – are almost always represented as sexually neutered or asexual, unless they behave like women, effeminate men or gay men (e.g., *Farewell My Concubine*, *M. Butterfly*).[11] If a Chinese female body always exhibits excessive sexuality, then a Chinese male body is always devoid of sexuality. Chinese men are seen as 'sometimes dangerous, sometimes friendly, but almost always characterized by a desexualized Zen asceticism' (Fung 1996: 183).

If images of the Chinese men are largely absent or feminized in the commercial sector of mainstream white straight society, what about Chinese gay figures in mainstream white gay and lesbian communities? In the gay world, the 'super macho' man embodies a form of hegemonic gay masculinity and defines the 'gay citizen', while the Chinese gay man who cannot conform to or perform this masculinity becomes one of several gay subordinate variants – a second class citizen. The 'golden boy' in traditional Chinese literature is a young virgin boy who is innocent, infantile, feminized or even androgynous.[12]

As described elsewhere (Kong 2002), this infantilized, feminized and 'golden' Chinese gay man has become the dominant image in Britain, and also in many Western industrialized societies. The free London-based gay paper, QX, features an advertisement for the Long Yang Club, which claims to be the only 'oriental' gay organization in Britain, states:

> The *Long Yang Club* continues to draw Orientals and their admirers to the *Star Bar* at *Heaven* each week from 9pm. If you haven't been then give it a try – but don't necessarily expect to get a Chinese take away.

The advertisement not only reinforces the stereotype of Chinese as restaurateurs but also exoticizes Chinese gay men as something like fast, quick and cheap – takeaway food.

Richard Fung (1995, 1996), a Canadian film maker and critic, has reflected on the social and psychological impact such typing has had. In his longstanding pursuit of 'looking for his penis', Fung argues that Chinese men (and also other Asian men) are always put to play the passive roles (i.e., the role of 'bottom', 'houseboy' or 'servant') in gay pornography – '. . . the problem is not the representation of anal pleasure per se, but rather that the narratives privilege the penis while always assigning the Asian the role of bottom; Asian and anus are conflated' (Fung 1996: 187).[13]

First, how, and in what ways, do Hong Kong gay men desire Westerners, or *gwailo* (鬼佬 Cant.) (see Chapter 3 note 13)? When my respondents were asked to talk about their desire for Westerners, they made similar comments about Western bodies. For example, Nelson (30, freelancer, in 1998), said, '*Gwailo* are more beautiful and nicer. And you can see many different types.'

> My ideal is the butch type. I am obviously looking for masculinity, someone who is masculine, but who can be sensitive and romantic at the

same time. I prefer . . . well, hunky really . . . which can be much easily found in *gwailo* than in Chinese . . . I don't know, maybe I've been subjected too much to those images presented in magazines.

(Jeff, 26, architect, in 1997)

The *gwailo*, or the white man, is seen as the desired image, or the standard against which we compare ourselves, and often our brothers. This 'native dreaming' for the West is translated into an 'imagined and desired whiteness' (Manalansan 1993: 68).

Second, among Chinese–white relationships, it is not uncommon to find that the Chinese party is younger, smaller and more feminine than his Western counterpart. It is almost impossible to find an older, stronger and more masculine Chinese with a young, slim blond. Western partners seem to take for granted that English is always to be the medium of communication, even if the Chinese counterpart's command of English is inadequate. Very few such Western partners seem to have any intention of learning any Chinese language, apart from a few words such as 'I love you' or 'I want to sleep with you', which facilitate 'exchanges'. The Chinese party thus seems to abide by his Western partner's lifestyle, very often without feeling oppressed.

Thirdly, Chinese–white, rather than Chinese–Chinese, relationships dominate the Chinese and East and Southeast Asian gay population in the London gay world. Interestingly, my respondents had experienced certain forms of hostility from other East and Southeast Asians in the gay community. As Jeff said, 'I felt this kind of hostility from them, and so the next time I went to Kudos, I would smile at them and say hello just to see how they would react.'

Kudos is a bar in Soho with a substantial East and Southeast Asian gay clientele. Jeff's comment is confirmed by my Thai friend Chai, who also experienced this kind of difficulty,

> I don't like going to Kudos. You know, there are a lot of Asians, some of whom are my 'hello–goodbye' friends. I always feel uncomfortable. I remember I was with them once and an Asian guy came to the bar. They commented on him even though they didn't know him. They commented on everything about him – his face, his body, his clothes, blah blah blah. If he was with a handsome white guy, we would say 'stone the bitch' . . . I joked about him as well. But then I suddenly realized that they would do the same thing to me behind my back.

This hostility reflects the men's irrational jealousy and envy – as if an East and Southeast Asian newcomer posed a potential threat, becoming the 'exotic trophy' usually consumed by 'rice queens', i.e. Caucasian men who are solely interested in Asian men.[14] This hostility also reflects the stratified nature of the gay community, in which discrimination might not always come from the dominant 'race' (white British) but from within the 'same' 'race' (Chinese, or Asian). This negative identification shows the predicament of eroticizing the

Chinese or Asian body (or the predicament of the 'sticky rice queen', i.e. Asian men going out with Asian men), as if the white body were the only object of desire. Under the disciplinary effect of the 'phallus-is-white' logic, the body from the 'East' is thus conflated with the feminine body. Leo (36, nurse, in 1997) said, 'Two Malaysian friends told me that if two Asian men had sex, they were really like two lesbians making love. I agreed with them. I only fancied *gwailo* . . .' As noted elsewhere (Kong 2002), perhaps the problematic is less about the image of 'passivity' or 'servitude', and more about how the meeting between the 'East' and the 'West' entails the 'East' always adopting the servant role. The consistency of this role and the lack of other possibilities lead us to believe that the uniformity reflects real social hierarchy, economic inequality and political domination. While the gay community operates a space for personal affirmation and reassurance and sexual liberation, it can also, paradoxically, reinforce and strengthen the racial, cultural and sexual tension and alienation, sometimes even more pronounced than that in the larger community (Fung 1996: 190).

Without attributing to Hong Kong gay men the derogatory ideas of 'otherness', 'lack' or 'failure', how might we describe their uniqueness and their difference – how might we go about thinking of them as men in their own right? Thus, instead of asking how Hong Kong gay men fall short of other hegemonic gay masculinities or of British (gay) citizenship, we should ask what Hong Kong gay men tell us about our assumptions of masculinity and citizenship in general. How do they offer us new insights into the conceptualizations of modern gay identity and sexual citizen? Western gay men seem to be the 'origins' from which the whole universe of 'gayness' has been defined, and post-colonial gay men are imagined to be the mere recipients of such values, living lives of a forever 'local' and negligible character. What might Hong Kong gay men tell us about gay men in London, New York, Paris or Berlin, rather than vice versa?

Like Lee *et al.* (2002) in their studies of Chinese migrant women in Britain, I will discuss three major types of Chinese migrant gay men in Britain and examine the sexual politics they have been employing in white-dominated British straight and gay societies.

Overseas 'bride'

The first type of migrant consists of those who came to Britain as overseas 'brides' of white British gay men. Martin was 27 when I first interviewed him in 1997. He had first come to the UK at 20 with a British man (Michael), who was then 40. They met in Hong Kong, and Martin flew to the UK with Michael because of his fear of the 1997 issue and his desire for love, romance and sexual freedom.

> Every day when I read news, I was scared . . . My heart was dead! People were just concerned about how Hong Kong economy would be damaged, but I thought about the right, the freedom, the right to freedom, and the freedom of speech, etc. Hong Kong was a very free society. You could

> say anything about Taiwan, China, etc., but after '97 you could not, you could only say good things about China, you could not criticize it . . . and I desperately wanted to leave Hong Kong . . . it was because of love. I just wanted to leave. Hong Kong was too small for me.

In retrospect, Martin's fear about 1997 was a bit exaggerated, but when he migrated to the UK in 1990, Hong Kong indeed had undergone a serious political crisis. Although the fear of political uncertainty over the 1997 issue had already triggered off a series of immigration tides throughout the whole of the 1980s, it climaxed after the 1989 June Fourth Incident. Martin's fear was real at that time. Moreover, homosexuality had only just been decriminalized in 1990 and Hong Kong society was still homophobic (see Chapters 2 and 3).

However, after Martin came to the UK he was bored to death, as he acted as a 'houseboy' and experienced the cultural shock between the restless, overcrowded, hectic urban life of Hong Kong and the tranquility and peacefulness of the English countryside.

> The first year, I did things like staying at home, shopping, sleeping and cooking . . . and the second year, the same! . . . Michael bought a flat in Ireland and he asked me to go with him. We then went there for one summer and I found I was so bored. No bars, no clubs, none whatsoever . . . I came from Hong Kong and was brought up in high-rise buildings with loads of people around. But here, within the 5km area, it was only me and him. I was bored to death. Every day, we woke up in the morning, and went to the beach and fishing . . . we went to bed at 8 p.m.! I found it was meaningless.

Martin, like Lee *et al.*'s (2002: 610–13) overseas brides among their samples of Chinese migrant women, heavily depended on the British man. His relative lack of economic and cultural resources and networks in the host country exacerbated his social isolation. The breakthrough was when some friends from Hong Kong came to study fashion in London. He followed them and studied art in London. 'I had two friends who came from Hong Kong and they studied fashion design in London. I then asked one of them, Can I study? He said, Why not?! That's how I started . . . I got a place in Chelsea . . .' This was also the time that he split up with Michael and went out with his long-term boyfriend Wolfgang, a German gay man, who was 42 when they first came together.

> . . . and around that time, I was about to split up with Michael. I knew Wolfgang for a long time, I knew him in Hong Kong . . . and we talked over the phone a lot about my relationship with Michael and he came very frequently to visit me in London. I think I was a grown-up, but he (Michael) did not like what I was doing, he was sort of fathering me and told me what I should do and what I should not . . . we then split up. . . .

> But with Wolfgang, we had some problems at first. He had a German boyfriend who was 20 years younger than him, so I couldn't stay with him. He rented a flat for me . . . and I always had to hide away. But you know, we couldn't escape. One day, Wolfgang was driving his car and his boyfriend was chasing after us on a motorbike . . . his boyfriend then suggested that they should separate.

It was the rather negative experience with Michael and this incident with Wolfgang that made Martin think that he should not depend solely on anyone.

> That's why I study . . . the higher the education you get, the farther you can go. . . . And to study for a degree, for me, is that when I can't depend on others, I can still depend on my degree. If I really need to work, I say if I really need to work . . .

Wolfgang was a rich man who could support Martin's travels to Germany every single weekend. Martin was happy to do this, and their open relationship led him to different transnational sexual experiences that he could hardly have imagined, especially within the much smaller gay community, and with the relative non-existence of the leather scene and Black men, in Hong Kong.

> It was much better with Wolfgang . . . but the problem is that he lives in Germany and I live in London. We only see each other on weekends . . . so every day I just go to school, I am lonely, I go clubbing and cottaging every day . . . and during the weekend I fly to Germany, we have dinner on Friday and then go out . . . we usually go to a park first . . . as appetizer . . . then a leather bar, and then clubs . . . we are open in our relationship, we swap our sexual partners and exchange our fantasies . . .
>
> . . . and I find myself fancying Black guys . . . in Hong Kong you can hardly find a Black guy – people will put pressure on you if you hang out with a Black man, I can't afford that kind of pressure . . . Hong Kong is so small, you only have a few choices to hang out . . . you see the same crowd everywhere you go . . . but in London, you can hang out with every type of man you want . . . if you can't meet a man in a bar, you can always go to another one. There are so many places to hang out.

He was heavily involved in the London gay leather and 'Black' scenes. Boldly referring to himself as a potato queen and a size queen,[15] Martin was clearly aware of his object of desire. He had always sought a father figure who, for him, would symbolically represent maturity, economic stability and material satisfaction. His small and skinny body had always contrasted with the bodies he found sexually desirable, which were usually hunky and big. However, he recognized the sexual stereotyping of ethnic minorities, but instead of rejecting it, he embraced it. He was well aware of his own 'exotic cultural capital' (c.f. Bourdieu 1984, 1986, 1989), which helped him to benefit from the white fetishization of coloured bodies. Consciously controlling his body, he knew how to fit into the white 'gaze'.

> I like older guys, maybe I have always been looking for a father type, maybe I want someone to take care of me, I don't know . . . In the gay world, your body is very important. If you are too hunky, you look too similar to them. They don't like you. If you dye your hair, you look too funky. You should keep your body slim and look cute.

He was very flexible in using his body in the fetishization of body types in the gay 'market'. However, a bad experience on a holiday in Miami drove him to pump up his muscles to fit the increasingly global market norm of the hegemonic body type: the muscular male athletic body. 'It was at that time when we went to Miami for holiday. We went to the famous Muscle Beach, and no one, not a single man looked at me. FUCK!!!! I then decided that I had to do something . . .' Infused with his disappointment in Miami and his increasing interest in the Black Caribbean gay community in London, he consciously transformed his timid oriental body into a dark muscular body. When I saw him in 2007, I was surprised by his 'body modification'. He looked like a Black man, with dark tanned skin, shaved head, and well-trained athletic body.

Martin was now working as an art curator, travelling among European countries. He got his EU passport through applying for same-sex partnership with Wolfgang in Germany. He also has got his British passport. He concluded our interview in 2007: 'In the UK, you can do what you really want to do. In the past ten years, I got what I wanted. It's about freedom . . . and fulfilling my dreams . . . I have gone through this: study, same-sex marriage, and work . . .' Martin seems to represent the most successful and exceptional example of this type. Chai, my Thai friend, is the other extreme. Chai was only 20 when I first met him in 1996. He was poorly educated and came to London in 1996 as the 'bride' of a British man. However, he was unlucky, as he was quickly dumped by his British boyfriend. He then worked in a Thai restaurant for a few months. One day he decided that he could not live that way. He then became a sex worker, through an escort service agency. He had many clients, and bought a flat and his own car. In 2002, when I went back to London for a holiday, he drove his car to pick me up and showed me his little Thai grocery store. I was happy for him. However, in 2007, when I went back to London on a research trip, he had changed. He had lost all his money through bad investments and through being cheated by friends and family. He had also lost his shop, his flat, his car and his Irish boyfriend. He was into heavy drug use. He was then living with other Thai sex workers in a small apartment in Soho. Before I left he was dragging as an executive woman, and asked me to lend him 20 quid to go to Madam JoJo's.[16] He said with confidence, 'I will be lucky tonight, don't you worry. I will pay you back!'

These overseas 'brides' had longed to leave their home countries. They had grasped the chance, with the high hope that 'marrying' abroad would offer an escape from poverty, constraining familial culture, a homophobic environment or political uncertainty. London was one of the destinations – not just a cosmopolitan city, but also a global gay city with a substantial gay population. London represents modernity and sophistication, romance and sexual freedom, wealth and upward mobility, and acts as a 'global gay magnet', attracting thousands of gay men.

However, because of the lack of familial and community support, the low social and language skills and the difficulties in getting jobs due to their legal status, such gay men are highly vulnerable to problems of social isolation, and their lives are closely tied to the British men who brought them in. While Martin was supported by economically secure men, and while his determination to study eventually led him to better life chances, others like Chai were not that lucky.

Without being part of an extended family or migrant community, the commercial gay scene seems to be the only social outlet for gay migrants. Far from being a supportive and resourceful network, the gay community can simply be a commercial market based on the 'twin motors of sexual desires and commodity' (Keogh *et al.* 2004b: 41). Engagement in sex work is thus one option. As Keogh *et al.* (2004a: 23) writes,

> if you are a gay migrant with social needs, gay community attachment in London today does not help you learn English, increase your job skills, find a job, find a home, find friends or love. On the contrary, it exploits the most capital you possess: your body. That is, your capacity to sell your labour or sex in order to earn a living. We conclude therefore that, at present, gay community attachment is a liability for less well-educated migrants.

Men who came with family

To send children to obtain universally certified education degrees and residency for the whole family has always been a strategy of many in the middle and upper-middle classes in Hong Kong, Taiwan and (more recently) mainland China (Skeldon 1994b: 11; Ong 1996, 1998). Thus the second type of gay immigrant I am going to discuss consists of those who came with family. Jeff is such a case.

Jeff came to the UK with his family when he was nine, as part of a familial strategy of advancement. His father, as the head of the family, maximized transnational business opportunities and relocated some family members overseas. This 'family biopolitics' governs the 'conduct of family members in the interest of ensuring the security and prosperity of the family as a whole' (Ong 1996: 748). Jeff was a 'parachute kid', as were his brothers, while his father shuttled back and forth to Hong Kong for business in the 1980s.

With his family in the UK, Jeff had to hide his sexuality quite carefully. He lived through the period when Section 28 of the Local Government Act of

1988 was enforced at school. Like most gay boys, he secretly tried out the gay scene and eventually came out through working in London in the 1990s.

> I knew I was gay but I repressed it during my entire period of study . . . I secretly looked at *Skies* magazine, and there was a small gay personal page . . . I did write once but nothing happened . . . I then started going out with girls and . . . I tried to convince to myself that I was not (gay) and also tried to prove to others that I was not (gay) . . .
>
> I studied at Bristol . . . and in that community it was quite hard to come to terms with it . . . Coming to London, opening up to the city environment through work, and I think actually being in London, was a major factor (for me to come out) . . . because you can actually do things without other people's knowing. So that's why I remember how I found out about Earls Court . . .
>
> Actually it was in *Time Out* – a very brief article on an area of a gay sector, whatever – and it just mentioned that Earls Court was big and beautiful blah blah blah and I hoped in my mind, despite feeling very very unhappy with the whole situation within myself . . . and felt that I should do something, otherwise I would continue to be very very unhappy . . . OK, so I went to Earls Court without anybody knowing and tried it out . . . I was really nervous and I went to *Clone Zone.* I had been there for about 45 minutes, I was really really nervous, but somehow I suddenly plucked up the courage to ask a salesman, 'Where is the nearest bar?', and he pointed it out to me . . .

It was around the same time that he came out to his best German friend, who was an out gay man, and he got into the gay subculture. However, he had great difficulty in coming out to his family, especially to his father, who, for him, presented the figure of the typical patriarch.

> I think my father was the most difficult person for me to come out to . . . I was in Hong Kong last February and I had to go and see those girls that my dad arranged for me . . . he was a heterosexual chauvinist and if he found out his son was gay, he would be quite disappointed . . . and maybe there was also some financial dependence ... since his death it has become much easier for me . . .

Arranged marriage is an old practice and was very rare in Hong Kong in the 1990s. This attempt at arranging a marriage reflects that his father's attitude was as a traditional and controlling Chinese man. Only after the death of his father did Jeff finally come out as a gay man to his whole family. But family was still a big issue for him, which is a characteristic that he regarded as 'Chinese'. He had been going out with Klaus, a German gay man, for six years. They split up in 2006, the trigger point being that he thought his boyfriend did not understand his Chinese way of handling family, especially as he had to take care of his mother and an elder brother who was mentally ill.

> Klaus doesn't quite understand when I come to terms with my Chinese background . . . he can't understand the whole family responsibility thing and I think, to him, it's very different. He is in a very different type of family, he is in a single parent family, but has a very close relationship with his mum . . . he only has to take care of himself, and his mum is a doctor and very independent . . . but I have to take care of my mum and my brother . . . who has been sick all the time. One day when I came to see him he was falling apart . . . letters scattered near the door, he didn't eat properly, dishes all around . . . but Klaus, he was not there when I needed him emotionally. He thought I shouldn't be responsible for my brother and my mum.

Apart from the family 'issue', Jeff has had no problem integrating into British society. He was the only respondent who insisted that he had never experienced any form of racism. He had an upper-middle-class background, and enjoyed the benefits of holding two passports, which for him was a matter of convenience.

> I am still proud of being a Chinese, I never let that go . . . so I still identify myself as a Chinese living in London . . . and use my British-ness . . . and my Chinese-ness to get things done . . . I am just a person who was coincidently born in Hong Kong and educated in England . . . and I think cultural identity is more a matter of convenience . . . I get the British passport therefore – lets me travel more easily . . . and I don't let go of my Chinese passport, as that's more related to convenience too . . .

Moreover, possessing virtually all the 'required' capitals of gay citizenship – rich, middle class, highly educated, with a British accent and a professional, muscular gym-trained body – he found himself to have no problems inside the white gay community. For a certain period of time Klaus was unemployed and stayed at home, acting more like a houseboy. Jeff was actually the one who supported the white man financially, treating Klaus as a 'houseboy'.

The relationship between 'race' and sexuality is a complex one, as they intersect with other categories of difference such as class, age, education, etc. Ho and Tsang (2000: 318, emphasis original) point out, 'In some situations, the "active–passive" sexual roles follow the lines of "colonizer–colonialized" and in other situations the opposite happens. In many instances, age and wealth and institutional forms of power are more important than race and colonial status' (see also Kong 2002).

Jeff's case seems to hold true to this argument. In fact, Klaus's later employment in some ways changed their relationship, and this seems to have been a reason for their separation:

> I think the whole dynamic of our relationship is different now. He's more independent . . . and I guess he was being a puppy and I could actually manage him . . . but soon as he's got a job and becomes more independent, he finally has a say in the relationship . . .

To sum up, the respondents who migrated to the UK early in their lives have to find a way to live with both the migrant Chinese culture and the urban gay culture. On the one hand, Chinese gay migrant men with family in the UK have to live within their distinctive 'parental culture' – as Chinese. The migrant Chinese community, like other ethnic communities, functions to preserve cultural tradition, offers economic support, and provides social identification. It is usually conservative and heterosexual, with a closely-knit familial structure. On the other hand, Chinese gay migrant men must engage with certain aspects of gay identity and sociality in the UK gay community. Despite its cultural repertoire of gay identification, friendship and romance, the gay community is also a sexual market, where Chinese may experience a brutal form of racism, in which being gay means 'being white'. The solution to this dilemma is neither total rejection of, nor total assimilation to, either one or the other. Rather, such Chinese gay men negotiate a space through slow, silent and subtle acceptance and rejection, disclosure and withholding.[17]

Independent migrants

The final group of migrants is the largest number in my sample. They had come on their own, with strategies of individual advancement, mainly through education or training, as well as for the hidden reason of realizing gay sexuality. After finishing their studies, they had decided to stay. While most could not succeed due to the various limitations of British immigration law, some managed to stay, either through work or through their same-sex relationships with their partners.

Nelson was 30 when first interviewed in 1998. He had come to the UK in 1994, at a time when he was tired of his work and, more importantly, was urged by his burning desire to escape what he perceived as the repressed situation of being homosexual in Hong Kong.

> I was so suffocated by my work and, more importantly, I could not come out in Hong Kong. I then decided to quit my job, and came to London to take a course on media. I wanted to throw everything away. I thought maybe I could forget my past love, and I wanted to have a break. It might sound a bit silly, but I wanted to find a relationship. I wanted to have a simple life.

Living in London, on the one hand, gave him the experience of cosmopolitan life and the freedom to fully realize his sexuality.

> I love Hong Kong. It is the place where I was born and where I was brought up . . . but it is too small . . . and people are too narrow-minded . . . here (England) is different – you are talking about many different races, different languages . . . it's multicultural. It's more sophisticated and I love to live in such an environment . . .
>
> Typical Hong Kong gay men are camp, very bitchy, and are too concerned about their appearance . . . that's why I found here (London) much more natural . . . I did find difficulty in identifying myself with Hong Kong gay men because I am not a campy or bitchy type of gay man. I am simply a man who loves another man! Living as a gay man in London is much more relaxed and natural than in Hong Kong . . .

However, living in London posed a serious challenge to him in relation to his minority status. It was not until he came to London that he started to rethink his own cultural identity and to discover the close relationship between 'race' and sexuality.

> I have always disliked China. I even rejected my own country . . . I think I am quite a typical colonial Hong Kong man . . . I think being a *hoeng gong jan* (香港人 Cant.: 'Hong Kong people') is superior to being a mainlander . . . but I guess I have changed my ideas since I came to London. When my own culture was despised or looked down upon by my British friends, I started to rebel against this humiliation . . . But then I realized that I know nothing about China, and I don't know how to defend my own country . . . Is Chinese medicine good? What is *jik ging* (易經 Cant.: 'A Book of Change')? In what ways do Confucian thoughts influence me? . . .
>
> Race and sexuality are parallel, like the film *M. Butterfly* [see note 11]. It talks about the white fetish for an oriental man . . . My present boyfriend, he is 43. . . . I have spent a lot of time trying to understand the meanings or motives behind his behaviour . . . So there is definitely a cultural conflict between us . . .

After a short relationship with one British man, he ended up going out with another one, Paul, a white British man 12 years older than he was. At that time his ambiguous status seemed to have led him to play a sort of 'houseboy' role, involving the tasks of cooking and gardening. He was quite frustrated about that period of time.

> I am now at a most uncertain moment in my life. In front of me is an empty land. Although someone is with me, I think I have lost any vision . . . I don't know how to function in this society. Well, I could be a typist or technician; earning a living is not a problem. Even if I don't work, I can still live here. But I want to find a position for myself.

The situation got worse when his mother in Hong Kong passed away.

> I was working freelance at a Chinese media company, but I had not got the work permit. It was around that time we applied for civil union . . . at first, the Home Office rejected our case, but we appealed . . . I could not work full time and had to be self-employed . . . and then my mum passed away in Hong Kong. It was the hardest part of the whole experience . . . I had always been very close to my mum . . . I could not go out of the UK. Because of the status, if I went back to Hong Kong, I would be very unlikely to get back here . . . but we finally decided that I should go back to Hong Kong. So I did . . . and after a series of very complicated legal procedures, I got back to the UK and I was holding tourist status, which again prevented me from working! It was not until we got the status of same-sex partnership that I got civil status and then was able to work.

Nelson and Paul eventually won the case for civil union, after which Nelson started to work in a Chinese media company. 'And then I got this job. The pay was not that good, but that was fine. At that time, I didn't care, I just wanted to work . . . after a few years, I was promoted to be a manager . . .' Getting British residency allowed him to work. Although he later split up with Paul, he did not feel that he had used his boyfriend for the purpose of settling in the UK.

> At that time, I guess we were too 'fast', because of the immigration issue – we were so determined to get me to stay in Britain and didn't think about other things . . . we had problems in sex . . . he is into open relationship but I am not . . . so we decided to split up at the end . . . but I don't think I used him . . . I never think that I used him to get the British passport. It's just that our relationship cannot work out . . .

After they split up in 2003, Nelson was in despair. He never got into the gay community in London, which he found too sexualized and alienating. More importantly, he knew he could not fit into the 'oriental' sexual type and had no intention to do so.

> After we split up, my love life was like a blank sheet! I was so scared to commit, but at the same time I was so scared to live a solitary life . . . it was really hard for me . . . and I didn't go out much . . . I have never really hung out in either the Hong Kong or the London gay scene . . . I don't like it . . . and I don't go to saunas as I am fat . . . and sometimes I just found casual sex through internet . . . I just worked until I met my recent boyfriend in 2005 . . .

Nelson, like many other respondents, turned away from the gay community and involved himself in work, finding more meaningful social interactions through other, mainly Chinese, friends.

Leo and Kenny are other examples of independent migrants. Leo was 36 when I first interviewed him in 1997. He had studied for O levels in the early 1980s and then did a degree in computing. After graduation, he did not get a job. He eventually managed to stay in the UK to study nursing, as there was a shortage of labour in the field. His social network was largely confined to the Chinese community. Another man, Kenny, seven years younger than Leo, came to London in the mid 1990s to study fashion and got freelance jobs after graduation. He worked at gay bars for a couple of years, hung out mostly with white men, and later became a flight attendant flying back and forth between London and Hong Kong.

To sum up, these men, like other migrants, have to face all the difficulties of finding jobs, shelter, lovers and a sense of belonging. Since they have left Hong Kong for reasons mainly related to their sexuality, they generally do not get active or full support from their families. Sexuality may be a burden as well as an advantage to them. Unlike the first group, who are financially supported by their partners, or the second group, who have come with their parental families, they have to depend much more on themselves. Although they might experience intense personal alienation, possession of the social capital of education helps them to survive and offers them a way out of the 'houseboy' scenario. Due to the increasing proximity among countries through technology, they do not have to cut off completely their ties with Hong Kong, and they maintain good access to Hong Kong society through regular trips to Hong Kong, mobile phones and the internet, etc.

Discussion and conclusion

This chapter has examined the complicated relationship between perceived race and sexuality in the context of queer migration by looking at Hong Kong gay men who migrated to Britain in the 1980s and 1990s. They came as 'brides', as part of their family's advancement plan, or as candidates with a deliberate strategy of individual advancement. Migration is always a complex act. Some had come as the result of conscious long-term planning while others did so opportunistically, with only poor planning. Some had clear goals of family and/or individual advancement. Yet others hoped to escape from poverty, constraining familial culture, political uncertainty and the repression of their homosexuality. The whole of their migration experiences should not be seen as simply a matter of individual efforts of resettlement, but as part of the state's policy of immigration control and reproduction of racial privilege.[18]

Even though Chinese are perceived as the 'ethnic model', and are subject to lesser institutional forms of racism than Black British, they still maintain a minority status in the white-dominated British culture. They are still under-represented in areas such as the political system and the mass media, and experience various degrees of difficulty in the job market, more than do their white counterparts. As migrants, they tend to accept the basic order of 'British first, Chinese second'.

Gay men who came with parents did so as a result of a collective family planning to expand transnational family business, to obtain overseas qualifications, and/or to obtain residency or citizenship 'insurance' in the face of the political crisis in Hong Kong. Most of them came to Britain at early ages. Due to the close ties with family, they had to live within two seemingly contradictory cultures – first, the Chinese culture, characterized by the familial network that signifies a culture of difference from that of the host British culture and a culture of similarity with other Chinese; and second, the urban British gay subculture of a global 'gay city' of sophistication and modernity, but one with a racial hierarchy, so that being accepted as a full member of the gay community means being cosmopolitan, middle class, and preferably white. Instead of totally rejecting, or assimilating to one culture or the other, they have struggled from within and sought to create new ways of being Chinese and gay.

Unlike gay men who migrated with family, the other two types came to Britain as a result of their own deliberate and conscious decisions – not only for the common reasons of poverty, social mobility and individual advancement through studying or training, but also for the hidden reason of escaping the homophobic culture of Hong Kong, with a burning desire to experience gay sexuality. They tended deliberately to cut themselves off from familial ties, and their lives in Britain have depended heavily either on the British men who brought them or on themselves. In a kind of racially discriminated-against sexual exile, they have had to struggle for survival. Through a man or through a degree, they have struggled to get British (or EU) passports and residency to help them to stay in Britain. Their success has depended on their individual social and economic backgrounds, and they have managed to survive variously as professionals, manual workers or even as sex workers. Without much support from their families, they have tended to move towards the gay community. Although the gay community can be a place to find friendship, love and romance, it can also act as a purely commercial market that operates on the basis of sexual stereotyping, racial discrimination and body commodification. With the racialized fetishism of gay male bodies, the Chinese gay man has been confined by the image of the 'golden boy'. While some passionately embraced this image, others rejected it outright and contested it. Willingly or not, they are caught in the web of domination inside the gay community, with which they have longed to identify. Although some are still heavily involved with it, others have moved away to other, mostly Chinese, communities and networks for support. The advancement of new telecommunication technology and their increasingly globalized way of life have helped them to live between different cultures.

Citizenship is not merely a political attribute but is also 'a process in which culture becomes a relevant category of affinity' (Rofel 2007: 94). Like Manalansan's (2003) Filipino migrant gay men in New York, my respondents have become caught in the dual processes of 'being-made' and 'self-making' of citizenship, which lie at the junctures of continuity and discontinuity for becoming Chinese British gay men. They thus juggle three cultures – the

British culture, which represents autonomy and sophistication as well as white superiority and racism; the Chinese culture, which materializes economic support and cultural identity but also represents familial pressure and obligation; and the specifically British *gay* culture, which symbolizes sexual freedom and liberation but at the same time is subject to sexual stereotyping and body commodification. The process of citizenship is thus 'neither a birthright nor is it about the romance of dissidence and resistance, but is about struggling to create scripts that will enable them to survive' (Manalansan 2003: 121) within the lines of class, family and race relationships, and among the practices and identities both of society in general and of the gay community in particular.

Every identity has a history. 'Gay' identity cannot be separated from other 'categories of difference' such as race and ethnicity, education and class background, sex and gender, age and physical embodiment which together make up the 'wholeness' of citizens, including gay citizens. The case of Hong Kong migrant gay men exemplifies the multifarious experience of gay citizenship in Britain.

Part III

China

Introduction

There is a well-established literature documenting the changing meanings of citizenship in contemporary China.[1] Scholars have argued that the concept of citizenship may have a different meaning than that provided in the Western conception of citizenship (e.g., T. H. Marshall's (1950) model). For example, Keane (2001: 2–3) and So (2004: 247–50) both point out that the concept of the citizen, due to its bourgeois legacy and associated connotations of individual political and civil rights, was seldom used in the PRC during the Maoist era, which emphasized so much the socialist goals of altruism, collectivism, mass mobilization, and class struggle. Unlike Marshall's conception of the evolution of civil, political and social rights towards a Western-style welfare state, the PRC, in the Mao era, restricted citizens' civil and political rights while granting massive social rights to its urban citizens, such as the rights to employment, housing, healthcare, childcare, and other benefits, within a work package administered through their work units (*danwei* 單位).

This mode of citizenship, which can be referred to as 'socialist citizenship', has gradually changed to one of 'market citizenship' with the various economic reforms, such as the 'Four Modernizations' and marketization in the economy, that have taken place since the late 1970s. The socialist project has given way to neo-liberal market economics, the selflessness ethic has been replaced by economic incentives, mass mobilization campaigns are no longer launched, and 'the iron rice bowl' (*tiefanwan* 鐵飯碗) has been replaced by the law of supply and demand. Economic governance has evolved as the primary mechanism of governance, has begun to roll back many of the social rights previously enjoyed by urban citizens and has substituted property and consumer rights, giving rise to the development of a new identity formation on the basis of economic and cultural citizenship (Keane 2001). To a certain extent, as noted by So (2004: 249), this market citizenship is similar to the 'enterprising citizenship' in Hong Kong, in the sense that governments in both the mainland and Hong Kong have limited social rights in order to promote competence in the market; nurture a strong sense of economic, or consumer, citizenship; and limit 'rights' to the civil and political rights endorsed through the discourse of law and order.

It is with this background that I situate my discussion of Chinese gay men in mainland China in the following two chapters. In Chapter 6, I will delineate the emergence of gay identity since the 1990s and how the newly emerged gay identity taps into the development of cultural citizenship. In Chapter 7, I will discuss the other side of this newly emerged gay citizenship through the life of the 'money boy' – that is, the rural-to-urban migrant who sells sex in cities and tries hard to change his own fate from that of a city marginal to that of an urban citizen.

6 *New* new China, *new* new tongzhi

12 July 2008 ***Saturday, 4 p.m., Guangzhou, China***

Saturday afternoon. I just interviewed two men today. Ah Ming, 42, lives in a small rural village near Guangzhou. He married twice, with two kids. He is computer illiterate and never uses the internet for social and sexual networking but finds other gay men through his mobile phone. Sexually explicit photos and messages are sent from friends' friends' friends, mediated by the new technology of mobile communication. I think this is a kind of 'gay Facebook' that connects one to another. What a good way to connect! I was amazed by the messages sent by his gay friends or acquaintances to him through his mobile phone that he showed to me. I asked him if his wife might accidentally pick up his phone and see the messages. He said, in a confident voice, 'No!'

And then I met Xiao Wang. He is a very typical bookish good-looking 25-year-old young man who comes from Sichuan. He studied at a university in Beijing and now works at a computer company in Guangzhou. He is now going out with a man, of course without letting his family know. But he insists that he won't get married for his family. He said, 'I will tell them if they force me to get married.'

After the two interviews, I was a bit tired. Xiao Guang, a staff of the NGO who helped me find respondents for interview, told me that I should take a rest. He said in a cheerful voice that one of their outreach team leaders, Ah Bei, was going to have a big birthday party tonight and asked us to join. He was very keen to tell me that we could go swimming, as there was a swimming pool in the housing estate. Going swimming on a private premise seems to be something special for him. Coming from a poor rural area in Guangdong, Xiao Guang, now 32, had just settled down in Guangzhou in 2006. He had moved to work in Shenzhen in 1993 and had later fled to Shanghai in 2004 to escape the family pressure to get married. After two years of separation with almost no communication, he finally came out to his family. He came down to work in Guangzhou to be closer to his family. Although his family knew he was gay, they still asked him to get married. Well, everyone has his own story![1]

We then took a train and arrived at a very nice private housing estate, with its own garden, club house and internal transport system. This is where Ah Bei is now staying. I was surprised by the development of Guangdong's economic prosperity, especially the emergence of the middle class, which subsequently has led to such a luxurious life. I wish I could have such a nice flat in Hong Kong! We saw Ah Bei and a bunch of friends in a swimming pool. We swam and played water sports, chasing each other. I had been so tensed thinking about my research, but now, I could finally take a break and relax myself in warm water under the sun.

Later on, we went to dinner at a restaurant inside the club house and they booked a room. I then met some of my previous interviewees, outreach workers, and also saw some new faces. We were, altogether, 20 people. Someone bought the birthday boy a pair of white wings. Ah Bei put them on. With his handsome face, he really looked like an angel. And then some of them took out wigs and took photos. I was shocked by their outrageous and flamboyant behaviour. They didn't seem to mind that the waitresses, those *dagongmei* (打工妹 'working girls') who served us, may have had a very clear idea of who we really were.

We went back to the flat. They then turned the birthday party into a big drag fashion show. These young men, aged mainly from early twenties to late thirties, mostly came from different places in China but had settled down (at least for the present) in Guangzhou. They had met one another either through the outreach work of the NGO or the internet. They all acknowledged their same-sex desire and identified themselves as 'gay', tongzhi, or *quan'neiren* (圈內人 'members of the circle'). Some had been out to their families, most had not and had no intention of becoming so. Some had got married, some had decided to get married, and some were still wandering, juggling their parents' expectations of their getting married and their own troubles of finding a boyfriend.

While some remained as audience, half of them rushed to the closet room and picked up clothes, dresses and accessories and came out with all sorts of glamorous gender performances – as a schoolgirl, as a lady, as an executive woman, as a cowboy, as a go-go boy, as a fairy, etc. That reminded me of the Ball in Harlem depicted so vividly in the documentary *Paris is Burning* (dir. Jennie Livingston, 1990), though on a much smaller scale. We were all into laughter, with flashes of photos all over the room to capture the moment. Harry, a US-educated businessman, said to me, 'Isn't it fun to be gay!'

What does it mean to be gay in China? Why is being gay always perceived as a family problem? How do Chinese gay men cope with their sexual identity in a neo-Confucian family setting, in which getting married and bearing children is still a norm, especially in rural areas? Is getting married the only solution for those like Ah Ming? Does coming out necessarily mean leaving home, like Xiao Guang, who fled to Shanghai as a wandering soul? Most of the gay men I met in China do not normally see homosexuality as a perversion; rather, they think that being gay is a kind of liberation, a 'fun' way of being human. If global gay identity, mediated through the process of globalization and the neo-liberal ideology, has swept over China and transformed gay identity from that of a perverted subject to that of a new kind of human subject

(Rofel 2007: 1), what does this new subject look like? In what ways does this new subject relate to the hegemonic state ideal of urban cultural citizenship and cosmopolitanism?

This chapter will, first, briefly consider the emergence of gay identities in China, situated within the changing sexual culture and the socio-political

Figure 6.1 The party (2008, author's photograph).

history of the past decades. I will then discuss the major problem Chinese gay men are facing, using 'coming out' as the key problem – as reported by my respondents who now live in Guangdong.

I will show that gay identity has been subordinated under various gendered and sexed social institutions such as the family, the work unit (*danwei* 單位),

Figure 6.2 The party (2008, author's photograph).

the police and the state. Among these, the family seems to be the dominant institution that the respondents have to deal with. In particular, they have to deal with their familial roles and the 'face' issue of the family. Coming out – as a strategy of accommodation and resistance – is thus the focal point of examination.

Figure 6.3 The party (2008, author's photograph).

I will then conclude that the coming-to-term of new gay identity in China has slowly shifted to involve a new understanding of homosexuality, not so much in terms of the medical discourse of perversion (though this is still the dominant model) but in terms of the idea of active self-fashioning.[2] Being gay thus means 'quality' (*suzhi* 素質), individuality and 'difference' – a new kind of humanity under the vigorous processes of globalization, neo-liberalism, cosmopolitanism and consumerism (Rofel 2007: Ch. 3).

Figure 6.4 The party (2008, author's photograph).

A brief history of the emergence of gay identities in China

Ancient China

There is a well-established literature that demonstrates a rather rich and relatively tolerant tradition for 'same-sex love' between men in ancient China. The stories of *yu tao* (餘桃 'the peach reminder') and *duanxiu* (斷袖 'the cut sleeve') present the two most famous and commonly cited euphemisms among the literati for male homosexuality (*nanse* 南(男)色 'south (male) colour'; and *nanfeng* 南(男)風 'south (male) wind') in Chinese history. These date back as early as the Zhou period (11th century BC to 221 BC) Although there was thus a celebrated rich homoerotic tradition, it is believed that homosexuality was always in a marginalized position in ancient Chinese culture, existing as peripheral to the gendered hierarchies of the Confucian family and marriage institutions (e.g., Van Gulik 1961; Chou 1971: 90–93; Bullough 1976: 300–310; Ruan and Tsai 1987; Ruan 1991: 107–20; Ruan 1997: 57–59; Samshasha 1997; Hinsch 1990).

A rich and even celebrated homoerotic tradition did exist in ancient Greece and Rome (Hubbard 2003), but this ended when Judeo-Christian thoughts and teachings, which condemned homosexual conducts (e.g., St. Thomas Aquinas' natural laws), came into power in the medieval period. Accounts of a wide range of homosexual practices (including, especially, the forms of 'trans-generational', 'trans-gendered', 'class-structured' and 'egalitarian' homosexuality, which operated with roles along the axes of dominant/submissive and active/passive) in ancient China (Hinsch 1990: 8–13) tend to point to a different model of selfhood. The most commonly cited explanation for this apparently is the prevalence of Confucianism, the dominant social and philosophical way of thinking in traditional China. In Confucianism, a person is defined as a relational self within a structured, socially reciprocal relationship network. Identity is thus not defined by the idea of essence, but rather is constructed around familial and kinship structures. If there is no essence of identity, but only morally right conduct inscribed by different social relationships, it can be argued that there is no essence of sexuality either, but only correct sexual behaviour, as defined according to different socially reciprocal patterns. Sexual behaviour is thus only condemned if one violates social expectations or is over-indulgent. If we follow this logic, it can be said that there is no 'homosexual' or 'homosexual identity' in traditional Chinese culture, as a homosexual identity presumes a distinctive type of individual who has a sexual desire for erotic contact with persons of the same gender. The emphasis thus was on doing (i.e., what one *does*, likes, enjoys, engages or indulges in, in sexual activities), not on being (i.e., what one *is*) (Hinsch 1990: 7; Kong 2000: 63–67).

A recent account along this line can be seen in Louie's (2002) theorization of traditional Chinese masculinity, which is manifested through two intertwining ideals. The *wen* (文) ideal refers to 'literary and other cultural attainment' (p. 10), manifested in a 'softer, cerebral male tradition' (p. 8) of the *caizi* (才子 'the talented scholar'), the *wenren* (文人 'the cultured man'), and the scholar-officials; while the *wu* (武) ideal refers to 'physical strength and military prowess' (p. 14) and is manifested as the *yingxiong* (英雄 'hero'), the *haohan* (好漢 'good fellow'), and the military-official. *Wen* and *wu* masculinities thus formed the opposing poles of the axis on which Chinese male identity was constructed. Both *wen* and *wu* masculinities were desirable, although the latter was always devalued, as Confucian culture downplayed physical potency. As argued by Louie (2003: 6–7), social morality concerning male sexuality was primarily concerned with the correct playing-out of hierarchies of power, within which men had to fulfil social expectations such as getting married and siring children; and secondarily with the containment of excessive sexuality (e.g., as manifested in masturbation, prostitution, etc.). In this regard, the gender of the sexual partner was not a matter of concern. Neither *wen* ('soft' or 'effeminate') masculinity nor homosexuality was seen as a threat to masculinity. As argued by Sommer (1997), adult males were seen as powerful and non-penetrable. A male homosexual was stigmatized if he assumed the role of being penetrated, as this represented the subordinate position assigned for women; and this was especially the case if he was an innocent youth, as both youth and the female gender represented powerlessness in an age hierarchy.

As a result, homosexuality was thus either treated as a transitional stage in the sexual life cycle of a man or as a legitimate practice for those who were, and remained, married and within the institution of the family. A heterosexual marriage with homosexual romance thus remained a possible outcome of a kinship-structured society. What this form of social organization rejected (and still rejects), however, is the emergence of a self-identified homosexual who lives his life independently of the heterosexual marriage institution, as most gays in the contemporary Western world do.

The Republican era

Homoerotic practices between men were enjoyed right up to the Qing Dynasty (AD 1644–1911), when homosexuality was brought under increased regulation in an attempt to strengthen the Confucian idea of the family – perhaps as a reaction against the permissiveness of the individualistic Ming period (Hinsch 1990: Ch. 7; Ng 1987, 1989).[3]

The end of the *duanxiu* ('cut sleeve') tradition seems to have come with the impact of modernity. The major changes in Chinese attitudes towards same-sex desires took place in the course of Westernization and modernization in Republican China. Dikötter (1995) observes that Republican China witnessed intense nationalism and rapid state building, in which the idea of proper control of sexual desire was the key to the development of the modern nation-state. Individual sexual desire was to be disciplined and bad habits eliminated, and couples were advised to strictly regulate their sexual behaviour in order to help bring about the revival of the nation.

As a result, sexuality was regulated under this official discourse in the name of social welfare and nation building, and marginalized premarital and extramarital sexual practices such as adultery, masturbation, homosexuality, prostitution and pornography were seen as 'shameless' or 'abnormal'.

In addition, the modern Chinese intellectuals of the time were keen to translate major Western theories and literature on sexuality into Chinese (e.g., Magnus Hirschfeld, Havelock Ellis, Iwan Bloch, Richard von Krafft-Ebing, Sigmund Freud, Edward Carpenter). Although early translations of Western literature offered ambivalent or even positive understandings of homosexuality, Ellis's medical theory of homosexuality, which dichotomized sexual normality and deviation, has gained hegemony since the 1920s through repeated citation and translation (Sang 1999, 2003; Kang 2009). This medical discourse of homosexuality has been dominant for decades and is still regarded as the major social understanding of homosexuality in China.

The Maoist period

In the Maoist period (1949–76) the state emphasized the collective – 'the people', 'the masses' – and the corresponding virtue of complete altruism, under the vigorous process of mass mobilization. First introduced by Sun Yixian (孫逸仙) in the early twentieth century, the term tongzhi was adopted and increasingly used in the Mao period to mean *comrade*, in conformity with communist practice.

In the name of revolutionary passion, this period is frequently referred to as a dark age of puritanical repression of sex (Ruan and Bullough 1989; Ruan 1991: 120–23; Wu 2003: 124–25). However, as noted by Jeffreys (2006: 3–4), along with other scholars (e.g., Hershatter 1996: 86–88; Honig 2003; Evans 1997), this period can also be read as a shift of the state's disciplinary power, stemming from the paramount state imperative of revolution. For example, as Evans (1997) shows, in contrast with the common thought that sex was a taboo subject, the state extensively produced official publications on female sexuality during the 1950s and early 1960s, although these were confined to physiological and moral dimensions of sex, and were prescribed according to a hegemonic model of reproductive sex within monogamous heterosexual marriage in the 1950 Marriage Law. Accordingly, the compulsory heterosexual marital reproductive model left little room for 'outside' sexualities (e.g., prostitution, pre- and extra-marital sex, pornography, homosexuality, etc.); constructed female gender as an effect of 'sexual difference'; and reinforced revolutionary Puritanism – '[t]he development of an official discourse of sexuality testified to the deployment of party-state power over individual, and particularly female, behaviour through the creation of uniform, normative standards of sexual conduct' (p. 7).[4]

In addition, in the medical discourse and the compulsory marriage ideology, homosexuality was not only pathologized and silenced, but was increasingly seen as deviance and crime. Homosexuality had increasingly been categorized as a type of 'hooliganism' (*liumang zui* 流氓罪) – an umbrella term that referred to a wide range of social misbehaviours. The homosexual as social outcast, characterized as a 'hooligan' (*liumang* 流氓), has thereby been a dominant, socially stigmatized image.[5]

The reform era

The reform period (1978–present) has witnessed a drastic change in terms of sexuality. The reform era, in contrast with the class struggle and mobilization politics of the Maoist era, has emphasized economic development, the 'Four Modernizations', marketization, agricultural decollectivization, land reform and so on. China has, in principle, aimed to turn from a Maoist 'rule of man' to a modern 'rule of law'.

The state has played a crucial role in shaping the new sexual culture. For example, Pan (2006: 28–36) argues that the one-child policy in 1980 was instituted principally to limit the birth rate, and that one of its unintended consequences implied that the reason for married people to maintain a sex life after the birth of a single child was not so much about reproduction as about mutual affection and pleasure. The introduction of the 1950 Marriage Law outlawed concubinage and arranged marriage, thus promoting free-choice, usually monogamous, marriage; and the revised 1980 Marriage Law has helped to replace love as relating to 'marital favour and gratitude' to that of romantic love, and many more. As a result, the ideas of 'sex for reproduction', and romantic love as mere 'petty-bourgeois sentiment' with a decadent capitalist undertone, of the Maoist era, have slowly been replaced by the idea of 'sex for pleasure' in the reform era.[6]

Although monogamous heterosexual marriage was set as the ideal, public discussions of sexuality have been largely enhanced by the emergence or re-emergence of new disciplines such as sociology, sexology, social work and law, as well as the advancement of new technologies such as the mobile phone, phone-in radio shows, telephone hotlines and internet chat rooms, which have subsequently opened up new sexual spaces, especially for young men and women, for social networking. Barmé (1994) worries that the new market economy might have transformed dissident voices into 'soft porn and packaged dissent', yet a process of 'sexual story telling' of all sorts is evident in the burgeoning market economy.[7]

It is in such a context that room has emerged for public discussion of homosexuality in the reform era. Drawing heavily on a medical and mental health approach, literature in the 1980s focused overwhelmingly on 'treating' homosexuality, especially in the context of the onset of the AIDS epidemic. After the introduction of the term 'hooliganism' in Article 106 in Criminal Law in 1979, homosexuality was increasingly placed under the umbrella of hooliganism even though it was not explicitly listed as a form of hooliganism.[8] So the homosexual oscillated between being a mental patient and being a hooligan, or was both.

However, in the 1990s, visible gay identities and communities slowly emerged, along with vigorous social, legal and economic developments (Wu 2003: 125–36; Rofel 2007: Ch. 3; Wei 2007): The 1997 revised Criminal Law deleted specific reference to the crime of hooliganism, and the Chinese Psychiatric Association removed homosexuality from the list of mental illnesses in 2001; and these developments have successfully unlocked homosexuality from pathological and deviant constructions. Increasingly, indigenous writings about homosexuality have portrayed homosexuality as a normal way of life (Wu 2003: 125–33).[9]

AIDS work has been implemented, since 1993, with 'men who have sex with men' (MSM) as one surveillance subject under the PRC's AIDS policy (He and Detels 2005: 826). Gay-affiliated non-governmental health organizations and national hotlines have been set up since 1992, with the help of transnational gay activists from Hong Kong, Taiwan and overseas. Although the major task of these endeavours has been HIV/AIDS prevention, they have given room for public or semi-public discussions about homosexuality, on such issues as coming out, social discrimination, public recognition, and mental health (Wu 2003:125–33; Rofel 2007: 85–89).

Media exposure of sexual minorities has been frequent (e.g., the TV talk show *Let's Talk*, featuring open gay individuals and experts, on Hunan TV in 2000) (Wu 2003: 132), accompanying the emergence of various gay consumption venues (e.g., bars, clubs, massage parlours, bathhouses, etc.) in big cities and the rise of the internet. All of these have allowed gay men and lesbians to identify one another through real and imagined communities.

As Jeffreys (2006: 1–12) cautions us, scholars such as Ruan Fangfu (e.g., Ruan 1991: 120–34; Ruan and Bullough 1989) tend to assume a big contrast between the alleged greatest repression of the Maoist 'party-police-state regime' and the seeming liberation of sexuality of 'open-door' China since the 1980s. This assumption should be qualified, however. Adopting a Foucauldian approach, other scholars have pointed out that 'liberated' sexual discourses since the 1980s have been 'generally tied to government-led agendas designed to promote modernization and social stability as the basis for prosperity, as well as to ensure the CCP (Chinese Communist Party)'s ongoing political legitimacy' (Jeffreys 2006: 4).

For example, Woo (2006) argues that the 1980 Marriage Law has empowered women (in particular) to initiate divorce in the case of deteriorating and usually exploitative relationships. However, female divorce litigants are usually disadvantaged in court due to their limited financial resources, as the responsibility for social efforts has been shifted from the Party-state to the individual litigant. People are now expected to pay individually for legal, social, medical and education services in the new and unequal 'socialist market' class society – services that were once theoretically (at least) considered to be their right as citizens of the previous socialist, prospectively 'classless', society. Farrer (2006) shows how the state has adopted a Western conception of sexual liberation and personal freedom and thus promotes adolescent sex education in secondary school – while at the same time suppressing the right of youth to engage in premarital sex by emphasizing traditional gender roles (especially that of female chastity). Erwin (2000) asserts that the apparent explosion of open discussion of sexuality over hotlines does not necessarily imply greater individual freedom but should be understood as an after-effect of both consumer capitalism and state power, which together 'promote modernization and social stability as a basis for prosperity and continuing political legitimacy' (p.170).[10]

In relation to homosexuality, the Beijing Queer Film Festival always seems to have problems of organization. The cancellation at the last minute of the first Beijing Queer Film Festival on the Beijing University campus in 2001 can be seen along these lines. Extensive media publicity for this festival, as well as the positive representation of gay identity in Beijing, seems to have provoked the Beijing University officials to view the event as an encouragement and promotion of homosexuality, resulting in the cancellation of the film festival at the last minute (Wu 2003: 137; *Queer China*, dir. Cui Zi'en, 2009). The 4th Beijing Queer Film Festival, in 2009, was caught in a dilemma of choosing a venue for screening. The final venue was in Songzhuang, a remote art commune in suburban Beijing. Although with this venue it was hoped that government intervention and media attention would be avoided, it was too remote, and this apparently affected the size of the audience.[11]

What are the stories of men who desire other men who are living through these broad processes of political change, economic reform and social transformation in China? Below are the stories of tongzhi in cosmopolitan Guangzhou (Canton), the capital of Guangdong Province, and in sub-provincial cities of Guangdong Province. Guangdong Province is situated in the southern part of China and is the origin of most of the early generations of the Hong Kong population. With a population of 9.6380 million permanent residents[12] in 2009 (National Bureau of Statistics of China www.stats.gov.cn/tjgb/ndtjgb/dfndtjgb/t20100301_402625749.htm, accessed 5 April 2009), Guangzhou City is one of the most populous cities in China.

'I'm the only gay in the village'

Lao Wu was born in 1957 in Guangzhou City and lived his early life during the Maoist era, when he found it very hard to be gay. He met his first love in his strictly sex-segregated secondary school, but it died out in the atmosphere of revolutionary collectivism. He got married in 1986, when he was 29, but now he and his wife are separated without divorce. He only came out to the gay world in 1993. When I interviewed him in 2008, he said in Cantonese:[13]

> I was in the senior year of secondary education, around the age of 15. I found that I liked the same sex. . . . It was in the Maoist era. We studied together, farmed together, swam together, played together and lived together. Of course, boys and girls were separated . . . I then felt close to

> one of my classmates . . . It was one of the happiest moments in my life . . . and I found it very natural . . .
>
> I realized that I had no interest in the opposite sex. I thought I was sick. At that time, no media whatsoever talked about homosexuality in society – or if any did, very negatively. I treated myself as a sick person . . . I tried to avoid the issue but I didn't dare to see a doctor . . . and I tried to correct myself. . . . I forced myself to like the opposite sex . . . I could talk to nobody . . . as I felt *ng gwong coi* (唔光彩 Cant.: 'disgraceful')[14] . . . At that time, I didn't know where to find other gay men. I didn't know any toilets or parks . . . it was not until the mid 1990s, then I knew these things. I answered some classified posts to find male friends in 1993 and later found the People's Park . . . anyway, before [in the 1970s and the 1980s], society was like a closed system . . . I thought I was the only gay person in the world . . .
>
> . . . and then I got married when I was 29. My dad, my mum and people from the *daanwai* (單位 Cant.: 'work unit') all asked me why I didn't get married. I had no reason to argue. After a few introductions, I then chose this woman. We have a daughter. She is almost 20 years old now.
>
> I guess the thought of my parents' generation is that you have to continue the lineage by getting married and having children. They don't understand that two men can live together . . . they are so determined to see you get married before they die . . . they kept telling me and my siblings that they could die peacefully if you kids all got married . . . well, we all did it . . . I had to satisfy them. My dad passed away and my mum is now 80.
>
> Oh . . . those were the days, I was so repressed . . . and you had to be extremely careful in choosing friends . . . if people in the *daanwai* (Cant.) knew that you were gay, the whole *daanwai* (Cant.) would discriminate against you . . . and even later . . . it was dangerous in those places – I mean in parks . . . in bathhouses . . . you were very easily blackmailed . . . or caught by the police.

Ah Ming (briefly mentioned at the beginning of this chapter) was born in 1966, almost ten years after Lao Wu, and spent his early adult life in the 1980s, when China had just started to implement a series of reforms. He had turned 42 in 2008, when I interviewed him. He and his brother Ah Jiang were born in the same year in a rural village in Guangdong. They both realized their same-sex desires when they were teens, and had some casual sexual encounters with classmates or villagers. They entered the gay world only when they went to Guangzhou for work and leisure. Ah Jiang married in 1993 and divorced in 1998. Ah Ming married in 1994 and divorced in 1998, but then married again in 2005. Both had kids.

They are both Cantonese speakers. Ah Jiang said:

> I knew I was gay when I was in junior middle school . . . I had some fantasy about men and then had sex with a classmate. We only used hands . . .

> and did it before we went to school . . . we still keep contact with each other . . . and of course we are both married . . . and I knew more about the gay world in the 1990s when I came to Guangzhou after I graduated from secondary school . . . there is a famous cottage near Beijing Road.
>
> I didn't want to get married. My family forced me to. They said everyone had to get married at this age, why don't you get married? . . . and then I got married in 1993 . . . I never told anyone about this . . . it's hard to tell your parents, it is something *ng gwong coi* (Cant.) . . . my wife was introduced by a cousin . . . we did court each other for awhile . . . and then after one year, I decided to get married. This was also because of the 'bonus' of getting married, so I thought it was OK . . . and then we registered . . . we didn't have sex much, we had some sex before the birth of our daughter, but after she was born I lost interest in having sex with her completely . . . and yes, it's she who initiated the divorce . . . she knew that I was gay . . . when she lost her temper, she used to say that I liked men . . . I then said I liked both sexes . . . well, I don't care much now. The society is different. Before, I felt like I was a *lauman* (流氓 Cant. 'hooligan') . . . a lot of discrimination . . . but now it's much better.

Ah Ming received the same family pressure as his brother,

> I guess I was seven or eight years old . . . I was taking a rest in a courtyard at night and the guy was wearing shorts. I then touched him, he didn't resist. He was about 20 years old . . . a villager . . . and then I did similar things with my classmates . . . I had no interest in girls . . . I think I really knew about the gay world when I came to Guangzhou . . . I came to Guangzhou every weekend . . . I then went to a public toilet, and I was so excited . . . to meet many men . . .
>
> It was in 1994, my dad introduced girls to me . . . I told him bluntly that I had no interest . . . but my dad insisted and said 'everyone has to get married, you should do the same!' He was very anxious about me . . . he then found a woman for me . . . I then went out with her for about a year . . . and then we got married . . . but we didn't get along . . . we have a son . . . but she decided to get a divorce . . . she said I was gay at the court . . . but the judge didn't care, I did not do anything illegal, did I?! . . . we then got divorced . . . she actually proposed divorce one year after we married . . . but I postponed it for three years . . . that's why we divorced in 1998 . . .
>
> In our village, you had to get married by the age of 30, you would be laughed at if you didn't . . . only men who are disabled, like dumb or deaf people, cannot find a woman . . . or else you are so poor that you can't afford one . . . people would just laugh behind your back if you didn't get married . . .

The early lives of these respondents tell us about the general situation of gay men living in Guangdong (and probably elsewhere in China) during the Maoist era and the early stage of the reform period. There are three issues that a lot of these gay men had to face.

The first consists of the general pathological and deviant discourses of homosexuality that were perpetuated in society, partly reinforced by the state and mediated through the mass media. Homosexuality was still regarded as a mental illness, which is why Lao Wu thought himself a sick person at the time. Although the PRC had no written laws explicitly criminalizing gay men, male homosexuals were easy to penalize under the umbrella term of hooliganism. Ah Jiang thought he was a hooligan when he was young, and used this euphemism for homosexuality from the government's official discourse. Moreover, as argued by Li (2006), administrative penalties and Party discriminatory sanctions, though they had no solid legal foundation, posed a real threat to male homosexuals in the past. Subject to individual attitudes towards homosexuality, the Chinese police could apprehend or interrogate any gay men brought to their attention and could report them to their work units (*danwei*) or to their families, and this would bring substantial consequences for their futures, such as in their chances for job promotion, housing allocation, and so on. Although my respondents did not have such experiences, Lao Wu revealed that he feared them, and other studies have indicated that these were not uncommon experiences for many gay men.[15]

The work unit (*danwei*) constituted the second major issue, as it served as a regulatory mechanism for homosexuality in mainly urban areas before the mid 1990s.[16] The *danwei* was the fundamental social unit of urban China under socialism. It was the source of employment and other material benefits for urban residents (the famous *tiefanwan*, 'iron rice bowl'), as well as the institution that provided its members with a complete social guarantee and welfare services, including housing, medical care, child care, catering. Thus, through the *danwei*, the whole urban population was regulated – housed, organized, policed, educated and surveyed. Each *danwei* acted as a community that provided its members' identity and social belonging.[17] It was such a close micro-surveillance, backed up by the bureaucratic cadres and tied closely to the family, that it gave little room for gay men to express their same-sex desires openly. As Lao Wu said, '. . . if people in the *daanwai* (Cant.) knew that you were gay, the whole *daanwai* (Cant.) would discriminate against you . . .'

The third issue was that of the family. As noted by Rofel (2007: 97–102), the family has always been seen as an indispensible site for establishing one's humanness, as well as one's social identity, in China. The family not only provides moral privilege and access to social and material power for men, but also shapes a sense that 'heterosexual' marriage (encoded by the 1950 Marriage Law and the revised 1980 version) is the precondition for becoming a successful citizen. The family had (and still has) great impact on Chinese gay men, especially in rural areas.

Chinese gay men had (and still have) to deal with two major issues related to the family. First, there is a familial role, which is manifested as that of the filial son, generally defined according to prescribed ways of showing love and respect to parents and the elderly. One major element is obedience to parent's expectations, and following the pressure to get married and thereby to fulfil the obligation to continue the family bloodline are both seen as signs of a good filial son. My respondents seemed to have been virtually speechless whenever their parents asked them to get married. For example, Lao Wu said 'I had no reason to argue . . . they [his parents] are so determined to see you get married before they die . . .' Ah Jiang said, 'They [his parents] said everyone had to get married at this age, why didn't you get married?' Ah Ming said, 'My dad insisted and said "everyone's got to get married, you should do the same!"' The filial role sons are expected to play is also enhanced by the material factor, especially in rural areas. It is the family division of material property by the parents that gives sons benefits if they get married. This is the reason Ah Jiang mentioned that he would get a 'bonus' when he got married.

Second is the issue of 'face', which is manifested as having two aspects or layers: *lian* (臉) is the moral face, the fundamental layer that represents the integrity of a person's moral character; while *mianzi* (面子) is the social face, which indicates one's social prestige, over and above *lian* (Hu 1944; Zito 1994: 119–20; Yan, Y.X. 1996: 142–49). Both function in interaction with other persons for their construction. *Diulian* (丟臉), or 'losing *lian*', is a 'condemnation by the group for immoral or socially disagreeable behavior' (Hu 1944: 46).[18] Thus one of the reasons why the respondents could not come out was the fear of 'losing *lian*,' as *lian* 'keeps up the consciousness of moral boundaries, maintains moral values, and expresses the force of social sanctions' (p. 50). In this sense, *lian* serves as the parameter of the closet, and maintains the heteronormative terms of the moral boundary.

In addition, public disgrace or ridicule of a socially disgraceful nature – for example, because of homosexuality – is bound to have an effect on the reputation of the family. So losing one's *lian* also implies losing the *lian* of the family, which inevitably leads to losing the *mianzi* of the family. This is why the respondents were all so afraid of the idea of shame – it was not so much their vulnerability in defending homosexuality as healthy or as normal as heterosexuality, but the degree to which being gay would bring shame upon themselves and their families. As Ah Jiang said, '. . . it's hard to tell your parents, it's something *ng gwong coi* (Cant.)'.

Under the official and dominant medical and deviant discourses of homosexuality and the all-encompassing surveillance systems of the *danwei* and the family, the respondents reveal the struggles of being gay in the past: a man who was confused about his sexual orientation thought of it as a mental illness or a social deviance; he was afraid of being caught by the police and had to be extremely careful about his behaviour; and so he had difficulty in finding other gay men. Although the homosocial environment gave room for them to experience same-sex desires, which usually resulted in casual sexual encounters, long-term gay relationships or lived with one's boyfriend independent of one's family were quite unimaginable. To act as a good citizen and a good son, the only possible option was to get married.

'I am what I am'

But how about the younger generations, those who were born in the late 1970s or the 1980s? Xiao Guang, who turned 32 in 2008, was born in a small rural village in Guangdong, and grew up in the 1980s. With junior secondary education, he worked as a manual labourer before but is now a staff member of an AIDS NGO. He had realized his same-sex desire when he was in primary school and identified himself as a gay man when he was a teen. He did not then find anyone with whom he could talk. The books he read usually discussed homosexuality as an illness. When he started to work in his late teens he confirmed his identity through some sexual acquaintances. Since then he had desperately wanted to find out more about homosexuality. He is also a Cantonese speaker.

> When I was in junior middle school I read some books . . . they were written by medical doctors and they always said that homosexuality was an illness that could be cured . . . I was so scared . . . I didn't know how to deal with it . . . I talked to no one . . .
>
> When I worked as a car mechanic, I knew I was gay . . . I desperately wanted to find out what it was. I then searched the internet . . . I didn't know how to search, I didn't type the word GAY. . . . I remember I typed AIDS . . . then a lot of websites about gays popped up . . . I literally came out through the internet . . . I then met a lot of friends through the internet . . . and got into gay bars, saunas, etc. . . .

In contrast with those of elder generations, Xiao Guang became empowered through the internet, which provided a significant way for him to identify with the imagined gay community. It was through the internet gay world that he found a lot of information and was subsequently led to the 'real' gay world.

Like Ah Ming and Lao Wu, Xiao Guang lived in a small village where coming out was still a big problem for him.

> Continuation of your lineage is a very important issue. I am the only son in the family . . . and I live in a rural village . . . I have a lot of pressure from my parents . . . they used to find some girls for me . . . I didn't want to see them . . . even if I did, I just said 'No, I don't like her!' . . . They just couldn't understand why . . . they said I was not a good son . . . and most of my classmates and friends got married and I had more pressure . . . and then it was that girl, she was really pretty and good. After I rejected her, my family knew that there must be something wrong with me . . . but I realized that my parents also have a lot of pressure from their friends and relatives . . . I always feel sorry for them . . . as I am not a good son . . .

Using Xiajia village in Heilongjiang as his primary anthropological site, Yan, Y.X. (2003) points out the great transformations that occurred in rural areas in the 1990s, of which the most salient features were the increased importance of the private family and the rise of individuality in courtship and family life. Rural youth seemed to have begun to exhibit more individualistic character, which was evident in their spouse selection, post-marital residence, fertility choices, conjugal relationships and even in a decline of respect and support for the elderly.

It may be true that women have a larger bargaining power in initiating divorce, as is reflected in Ah Jiang's and Ah Ming's cases. However, Yan's descriptions may not entirely apply to the case of rural gay men. If a rural man is reluctant to find a spouse, arranged courtship, rather than free spouse selection, is still common. That's why most of the respondents, such as Xiao Guang, had had the experience of arranged courtship by their parents at one time or another. Moreover, although there might be a decline in overall filial piety, especially with regard to support of the elderly, rural gay men are still vulnerable to the compulsory marriage system, as it seems to be defined as the core filial duty. Younger generations still think that homosexuality is regarded as something of *diulian*, *ng gwong coi* (Cant.) or *taibuqitou* (抬不起頭),[19] in relation to their parents.

So what options have opened up for Xiao Guang?

> I then moved to Shenzhen . . . and later I met some friends, and there was a possibility to move to Shanghai . . . without saying goodbye to my family, I fled to Shanghai – for two years . . .
>
> I think I started to change when I moved out and worked in Shenzhen. I saw a lot of people from overseas companies, and then in Shanghai as well, I saw a lot of things, I met a lot of people, and I learned a lot . . . It is a great transformation for me, moving from one city to another, and I came to accept my own sexuality . . . but sometimes it's more than being gay, it's how you accept yourself, not just in sexuality but many other aspects . . . you should be true to yourself . . .
>
> . . . Now, my family knows that I am gay, but they still want me to get married . . . I still think that failure to get married is a sign of a bad son. . . . But what I can do is be nice to them. I am poor, so I can't give them more money, but that's not important, the most important thing is that we can now talk with no boundaries, and I love them.

China has witnessed the unprecedented growth of a rural-to-urban migrant population, known as the 'floating population' (referred to as 'internal migration' and 'mobile population'), as a result of the series of reforms since the 1980s.[20] Its size has been progressively increasing, and is estimated to have gone from 58.4 million in 1996 to 63.8 million in 1999 (Goodkind and West 2002: 2241), to 98 million in 2005 (Li *et al.* 2007: 31), and to 225 million in 2008 (http://news.cnfol.com/090325/101,1277,5640448,00.shtml, accessed

13 April 2009), and it is projected to reach 300 million by 2015 (Amnesty International 2007: 2). Within this visible floating population of rural migrants is a silent or invisible queer migration. This seems to be a legitimate way of coping with homosexuality and also a way to realize sexuality (see Chapter 7). Xiao Guang first moved to work in Shenzhen and then in Shanghai. These migrant experiences not only helped him accept his sexuality but also nurtured a new sense of selfhood, one that stressed individuality.

To sum up, what contrasts Xiao Guang's story to the earlier narratives are the rise of the internet as the major means for sexual identification; the possibility of migration, which provides conditions for rural youth to cope with homosexuality; and the association of the idea of individuality with being gay, permitting self-expression and the finding of one's 'true' self.

Qiang Ge was born in 1977 into a rather large family, with parents and three siblings, in a small rural village in a hill area of Anhui Province. He had a very difficult time when he was young in facing his sexuality. He stayed in his home village till the completion of post-secondary education and then moved out to the city. In 1995 in Jiangsu Province he met his first love, who turned out to be his lifelong partner. They have been living together since 1998.

> I met my boyfriend in 1995 when I went out to work in Jiangsu. I was instantly attracted to him. We had been together for quite some time, but then, I remember very clearly, it was in 1997, I read an article from a magazine. It reported a homicide case in which a male homosexual burned his boyfriend to death when his boyfriend decided to get married. The gay man then killed himself. The article was written in such a negative way that you just found being gay to be a bad, psycho, pervert thing . . . at that time, I believed firmly what was said in the mass media . . . I thought, they were right, that is, two men together had no hope, no future . . . I told my boyfriend and tried to break up with him and even tried to convince myself to love women, and thought that getting married might be the right thing to do . . .
>
> And I thought Guangzhou was a tolerant and open city . . . that's why I moved here . . . at that time, I thought what I should do was move away from home, the farther the better, so I could lessen the pressure of being gay.
>
> I guess my real enlightenment happened around 1999 or 2000 when I used the internet. For me, the real enlightenment never came from education, but the internet . . . I saw so many gay websites . . . and a new world suddenly opened up to me . . . before, I felt I was the only gay man in the world – or (that there were) two, with my boyfriend . . . I didn't know there are so many gay men in the world . . . I felt not so lonely . . . and I then read a lot of books, some from overseas, like Kinsey's reports, some from China, like books written by Li Yinhe . . . I then realized that being gay is not sick, is not illegal, but normal . . .

> It was in 2005, I told my younger sister. She of course couldn't believe it, as she thought male homosexuals were all psycho type of persons, how come you are one of those? She said, you are my brother, I know you, you are absolutely fine and normal . . . so she couldn't cope with it the first time, as there were two contrasting images: an abnormal mental patient and her healthy normal brother . . . she was so disturbed . . . but then she was fine . . . she told our elder sister, who told our elder brother, and he told our dad . . . well, they [his family] did think that homosexuality was something of *diulian.* Before I came out to them, I simply told them that I wanted to live on my own . . . but now they know. I think they are fine now, but even if they can't accept me, they can't change me . . . I am a strong person, I am what I am . . . I go home once a year . . .

His narrative also reflects the increasing importance of the role of mass media and the internet in gay lives in China. It was the media – in particular, the internet – that Qiang Ge said had opened his eyes. Migration was a way for him to cope with his sexuality. Coming out was not a totally negative experience, and it tended to confirm his individuality.

These two stories exemplify the impacts of broad social transformations on gay lives in contemporary China. First came the deletion of hooliganism as a crime in 1997 and the removal of homosexuality from the list of mental illnesses in 2001, which lessened social discrimination against, and stigmatizing of, homosexuals as perverted and deviant subjects. Yet attitudes do not change so quickly – Qiang Ge's sister held two contrasting images of homosexuals: the societal one of a 'perverted individual', as well as her own experience of a 'normal and loving' brother.

Second, the economic reforms have lessened the state's control of civil society and have led to the emergence of the mass audience of popular culture (and, later, that of the internet). This gives room for the creation of numerous public spaces in the mass media and popular culture that have resulted in more positive representations of homosexuality in magazines, newspapers and academic manuscripts, and on radio talk shows, TV programmes and so on. For example, Qiang Ge was able to read the Kinsey Report and books written by a famous Chinese sociologist, Li Yinhe, who wrote quite positively about homosexuality.

The rapid increase of gay consumption venues such as bars, clubs, bathhouses, karokes, massage parlours, etc., and the rise of information technology (e.g., telecommunication by pager, and later by mobile phone and the internet), have been significant forces for identification of a 'gay community', both in a real and an imaginary sense. Although gay community has its own logic of discrimination, as seen in Chapter 3 and also in the next chapter, most of the respondents had been empowered through gay communities and the internet. Xiao Guang said he had literally 'come out from the internet', and Qiang Ge said his real enlightenment was not through formal education but through the internet.

The economic reforms have had other impacts, in both urban and rural areas. The role and significance of the *danwei* in cities has lessened since the mid 1990s.[21] With respect to the rural population the impact has meant the creation of the massive floating population. Rural youth have moved to big cities for work. This unprecedented growth of rural-to-urban floating migration allows a lot of rural gay men to escape from their family and kinship networks.

As a result, young gay men have more choices for handling their sexuality. Although getting married is still a norm, especially in rural villages, young gay men have different strategies for dealing with it. Lying, especially for young respondents, seems the best way of assuring that their families suffer as little as possible. As one respondent said, 'My parents would think that they *taibuqitou*, there would be a lot of gossip . . . so I will not admit it (homosexuality) – even if they suspect, I won't tell, I will just deny it.' Another commented, 'Whenever I phone back home, I just avoid talking about it.' Others use the 'no-time-no-money formula', in reference to the high bride wealth and lavish dowries that marriage may involve. As discussed in Chapter 4 in the Hong Kong context, such tactics can be seen as 'the weapon of the weak', and this could be read as 'subversive', in the sense that these tactics undermine the marriage institution even though they do not explicitly challenge either it or the hegemonic family values. However, the problem is how long their families will believe such lies and excuses. Young gay men seem to hope that their families, even if they know the truth, will acknowledge their sexuality in silence, or admit it through hidden consent, without openly challenging them.

Nevertheless, there are more and more young gay men who come out to their families, and who live their lives around their gay friends and in gay communities, as illustrated by the account that opens this chapter. Ah Bei, the birthday boy of this account, was 25 in 2008. He was born in Xi'an, the only child of the family. He graduated from a university in Xi'an and went to Guangzhou in 2005, where he was working for a media company. He was one of the respondents who seemed to have little problem in coming out to most of his family members, friends and colleagues.

> I remember I was very young, probably only three years old. I saw a full male body in an acupuncture drawing – the full frontal, the back and the side, all together three pictures . . . it was the first time in my life, from my memory, that I was very clear to myself that I had a strong desire for the male body . . . maybe my dad was a psychiatrist, I knew the medical knowledge when I was very young..and I read quite a lot of books about it . . . I had no such problem of coming out . . . I was pretty out in secondary school . . . and I was very out in university . . . so university was not a place for sexual identification, but a place where I joined in tongzhi activities, volunteered myself to help, and dated boys . . .
>
> I have told my bosses – I have worked for two companies so far, they both know, plus my colleagues . . . we have been getting along very well

> ... even when I was in Xi'an, my classmates and friends knew, they are all heterosexual, and I think we can communicate even better if they know I am homosexual ... and now, you can see a lot of gay stories on television, especially Phoenix TV – quite objective and positive – for example, tongzhi love, or a tongzhi couple who have been living together for more than a decade, what they have been going through, etc.

Since being single has become more of an option, getting married has now become a negative and irresponsible act. Men in rural areas have tended to treat women as functional – there to carry out the domestic chores of cooking, washing, and reproduction rather than as human beings for communication and affection. Older respondents such as Ah Ming, Ah Jiang and Lao Wu all seem to have treated their wives in a traditional and rather misogynous way. Perhaps in this misogynous way they were able to cope with the conflict between homosexuality and heterosexual marriage, and either remained ignorant of, or ignored, their wives' emotional and sexual needs. However, the strategy of marriage was criticized by many of the younger respondents. For example, Qiang Ge said,

> I will never get married because of my family. I think this is something very irresponsible ... it only tells you that you are not true to yourself and you cannot truly identify yourself ... you do not have a firm belief in how you want to live your own life ... if you can really face yourself, really want to live your own life ... then you will discover that the so-called societal discrimination is not such a big thing ... getting married (with a person of the same sex) is our right, not an obligation, like with a woman.

However, not all respondents had such a negative attitude towards marriage. Two narratives arise concerning the idea of marriage: one involves the idea of marriage of convenience; the other, the idea of the security of heterosexual marriage. As marriage is still a big thing, finding a lesbian to marry is one option that respondents frequently mentioned. Robbie, 22 in 2008, born in Hunan, was now in his third year of university study:

> My mum knows that I am now with my boyfriend ... my dad doesn't know ... he is a very stubborn person, and he *ai mianzi* (愛面子) ('loves face'), so it would be very difficult for him to cope ... but my mum and my sister know and they like my boyfriend ... my boyfriend's dad passed away, but his mum knows that he is with me. His mum is fine with me ... my mum is now ok, provided that I should get married with a *lala* (拉拉) (local parlance for lesbian). And I will ... because I also like children. And I should definitely follow my mum's request ... My boyfriend indeed is planning to get married with a *lala*. His mum says the same thing – 'Once you get married and have children, I don't care about

> the thing between you and Robbie'. For me, the ideal would be me and my boyfriend living with a *lala* couple . . .

Robbie sounded a bit naive and idealistic – others have expressed the impracticalities or complexities of such an arrangement, such as those involving legal procedures, the cheating of a sham (sometimes call 'convenience') marriage, the problem of separation at a later stage, the custody rights to children, etc.[22]

Other respondents, who have been out to the gay community for a while, have realized that sex among men is very easy but long-term relationships between men are not. A retreat back to heterosexual marriage seems to be an attractive option for them. Xiao Kai, 21 in 2008, was born in a rural village in Guangdong and was a university student. He was going out with a man, but he had a deep belief in heterosexual marriage.

> Maybe I come from a rural village, my family will definitely want me to get married. And I do think marriage is the final destination of a man. I don't think that tongzhi love can last long . . . so I will get married . . . partly because of my parents, partly because of myself . . . I never have sex with women, but I guess I can accept women, at least psychologically . . .

Ah Ming married in 1994, had a son and got divorced in 1998, thus technically fulfilling his filial duty. However, in 2005, he remarried.

> Yes, I married in 2005 again . . . well, I didn't want to, but my sister-in-law introduced her to me, she is her relative . . . well, she is nice . . . she is a very nice woman, and she is nice to my friends too . . . we now live apart – she lives at home and I live in my company, which is just one block away . . . we are close . . . before the birth of our son, we did have sex . . . but now, we don't . . . well, I do want to live with a man, but it's not allowed by law, and it will just be a weird idea for people . . . but I am fine with my wife and kids . . . eventually I think I quite like it . . .

The desire for companionate heterosexual marriage is very strong for these men, and means a sense of security, protection, and comfort. Like their Hong Kong counterparts (Chapter 4), they tend to assume that a monogamous relationship is the ideal form of relationship. Since this cannot be easily found with a man, they don't mind finding it with a woman. The reason for getting married, then, is less about family pressure for them, and more about the desire for security, which they believe can only be found within the heterosexual marriage institution.

With regard to same-sex marriage, my respondents had two opposing views.[23] One view was that the major obstacles for homosexuals were the pressure to getting married and achieve social acceptance, not legal protection.

Respondents who held this view thought they would not benefit much from same-sex marriage. As Xiao Kai (aged 21 in 2008, university student), said, 'It is not necessary, what I am concerned with is my parents' expectation and how people look at them . . . it would be very *buguangcai*. If your relatives and friends know about this, it's very *diulian*.' The other view, however, was that formal recognition of homosexual rights was of paramount concern. As Ah Jiang said, 'I like same-sex marriage, it's like a protection, you don't fool around, it stabilizes a relationship, and it's healthier'. Qiang Ge held strongly to this view:

> Marriage is a right, not an obligation. From the angle of homosexual rights, same-sex marriage is very important . . . it tells us that you, like the majority of heterosexuals, enjoy the same right. If you want to get married, you know the right is there and you can exercise it by registering it openly. If you don't want to get married, the right is still there.

My respondents' opposing views on same-same marriage tend to reflect ambivalent stands, and perhaps even a paradox in the debate. Recognition of same-sex marriage, through an example of claiming equal rights for homosexuals, presupposes a legal homosexual subject, which, when articulated publicly, might lead to more governmental control, as in the case of HIV surveillance, which has targeted MSM as one of the high risk groups since 1993. Moreover, such a legal subject underscores a homosexual identity, which inevitably enhances the tension of coming out to family and society – which is still believed to be the major obstacle and pressure – rather than legal discrimination, for tongzhi in China. Furthermore, as is rigorously debated in the Western literature, recognition of equal rights often means assimilation to the conventional heterosexual marital model, a way of life that may not been endorsed by all tongzhi.

Needless to say, the coming-out issue is still a dominant one for most Chinese gay men. As discussed in Chapter 4, the Western coming-out model is usually a 'confessional model' (Foucault 1980: 53–73; Boellstorff 2005: 201–9). Not to come out – to remain in the closet – is usually seen as a negative and inauthentic way of being oneself. Although coming out is a political act that challenges the notion of compulsory heterosexuality, Bell and Binnie (2000: 104), using Butler's argument (1993: 226–30), remind us it is necessary to ask for whom being out is an available and affordable option before it can be claimed as a universally necessary part of a gay sexual citizenship. Seidman *et al.* (1999) point out that the closet should not be seen as negative and repressive just because it preserves the power of heterosexism and may tend to fashion a self-loathing homosexual. Closet practices may also be seen as positive, as they avoid the risks of unintended exposure and create a 'protected' social space that permits the individual to fashion a gay self and to navigate a path between the straight and gay worlds. In China, before the reform era, it is almost impossible to imagine a gay life involving moving out of the family and living independently without parents' approval. Even in contemporary times, this is not an easy option.

Then, too, coming out should not be treated as more authentic than staying in the closet. Some of my respondents (e.g., Xiao Kai, Ah Ming) do not necessarily consider homosexuality and heterosexuality to be two contrasting ways of being, between which one has to choose, but see a combination – heterosexual marriage supplemented by homosexual romance – as an option.[24]

Wong (2007) argues that the Western way of 'coming out', for some Chinese scholars (she uses Chou (2000) as an example), is always seen as a problem for tongzhi because it usually implies leaving home (family and parents) and is based on an individualistic notion of selfhood. I agree with Wong (2007) – that 'coming' out and coming home need not be treated as opposing strategies. The narratives of the respondents present a diversity of the experiences of coming out in the Chinese context. For example, Xiao Guang's first coming out actually involved leaving home and moving to Shanghai, but his recent move back to Guangzhou was a partial 'coming home', as Guangzhou is nearer his family.

Being gay as cultural citizenship

Perhaps the greatest difference between the younger generations and the older generations is the rise of individuality, which ties into the notion of cultural citizenship. In the Maoist period, the discourse of citizenship gave way to a discourse of class. An individualistic perspective on citizenship – the idea of an individual citizen who possesses civil, political and social rights – was replaced by a state-centric view of citizenship (So 2004: 247–50). Individual desires were subsumed in the great drive for collectivism, and in revolutionary passion. Homosexuality was thus constructed as a pathological and 'hooligan' trait, which rendered gay men second class citizens.

In the reform period, the mode of citizenship has changed from 'socialist' citizenship to 'market citizenship', in which economic discourses – '"smashing the iron rice bowl", the law of value, supply–demand economics, material incentives, efficiency, maximization of profit, and so on' (Keane 2001: 8, emphasis original) – have all been emphasized. As argued by Keane (2001), economic prosperity facilitates property rights reform, which has given rise to changing social relations that engender new identity and identity formations such as cultural citizenship and 'do-it-yourself' (DIY) citizenship. While cultural citizenship is exemplified by the idea of commonality, with a desire to claim various rights by various minority groups, DIY citizenship (Hartley 1999: 154–59), like the 'technologies of the self' suggested by Foucault (1988), centres on the idea of difference and signifies a new citizen-subject created through a process of active fashioning. The 'new socialist citizen' is thus one who struggles between the collective sense of the people and the sense of the individualized economic actor, both as producer and consumer – between the altruistic 'Lei Feng spirit'[25] and the enterprising entrepreneur; between 'spiritual civilization' and 'material civilization'; and between the pragmatic and the ideological. It is with such a new construction of citizenship that the homosexual is couched as a 'cultural citizen' and has emerged as representing a new kind of humanity, rather than as a pathological or deviant subject. When asked about what 'gay' meant to him, Qiang Ge gave a lengthy discussion.

> People in rural villages are very conservative . . . [What do you mean conservative?] I mean that they cannot bear difference. If you act differently, people would discuss you . . . in rural villages, doors are always open, you greet your neighbours . . . and so gossip is very serious . . . I remember, in the 80s, my sister, who wore a dress, was criticized – 'It's outrageous, how come she wears a dress?' . . . so, in villages, you cannot express your individuality . . . it's a very repressed personality, a repressed humanity . . . people would gossip about people who got divorced or had pre-marital sex . . . well, now it's better . . .
>
> I was born in the 70s. I was very young, so I didn't know much, but society seemed to be a very closed-ended system . . . in the 80s, various kinds of reform had just started, people were still talking about whether a person could open a factory, whether it was fine to employ workers – those kinds of things . . . there was no room for discussing homosexuality . . . and before 1997, homosexuality was still the crime of hooliganism . . . imagine: even if you had found a man, you were always living under the great white fear of being caught . . . and now things have changed – before you just wanted to be the same, but now you want to be different.
>
> Being gay . . . gives me a lot to think about . . . if I were heterosexual, I don't think I would be that reflexive . . . it's being independent, mentally . . . I think, being a minority, we have the right to speak out . . . society should allow different voices . . . AIDS patients should have their own voices and rights, hepatitis B patients should have their own voices and rights, gay men should have their own voices and rights, women should have their own voices and rights . . . plurality and difference is definitely one major theme of this epoch . . .
>
> For me, being gay represented struggle, pain and repression; and then it represented relief; now it's all about happiness . . . I don't know, maybe in the future it will represent pride . . .

Qiang Ge argues that the major difference between the present and the past generations lies in the idea of individuality. In the past, people were fused together through collectivism, and were encouraged towards complete altruism and the ideological battle between classes, and this created 'the people' as subject, at the expense of individuality. At present, however, younger generations stress individuality, difference and the right to be an individual, including a minority individual. This notion of DIY citizenship echoes many respondents' remarks about the significance of being gay. Ah Bei proudly said, 'For me, being gay means culture, enrichment, plurality and passion.' Being gay thus symbolically represents a new kind of humanity – one that taps into the sophistication, liberation and modernity that run throughout cosmopolitanism, neo-liberalism and globalization of popular culture (Rofel 2007: Ch. 3).

When I first met Xiao Guang, he showed me the videos that he made in Shanghai. All were gay love stories. Some were camouflaged, like MTV, with dubbed pop songs as background music; others were more like the documentaries one can easily find at a gay and lesbian film festival. I was surprised by the high quality of the videos he had made. These self-expressive productions in media form seem to exemplify DIY citizenship in the China of the twenty-first century:

> I think I was a person with a very low ego, and a narrow-minded person. I was an introvert. I didn't like to talk, and I never could talk clearly and vividly . . . I was a very confused person . . . coming to Shenzhen and then Shanghai helped me a lot . . .
>
> I like to take photos . . . because I want to express my point of view, I want to express something that is beyond language . . . maybe I am not good at writing or talking, that's why I chose photos and videos . . . I have a very strong urge to express myself . . . when I was in Shanghai, I made those videos that I have shown you . . . I don't think they are art, but just a way of documentation . . . I wanted to make videos about AIDS, about tongzhi's lives, about the struggle of a gay man, the sadness, the loneliness . . . that's why I always shaded my videos in a particular blue tone, to represent the mood . . .

Discussion and conclusion

If 'New China' meant the rule of the Communist Party in 1949, '*new* New China' signifies the post-Mao era of neo-liberal political economy since the late 1990s (Lee 2008: 41–44). Even though in many ways it may be similar to New China, this *new* New China is now presenting itself as a modern, open and global society, triumphantly advertised in the spectacular opening ceremony of the Olympic Games in 2008. But what are the freedoms and pleasures, as well as the dangers and domination, that can be imagined for Chinese people in general, and gay men in particular, in this globalizing *new* New China?

This chapter has tracked the changes in sexual culture in *new* New China, with homosexuality as an example – changes that have accompanied the turn of China from the Maoist 'rule of man' to a modern 'rule of law', and various economic and social reforms, over the past few decades. The changes in law and the economic reforms have resulted in a lessening of state monitoring of private life, and have created a new social environment for (especially young) people to engage in sexual and romantic interaction. Widespread practices outside long-term monogamous heterosexual marriage include the so-called

Western style courtship, pre- and post-marital sex, cohabitation, divorce, etc.; the upsurge of blatant forms of prostitution and pornography; and increased public discussion and advice on intimate and sexual issues in the mass media – to name but a few. China is witnessing a liberalization of attitudes towards sexuality and a rise in individualism. Although we should be cautious about how the state and the market both enable and limit the development of sexual cultures, new sexual spaces and new sexual stories have been emerging. It is with this background – the change in law (especially the deletion of hooliganism in law and the removal of homosexuality from the list of mental illness); the deregulation of private matters, especially in the work unit and the family; the rise of the mass media; the emergence of gay consumer markets and communities; and the advancement of new communication and information technologies, from mobile phones to internet chat rooms – that we have witnessed a proliferation of gay identities and communities since the 1990s. In an interesting twist, tongzhi, a communist term that implies 'similarity' and a common will for altruistic revolutionary passion, has now been transformed to mean gay men and other sexual minorities, and also to represent a notion of 'difference', a queer trace of individuality and cosmopolitanism.

Although the medical and deviance discourses of homosexuality are still compelling, the male homosexual has slowly been dissociated from the image of a pathological and deviant subject and has become a cultural citizen, who can be a good citizen – knowledgeable, civilized, cosmopolitan, and of 'good quality (*suzhi*)'. This of course is a good development – but again, we should be careful as to how the state and the market both liberalize and restrict the development of gay spaces, and as to who is now being marginalized under the hegemonic ideal of cultural (urban) citizenship.

In the present situation, in which organizing and/or unionizing *anybody* in China is illegal for anyone but the Party or the government with the Party's approval and leadership, organizing or unionizing gay people seems to be impossible. This makes the fight for gay rights in any collective sense difficult, and thus also suppresses the development of a collective gay citizenship. Gay venues are still occasionally raided or are forced to close down by the police. Most queer-affiliated NGOs camouflage themselves as health organizations in order to get permission to implement their work, after which they remain subject to surveillance by the government.

However, new stories and narratives of structuring personal life (i.e., a process of gay self-fashioning as a form of DIY citizenship) are emerging: narratives of remaining single, of heterosexual marriage with homosexual romance, of marriages of convenience (gay men and lesbians), or even of same-sex marriage, etc. However, the increasing adoption of a Western model of gayness and the appropriation of a new cultural citizenship marginalize these and other subjects and practices. Although for this research I have not interviewed the wives of my informants, the ideal of heterosexual marriage proposed by some gay men implies that women may remain marginalized subjects. Their emotional and sexual needs can seemingly be left unattended by gay husbands, although women may now have increased social and legal power in marital affairs, as is reflected by their increasing initiation of divorce to end 'failed' marriages. For gay men, staying in the closet becomes a new way of losing face (*diulian*), as it implies an inauthentic self contradicted by the new definition of gay authenticity, which stresses individuality, expression and pride.

Meanwhile, those who cannot attain the new hegemonic ideal of cultural citizenship are being marginalized. Among them, 'money boys' – young Chinese men, usually rural-to-urban migrants, who engage in commercial sexual exchange – seem to be the subject of multiple levels of discrimination in both straight and gay communities. This is the issue that I will now turn to in the next chapter.

7 Sex and work in a queer time and place[1]

> I was a salesman in an electronic shop. But those days were very boring. You got up in the morning, lunched in the afternoon, went home after work, then slept. Go to work, off work, sleep . . . everyday, you repeated the pattern, very boring and very exhausting . . . and at the end, you got only 1,000 yuan a month. For me, I just did one or two clients, then I could earn the same amount as a whole month's salary of a *dagongzai* (打工仔)!
>
> (Ah Jun, 20, ambivalent about his sexual orientation, full-time brothel worker, 3 years, Shanghai, interview in 2004)

> Living standard is very high in Beijing. As a rural migrant, you have to rent a room, buy clothes, etc . . . and if you don't know how to dress, how to act . . . it reflects that you are low *suzhi* (素質) . . . people would look down upon you . . . you have to live up to this urban ideal . . . and also you cannot enjoy a lot of benefits – the basic costs are greater than those for a local . . . like when you are ill, you have to pay extra.
>
> (Ah Tao, 32, gay, full time independent, 8 years, Beijing, interview in 2004)

> I met a client . . . he was so gorgeous, I was instantly attracted to him. I worked very hard that day . . . ha ha . . . the next few days, I so missed him . . . I called him out for dinner, I could sense that he also liked me . . . But . . . he admitted it (that I was an MB), that's why we couldn't (go out then) . . . I felt terribly sad and disappointed. I still keep the money that he gave to me, I haven't used it, just kept it . . . oh, it was really hard for me . . .
>
> (Ah Ji, 24, gay, freelancer, 6 months, Beijing, interview in 2004)

Why do men engage in sex work? To what extent does male prostitution relate to homosexuality, poverty and migration? What are the gains and what are the losses for men who do sex work? What is the state's policy on prostitution, especially the prostitution of men who have sex with men? In what ways do men who sell sex in China relate to citizenship?

This chapter continues the examination of contemporary gay life in China and presents one of its special features – the 'money boys' (MB), the local parlance for men who offer sexual services to other men in exchange for money and/or other rewards, a term used in the gay community as well as by the men who sell sex themselves. I will first outline the emergence of male prostitution in the 1990s and consider the effect on it of the socio-political changes since then. 'Money boys' are part of the still-growing rural-to-urban migration that has resulted from the series of reforms since 1978.

These 'money boys' are a new form of urban subject. Although sex work provides higher incomes and other benefits (e.g., sexual pleasure, control of work, self-esteem) than most work for rural migrants, money boys are caught up in a complex web of domination and power not only in society at large, but also in the gay community. As transient labourers and queer subjects, money boys struggle and negotiate a notion of identity, with the dominant goal of urban citizenship, which involves issues of class, work, gender, sexuality, migrancy, etc.

Same-sex prostitution in China

Discussion of 'prostitution' as such is mainly focused on female prostitutes.[2] In her excellent detailed and historical study of female prostitution in modern Shanghai, Hershatter (1997) argues that female prostitution, in contrast with the sophisticated and urbane images of courtesans with upper-class clientele in the late nineteenth and early twentieth centuries, was increasingly represented as dangerous, disorderly and diseased during the Republican era. Female prostitution, in China, was identified, under the strong influence of Western-inspired ideologies of nationalism and modernization, as unhealthy, and to be eliminated for the sake of the family, and as a national shame and a weakness that should be eradicated for the sake of the nation.[3]

Hershatter (1997) continues to argue that in the Maoist period, great efforts were made to eradicate female prostitution, which was depicted as a remnant of imperialism, a sin from the West, a brutal form of sexual exploitation of women and an obstacle to socialist revolution. Massive propaganda and radical measures were taken, such as the closing down of most brothels and the sending of female prostitutes to re-education centres, etc. The government claimed to have been successful in this effort. However, in the reform era, the government has been forced to acknowledge a widespread resurgence of female prostitution as a result of greater economic disparities, increased relative poverty and rural-to-urban migration, and a changing sexual culture.[4]

Study of male prostitution is relatively rare, but male prostitution (serving men)[5] has been evident throughout Chinese history, and a highly developed system of male prostitution was documented for the Song Dynasty (AD 960–1279) (Van Gulik 1961: 163; Samshasha 1997: 130–34; Hinsch 1990: 92–97). Since the 1990s, male prostitution has also caught government and media attention, partly because of the rapid increase of visible gay consumption venues such as bars, clubs, massage parlours, saunas, karaokes, etc. and partly because of the upsurge of HIV infection among the MSM population (China Ministry of Health *et al.* 2006: 2; Zhang and Chu 2005; Wong *et al.* 2008; Kong 2008).

The state would like to eliminate all prostitution and make special efforts to crack down on sex-related businesses and parties. Male prostitution complicates the situation, as the organization of the male sex industry always involves the element of homosexuality, which carries further social stigma. However, the state's market-economy ideology emphasizes 'material civilization' (as contrasted with 'spiritual civilization'), which is manifested best in terms of consumerism and the encouragement of the commodification of almost everything, including both female and male bodies, and which unintentionally encourages rural and semi-rural young men and women, especially, to enter the sex industry.

At present, third party prostitution (i.e., organizing, inducing, introducing, facilitating, or forcing another person to engage in prostitution) is a criminal offence in China, punishable by a number of years of imprisonment, with possible fines. First party prostitution is not criminalized but is regarded as socially harmful, and both female prostitutes and their clients are subject to periods of reform detention, also with possible fines (Jeffreys 2007: 154). In 2004, 34-year-old Nanjing City native Li Ning was sentenced to jail for eight years and fined 60,000 *yuan* for organizing male–male prostitution services. Since this widely publicized case, and similar cases, the government has tended to treat same-sex prostitution in the same manner as heterosexual prostitution, and has implemented *yanda* (嚴打 'hard strike')[6] campaigns against same-sex prostitution as a result of the rapid rise of HIV/AIDS infection in the commercial sex industry, and as a way to regulate the 'inappropriate' range of same-sex sexual activities.[7]

Becoming a money boy[8]

In China, men who serve men are most commonly called 'money boys'. Other frequent terms are *yazi* (鴨子 'duck'), *haizi* (孩子) or *xiaohai* (小孩) (both meaning 'child'), or simply called *maide* (賣的 'for sale'). Men who serve women are also called *yazi* ('ducks'), or *shaoye* (少爺 'young masters').[9] Although some of my informants serve both genders, their predominant clientele is male.

There are many types of men who sell sex,[10] but four are common in China. The first type is the full-time independent worker or street hustler, who mainly works on his own, hustling in public areas such as parks and bars and through the increasingly popular cyber channels of the internet. These venues usually provide opportunities for money boys to meet potential clients. Sex normally takes place elsewhere (e.g., in hotels), after negotiation has been carried out. The second type is the full-time brothel worker, who usually works under an agent at a sex venue (e.g., a male brothel or massage parlour). Clients can choose boys, and sex and/or erotic massage may take place in a room or cubicle inside the venue, or clients can buy the boys out (*chutai* 出台) for a few hours, or even to stay overnight elsewhere. These boys usually live at the venue and are kept by a pimp (called *jingli* (經理 'manager'), *laoban* (老板 'boss'), *mamasan* (媽媽桑) or *laolao* (姥姥), in local parlance), and cannot go out without permission. The third type is the part-time or freelance worker, including the worker who has 'quit' the job but who freelances occasionally when he is short of money or is requested by old clients. The final type is the houseboy (*beiyangde* 被養的, in local parlance) – i.e., a boy kept by a sugar daddy.[11]

Ah Yang, aged 22 in 2004 (ambivalent about his sexual orientation, junior middle-school education) has the most representative story as an MB. He was a brothel worker in Beijing but was unemployed at the moment of interview, as the brothel (camouflaged as a bar/restaurant) had just been raided by the police.

> I was born in a small village in Jiangsu. I finished junior middle school and worked as a waiter and a factory worker, but the wages were far too low, only about six or seven hundred *yuan* per month. I then decided to leave my hometown. I chose Beijing, as it was one of the four municipalities of China.[12] Wages should have been higher than in other areas. That's why I came to Beijing . . . And then I got a job in a computer factory through a friend. The work was to assemble electronic parts. They only provided one meal, and I didn't have much left after a month, not to mention sending money back home. I thought, as I was moving out to work, I had to send some money back home. I really wanted to earn more money . . . and then I got in contact with this [industry] through a friend, that's how I started . . . this job is much better than others . . . I have been working as a MB for half a year. I worked for two bosses before, now I am working for Manager Sun, but the bar was just raided by the police, so I just hang in there . . .

As a result of the unprecedented growth in the floating rural-to-urban migrant population (Solinger 1999; Goodkind and West 2002; Li *et al.* 2007; Amnesty International 2007), young rural men with diverse backgrounds – part of this massive floating population, with ages ranging from early twenties to early thirties, mostly single and homosexual, with diverse educational backgrounds ranging from poorly-educated to university level – have increasingly entered the sex industry and offered same-sex sexual services to other men. My informants were among them.[13]

My informants' work histories are complex. Before entering the sex industry, most had worked at many, usually temporary menial, low paid, long-hour jobs, such as in manual construction work, manufacturing or heavy industry (e.g., car mechanic, factory worker), or in the retailing and catering service industries (e.g., chef, waiter, hotel bellboy, security guard, salesperson, barber). They had entered the sex industry through friends in their home towns or through contacts with agents whom they met at gay bars, in parks, on the internet or in shops (Kong 2005a). Ah Yang, quoted above, is one of these –

a young man in his early twenties, with average education, who had desperately wanted to move out from his rural home, hoping for a brighter life in the cities, but ended up working as a factory worker with a very low wage, and came to realize that urban life could be as hard as rural life.

However, the city represents not only opportunities for work, but also other opportunities. I met Xiao Jin through his former brothel manager, Mr Sun, in Beijing in 2004. Xiao Jin was then 27 – a bit older than other brothel workers, who were usually in their early twenties, but he was very well mannered. He was poorly educated, having grown up in a small village in Jiangxi. He was gay, and had had a boyfriend for six years, but his boyfriend had passed away in 2003. Desperate for money and a new life, he fled to Beijing and worked as an escort for half a year. He had then quit the job and started a small business, but he continued to freelance with some regular clients.

> After he passed away, I didn't know how to face the city anymore . . . and I didn't know how to face people from the *danwei* (單位), as they knew my relationship with him . . . and there were so many memories . . . I then quit my job and fled to Beijing . . . I wanted to start a new life . . . I needed to survive, I had to depend on myself . . . so I started working for this . . . and why choose Beijing? I think: this is the capital of the country, it's a big city, with a very long history. I find it a very tolerant city . . . sometimes, at night, when I walk down the road, I find there is something behind this city, behind modernity and sophistication, behind those walls and bricks, there is something special that I can't tell, but it is liberating . . .
>
> I knew of this kind of job through the internet . . . so I thought, ok, first, I have nothing, I have to start from scratch, I need to survive. I depended on no one but myself . . . second, I just wanted to be 'not myself' . . . doing this could distance myself from my old self . . . I wanted to have a complete change . . .

For Xiao Jin and many other money boys, big cities like Beijing and Shanghai represented modernity, sophistication and freedom. It was the ideal place for them to forget their pasts, and they believed that they could experience a new world, different from that of their home towns. For Xiao Jin, the past was his lost love with his passed-away boyfriend and the difficulty of handling his homophobic colleagues. For Ah Tao, a 32-year-old gay man who had junior middle-school education and had been an independent worker for eight years, who had settled in Beijing, it was the homophobic environment of his home village and the desire to experience sexuality in big cities. When I interviewed him in 2004, he said,

> My family was very poor. I had no other options to earn money apart from leaving home. . . . And I desperately wanted to leave [my home town]. My home village is very rural, small and conservative . . . There is no such platform (*pingtai* 平台) for you to survive. The whole atmosphere is very

> repressive. They don't understand you . . . They would think that it [homosexuality] is a sickness, a perversion – they would take me to see doctors! . . . and my family always ask me when I will get married. That's why I haven't gone back home for four years. I don't know how to answer them . . .

Discussions of migration suggest that a variety of push and pull factors – structural, social, economic and even cultural – motivates the continuous tides of internal migration. The shortage of land, improper land use, and the surplus of labour in rural areas push migrants to leave their hometowns. The demand for labour for urban construction, both by the state and the private sector, and the widening rural–urban income disparity, attract them to come to cities (e.g., Li 1996: 1124–33; Mackenzie 2002: 308–9). Some studies offer plausible explanations of how rural youth are caught by a specific subject formation of citizenship in the reconfigured rural–urban distinction of the post-Mao development discourse under the ideology of 'globalizing China' (e.g., Solinger 1999; Zhang 2001; Pun 2003, 2005; Yan, H.R. 2003a, 2003b). In addition to these factors, there seem to be hidden reasons for migration – namely, that migration provides a way to cope with homosexuality, away from the homophobic village or work environment; as well as being a way to realize, in the big cities, the desire for sexual, material and affective self-interest.[14] Migration for these young rural migrants meant so much – it was a way to earn money, a way to experience a new world, a way to realize gay sexuality, and a way to escape from the rural homophobic environment, and especially from the familial pressure to get married.

However, my informants were quite disappointed once they came to big cities such as Beijing and Shanghai. As rural migrants, economic hardship meant many things to them – not only basic survival in the city, but also their continual support for their parental families and for siblings' tuition fees, and/or to repay family debts incurred from misfortunes that included natural disasters and illnesses. Sex work thus provided an attractive option for them. Nearly all treated sex work as a source of income, and engaged in it for a specific primary purpose: money.

Ah Tao continued his story, telling of how he came to realize that his body could be a means to earn money:

> My family background is not good, I have no other option but to do this. This is a fast track for earning money . . . I didn't realize that I could be a money boy . . . before, I just wanted to play with other men, it was more a biological need. When I came to Beijing, I realized that the world was so big, and you could actually use your body to earn money . . . so I started doing it . . .

Can sex work provide the solution for these rural-to-urban migrants? Can money solve their problems? In the following section, I will discuss the complexity of the three major interlocking identifying characteristics of money boys – rural migrancy, the nature of their sex work and their sexual orientations – in order to show how they must struggle with the confines of the hegemonic ideal of urban citizenship.

Subjects of triple discrimination

Being a rural-to-urban migrant

Rural-to-urban migrants are denied various rights as urban citizens, primarily due to the household registration (*hukou* 户口) system. This is a unique system, based on locality and family background, which has been in place since 1958, according to which rural migrants are not entitled to obtain the same benefits as local residents of cities – benefits such as government-subsidized housing, healthcare, employment, education for children and many more.[15] Although the Chinese government has proposed some changes and reforms to the *hukou* system since the late 1990s, the problems have not been resolved and situations vary from one city to another (Li and Piachaud 2006; Zhu 2007[16]).

As some literature suggests (Amnesty International 2007; Li *et al.* 2007), rural-to-urban migrants have suffered from discrimination, as well as from stigmatization, in virtually all aspects of their lives – discrimination in the legal system, the economic system (e.g., in the factories) and the social welfare system (e.g., healthcare, housing, education of children). They are discriminated against by various agents, such as policemen, government officials, employers, landlords, local residents, etc. With very little chance of gaining permanent urban residency, and thus full access to various rights, migrant workers are deprived in employment (e.g., through denial of labour contracts; forced overtime, denial of holidays; unpaid, underpaid or delayed wages; and even through denial of the right to leave employment), in housing (e.g., through exclusion from housing subsidies), in health care (e.g., through lack of access to health information and treatment) and in education (e.g., through the lack of education rights for immigrant children) – to name but a few types of discrimination.

Guang (2003) argues that state practices and popular culture have both contributed to the formation of a new urban identity at the expense of the production and reproduction of a homogenous category of rural migrants. On the one hand the state, using the excuse of the 'city image', has maintained 'urban orderliness' by disciplining the city's marginals – 'beggars, vagabonds, petty criminals, migrants of the three withouts,[17] and other shabby-looking individuals' (p. 631). On the other hand, popular culture, as manifested in youth magazines, has radically contrasted the image of urban citizens (Guang uses the Shanghainese as an example), who are 'shrewd, self-reliant, calculating, tolerant, comprador [sic], respectful of highbrow culture, and open to foreign influence' (p. 632); with that of the backward-looking, provincial, rural migrants, who are either lazy and only 'spend their nonworking hours on sleep, rest, and meals' (p. 629) or are simply mindless workaholics who 'repeat the dorm-to-work-and-back-to-dorm cycle' (p. 629) of hard life. It is through such a radical binary division between the two – 'cosmopolitan versus agrarian, spiritual versus economic, highbrow versus lower class, etc.' (pp. 632–33) – that rural migrants are placed at the lower end of the hierarchy of urban residence. The *hukou* system thus contributes to and/or combines with other factors – their insecure or even illegal status, their lack of knowledge and lack of rights, their social and economic differences with local residents, their sense of social isolation and cultural inferiority – and thus contributes to the vulnerability of rural-to-urban migrants living in cities.

Although moving out from his hometown was a dream for Ah Tao, he, like other rural migrants, soon realized the difficulty of living in a city. Due to his rural *hukou*, he could not enjoy various social and medical benefits. More importantly, perhaps, his rural status, which was embodied in the way he looked, his accent, and the assumed low 'quality' (*suzhi*) he possessed, marked him off from the cultural formation of an urban citizen. He thus served as a marginal subject in terms of the rural–urban dichotomy. As cited in the beginning of this chapter, he complained that the living standard was very high in Beijing, and he had to rent a room, buy clothes and dress well, in order to live up to the urban ideal and escape the bad label of 'low *suzhi*'.

So how do the money boys respond to these disadvantages? Some of the respondents argued that urban citizens were rude and snobbish, while people from rural areas were more authentic and sincere. Xingxing, aged 23 in 2004, gay, with senior middle-school education, who had been freelancing as a MB for six months through parks and the internet in Shanghai:

> People from rural areas have *suzhi*. For example, if you asked directions on the street, people would sincerely show you the way. In a bus, they would give way to the elderly. But in Shanghai or in Guangzhou, I don't see much of this. City people are rude and snobbish . . . they are actually of lower *suzhi*.

Being a rural migrant is thus not always seen negatively. Xingxing, like other MBs, said he would make use of his rural status to package himself according to his value in a higher currency – as innocent, naive, obedient, clean, etc. Nevertheless, rather than rebel against the urban ideal and use their rural status as a currency in the market exchange for sex work, most money boys actively promote themselves and attempt to become urban. Ah Qing (aged 22 in 2004, gay, with junior middle-school education) came to Shanghai from a small village, and had appropriated a discourse to refashion himself as an urban citizen.

> A good MB is a good urban citizen. He should be one who is good at calculation. He knows the steps of how to cruise a man – not by doing things illegally like theft, murder, etc. but by using his capital . . . he should

> earn more money, which can support him for living a good life. That is, he should have his own flat, dress well, look good. It is better if he has computer skills and can speak English . . . these are all the qualities he has to possess . . .

This image of a good citizen echoes the newly emerging image of being gay, and many are keen to perform as a 'proper' gay. As Xiao Tui (aged 22 in 2004, gay, senior middle-school education) said: 'In Shanghai, you can see a lot of gay men. They dress very well, with all the big labels, accessories, etc . . . this is how you should look!' Engaging in sex work provides the material conditions for them to live up to the high standards of the cities, while performing as a 'proper' gay provides the cultural condition for them to present themselves as cosmopolitan subjects. Both enable them to negotiate a notion of cultural citizenship that upgrades their status from that of rural-to-urban migrant. However, engagement with these two 'new' identities poses new challenges for them.

The nature of sex work

As previously mentioned, money was the principal and initial reason given for entering the sex industry. However, when asked about other rewards than material ones, respondents mentioned aspects of satisfaction that can be classified according to three categories: sexual pleasure from work and ensuring gay identity; control of work, such as flexibility and freedom in the job; and self-esteem and self-development for upward mobility.

Ah Dong, (aged 26 in 2004, gay, senior middle-school education) had worked as a freelancer in Beijing for half a year.

> I don't just work for money. It's because we are quite repressed sexually, and at our age we have our own biological needs . . . and in front of my clients I can be relaxed and say I love men! I am a tongzhi! I think this job is a psychological balance for me – it's a way to meet friends, a place where I can relax. It's a stage where I can lead a show, a show of self-expression.

The respondents, especially those who were gay or ambivalent about their sexual orientation but were interested in men, frequently mentioned the sexual pleasure of the job and associated it with a confirmation of gay identity and a model for male sexuality.

Another type of satisfaction was found in their control of their work, in contrast to what was experienced in other menial and tedious jobs. Ah Wei (aged 25 in 2004, gay, junior middle-school education) worked on his own and found clients mainly in bars. He had been working as a full-time independent MB for eight years. He had just returned to Beijing from Shenzhen:

> Freedom! For other jobs, you have to work on time; for this job, you can sleep whenever you want, eat whenever you like, it's quite free really . . . and if I have money, I will only choose those clients I like to talk to – if they want to go for it, that's fine; if not, that's still ok . . .

Quoted in the beginning of this chapter, Ah Jun (aged 20 in 2004, ambivalent about his sexual orientation, junior middle-school education) was born in a village in Shenyang. He had worked in Beijing and Chengdu before and was now settled in Shanghai. He had worked mainly in brothels for three years. He had had a chance to leave sex work through a client's support: 'I had been working as an MB for three months, and then a client told me not to do this anymore. I then quit, and he rented a flat for me and found a job for me.' But he found it boring to work as a salesman in an electronics shop, and he had earned much more as a MB than as a salesman. He eventually decided to stay in the brothel:

> I told him one day that I couldn't live that sort of life. He was very angry and upset. He asked me to move out of the flat once the lease was due. I then went back to the brothel . . .

The third type of satisfaction is self-esteem and social mobility. Xiao Yu (aged 26 in 2004, gay but married a woman, primary educated), a freelancer who stayed in Beijing, said:

> I worked purely for money. I owed money to others and I was very anxious, that's how I got into this job . . . but once I got into this job, I found I had learnt something more. I have known a lot of people through this job. They have come from all sorts of classes, they were helpful to me . . . I was a very ordinary, average *dagongzai*. But since I have worked at this (job), I have known a lot of things. I have learnt a lot of things from the upper class and I have been in and out of a lot of luxurious places . . . the change was fundamental, from inside to outside . . . and I know this social networking will be very useful for my future . . . this is my major gain!

Xiao Yu was then running a salon with a friend and also working as an insurance salesman. Social networking was definitely a very important asset for him.

Qualitative or ethnographic studies in other countries have shown that male prostitution, generally, offers a relatively attractive alternative when compared with other ill-paid, repetitive and demoralizing menial jobs, not just in terms of monetary reward but also in terms of other perceived benefits such as sexual pleasure, control of work, flexibility and freedom, self-esteem and social mobility.[18] This seems also to be particularly the case for money boys in China. Emphasizing these benefits may be a coping strategy that money boys employ to justify their engagement in this highly stigmatized job.[19] By doing so they assert that they are not just money machines, but can escape the destiny of becoming a *dagongzai*, which appears to them to be the overwhelming prevalent outcome of rural-to-urban migration, and can live up to the ideal of urban citizenship.

However, sex work entails a lot of risks and dangers. Due to the government's *yanda* campaign, my informants were constantly worried that they might be caught by the police and sent back home. As sex work involves intimate contact with clients, they ran the risk of contracting sexual diseases. Although no HIV/AIDS cases were reported, some had contracted various sexually transmitted diseases such as crabs, herpes, syphilis, gonorrhea and urethritis; and the absence of HIV/AIDS cases should be qualified, as more than half of them had not had an HIV test, partly because they believed they had taken sufficient precautions, so that health checkups were unnecessary, but more importantly because their rural *hukou* required higher payments for medical care, and because they did not want to disclose their same-sex sexual activities to medical professionals, fearing that any medical results might be reported to the government. Thus it is the interlocking of their three identities – as rural-to-urban migrants, as homosexuals and as prostitutes – that makes their lives difficult.

Two features of hardship are salient in their daily working lives, the first being encounters with bad clients, or undesirable ones – i.e., clients who are demanding, rude, rough or even violent.[20] Ah Jun said:

> Some brought you out and you had to drink with them and took pills with them, they wanted to get 'high' and then brought you home and had sex with you . . . they could then do it many times . . . day and night . . . and they asked you to lick here or there, do this and that . . . a lot of demands . . .
>
> Sometimes they would say you didn't give them a good blow job and accused you of your low quality service and rang to your Laolao and asked Laolao to bring another boy . . . I then went back without getting any money, and was scolded by Laolao, who thought I didn't do good. The client had got two boys to serve him – paid for one but had two boys! It always happens, especially when you meet *laoyoutiao* (老油條 'a slippery customer') – who find money boys on a regular basis. They know the trick!

Xiao Bao (aged 20 in 2004, gay, junior middle-school education) formerly worked at massage parlours but now had been kept by a man for a year in Shanghai. He spoke of his fear of street hustling.

> Working in parks is dangerous. Some people don't come to parks for an MB, but for robbery. They would bring you to come and rob your money. We have our mobile phones and a few hundred *yuan*, that's all we have. If we are robbed, we are dead!

The second hardship feature is that most of them experienced feelings of meaninglessness about their jobs. As Ah Jun said:

> I think I kind of abandon myself. I don't want to learn anything. If I have business [meaning clients] I work; if not, I just watch television, play cards, etc. Every single day I am idle, I don't know how a day is spent . . . time just passes . . . I can't think about the future, I don't know what it will be . . . I just hang in there . . .

As contrasted with the disciplined labor of *dagongzai*, who are anxious about the 'too much work, too little time' production formula, money boys live according to an opposite work logic, that of 'too much time, too little work'. Furthermore, any idle time they commonly experience is not quite the same as idle time for *dagongzai*, as they must always be ready for a sudden call from clients, managers or sugar daddies, so that it is difficult to say when they are at work and when they are off work. The work demands full awareness, even when they are on idle. This psychological discomfort sometimes drives them crazy. As Ah Wei said, 'You are not happy, you feel emptiness and meaninglessness. When I was in Shenzhen, I took drugs every day with friends. You felt so empty, you felt so uncomfortable.' Ah Wei indulged in soft drugs, but others were into gambling with cards or mahjong. Writing mainly in reference to female sex workers, but applicable to male sex workers, Brewis and Linstead (2000a) rightly point out that 'managing time as a prostitute can be compared to managing time in other occupations where boredom is a problem and psychological survival is a paramount concern' (p. 87).

One major coping strategy is to disassociate from the job. My respondents viewed their engagements in sex work differently. Some adopted a sexual-victim identity, arguing that they were losers, seduced and cheated by the 'false' love of pimps. Ah Ji (aged 24 in 2004, gay, university education) said, 'I love him (the pimp) but I also hate him. I hate him because he dragged me into this circle. He made me become an MB . . . my life is ruined.' Others insisted that this was not 'work', just a means to earn money – Ah Gang (aged 22 in 2004, ambivalent about his sexual orientation, senior middle-school education): 'This is not a job, it's just a tool to make money.' Still others stressed that it was simply a way to meet 'friends' and have fun, downplaying the basic logic of the exchange of their body for material rewards. For example, Xiao Bin (aged 22 in 2004, gay, junior middle-school education) said, 'You meet a lot of people, from all walks of life, making friends . . . I never treat it as a job, it's just an entertainment.' Some others treated it as an ordinary job, with gains and losses, such as Ah Tian (aged 20 in 2004, ambivalent about his sexual orientation, senior middle-school education), who said, 'This is just like any other job, plus earning a bit more money. That's it, really.' Finally, some even viewed themselves as entrepreneurs who treated sex work as a business and a platform from which to reach higher goals. Such was Xiao Jin (aged 27, gay, primary school education): 'This is just a springboard for me, it's not just about earning money. In this job, you have a lot of opportunities. If you know how to grasp the chances, you can jump out of the loop.'

These diverse interpretations of sex 'work' not only juxtapose and contradict the apparent binaries of public/private, work/leisure, love/sex, client/friend, etc.

that underline the logic of production (work), consumption (leisure) and intimacy (love), but also provide coping strategies for handling this highly stigmatized job with its intense emotional toll.

It is apparent that sex work, in terms of the life cycle, is rather short term, as the sex industry is constantly looking for 'fresh meat', so that the longer one is in it, the less one earns. Sex workers know their time is running out. Xiao Bin's (aged 22 in 2004, gay, junior middle-school education) comment is shared by most money boys: 'This won't last long. This is *chi qingchun fan* (吃青春飯 'eating the rice bowl of youth'). You just can't do it when you get old. No one will come to you.' They all agreed that 'you get in, make quick money, and get out of it'. Their bodies would all run out of opportunity for prosperity, and most would be quite unable to realize prosperity, as the prospectus of sex work is rather limited, leading only to becoming a pimp or manager, which involve totally different skills – and managing sex workers (i.e., third-party prostitution) is a criminal offence in China.

My informants were highly mobile, transient and temporary, and moved back and forth from one occupational setting to another, from sex work to other jobs, and from one city to another. For example, Ah Wei was born in Shandong. He came to Beijing in 1996 and found work as a salesman in a boutique through a friend. He later found out that the boss was a gay man, and the boss became his sugar daddy for two years. Ah Wei later hustled in parks and bars and worked as an escort or brothel worker in many places like Shenzhen, Hong Kong, Zhuhai, etc. Later he returned to Beijing in 2004 and worked on his own.

No matter how they look at their work, others seemed to have a fixed view of them. The social stigma of prostitution, partly induced and reinforced by the government's *yanda* campaigns, is strong. Prostitution has always been framed as a 'deviant occupation', especially for men, and legal persecution and moral condemnation define prostitution as an illegal and immoral institution, so that prostitutes are constructed as dangerous, undesirable, deviant and diseased individuals.

Hiding their work seemed to be a common strategy for dealing with social discrimination against prostitution. They were very reluctant to tell others about their work. They usually lied to friends and families, saying that they worked at other jobs. Ah Tian (aged 20 in 2004, ambivalent about his sexual orientation, senior middle-school education), who had been working as a full-time brothel worker for one year), said,

> No, all my friends and my family, they don't know what I am doing . . . I lied to them. I said I was working as a waiter in a restaurant . . . I won't tell them (what I am doing) . . . they will definitely discriminate against me.

Many, like Ah Tao, used migration as a strategy to hide their work identities, as they had left their home villages and went home only occasionally.

Although they may be able to live in a closet in front of their families, friends and colleagues if they have other jobs, they cannot do so in the gay community, as gay men are their potential clients. The gay community has a negative impression of money boys (Jones 2005: 159–60, 2007: 102–3; Rofel 2007: 103–6, 2010). Most of my gay respondents in Guangdong expressed quite negative impressions of money boys. Ah Ming (aged 42 in 2008, self-employed gay man who married twice, whose story appeared in the previous chapter) complained about them:

> I had such bad experiences . . . they looked very pitiful and said they were students, they had no money. I then gave them money, a few hundred *yuan*. I didn't mind giving them money or paying for their dinners, but I hated that they cheated on you – they were dishonest. . . . There was one time in a park. He was following me, I thought he fancied me, and he winked at me, so we did it. While he was blowing me, he was taking my wallet without my notice . . . and then there was another time . . . I was taking a shower, and he just took my cell phone and left . . . I think, altogether, I lost about ten mobile phones . . .

In fact, what Ah Ming reports is often true. Some of my respondents admitted to me quite frankly that they cheated and stole money from clients. Ah Yuan (aged 25 in 2004, gay, senior middle-school education) who had been a full-time independent hustler in parks for one and half years in Shanghai, told me,

> At one time I stole a lot of money. [How much?] A few thousand *yuan* – but for me, it was a lot. I was so happy . . . but then I was caught by the police a few days later and was investigated . . . but they didn't find anything, and I was released later!

Ah Wei said:

> It's easy to cheat clients of their money. But you have to wait – not the first few times . . . wait till he becomes your friend . . . and say you have some family problems, you have to go home . . . like your dad or mum is sick, so you need money to buy tickets . . . or you simply say you lost your mobile, etc.

If the reports of a lot of gay men about money boys' misconduct are true, it is equally true that the same applies to gay clients, as the misconduct of clients is not uncommon. The gay community tends to emphasize the former and ignore the latter. Using the term *suzhi*, the gay urban community tends to equate both rural migrants and money boys with thieves, thugs, gangs and blackmailers, and lumps them in the homogenous category of 'low *suzhi*' citizens. The issue of *suzhi* generally comes up in relation to desired children, under the restrictions of population control (Anagnost 2004), and in relation to the desired bourgeois lifestyle, as distinct from the rural, under neo-liberal governmentality (Yan, H.R. 2003a).[21] However, Rofel (2010) succinctly argues that the use of the term in the gay community reveals the newly exclusionary force of gay men in China, who are keen to draw a boundary, under the influence of neo-liberalism and cosmopolitanism, to separate themselves from money boys – a separation that encodes a difference between licit and illicit desires, between good and bad homosexuals, between love and money, etc. As a result, money boys are alleged to contribute to the overall *luan* (亂 'chaotic') situation of the gay community.

Being gay

Like other rural gay men, as discussed in the last chapter, the gay money boys I interviewed expressed fear and worry about their sexual orientation. Most had not come out to their friends or families, and worried that their friends or family members would not accept their homosexuality, as they thought people would consider homosexuality to be abnormal, sick or perverted. They were afraid that the news would break the hearts of friends and family and worried that they would distance themselves from them. They were reluctant to face their families, believing their gayness would bring shame to their families and lead to the loss of face. They, too, were constantly pressured by their families to get married.

Although moving to cities gave them a lot more space to experience gay sexuality and identify themselves as gay men, gay identity has increasingly been associated with consumption, so that they had all learnt how to consume and look 'gay' in order to live up to the ideal of gay citizenship, as well as to become visible and marketable objects of consumption for their gay clients. As Xiao Tui said, 'You have to buy clothes, cosmetics, etc. A gay has to take good care of himself. You have to look good in being gay.' They had invested a lot of time and money on clothes, accessories, hairstyles, etc., as necessary 'work expenses' in order to perform as 'proper' gay men.

However, gay identity sometimes clashes with work identity and puts money boys in a more vulnerable position, both emotionally and physically. Engagement in sex work means performing erotic labour and drawing boundaries between public and private selves – between what they sell and what they don't sell, between which areas of their bodies are allowed for access and which are off limits.[22] A lot of money boys make great efforts to maintain these boundaries. My informants told me that they did not believe in 'true love' between men in the gay world in general, or with gay clients in the sex industry in particular. Ah Jun's remark was very typical of what I heard from my respondents.

> Since I have got into the (gay) circle, I have realised that there is no true love between tongzhi. Two men living together – no matter how much they love each other, how much they want to commit to each other, they will be set apart in the end . . . and in this circle (the sex industry), I think it's stupid to fall in love with a client . . . this is also taught by

> Laolao (his boss) – he always tell us not to fall in love with clients and . . . even with anyone.

One derivative of this attitude is the separation of sex from work and from love. Like the men reported in Browne and Minichiello's (1995, 1996a, 1996b) study of male sex workers in Melbourne, my informants separated 'work sex', which was regarded as 'meaningless' and with affection shown only as a performance, from 'personal sex', which was regarded as passionate and intimate, carried out only with their non-paying affective partners. As Ah Wei said:

> Big difference. With clients, if he wants anal intercourse, I will lie down and let him do me. If he wants a blowjob, I will give it to him. But with my boyfriend I will be very active. Even if he doesn't request anything, I will do it for him . . . and even if we hug each other, you will feel the passion.

Despite the above, however, almost all the money boys I interviewed told me that they had crossed the boundary, one time or another. Ah Ji (aged 24 in 2004, gay, university student) fell in love with the brothel manager and worked for him for half a year. He never treated sex work as a means for making money, but more as a way to find a boyfriend. As cited in the beginning of this chapter, he was in great pain once when he encountered a client whom he could regard as 'heaven trade' (c.f. Browne and Minichiello 1995: 610–11) – that is, a client who represented the worker's fantasy and symbolizes a 'potentially happy future'. Such clients represent something more than just money. They are special encounters for the worker.

On the one hand, most informants knew that it was difficult or even impossible to find 'true love' in the gay and the sex work communities, but on the other hand, they seemed to dream of a happy future, brought by a client with whom they could find 'true love'. The emotional damage brought by this contradiction from such encounters can be something unbearable, when love enters the realm of 'work'.

A more serious outcome may result when they blur the boundary between work and friendship. Although they all reported condom use at work, they sometimes broke this rule, especially if they treated the client as a friend. Ah Gang (aged 22 in 2004, ambivalent about his sexual orientation, senior middle-school education) who had been a full-time brothel worker for one and a half years, said, 'I did it once (unprotected sex), I didn't use it (condom). I was a bit drunk, and the feeling was quite good, and he was an old client.' Ah Wei said, 'I have known him for a long time, more than half a year, and he is my regular client. He said he didn't like condoms and he tested negative so we didn't use it.'

With ambivalent work identities, they very easily began to consider a customer as an 'old' customer after a few visits. They then began to regard him as a friend after further visits. Ah Lin was 22 in 2004, gay, with a senior middle-school education, and had been working in the industry for two years. He was being kept by a man, his ex-client, in Shanghai. The conversation below reflects his double standard concerning using condoms for his present boyfriend/ex-client and his ex-boyfriend.

Ah Lin:	. . . yes, of course I always use it (condom) when I am working. But the year when I was living with my boyfriend, we didn't.
Interviewer:	But he was also an MB right?
Ah Lin:	Yes . . . when he was working, he used it, he just didn't use it with me.
Interviewer:	Why?
Ah Lin:	Because we treated each other as BF ('boyfriends').
Interviewer:	So, you don't use condoms with your BF?
Ah Lin:	He said that if we didn't 'mess it up', we didn't need to use a condom.
Interviewer:	But how do you know that he didn't 'mess it up' himself?
Ah Lin:	Well . . . I . . . trusted him.
Interviewer:	So do you use a condom with your present BF?
Ah Lin:	Oh, yes, because I always treat him as my client . . . Although he treats me as his BF.

The condom holds a special symbolic meaning for these money boys. It seems to be the way to demarcate their work and their private selves. They insisted on practising safer sex at work but broke the rule when the client was a regular client who was more like a friend. They seldom used condoms with their wives or girlfriends (if they had them) or boyfriends. Information about the sexual behaviour of their partners is unknown, but it is doubtful that all their non-paying affective partners had had no sex with others or practised safer sex all the time. Unprotected penetrative sex in the context of affective relationships seemed to have a significant symbolic meaning for these workers, for whom the underlying operative logic was work = risk = unsafe and love = trust = safe. Having unprotected sex with love, ironically, thus becomes the most dangerous sex act. This finding conforms to those of other studies: sex workers may be more at risk of HIV infection in the context of their private sexual lives than in their work lives.[23]

Discussion and conclusion

The traditional portrait of the male prostitute in international literature depicts him as a powerless young man trapped by personality defects, childhood traumas, and family dysfunction in a cycle of self-loathing, poverty and cultural deprivation (e.g., Coombs 1974: 784). The male prostitute usually identifies himself as heterosexual, emphasizes the material rewards of the work, denies getting sexual pleasure from the sex, performs only as a fellator, and despises, or is even physically violent to, clients (e.g., Reiss 1961). Similarly, in the Chinese literature, Choi *et al.*(2002) reported that money boys in China engaged in 'survival sex' and, in order to please clients, rarely used condoms. He *et al.* (2007) and Wong *et al.* (2008) showed that the major motivation for becoming money boys was economic survival. Their respondents had engaged in high-risk behaviour, suffered from depression, were dependent on substance use, and had been exposed to past or current sexual abuse or violence.

Building on later works in international literature which have acknowledged male prostitution as legitimate work and have examined men's involvement in sex work as a result of a number of factors, such as migration and considerations of financial gain, sexual pleasure, affection and freedom in the context of personal and structural constraints (e.g., Calhoun and Weaver 1996; West and de Villiers 1993; Browne and Minichellio 1995, 1996a, 1996b),[24] I have argued that my findings show most respondents to have been rural-to-urban, young, single homosexuals who came to big cities for various reasons – not just for work and to experience a cosmopolitan life, as have been succinctly discussed in migration literature (e.g., Solinger 1999; Zhang 2001; Pun 2003, 2005; Yan, H.R. 2003a, 2003b), but also to experience gay sexuality and to escape from the homophobic rural culture, and especially from the familial pressure for marriage (Kong 2005a, 2008).

A discourse of citizenship always entails the issue of exclusion as well as that of inclusion. Rural-to-urban migrants are caught in a specific subject formation of citizenship associated with the reconfigured rural-to-urban distinction of the post-Mao development discourse in the ideology of 'globalizing China'. Rural-to-urban migrants, as well as other city marginals (e.g., farmers, criminals, ethnic minorities, the urban poor, as described in Fong and Murphy 2006), have to deal with the state's efforts to transform them into model citizens (Guang 2003). The case of money boys shows the complexity of this process. In particular, the hegemonic ideal of citizenship, induced and reinforced through the state and popular culture, tends to construct rural migrants as 'backward', 'low class' and of 'low quality'; to define sex work as 'immoral', 'dirty' and 'diseased'; and to proscribe same-sex sexual activities as 'immoral', 'perverted' and 'sick'.

Rural-to-urban migrants, generally, are deprived, unofficial urban residents. They cannot gain permanent urban residency and are deprived of social welfare and social benefits, and so become culturally stigmatized as of low *suzhi* – all of which makes them vulnerable in different aspects of life, including employment, housing, health care, and many others. Although rural-to-urban migration was their dream, and a way to cope with their homosexuality, those who have become money boys have to pay a high cost in attempting to live up to the urban ideal.

Desperately seeking an alternative to the dead end of becoming a *dagongzai*, rural male youths who engage in sex work receive monetary rewards as well as other satisfactions such as sexual pleasure, self-esteem, freedom and control over work; and perhaps even a social mobility that seems to decrease the economic, social and cultural poverty that most rural-to-urban migrants commonly experience. Performing as a 'proper' gay citizen may also help them to increase their self-esteem, as homosexuality is slowly being dissociated from pathology and deviance and is increasingly associated with cosmopolitanism and urbanism. This helps them negotiate better positions within the confines of the ideal of urban citizenship. Yet it is precisely these two new identities – sex worker and gay – that create new problems for them.

Prostitution can be a double-edge sword: it provides pleasure and excitement, but also creates dangers and risks. Although prostitution can provide monetary and other rewards, risks range from being caught by the police to various forms of vulnerability, such as physical and sexual violence and psychological and emotional discomfort over the short career cycle and the unstable working environment.

Dissociation from prostitution may help money boys to cope with it. Such dissociation may involve adopting an occupational discourse (as business or as work). Most respondents treat sex work as a tool to make money, assume an innocent victim position, or simply regard it as a way to meet more 'friends'. Such an ambivalent 'work' identity not only complicates and even contradicts the binaries of public/private, production/consumption, work/leisure, love/sex, client/friend, etc., but also protects them from the stigma of sex work, with its intense emotional toll – although such ambivalence entails various risks and dangers. They may be quite successful in hiding their status of being money boys from their families, friends and colleagues, yet they cannot hide from the gay community, as gay men are potential clients. They encounter brutal discrimination and are placed at the bottom of the hierarchy of gay citizenship.

As regards homosexuality, rural gay money boys have the same problems, discussed in the last chapter, as other rural gay men – the pressure to get married and the difficulty of coming out to their families and relatives. They seldom go back home. Living in cities gives them more space to live as gay persons, even though they have to live up to the gay citizenship fashion that links gay identity to consumption, urbanism and cosmopolitanism.

For many gay money boys, engagement in sex work is not solely for money, but relates to their sexual orientation. Although they know the importance of maintaining boundaries when performing erotic labour, most of them have crossed the line, risking emotional tragedy and even exposure to the life threat of contracting HIV/AIDS. Far from being merely a matter of moral condemnation, the notion that *biaozi wuqing* (婊子無情 'the whore is heartless') is indeed a professional ethic that needs to be upheld (Ho 2000: 285).[25] Although they have been told and even trained by pimps that they should not fall in love with anybody, it is ironically their hunger for 'true love' that drives them to cross these boundaries over and over again.

For a number of reasons – state laws restricting access to permanent urban residency, the *yanda* government policy on (same-sex) prostitution, the short life cycle of the sex industry, and the rural homophobic culture – money boys become transient labour, moving back and forth between occupational settings and cities, and from sex work to other work. Money boys are transient queer subjects who live in 'queer time', 'outside of reproductive and familial time as well as on the edges of logics of labour and production' (Halberstam 2005: 10), in the 'queer places' – parks, brothels, massage parlours, clients' owned flats – that do not and never will belong to them, and which others have abandoned.[26] They live in secrecy and receive little help from those in their social networks unconnected with their work or sexuality, which subsequently leads them to live confined within a closed circuit (i.e., their world becomes tightly connected with their occupation and/or sexuality).[27]

Male prostitution is a contested, negotiated arena of power, and the identity of the prostitute involves a strategic self that constantly negotiates risks and dangers, excitements and gains, hopes and disappointments in the process of commercial sexual transactions. The case of money boys exemplifies an urban formation of such a strategic self in contemporary China. They are deprived of many aspects of life due to their migrancy, although some make use of their rural status to mark themselves up as innocent, clean and obedient. Compared to other rural migrants, their financial situation is generally better, and they escape the destiny of being *dagongzai.* However, sex workers are vulnerable to various kinds of physical violence, sexual risk and psychological discomfort. Although migration helps a lot of gay men escape from homophobic rural culture, gay MB identity not only drives them to conspicuous consumption but also presents the dangers of sex work, including emotional tragedy and even threats to life.

The interlocking effects of three identities – those of rural-to-urban migrant, sex worker and a man who has sex with other men – produce the complicated 'bare life' of the money boy. Like other city marginals, money boys struggle for an identity in the hierarchy of urban citizenship along the lines of class, gender, sexuality, work and migrancy and according to the binaries rural/urban, high quality/low quality, moral/immoral, healthy/diseased, etc. They are thus caught in webs of domination of the processes of liberalization, modernization and cosmopolitanization in globalizing China. In my last interview with Ah Jun, he told me softly, 'Maybe one day I will meet a man who really loves me and will support my study. I will then go back to school, get a diploma, and find a good job! Well . . . I know it won't happen.' Being a money boy is both to have a dream, and to know well that it will never come true.

Conclusion

Transnational Chinese male homosexualities and citizenship

With the great pace of globalization, de-colonization and neo-liberalism, modern homosexualities have emerged in contemporary Chinese societies. This has meant the creation of different hybridized gay identities – such as the cosmopolitan and conspicuously consuming 'memba' in Hong Kong, the diasporic and femininized 'golden boy' in London, the urban 'tongzhi' and the 'low quality' 'money boy' in China – all of whom are caught up in the transnational flow of global queer culture.

In this book I have taken a look at these newly emerged identities and examined how these Chinese gay men become sexual citizens under different political, economic, social, cultural and historical circumstances in the three locales of Hong Kong, London and China (major sites: Guangdong, Beijing and Shanghai) within the constellation of global culture. It is through these newly emerged queer subjects that I have been able to rethink the new direction of the queer movement for combating social discrimination and fighting for equal rights, to examine the pleasures and dangers of the celebration of queer popular cultures and consumption venues, to understand the tension between the almost universal coming-out model and the seemingly omnipotent family bio-power, and to realize the possibilities of experimenting with alternative families and intimate relationships.

I began with a discussion of the notion of identity. Modern Western theories of identity usually have assumed a stable, unified and identifiable human subject, and so in studies of gender, sexuality and race/ethnicity the categories 'woman', 'man', 'straight', 'gay', 'Occidental' and 'Oriental' have all been assumed to represent relatively stable, unified and identifiable human types.[1] Disputes have occurred about the origins of such subjects (natural or social), changing social forms and roles, their moral meanings, and political strategies of repression and resistance. Drawing on the insights of deconstruction, queer theory and Black feminist thought, I have argued for the notion of Chinese gay male identities, the construction of which is viewed as plural, unstable and regulatory. Sexual identities are always multiply formed, with various identity-components or categories of difference (e.g., sexual orientation, race and ethnicity, class, age, nationality, gender, ability and so forth) intersecting and combining with one another. However, the multiplicity of these sexual identities consists not merely of the additive experiences of these categories of difference, but rather is the result of multifarious and contradictory forces of oppression (i.e. in the intersectionality of differences), within specific institutional arenas, at any given time. Sexual identity should therefore be understood in terms of this politics of difference in order to avoid the denial of the multiple ways of experiencing homosexual desires, which a unitary notion of identity tends to assume. Moreover, rather than viewing the affirmation of (gay) identity as liberating, I have argued that identity construction entails disciplinary and regulatory effects, as any unitary definition of selves and behaviours must exclude a range of possible ways to frame the self, the body, desires, actions and social relations. My aim is not to abandon identity as a category of knowledge and politics but to render it permanently open and contestable. It is hoped that this will encourage a culture where multiple voices and interests are heard and allowed to shape queer life and politics.

The politics of difference model fits into a post-structuralist power-resistance paradigm, for which I mainly employ Foucault's (1980, 1982, 1988, 1991) works on bio-power, governmentality and the arts of the self, in order to understand the formation of identity and citizenship of non-Western non-normative genders and sexualities, using Chinese gay men as an example. Following Foucault's conception of power as both repressive and productive, I have argued that multiple fluid and complex forms of domination, or 'scattered hegemonies' (Grewal and Kaplan 1994: 7) – e.g., heteronormativity, patriarchy, sexism, racism, nationalism etc. – actively administer, regulate and reify sexuality on different levels – the systemic, the community and the personal – in our everyday lives, and on a transnational scale. It is through these disciplining gazes of surveillance at all levels that we are constituted as sexual citizens.

However, these sites of domination are also sites of resistance; and the scope of domination and the scale of resistance are both subject to the political, social and cultural circumstances of a particular locale, as well as to the position of the subject, who may possess various forms of capital. The results, either through overt and visible political action and/or the covert and invisible 'politics of the weak', are the making of queer identities, citizenships and counterpublics; and their increasing visibility in political agendas, in representations in cultural spheres, in the establishment of consumption venues, in the emergence of fleeting and ephemeral queer 'zones', and in the various 'experiments in life' of alternative intimacies. It is through the interplay between the personal biographies of some Chinese gay men and their engagement with social institutions – including the state, the market, the mass media, the popular culture, the civic community, the family, marriage etc. – that we can see how they derive tactics to negotiate – through resistance, re-definition, accommodation, rebellion, etc. – a range of possibilities for the gender and sexual practices that inform their lives.

In its broadest sense, this book is an attempt to understand non-Western non-normative genders and sexualities in relation to the thesis of globalization.

Inspired by Inda and Rosaldo (2002: 9–26) in their critique of cultural imperialism, I view globalization as a complex and unequal process which can be understood as involving three interconnected 'traffics' of queer identities – the 'traffic of the West to the rest' (of the world), exemplified by the global (read 'Western') queer body, identity, capital, rhetoric etc. that circulates to a non-Western city such as Hong Kong; the 'traffic of the rest to the West', exemplified by Hong Kong gay men who migrate to London; and the traffic among 'the rest', exemplified in queer circulations among and within Asian societies, and especially between Hong Kong and China, in generating queer identities, desires and citizenries.

My starting point has been Hong Kong, a city deeply implicated in and integrated into global processes, due to its colonial history. I have highlighted three sites of domination/resistance – namely, the state, the civil society and the private sphere – for analysis.

The state has played a crucial role in regulating sexuality, and the state is the first site of domination/resistance that I have examined. The emphasis on the state also highlights the shift from identity to cultural citizenship, as an examination of the relationship between the state and identity brings up the question of the preconditions for how a person can become a 'valid' and full member of a nation-state, and exposes how such prescriptions for cultural citizenship are established and circulated, thus allowing us to envision how these latter can be successfully transgressed.

Hong Kong was under a colonial government, which followed English law, which rendered homosexuality a criminal offence in Hong Kong for the first time (1842–1990). The decriminalization of homosexuality in 1991 is believed to have been a complicated and strategic response to various political and historical factors, and should not be seen as approval of homosexuality, or as endorsing gay rights or recognizing a gay lifestyle. Nevertheless, the decriminalization of homosexuality has had numerous effects: it has protected gay men who engage in certain private sex acts, it has triggered the mushrooming of gay and lesbian groups and queer cultures, and it has nurtured a new citizen-subject, 'the homosexual'. However, it has also differentiated between 'good' and 'bad' homosexuals, by confining sexuality to a private realm and punishing those who violate the distinction; and has also contributed to the development of an apolitical and hedonistic gay subculture.

The state in Hong Kong has shaped the contours of lesbian and gay movements. In contrast to the Western literature on sexual citizenship, which tends to assume heterosexuals to be full citizens, I have argued that Hong Kong people, homosexual or not, have always only been able to attain partial citizenship, under both the colonial rule and the present SAR administration. Under these two governances, Hong Kong people have tended to shift from a colonial citizenship, defined as applying to law-abiding subjects; to a self-enterprising citizenship, defined as applying to self-reliant subjects. It was the colonial government, in the name of 'respect for local culture', that depoliticized Hong Kong society through the 'minimally-integrated socio-political regime' (Lau 1982) and emphasized law-abiding citizenry; and it is the SAR government, in the name of 'harmony' and 'moderation', that has opposed any 'radical' democratic change (e.g., the implementation of universal suffrage); has emphasized the importance of self-reliance, self-help and self-improvement; and has cultivated a specific ethic of self, and of the citizen as 'an apolitical and yet productive economic subject' (Ku and Pun 2004: 2).

It is under these colonial conditions that we can have a more nuanced understanding of the notion of sexual citizenship, manifested in three major contested areas, as stated in Chapter 1, namely, those involving the question of whether sexual citizenship means setting up the standard of 'normal citizen' for lesbians and gay men to follow or whether it provides a possibility to challenge the heteronormative definition of queer life; the question of whether sexual citizenship, interlocked with the pink economy, manifests in a cosmopolitan and class-based consumer citizenship that facilitates cultural belonging and identification, or whether it marginalizes queer bodies along the lines of class, gender, race and ethnicity, age, body types, place of origin etc.; and the question of whether sexual citizenship universalizes the coming-out model and same-sex marriage (crystallized in the notion of monogamy) and thereby marginalizes 'alternative intimacies' that are widely practised in queer (especially gay male) communities.

With regard to the first question, I have argued that the tongzhi movement, especially in the past, tended to buy into the language of the government and to advance as a non-confrontational and assimilationist movement, suppressing any radical and transgressive politics. The movement promoted and encouraged a notion of sexual citizen not much different from that of the law-abiding colonial subject – one who is highly discreet, pro-establishment and conformative. The recent IDAHO events, since 2005 and the Pride Parades since 2008, have been promising and encouraging, as they have involved struggles between assimilation and confrontation and have advocated a notion of the sexual citizen as one who could be either 'normal' or 'perverted'; have sought equal rights but have emphasized queer difference; and have asked for inclusion into the mainstream but have also challenged social heteronormativity. Moreover, their call for a coalition politics that brings different parties – queer and non-queer – can be seen as a more appropriate strategy that goes beyond identity politics to integrate under a broader umbrella of democratic movement. The urgent agenda for queer activists in Hong Kong, however, is their continual battle to reconcile the tension of the first question, which crystallizes into the threat of heterosexualization of queer life, as opposed to the articulation of the subversive potential of queer critique of society. That is, tongzhi activists have to find a way that is sensitive to the political and cultural environment, taking seriously the tensions between confrontational politics and 'social harmony'; between Western queer politics (especially the coming-out model) and the disciplinary Chinese family biopolitics; between the ideas of 'good' homosexual citizens, on the one hand, and 'bad' and 'dangerous' sexual dissidents, on the other; as well as the tensions according to internal schisms within the queer community along the lines of gender, class, age, etc.

As the literature criticizing the allegedly apolitical culture of Hong Kong has successfully shown to us, Hong Kong people have tended to seek non-traditional channels to mobilize their discontents (Lam 2004), and to direct themselves towards economic consumption or cultural production (Abbas 1992). Likewise, with political institutional channels blocked, queer energy has been diverted to other spheres, particularly the civil and private spheres, where we can find vibrant queer subcultures and subversive sexual practices, passionate engagements in cultural production and the creation of queer worlds, die-for-it bodily consumption performances and queering of public spaces, and sexual practices that subvert conventional definitions of intimate relationships and family.

Civil society is thus the second site of domination/resistance, in relation to which I have examined the sexual politics and citizenship-making of Hong Kong tongzhi. Although governance limits the nurturing of critical mass through civil education and in academia, a more vibrant queer cultural world has been emerging in the mass media and popular culture. It is the tongzhi movement in the cultural sphere that has successfully transformed the traditional pathological deviant personage of the homosexual into a cosmopolitan and transnational queer cultural subject. Although homophobic discourses saturate tabloid newspapers and other media channels, a new trend of homophilia has appeared in mass media and popular culture – not so much in mainstream culture, but in independent, non-profit cultural productions. The cultural representations of the kaleidoscopic lives of tongzhi citizens, manifested vividly in films, popular music, theatre, fiction, blogs and many other cultural forms, have offered a subversive challenge to the 'normal' life of a citizen, heterosexual or not, whose assumptions about normal/perverted, heterosexual/homosexual, masculine/feminine, good/bad etc., have all been questioned and potentially redefined.

However, the queer cultural world, as part of the civil society, cannot be treated as autonomous, as it has been subject to various constraints, such as those of governance and censorship, commercial considerations, funding and sponsorship, and a backlash from some Protestant Christian- and Catholic-based NGOs that are actively and openly against non-normative genders and sexualities. This can be seen in the warning given by the government to RTHK over the programme 'Gay Lover', in the censorship of certain artworks in the exhibition organized by Nutong Xueshe (女同學社), and in the dilemma of over-presentation of mainstream Western commercial blockbusters (usually middle-class gay man stories) and under-presentation in alternative, independent and local films and films about lesbian, transgendered and working-class sensibilities in HKLGFF. It is this interplay of various forces that causes us to be more cautious, and to qualify the seemingly queer visibilities in Hong Kong cultural space.

Perhaps the most developed aspect of the queer world is the substantial queer consumption infrastructure, and perhaps the most established aspect of sexual citizenship among Hong Kong tongzhi, particularly among memba, is the notion of consumer citizenship. This consumer gay citizenship, linking gay identity with leisure and lifestyle membership, can be seen as a typical example of the allegedly 'apolitical', but productive, economic subject of the Hong Kong citizen.

It is from here that we can address the second contested area of sexual citizenship, that of the pink economy. Queer consumerism is a powerful assertion of queer economic power, and this seems to be a major queer form of power, as society still constrains the civic, political and social rights of tongzhi. But this queer power ironically rests on the global pink economy – involving, in particular, transnational middle-class sensibilities – and the global, hegemonic cult of gay masculinity. This style of queer citizenry sometimes serves less to promote cultural uniformity and identification than to act as a divisive force. The result is the creation of a hierarchy of gay citizens[2] – an inequality of transnational middle-class memba, gay expatriates and potato queens, new Chinese gay-migrant and money-boy 'margizens', and other gay subordinates defined along the lines of age, body type, gender performance etc. By adopting a 'flexible gay citizenship', Hong Kong memba negotiate – conform, resist, redefine etc. – cult gay masculinity, and use their embodied capital to find a suitable identity to help them manoeuvre among differentially empowered queer spaces.

Feminists have long been telling us that 'the personal is political', and so the private sphere is the third site of domination/resistance that I have investigated. This is also the third contested area of sexual citizenship, where sexual citizens are linked to the private realm of intimacy. The model of the citizen is implicitly based on a dominant script of long-term monogamous heterosexual pairing legitimatized in the marriage institution and exemplified in the nuclear family as the basic unit of society. I have argued that 'family biopolitics' (Ong 1993, 1996, 1999) can be seen as a tool of state discipline, through which a series of family practices and ideologies regulate healthy, productive, reproductive and heterosexual bodies. Familial heteronormativity, a derivative of such biopolitics, is produced via the family institution (characterized by utilitarianistic familism, or the 'harmonious family' under the SAR regime) and embedded in the couple relationship (characterized by monogamy).

Coming out has always been difficult for queers, as it is a lifelong process and requires repeated practices and performances (to 'out' or not to 'out') in everyday lives of compulsory heteronormativity. The classic Western coming-out model is usually based on an individualistic idea of selfhood that legitimizes an 'out' person as the proper sexual citizen. I have questioned this coming-out act as a universally necessary part of sexual citizenship, using my respondents who are Hong Kong memba as examples. The coming-out model seems to clash with the notion of the relational self embedded within the Chinese family. Memba have tended to negotiate gay identities through tactics that range from total closeting, mediation through getting married, lying, ambiguity, 'no-time-no-money' excuses, silence and redefinition of the filial son on the one hand; to total coming-out on the other – in order to create personal sexual spaces within the parameters of familial heteronormativity prescribed by family biopolitics.

Hong Kong memba are not particularly keen to discuss same-sex marriage, but they passionately engage in various intimate projects that distance themselves from the heterosexual hegemony of 'doing' courtship, marriage, intimacy and family practices, all of which are centred around the notion of monogamy. They embrace the idea of 'family we choose', which includes not just family of origin but also 'family of choice', the latter consisting of a bunch of people (e.g., boyfriends, close friends), that blurs the boundaries between the non-erotic and the erotic, the sexual and the non-sexual, and contests the conventional meanings of 'lover', 'friend', 'partner', 'family' etc. A call for such a politics of friendship and family, as noted by Bell and Binnie (2000: 134), is thus a call for the remaking of sexual citizenship. Moreover, juggling the romantic and sexual adventure scripts, and the feminine and masculine scripts of courtship, Hong Kong memba couples venture out – either together or separately, openly or in secret, with explicit or implicit rules – to engage in different forms of relationship, ranging from fleeting casual sexual encounters ('2 + many' model) to 'quality' secondary relationships ('2 + 1' model). It is through these practices of alternative intimacies, lifestyles and experiments in life that they go beyond the metaculture of compulsory monogamy.

While Hong Kong has presented the first example of sexual citizenship and identities of Chinese gay men, London and mainland Chinese cities give us more insights for understanding the effects of differential processes of globalization on Chinese gay identities. Living in London, Hong Kong gay male migrants are living in the capital of their former colonizer, Britain. Although much literature assumes globalization to be simply a flow 'from the West to the rest', Inda and Rosaldo (2002) rightly point out that the reverse traffic of people, goods, images, ideas, capital etc. to the West also takes place, constituting 'a monumental presence of Third World peoples in the metropolises of the West' (p. 18). Thus another dimension for looking at globalization is that of the flow from 'the rest' (i.e., the non-West) to the West. The London chapter is a story of why and how queer migrants live in the West.

The three types of Hong Kong gay male migrants – overseas 'brides' brought to the UK by English boyfriends, those who migrate as part of family advancement plans, and individuals with deliberate strategies for personal advancement – have tended to face different issues concerning sexual citizenship that arise from the different interplay of the state, civil society, and private sphere that takes place in London.

The state, again, plays a crucial role in the formation of this diasporic queer subject. As ethnic minority members, Hong Kong gay male migrants are subject to the discourse of race and ethnicity, and to various immigration and naturalization laws. Although Chinese are perceived as the 'model ethnicity', they are still under-represented in the political arena, lack visibility within popular culture and are more easily likely to encounter ceiling effects in occupations. Within the hierarchy of an 'ethnocracy', they are caught between British and other ethnic minorities, such as the Asian/Asian British and Black/Black British, and other 'margizens' such as new European migrants, illegal migrants and refugees. In this ethnocracy, a basic order of 'British first, Chinese second' tends to be the rule.

These Hong Kong-Chinese gay male migrants, on the one hand, benefit from the lesbian and gay movements in the UK. Some of them have gained British passports through the recent implementation of the Civil Partnership Act 2004, which has allowed them to gain residency status. They enjoy the well-established London queer subcultures and communities that have given them remarkable cosmopolitan and transnational queer experiences they had thought they would never experience in places such as Hong Kong. However, they are also subject to a brutal sexual stereotyping and marketization of racial queer bodies inside the British gay community, in which the hegemonic British gay citizen is constructed as a middle-class, cosmopolitan, masculine white body, and the Chinese gay man appears as a silent and feminine 'golden boy', a second class British gay citizen.

Within the private sphere, 'interracial relationship' is always a prominent theme in queer diasporas, and it has been discussed at length in (especially American) queer Asian diasporic studies (e.g., Eng 2001, Eng and Hom 1998; Leong 1996). Through the narratives of my respondents, I join the debate and question the logic of 'desired and imagined whiteness'. Hong Kong-Chinese gay men in Britain have derived tactics, passionately embracing or outright rejecting the 'golden boy' imagery, or finding ways to modify, redefine and negotiate gay relationships that accommodate desires strongly implicated in racial ideologies and sexual discourses.

Hong Kong gay male migrants thus must juggle three cultures – British culture, which represents autonomy and sophistication but also signifies white supremacy and racism; Chinese culture, which is materialized as economic support and cultural identification, but which also highlights familial pressure and obligation; and British gay culture, which symbolizes sexual freedom and liberation but also intensifies sexual stereotyping and marketization of bodies – in order to form a diasporic citizenship within which lines of class, family and 'race' intersect.

In mainland China we find another 'traffic' of globalization, which is often neglected: the traffic within 'the rest' – that is, in 'those circuits of culture that circumvent the West – those which serve primarily to link the countries of the periphery with one another' (Inda and Rosaldo 2002: 22). In her study of mass media and transnational subjectivity in Shanghai, Yang (2002) argued that popular culture in Shanghai had been dominated, recently, less by Western than by Hong Kong and Taiwan cultures. She states, '. . . it is no longer adequate for critical theory to identify *capitalism* only as a *western* force. What post-Mao China is encountering is the regional or transnational ethnic capitalism of overseas Chinese in Hong Kong, Taiwan, and Southeast Asia'

(p. 337, emphasis original). This economic development has obvious cultural implications. In the present work, I address the transcultural circulation of sexualities between and within Chinese cultural areas. In particular, I discuss how the invasive Hong Kong queer culture, in accompaniment with Western queer culture, has been influencing queer culture in mainland China.

China has undergone tremendous changes in the past few decades. Chinese people have shifted from 'socialist citizenship' in the Maoist era to 'market citizenship' in the reform era. *New* New China is now presenting itself on the world stage as a modern, open and global society. Various changes – such as the deletion of hooliganism in 1997 and the removal of homosexuality from the list of mental illness in 2001; the lessening of state regulation over private matters within the work unit and the family; the rise of national AIDS work, which includes hotlines and health workshops facilitated by transnational networks of queer activists from overseas, as well as from Hong Kong and Taiwan; the rise of the mass media, internet and other communication technologies; and the emergence of queer consumption venues in big cities – have not only contributed to the proliferation of gay identities, such as 'tongzhi' and 'money boy', but have also facilitated new sexual, romantic and commercial exchanges and interactions since the 1990s. The *new* new tongzhi has emerged – one who has slowly dissociated himself from the image of a pathological and deviant subject and has approached the image of urban good citizen, who is knowledgeable, civilized, cosmopolitan, and of 'good *suzhi* (素質)'.

However, the state, now infused with neo-liberal ideologies, still both enables and limits the development of (homo-)sexual cultures. It remains repressive, as can be seen from the frequent raids of gay consumption venues such as bars, clubs and cafés; from the 'hard-strike' campaign against male prostitution; and from the censorship of queer visibility in popular culture, such as in the cancellation or prevention of the opening of the Tongzhi Film Festival in Beijing. 'Social movement' and 'human rights' are hypersensitive terms, as they continue to have a special connotation in China because of the past history of political turmoil. Organizing or unionizing is not easy, and this makes a collective fight for gay and lesbian rights, or a fight at the institutional level, difficult, thus prohibiting the development of a collective tongzhi citizenship. Most queer-affiliated NGOs in China thus have to camouflage themselves as AIDS NGOs, which, on the one hand, are officially approved and financially supported, but on the other, are under close control and surveillance by government officials.

At the community level, established queer consumption venues have followed those in Hong Kong and other developed cities, where the sexualization and marketization of queer bodies are almost the norm. This is particularly prominent in China in the development of the sex-worker scene. While the *new* new tongzhi has been struggling to become a chic new urban subject, the money boy, with a complicated identity of rural-to-urban migrant, sex worker and man-who-has-sex-with-man, is constructed as a subordinate queer transient urban subject who is desperately seeking a 'proper' gay citizenship that he always fails to attain.

In the private sphere, Chinese gay men, like their Hong Kong brothers, are still struggling with the coming-out issue within the neo-Confucian family setting. Although the dominant script remains staying in the closet and marrying a woman, new narratives of the *new* new tongzhi have been emerging, which involve the question of coming out to family, remaining single, marrying a lesbian, or even same-sex marriage, and which thus emphasize individuality, difference and equality. The same-sex marriage discussion highlights the tensions inherent in the concept of sexual citizen. Whether the fight for equal rights highlights the visibility of a homosexual subject, a subject position assumed for the model of sexual citizen, and thus attracts more surveillance from government; and whether recognition of same-sex marriage may protect tongzhi legally only, at the cost of family and societal disapproval rather than that of legal discrimination; seem to be the major obstacles for most tongzhi.

* * *

Travelling among these three sites, I have demonstrated the dual process of citizenship making – being-made and self-making, under a power-resistance paradigm – using Foucault's notions of governmentality, bio-power and the techniques of the self. On the one hand, Foucault's biopolitics, as manifested in various 'scattered hegemonies', has proved to be constraining on gay men's lives; however, on the other hand it is precisely by acquiring such a stigmatized identity of sexual citizen that my respondents have been 'liberated', and have been put on the path to defining and developing a new life.

In examining these three sites, we can understand more fully the relationship between sexuality and neo-liberal governance. The state proves to be a major institution that we should pay more attention to. The state apparently seems to be retreating from regulating private life. However, it is both an enabling and a limiting institution. It sanctions certain forms of non-normative sexual acts and intimacies, which can be seen, for example, in the UK, decriminalization of homosexuality, equalization of age of consent and enactment of civil partnership; in Hong Kong, decriminalization of homosexuality and equalization of age of consent; and in China, deletion of hooliganism from criminal law and removal of homosexuality from the list of mental illnesses. However, the state has also defined the rights of sexual citizens according to its own controls and regulations, such as the effects of decriminalization of homosexuality in creating public/private dichotomies for homosexuals and the link to the development of an apolitical queer subculture, in both the UK and in Hong Kong; and in the frequent raids of gay consumption venues, hard-strike campaign against male prostitution, and censorship of queer visibility in popular culture in China. We should note that the state maintains a close relationship with the market, especially in its endorsement of neo-liberal ideologies, which nurtures a self-regulating neo-liberal queer subject who has internalized these norms in becoming a responsible and respectable citizen. However, these norms also serve to demarcate a new boundary between 'good' and 'bad' citizen in the process of normalization of the sexual 'other', and to exert new disciplining effects on NGOs and the family.

As concerning NGOs, we should be careful of how the state strategically allies with certain NGOs for a 'reign of civility and respectability' in which sexual acts, identities, information and exchanges are regulated.[3] Examples of this include the censorship cases in Hong Kong and state control over queer NGOs through provision of funding and support, with consequent accountability and dictatorship over these NGOs, in Hong Kong and also in China, where most queer NGOs have to camouflage themselves as health organizations (especially, as organizations concerned with AIDS) sanctioned by the government. As for the family, we should be cautious of how the family may act as a tool of state governance in regulating 'healthy' and heterosexual bodies at the expense of queer offspring.

In civil society, we can see the sexual politics of lesbians and gay men in various queer movements in different locales. Here we see the fight against discrimination by gay men and lesbians, especially in Britain, where they have successfully promoted endorsements of an age of consent and civil partnership that have benefited Hong Kong gay migrants. Tongzhi movements in Hong Kong and in China take a different path, strongly shaped by (post-)colonialist and socialist ideologies, respectively. Lesbian and gay movements have developed differently in difficult locales, all of which are sensitive to national socio-political and historical contingencies, so that the Western model for such movements should not be taken as a universal standard for judging queer movements in other non-Western societies.

The mass media and popular culture have played pivotal roles in shaping the relationship between sexuality and cultural citizenship, as can be seen in the increase of positive queer visibilities, as opposed to the stereotypical representations of gay men and lesbians of the past, in all three locales. Yet the notion of citizenship is always about both inclusion and exclusion and the resultant hegemonic imagery of a cosmopolitan, middle class, urban and global queer subject – but also about the under-representation of certain queer bodies and gay subordinates along the lines of age, class, 'race'/ethnicity, migrancy, body type and gender performance.

Inside the queer world, marketization of queer bodies is very prominent. It works according to the logic of 'scattered hegemonies', such as pink economy, cosmopolitanism, cult gay masculinity, racism, urbanism etc., in all three locales. Although the gay community provides substantial cultural space in which gay men can identify with one another through sexuality, language and values, we should note that it is also the site where queer bodies are commodified, exoticized and eroticized. Such are the 'golden boy' in the London gay scene and the 'money boy' in the mainland Chinese gay scene.

The private sphere is where we find love and intimacy, but it can also be a site of domination and of the reproduction of familial heteronormativity.

Coming-out is still a big issue for Chinese gay men, and their various tactics employed in dealing with their sexual identities are always worked out within the parameters of family biopolitics. Yet again, we have to question the arbitrary formula that equates Chineseness with the family institution and the question of what purposes this serves. Although some respondents appropriate this formula and live in the closet or even claim to be 'good' sexual citizens, the private sphere is also a site where we can see practices of subversion – those of the subversion of sexual norms in the redefinition of family and in the formation of intimate relationships, such as by remaining single, or by entering into a marriage of convenience or a same-sex marriage, by adopting the 2+1 model or the 2+ many model, and probably in many more ways.

Through examining the three sites we not only can come to understand more fully the relationship between sexuality and neo-liberal governance but also that between sexuality and globalization; and this is the final question asked in Chapter 1. The vision of globalization usually assumes a smooth homogenous process that constructs non-Western subjects as passive agents of cultural reception. This hypodermic model of cultural effects ignores how non-Western subjects customize Western culture. In relation to homosexuality, this means that the notion of global gay identity usually assumes that non-Western gay men are cultural dupes who passively buy into a Western gay culture that governs globalized queer culture.

However, in this book I have attempted to understand how Chinese gay men transform – interpret, translate and appropriate – ostensibly Western notions of homosexuality and take them up for life in a Chinese context. I reject both the universal version of gay global (read 'Western') origin stories, which renders Chinese gays as located 'forever in the place of deferral arrival' (Rofel 2007: 91); and the impossible search for an 'authentic' root of indigenous Chinese homoerotic tradition. I have sought a way that goes beyond the reductionism (involving either side of the binaries 'similitude/difference' or 'homogeneity/heterogeneity') of contemporary Chinese gay identities (e.g., memba, tongzhi, golden boy, money boy). I have done this by viewing the 'West' and the 'East' (read: 'Chinese'), or the global and the local, as arbitrary and imaginary cultural locations. Gay identities, no matter global or Chinese, are both fictional and strategic, subject to the act of positioning. In other words, instead of asking how Chinese gay identities fall short of the global hierarchy of gay identities, masculinities and citizenships, it may be more productive to ask why Chinese gay identities are placed on the lower end of this global political queer economy, how they sustain this inequality, and to what extent they challenge our presumptions of what is meant by being gay, masculine or even sexual in the first place. It is this 'misfit' that gives us queer insights to understand the geopolitical context of global queer politics. Moreover, looking at the various Chinese gay identities on a transnational scale also helps us to debunk the myth of Chineseness – as if being Chinese were something essential, fixed or universal, instead of meaning something different in different localities. It is this cultural logic of reconfiguration, which maps out the complicated 'social process of discrepant transcultural practices' (Rofel 2007: 94), that gives us more queer insights to grasp the various meanings of 'Chinese' gay identities, practices and desires in the constellation of global queer culture.[4]

* * *

I have combined the sociology of homosexuality and queer theory to map out on a transnational scale that has enabled me to understand the self-identities of some Chinese men marginalized as gay, memba or tongzhi, as well as the process of making sexual citizenship among these men, and the rethinking of queer politics as constituting a form of social and democratic movement. Throughout this book, I have paid attention to the social–structural order in the formation of identity and citizenship, while remaining sensitive to how language, rhetoric and discourses have textualized our lives. I have employed the life history approach, which emphasizes the complexity of human experience, the concreteness of everyday life, and the reflexive elements of human agency – how subjects mediate the process of globalization, especially in its unequal transnational flows, through a material analysis of socio-historical circumstances, in order to understand non-Western non-normative genders and sexualities.

The arguments that I have developed in this book are inevitably incomplete. In addition to the small size of my sample and the research limitation of focusing on gay men only, my analysis is also limited by my attempt to capture the continuing transformation of moving subjects, some of whom were even interviewed repetitively over a decade. I have tried to grasp at best the 'partial truths' (Clifford 1986: 7) of the 'wholeness' of my respondents' narratives at certain ethnographic moments of contingency – those 'of language, rhetoric, power, and history' (p. 25). Moreover, I have been caught by the problem of representation in the tension between my authorial status, in which I have tried to represent my respondents 'truly', but I may have over-represented my own voice (Denzin and Lincoln 1994: 577–78; Krieger 1991: 5). More fundamentally, I have run the risk of overstating my theoretical position, which on the one hand criticizes the (Western) power/knowledge regime of sexuality, but on the other hand (despite the fact that this is a piece of 'minor writing'[5]) may in itself have become another 'grand narrative'. This is because, in suggesting some absolute 'truths' about Chinese gay male sexuality, I have subjugated other voices.

Despite these shortcomings, I have highlighted the multiple frames of reference and diverse systems of thought and action that have shaped homosexuality over the course of recent decades in Hong Kong, London and China. I have explored a number of key contexts in which homosexual experiences have taken shape, and have linked these to the broader processes of historical change in which they are necessarily situated. Furthermore, I hope to have shown how the 'universal' (read: Western) rhetoric and styles involved in the continuation of Chinese culture and traditions have had profound impact upon the Chinese gay male body. It is only within this constellation of global queer culture that terms such as 'memba', 'golden boy', 'potato queen', 'tongzhi', 'money boy', and so forth can even be imagined, let alone eroticized and exoticized. Yet in between the connected spaces of the global and the local, the present and the past, the familiar and the 'exotic', a third space for multiple voices has, I hope, been created.

Appendix

Methodological note

During 1997–98 I interviewed 34 Chinese gay men, in Hong Kong and in London, and re-interviewed one-third of them ten years later, in 2007–8. I also interviewed another 26 Chinese gay men (11 in Hong Kong and 15 in Guangdong) in 2007–8, for a total of 60 life histories. I found my interviewees mainly through personal contacts and referrals from tongzhi organizations in Hong Kong, such as the Chi Heng Foundation, Midnight Blue, Hong Kong Rainbow, and then through the snowball technique. I tried to interview people with as diverse backgrounds as possible (in terms of age, education, marital status, family status, occupation, etc.) in order to reflect the diversity of the population. In addition, from 2004 to 2005, I interviewed 30 other Chinese men who have sex with other men in exchange for money, in Beijing (n = 14) and Shanghai (n = 16), and their stories appear in Chapter 7.

I am aware that it is impossible to obtain a 'representative' sample of a stigmatized population, and so I do not claim that my interviewees are representative of the Hong Kong gay male population, the British Chinese gay male migrant population in London, the Guangdong gay male population or the male sex worker population in China.

I followed standard procedures for sociological interviewing, and explained carefully the nature of the study, emphasizing confidentiality and anonymity and seeking consent before all interviews. All names that appear are pseudonyms, and I have made minor alterations of biographies in order to protect the identities of my informants. The interviews were open-ended, with interview guides as agendas, which I followed (with slight modifications) from case to case. After the interviews, all tapes were transcribed and the data were coded. Guided by a grounded theory approach (Glaser and Strauss 1967) and following Ryan and Bernard's (2000) framework, data analysis included identifying themes, building codebooks and marking texts. Themes that occurred repeatedly in most interviews were identified, compared and analysed in relation to those in the existing local and international literatures.[1]

During the interviews, as well as during the writing process, I have been aware of the post-structuralist critique of traditional 'scientific' methodology, which can broadly be seen in terms of the problem of representation, of legitimization, and of ethics.

The first problem is the problem of representation. According to Denzin and Lincoln (1994: 577–78), it consists of two separate but related questions: one is the question of the subjects being studied – that is, the other (Who is the other? Who is being represented?). The other is the question of author's/researcher's place in a text or field – that is, who can speak for the other, from what position and on what basis?

Homosexuals have typically been cast into the role of the other and have usually been misrepresented in interviews. As I, and others, have argued elsewhere (Kong *et al.* 2002: 240–45), there have been three waves of study of the 'homosexual' in North America and Europe over the past 100 years: the 'traditional', the 'modernizing' and the 'postmodern'. Briefly put, traditional 'homosexual' research relied on a form of positivism that drew a sharp distinction between the knowing subjects (i.e., the researchers) and the objects of study (i.e., the interviewees or informants). Through standardized interviews, ostensibly disinterested researchers obtained seemingly 'objective' accounts of the nature of homosexuality. Until the latter third of the twentieth century, social scientists studied homosexuals – initially, as 'perverted'; then as 'sick'; and finally, as 'different' persons. The rise of the lesbian and gay movement from the 1960s onwards has triggered a new understanding of homosexuality and a new research direction ('the modernizing tale'). A hermeneutic or interpretive perspective has emerged, and the interview has increasingly become a tool for self-identification and 'coming out'. More and more self-identified gay researchers have carried out interviews, collapsing the old split between the subject/researcher and the object/researched, and these have begun to imply that only gay and lesbian researchers could conduct interviews, because of their more 'authentic' understandings of other gay men and lesbians. The more recent 'postmodern' or queer critique problematizes this, however, and problematizes the subject of inquiry ('the homosexual'), the nature of inquiry ('the interview'), and the inquirer him/herself ('the researcher'). In particular, the queer critique of the practice of having gays and lesbians interview other gay men and lesbians questions how often the gay and lesbian experiences represented are merely a reproduction of the experiences of white, middle-class, Western gay men and lesbians. Who are being excluded in the process of interview?

I would say that I have the advantage of, to some extent, representing 'Chinese gay men', as I am 'one of them'. When I study the identity of Chinese gay men, I study something that is as much a part of me as it is of the people I interview, and what I have learnt as a result of my study is as much a contribution to my own self-understanding as it is to social understanding. As an 'insider', I found greater acceptance by the interviewees, and so it was easier to establish rapport with them. However, being an 'insider' does not mean that I can claim to truly represent Chinese gay men. On many issues I am quite different from my respondents due to differences in class, age, education and other socio-cultural factors; as well as in relation to different ideas and goals concerning political activism, cultural politics and social intervention – so that, at times, I felt more like an 'outsider'. My particular experience of being simultaneously an insider/outsider confirmed my post-structuralist understanding that gay identity entails no coherent 'essence', but is a contested construction that intersects an individual's other social identities and categories of difference.

Another concern in queer interviewing is the increased awareness of the need for self-reflexivity. As Bourdieu (1992: 68–72) suggests, reflexivity provides much greater awareness of the entire intellectual (including interviewing) process. We need to examine the subject of the research, along with the social locations in which research knowledge is produced, as well as a much fuller sense of the spaces – personal, cultural, academic, intellectual, historical – that the researcher occupies in building that knowledge (Kong *et al.* 2002: 249–51). I have constantly asked myself about my own identities in the process of interviewing and writing – the identities of tolerant researcher, co-participant in self-disclosure, and representative of the experience under consideration.[2]

Perhaps more fundamental and important is the idea that representation always involves a kind of self-representation (Krieger 1991: 5, 1985[3]). That is, the interviewees' presentations are always directly connected to the situated writing self of an author/researcher, the 'I'. Whether the voice of an author/researcher is manifest or not, s/he always presents a unique self in the text and claims to have some pervasive authorial functions over the other subject matters that are being interpreted (Denzin and Lincoln 1994).[4] Strathern (1987) says bluntly, 'There is no evidence, after all, that "we" have stopped attributing our problems to "others"' (p. 269, emphasis original). I do not think that we can completely resolve this dilemma, but a life history approach that emphasizes 'other' voices might neutralize some of these authorial effects. In writing up the interview data, as Foucault's power/knowledge paradigm reminds us, I am aware of the fact that I am producing, not simply describing, the identities of the respondents, and I am also aware of my authorial voice in relation to the multiple voices of the respondents through the production of queer knowledge about Chinese gay men.

The second problem is the problem of legitimization and authenticity – what used to be called validity.[5] At the simplest levels, respondents may lie or attempt to please the researcher in order to be positively evaluated (Plummer 1983: 102). Even if they are assumed to give 'authentic' answers, problems still exist. As a large part of interviews take the form of retrospective accounts (e.g., involving the feelings interviewees first had when they found men attractive, of how they first came out, of how they felt when they had their first sexual experiences or romances, of how they first experienced the gay scene, etc.), the interviewees were required actively to reconstruct their pasts in order to give consistency to their present selves. Problems of memory and accounting enter here (Plummer 1983: 105–6; see also Thompson 1988: 110–17). Moreover, even questions not asked about the past (e.g., about what being gay means, or what opinions they had of love/sex at the time of interview) still required them to create coherent stories through a narrative device. As Stein (1997: 202–5) has argued, the life history method emphasizes the ambiguity and contradictions of their 'lived experiences', yet might neutralize the tendency to give a more 'balanced' picture.

Any attempt to overcome the 'authenticity' problem of the narrative, however, risks falling into the trap of positivism, which claims that the 'truth' of the past can be revealed by 'objective' methods. Postmodern sensibility reads (epistemological) validity not as validity-as-authority, but as 'a text's desire to assert its power over the reader' (Denzin and Lincoln 1994: 579). Various kinds of postmodern sensibilities for 'queer interviewing' suggest themselves (Kong *et al.* 2002: 248–49). If postmodern sensibility can be read as a political act which challenges the power/knowledge regime of society, this book is itself, to paraphase Deleuze and Guattari (1986: Ch.3), a minor(ity) writing that attempts to disturb the Western hegemonic claims of identity, body, sexuality and the self of homosexuality. If postmodern sensibility leads to a shift in writing strategy for the representation of interview materials, I attempt to integrate the ideas of 'otherness', 'marginality' and 'resistance', and sociological analysis. That is, I offer a constant critique of positivist methods of study by showing how my sociological enquiry of Chinese sexual identity and citizenship-making is led by my 'vested interests'. I show my persistent doubts about the universalizing drift of reason by situating myself in (relatively) specific times and locations in Hong Kong, London, Guangdong, Beijing, Shanghai, etc., and attempt to unmask compulsory heteronormativity in our daily lives by examining the power/knowledge regime of sexuality though the voices of my interviewees. I thus blur disciplines (e.g., sociology and queer theory, with a nod to cultural studies, anthropology, etc.) and subject matters (e.g., those of 'hard core' sociology and (auto)biography). Perhaps what I am trying to do is to revive sociology as a creative and imaginative process of understanding society – the promise made by a traditional sociologist, who tried to grasp the 'interplay of man and society, of biography and history, of self and world' (Mills 1959: 4).

The final problem is the problem of ethics. Although it may be cozy and pleasant to see interviews as simply a matter of technique, I hope to develop an appreciation of my respondents' lives, the relationships formed in the field, and a clearer understanding of myself. This requires a finely tuned aesthetic that is sensitive to the specific cultural meanings of erotic experience, and to individuals and groups who share a history, culture and social–structural position.

Profile of interviewees

Table A.1

Old Interviews (interview during 1997/98): Hong Kong (HK)/London (LN)					
	Name (Pseudonym)	*Age*	*Education*	*Occupation*	*Remark*
1	Adam	46	Degree (Psychology) (US)	Publisher	Back to HK in late 1970s
2	Alan	36	Secondary (HK)	Dancer	
3	Alex *	33	Post-secondary (HK)	Computer analyst	
4	Aron *	33	Matriculated (HK)	Para-medical professional	Migrated to Toronto in 1999
5	Barry	22	Secondary (HK)	Bank teller	
6	Ben	38	Secondary (HK)	Self-employed (Transport)	
7	Bobby	23	Degree (Fashion) (UK)	Student	Studied in the UK
8	Brian	22	Degree (Business) (UK)	Student	Studied in the UK
9	Calvin	32	Post-secondary (HK)	Para-medical professional	
10	Charles	23	Degree (Marketing) (Australia)	Flight steward	
11	David	43	O-Level (UK)/Dip (HK)	Self-employed (Catering)	
12	Dennis	22	Secondary (HK)	Bank teller	
13	Edward	25	Degree (Econ) (Australia)	Manager trainee	
14	Eric *	48	Degree (Medicine) (UK)	Medical doctor	Back to HK in 1985
15	Frank *	35	Secondary (HK)	Unemployed	Now: Insurance sales
16	George *	24	Degree (Art) (HK)	Artist	
17	Ivan	22	Degree (Literature) (HK)	Manager trainee	

	Name (Pseudonym)	*Age*	*Education*	*Occupation*	*Remark*
18	James *	22	Degree (Art) (HK)	Student	Now: Freelance designer
19	Jeff *	26	Degree (Architecture) (UK)	Student	Now: Architect, settle in LN
20	Jonathon	33	Diploma (Art Admin.) (UK)	Student	Back to HK in 1999
21	Kenny *	29	Degree (Fashion) (UK)	Student	Now: Steward, settled in LN
22	Leo *	36	Degree (Computer) (UK)	Student	Now: Nurse, settled in LN
23	Martin *	27	Degree (Art) (UK)	Student	Now: Curator, settled in UK
24	Matthew	38	Secondary (HK)	Self-employed (Garment)	
25	Nelson *	30	Diploma (Media) (UK)	Freelancer	Now: Manager, settled in LN
26	Norman	17	Secondary (HK)	Student	
27	Peter	26	Secondary (HK)	Policeman	
28	Richard	20	Dip (Communication) (HK)	Student	
29	Robert	20	Degree (industry) (Australia)	Student	
30	Russell	36	Master (comm.) (HK)	Freelance writer	
31	Samshasha	43	Degree (US)	Translator	Deceased
32	Stuart	35	Secondary (HK)	Construction worker	
33	Terry	25	Secondary (HK)	Escort	
34	Tony	21	Special education (HK)	Clerk	

* Re-interviewed during 2007/08

contiued over the page . . .

Table A.1 . . . continued

New Interviews (interview during 2007/08): Hong Kong (HK)

	Name (pseudonym)	*Age*	*Education*	*Occupation*	*Remark*
35	Bill	23	Degree (HK)	Program manager	
36	Bowie	23	Degree (Engineering) (HK)	Student	
37	Christopher	18	Secondary (HK)	Student	
38	Eddy	23	Diploma (Imaging) (HK)	Editorial assistant	
39	Ian	22	Degree (Linguistics) (HK)	Student	
40	Jason	20	Matriculated (HK)	Program manager	
41	Joey	22	Degree (Literature) (HK)	Student	
42	Josh	22	High Diploma (HK)	Program trainee	
43	Sunny	19	Secondary (HK)	NGO helper	
44	Wing Gor	60	Primary (Macau)	Retired/NGO volunteer	Came to HK in 1968
45	Yan Gor	66	Secondary (HK)	Retired (formerly clerk)	

New Interviews (interview during 2007/08): Guangzhou (GZ)

	Name (Pseudonym)	*Age*	*Education*	*Occupation*	*Born in*	*Remark*
46	Ah Bei	25	Degree (Xi'an)	PR manager	Xian	Came to GZ in 2005
47	Ah Jiang	42	Lower middle	Security guard	Guangdong	
48	Ah Ling	25	Postgraduate (GZ)	Student	Fujian	Came to GZ in 2006
49	Ah Ming	42	Lower middle	Self-employed	Guangdong	

	Name (Pseudonym)	*Age*	*Education*	*Occupation*	*Born in*	*Remark*
50	Harry	42	Degree (Shanghai/US)	Freelancer	Shanghai	Travels around China
51	Lao Wu	51	Upper middle	Transport	Guangzhou	
52	Qiang Ge	31	Post-secondary	Self-employed	Anhui	Came to GZ in 1998
53	Robbie	22	Degree (Hunan)	Student	Hunan	Came to GZ in 2005
54	Xiao Feng	25	Lower middle	Unemployed	Fujian	Came to GZ in 2008
55	Xiao Guang	32	Lower middle	Program manager	Guangdong	
56	Xiao Hua	18	Primary	Unemployed	Sichuan	Came to GZ in 2006
57	Xiao Jie	20	Degree (Guangzhou)	Student	Guangzhou	
58	Xiao Kai	21	Degree (Foshan)	Student	Guangdong	
59	Xiao Shu	33	Lower middle	Dancing teacher	Guangzhou	
60	Xiao Wang	25	Degree (Beijing)	Computer analyst	Sichuan	Came to GZ in 2005

Table A.2

Interviews with men who sell sex (2004/05) Beijing (BJ)/Shanghai (SH)

	Pseudonym	*Age*	*Education*	*Sexual orientation (self-identified)*	*Type of sex work at the time of interview*	*Length of engagement in sex work*
Place of interview: Beijing						
1	Ah Dong	26	Senior middle	Gay	Freelancer	6 months
2	Ah Gang	22	Senior middle	Ambivalent	Full-time brothel	1.5 years
3	Ah Hao	25	Post-secondary	Straight	Freelancer	3 years
4	Ah Hong	20	Junior middle	Ambivalent	Full-time brothel	6 months
5	Ah Ji	24	University	Gay	Freelancer	6 months
6	Ah Ping	30	Primary education	Gay	Freelancer	8 years
7	Ah Tao	32	Junior middle	Gay	Full-time independent	8 years
8	Ah Tian	20	Senior middle	Ambivalent	Full time brothel	1 year
9	Ah Wei	25	Junior middle	Gay	Full-time independent	8 years
10	Ah Yang	22	Junior middle	Ambivalent	Full-time brothel	6 months
11	Dou Dou	22	Senior middle	Gay	Full-time independent	6 months
12	Xiao Bin	22	Junior middle	Gay	Full-time brothel	6 months
13	Xiao Jin	27	Primary education	Gay	Freelancer	6 months
14	Xiao Yu	26	Primary education	Gay (married)	Freelancer	6 months

	Pseudonym	*Age*	*Education*	*Sexual orientation (self-identified)*	*Type of sex work at the time of interview*	*Length of engagement in sex work*
Place of interview: Shanghai						
1	Ah Bing	22	Post-secondary	Ambivalent	Full-time brothel	1 year
2	Ah Jian	25	Post-secondary	Gay	Freelancer	2 years
3	Ah Jun	20	Junior middle	Ambivalent	Full-time brothel	3 years
4	Ah Li	22	Post-secondary	Straight	Freelancer	1.5 years
5	Ah Lin	22	Senior middle	Gay	Kept by a man	2 years
6	Ah Ming	23	Senior middle	Straight	Full-time independent	3.5 years
7	Ah Qiang	25	Senior middle	Gay	Freelancer	2 years
8	Ah Qing	22	Junior middle	Gay	Full-time independent	1 year
9	Ah Si	21	Senior middle	Gay	Freelancer	1.5 years
10	Ah Wen	19	University	Gay	Full-time independent	1 year
11	Ah Xian	23	Senior middle	Gay	Full time brothel	1 year
12	Ah Yuan	25	Senior middle	Gay	Full-time independent	1.5 years
13	Xiao Bao	20	Junior middle	Gay	Kept by a man	1 year
14	Xiao Chao	23	Senior middle	Ambivalent	Full-time independent	3 years
15	Xiao Tui	22	Senior middle	Gay	Full-time independent	6 months
16	Xing Xing	23	Senior middle	Gay	Freelancer	6 months

Glossary

Mandarin romanization (pinyin)

(http://humanum.arts.cuhk.edu.hk/Lexis/Lindict/)

Terms

Table G.1

Terms		
Pinyin	*Chinese*	*English meaning**
ai mianzi	愛面子	'love one's face'; concern about the face issue
beiyangde	被養的	'being taken care of or being supported by'; kept by a client in the context of sex work
biaoziwuqing	婊子無情	'the whore is heartless'
buguangcai	不光彩	'not bright'; disgraceful, disrespectful
caizi	才子	'the talented scholar'; a form of *wen* masculinity
changzhu ren kou	常住人口	'permanent resident'
chi qingchun fan	吃青春飯	'eating the rice bowl of youth'; earn money by means of youth
chutai	出台	buying out in the context of sex work
dagongmei	打工妹	'working daughter'; a female worker
dagongzai	打工仔	'working son'; a male worker
danwei	單位	'work unit'
diulian	丟臉	'lose face'
duanxiu	斷袖	'the cut sleeve'; a euphemism for male homosexuality in traditional Chinese literature

gongmin	公民	'public people'; a term for citizens
guanxi	關係	'relationship'
guomin	國民	'national people'; a term for citizens
haizi	孩子	'child'; refers to male prostitute in the male sex work industry in China
haohan	好漢	'good fellow'; a form of *wu* masculinity
hukou	户口	'household registration'
jingli	經理	'manager'; pimp in the context of male sex work in China
jintong	金童	'golden boy'; young virgin boy in traditional Chinese literature
kaifang	開放	'opening up'; refers to the policy of 'opening' China to the outside world, beginning in 1978
ku'er	酷兒	'cool child'; Taiwanese mutation of 'queer'
lala	拉拉	'lesbian', used mainly in China
laoban	老板	'boss'; pimp in the context of male sex work in China
laolao	姥姥	'grandmother/old woman'; pimp in the context of male sex work in China
laoyoutiao	老油條	'old fried bread stick'; a cunning fellow who knows how to manipulate rules; a slippery customer
Lei Feng	雷鋒	a soldier of the People's Liberation Army; a national hero; a model citizen
Li Ning	李寧	a man who was sentenced to jail for organizing male-male prostitution in China in 2004
lian	臉	'face'
liumang	流氓	'hooligan'
liumang zui	流氓罪	'hooliganism'
luan	亂	'chaotic'
maide	賣的	'for sale'; person who sells sex
mamasan	媽媽桑	'mother' (Japanese usage); pimp in the context of male sex work in China
mianzi	面子	'face'
nanfeng	南(男)風	'south (male) wind'; a euphemism for male homosexuality in traditional Chinese literature ('south' and 'male' are homophones)

nanse	南(男)色	'south (male) colour'; a euphemism for male homosexuality in traditional Chinese literature ('south' and 'male' are homophones)
Nutong Xueshe	女同學社	a tongzhi organization in Hong Kong
pingtai	平台	'platform'
quan'neiren	圈內人	'members of the circle'; self-label in the gay community in China
renmin	人民	'people'; a term for citizens
saohuang	掃黃	government's efforts to eradicate prostitution
shaoye	少爺	'young master'; refers to male prostitute in the male sex work industry in China
shimin	市民	'city people'; a term for citizens
Sun Yixian	孫逸仙	the father of the modern Chinese nation
suzhi	素質	'quality'
taibuqitou	抬不起頭	'cannot lift up one's head'; shamed, shameful
tiefanwan	鐵飯碗	'iron rice bowl'; guaranteed employment
tongxinglian	同性戀	'homosexuality'
tongxinglianzhe	同性戀者	'homosexual'
tongzhi	同志	'comrade'; queer
wen	文	'culture'; cultural, scholarly, civilized, a dominant form of Chinese masculinity
wenren	文人	'the cultured man'; a form of *wen* masculinity
wu	武	'martial prowess'; martial, military, force and power, a dominant form of Chinese masculinity
wuliao	無聊	'idle'; bored
xiaohai	小孩	'child'; refers to male prostitute in the male sex work industry in China
yanda	嚴打	'hard-strike'; short term for 'hard strike against serious crime' (e.g., prostitution); sometimes translated as 'stern blows', 'severe blows'
yazi	鴨子	'duck'; male prostitute
yingxiong	英雄	'hero'; outstanding male, a form of *wu* masculinity
yu tao	餘桃	'the peach reminder'; a euphemism for male homosexuality in traditional Chinese literature

yunu	玉女	'jade maiden'; young virgin girl in traditional Chinese literature
zhixiashi	直轄市	'direct-governed municipality'

* The Chinese terms translated here are mainly used in mainland China. A direct literal translation of a Chinese term is given first, if possible, and put in quotation marks, followed by a more semantic interpretation of the term. The interpretation is brief, and should be used for quick reference only. Readers are advised to refer to the main text for a fuller explanation of the terms.

Phrases

geming shang wei chenggong, tongzhi reng xu nuli

革命尚未成功, 同志仍需努力

The revolution has not succeeded yet; comrades should fight for it until the end.

Yanli daji yanzhong xingshi fanzui

嚴厲打擊嚴重刑事犯罪

Hard strike against serious crime

Cantonese romanization

(http://humanum.arts.cuhk.edu.hk/Lexis/Canton/)

Terms

Table G.2

Cantonese	*Chinese*	*English**
baau yi naai	包二奶	to keep a second wife
caufui	溙魁	'taking care of a ghost'; going out with a Westerner
daan wai	單位	'work unit' (= Mandarin *danwei*)
Ga Bin	家變	'A House is not a Home'; a popular TV soap drama in 1977 in Hong Kong
gamgong Barbie	金剛芭比	'King Kong barbie doll'; muscular gay man with usually feminine mannerism; (= English 'muscle Mary'); used mainly in Hong Kong gay community
gamcing	感情	'affection'; love, romance
gei	基	'gay'
gei lo	基佬	'gay bloke/gay man'
gwailo/gweilo	鬼佬	'ghost-man'; foreigner, usually refers to a Westerner
hoeng gong jan	香港人	'Hong Kong people'
jat zai	1仔	'1 boy'; 'top' boy; usually refers to the role of penetrator in anal intercourse
jatgaajan	一家人	'all in the family'
Jik Ging	易經	*A Book of Change*; a classical Chinese text (= Mandarin *Yi Jing*); well known as *I-Ching* in Wade-Giles romanization
jikjan caang tungzi	直人撑同志	'straights back up gays'
koinim maan wa	概念漫畫	'conceptual comics'
lauman	流氓	'hooligan' (= Mandarin *liumang*)
ling zai	零仔	'0 boy'; 'bottom' boy, usually refers to the role of being penetrated in anal intercourse
memba	no equivalent	'member'; self-label of gay man used exclusively in the Hong Kong gay community
nggwongcoi	唔光彩	'not bright'; disgraceful, disrespectful (= Mandarin *buguangcai*)
noeng	娘	old fashioned

sai jan	西人	'Westerner'
Sun Yat-sen	孫逸仙	the father of the modern Chinese nation (= Mandarin SunYixian)
toi ng hei tau	抬唔起頭	'cannot lift up one's head'; shameful (= Mandarin *taibuqitou*)
tungsinglyn	同性戀	'homosexuality' (= Mandarin *tongxinglian*)
tungsinglyunze	同性戀者	'homosexual' (= Mandarin *tongxinglianzhe*)
tungzi	同志	'comrade'; queer (= Mandarin tongzhi)
zyut wat si cyu	啜核私處	'witty private parts'; the title of an artwork in In/Out: Hong Kong Tongzhi Art

* The Chinese terms translated here are mainly used in Hong Kong. A direct literal translation of a Chinese term is given first, if possible, and put in quotation marks, followed by a more semantic interpretation of the term. The interpretation is brief, and should be used for quick reference only. Readers are advised to refer to the main text for a fuller explanation of the terms.

Notes

Introduction

1 The second gay pride parade had just been held on 1 November 2009 and about 1,800 people turned up.

2 In discussing the relationship between sexuality and citizenship in Britain, Richardson (1998: 88–95) argues that lesbians and gay men are only 'partial' citizens in terms of political, social and civil rights. I will argue, in Chapter 2, that in Hong Kong, whether homosexual or not, people have always been only 'partial' citizens, due to the nature of colonial and post-colonial governance.

3 See my earlier account for this 'apolitical' character of the Hong Kong tongzhi (同志) movement in Kong (2004); see also Ho (1997: Ch. 6); Ho and Tsang (2004a). This issue will be discussed in full in Chapter 2.

4 Following Foucault's (1982, 1988, 1991) notion of biopolitics, Aihwa Ong, in her various writings (e.g., 1993: 753–62, 1996: 748–49, 1999: 117–19), proposes what she calls 'family biopolitics' to understand the relationship between the state and the Chinese family. In particular, she argues that 'family politics' is a set of 'rational practices that regulate healthy, productive bodies, and their deployment in flexible capitalist activities' (Ong 1993: 755), which links the Chinese family with colonial rule, modernity and global capitalism. In this book, I extend her idea and argue that familial heteronormativity, as a derivative of 'family biopolitics', can be seen as a tool of state and familial control over queer (especially gay male) bodies. See Chapter 4 for full discussion.

5 Hong Kong has always been a migrant city and its residents have traditionally been highly mobile. The 1997 issue triggered off a series of visible and salient migration tides in the 1990s that have caught the attention of academic study. See for example collections in Skeldon (1994). See also Ong's (1993, 1996, 1999) groundbreaking notion of 'flexible citizenship' to describe some Hong Kong people (especially wealthy businessmen) who hold different passports and shuttle among cities around the world for better family advancement. The issue of queer migration will be discussed in more detail in Chapter 5.

6 Well-known literature has been devoted to describing the rapid changes in China since the economic reform, and has particularly drawn out the problems and issues of social and cultural margins in this series of transformation. See for example collected articles in Perry and Selden (2000), Blum and Jensen (2002), Fong and Murphy (2006).

7 See, for example, Farrer's (2002) discussion of the vibrant young sexual culture in Shanghai within the emergence of a market-based economy since the late 1970s; Rofel's (2007) discussion of how both the Chinese government and its people (including gay men and lesbians) have been passionately engaging in a 'desiring project' that fashions a new human being in the era of globalizing China. See also

Jeffreys' (2006) collection of articles on the various issues and problems of the changing sexual cultures in contemporary China.

8 See stories documented in Li (1998: 228–37); Ah Qiang (2008); Chou (1996a: 38–62; 101–21).

9 I have drawn insight from Agamben (1995), who argues how a human being, born as 'bare life', must be transformed, through the state and politics, to 'good life'. In his words, 'The peculiar phrase "born with regard to life, but existing essentially with regard to the good life" can be read . . . almost as if politics were the place in which life had to transform itself into good life and in which what had to be politicized were always already bare life. In Western politics, bare life has the peculiar privilege of being that whose exclusion founds the city of men' (p. 7, emphasis original). I learnt from his Foucauldian argument about how the sovereignty or the state has an encompassing power over 'life', but also was fascinated by the idea of exclusion and inclusion of citizenship and the distinction between bare/good lives. I think, to a large extent, money boys in China, which will be discussed in Chapter 7, have long been keen to be included in the 'good life', or 'quality' (*suzhi* 素質) life of urban citizens, but their efforts have always been in vain.

10 I draw upon Appadurai's (1996: Ch. 2) description of five 'scapes' – ethnoscapes, technoscapes, financescapes, mediascapes, ideoscapes – that characterize the various flows of people, goods, capital, images and ideologies in his thesis of 'global cultural economy'. See Inda and Rosaldo's (2002) introductory chapter, which teases out the major debates and dynamics of globalization; see also their updated version (Inda and Rosaldo 2008).

11 I borrow Parker's (1999: 218–21) creation of 'homoscape', as an extension of Appadurai (1996)'s five 'scapes', to refer to the global flows of queer images, ideas, bodies, capitals, technologies, within the global queer cultural economy.

12 I understand that lived experiences of Chinese gay men are very different from those of lesbians and other sexual minorities such as bisexuals, transsexuals, transvestites, sadomasochists and so forth. Due to the research limitation that I solely interviewed gay men, I have limited myself to the discussion of Chinese gay male sexualities. However, in theorizing gay space, identity, practice and desire (in short 'same-sex male sexualities') in relation to globalization and citizenship, I am aware of the possibility of having privileged it over other sexualities.

13 See, for example, Massey (1994), Ferguson (2006) and Trouillot (2001) in their critiques of globalization, which will be explained fully in Chapter 1.

14 For general discussion of using 'transnational' over 'globalization', see Hannerz (1996: 6); Ong (1999: 4–8); Grewal and Kaplan (1994: 1–33). On theorizing transnational study of sexuality, see Grewal and Kaplan (2001), Farr (2007), Blackwood (2005). See Chapter 1 for fuller discussion.

15 See Fraser's (1992: 123) discussion of the creation of 'subaltern counterpublics' and Warner's (2002: 112) discussion of counterpublics, which both stress the differences inside civil society. See Chapter 1 note 30 for fuller discussion.

16 Leung (2008) revitalizes the tension between 'theory' and 'queer' and articulates the tension between academic, global, English writings, on the one hand; and non- or quasi-academic, local, Chinese writings, on the other. By archiving the queer feelings of three such Hong Kong writers on local queer writings, Leung hopes to offer an intervention to localize the global phenomenon of queer theory. See Chapter 1 note 18.

17 Ho and Tsang (2007) argue that the dominance of elite (usually English-writing) discourse on sex and sexuality in Hong Kong is evident, but that it has been challenged by local everyday-life language, in which lies the possibility of a new space for understanding Chinese sexuality.

18 See Chapter 1 for a fuller discussion of new Queer Asian studies.

19 I have gained insight from Inda and Rosaldo (2002, 2008), in their critique of cultural imperialism in terms of three flows of globalization: the cultural domination of Western cultures in non-Western societies, the presence of non-Western cultures in Western societies, and the cultural domination among and within non-Western societies.

20 In the introduction of *Scattered Hegemonies*, Grewal and Kaplan (1994) challenge the Eurocentric view of postmodernism, seeing it as an internal debate within a Euro-American standpoint, and argues that postmodernity should be understood as a set of complicated social, economic, political and cultural relationships that produce specific discourses of space, time and subjectivity in multiple sites on a transnational scale and under a particular time frame. The notion of a multiple, fluid and interlocking structure of domination – what they call 'scattered hegemonies' – challenges the grand narrative of cultural imperialism in globalization through articulation of multiple and transnational identities and subjectivities, and this enables them to spell out a transnational feminist critique. I borrow their idea to fashion a transnational queer critique of Chinese gay male identities embedded in multiple, fluid and intersecting transversal locales.

21 See also Cvetkovich (2003)'s theory of archiving queer traumas and (lesbian) feelings and the application to Hong Kong of local queer writings and cultures by Leung (2008, 2007).

22 See Chapter 5 note 2 for an explanation of the different connotations of the word 'Asian' in different locales.

Chapter 1: Study of Chinese male homosexualities

1 I borrow these questions from Manalansan (2003: 5). The book is a brilliant exemplary work of 'new queer studies', examining the politics of transnational queer identity using Filipino gay immigrants in New York City as an example. Manalansan offers a critique to Altman (1996b) and Adam *et al.* (1999), whose works seem to unify the notion of global gay and conflate global gay identity with white gay male identity under globalization of queer identities. It is interesting to note that Manalansan's questions 'Whose Gaze/Whose Gay?' seem to be a critical reflection of Altman's 1997 article entitled 'Global Gaze/Global Gays'. See also Rofel (2007: 89–94).

2 Mainly employing the scientific and positivistic approach, essentialists argued that one could 'discover' or 'deny' one's 'true sexuality', and attempted to explain the properties of sexuality by referring to 'an inner truth or essence – a uniform pattern ordained by nature, not connected to values and emotions' (Stein 1997: 203). As argued by Weeks (2003), this is *reductionistic*, as it reduces the complexity of human behaviours to imagined simplicities of its constituents; and it is *deterministic*, as 'it seeks to explain individuals as automatic products of inner propulsions, whether of the genes, the instinct, the hormones, or the mysterious workings of the dynamic unconscious' (p. 7).

In the case of homosexuality, the early discussions of these scholars were preoccupied with the question of its origin: what makes a person homosexual? They studied 'homosexuals' initially as 'perverted', then as 'sick', and finally as 'different', persons. For these theorists, someone simply 'is' a homosexual. Such research usually had strong clinical implications, with or without sympathy. The male homosexual was perceived as a pathological abnormal human type, as 'the other', who was forced to talk about what made him that way and just how different he was (Kong *et al.* 2002: 240–42).

3 As noted by many (e.g., Seidman 1996: 14–15; Plummer 1998: 607), this was the neo-functionalist framework advanced by British sociologist Mary McIntosh in her 1968 article 'The Homosexual Role', which broke from the mainstream view and proposed homosexuality as a natural, biological and psychological state. Instead of asking what made a person homosexual, she asked what social conditions gave rise to the idea of homosexuality as a distinctive human identity. The article thus shifted the focus from the study of a universal homosexual desire to an historical analysis of the rise of homosexual identities and subcultures.

4 Epstein (1987) gives a comprehensive review of the debate. See also collected articles in Nardi and Schneider (1998).

5 This social–structural approach relativized the conception of gay identity and argued that the late nineteenth-century Western experience of same-sex intimacies was historically unique, sketching different ways of 'making' the homosexual identity – e.g., in the emergence of male transvestite social clubs and homosexual coteries in major cities such as London at the end of the seventeenth century that provided a cultural context for the development of homosexual identity and community (McIntosh 1968; Bray 1988); in the professionalization of medicine, intricately associated with the changing legal and moral situations, that led to the construction of sexual categorization (e.g., the category of 'homosexual') and to the efforts at social organization and regulation it evoked in the nineteenth century (Weeks 1981: Ch. 6); and in the rise of capitalism, which nurtured the construction of a personal life outside the heterosexual family, based on one's sexuality (D'Emilio 1983; Greenberg and Bystryn 1984; Adam 1985).

6 See also Plummer (1975: 131–52), who describes the process of becoming homosexual through four central stages: sensitization, signification, coming out and stabilization; Troiden (1979), for whom they are sensitization, dissociation and signification, coming out and commitment – and in his later revised version (1988: 41–58), in which they are sensitization, identity confusion, identity assumption and commitment. See also Warren (1974: Ch. 7).

7 Apart from the 'Foucauldian Deluge', Plummer (1998: 608–9) mentioned that another major force that interrupted an empirical sociology of lesbians and gay lives was the arrival of AIDS, which generated its own research momentum almost exclusively on AIDS-related issues and left little room for anything else to be considered and researched.

8 The famous quote by Foucault (1980: 43) is: 'The nineteenth-century homosexual became a personage, a past, a case history, and a childhood, in addition to being a type of life, a life form, and a morphology, with an indiscreet anatomy and possibly a mysterious physiology. Nothing that went into his total composition was unaffected by his sexuality . . . The sodomite had been a temporal aberration; the homosexual was now a species.' Foucault's (1980) idea of the medicalization of sexuality as leading to the rise of homosexual identity is very similar to Weeks' (1981: Ch.6) idea of sexual categorization leading to the construction of the category of the homosexual.

9 Hennessy (1995) distinguishes three uses of the term 'queer': for a newly emerging theory in the realm of cultural studies (i.e., queer theory), for an avant-garde gay and lesbian subculture, and for a new form of radical sexual political activism (e.g., Queer Nation). Here, I refer to queer theory in academia. Several canonical works are emblematic of a 'queer twist' in academia: e.g., Sedgwick (1990), Fuss (1989, 1991), Butler (1990), de Lauretis (1991) and Warner (1993). Although many of these writers exhibit disagreement and divergence in their queer views, Seidman (1995) argues that they all share certain broad commitments, which can be summarized as follows: '. . . they draw heavily on French poststructural theory and

deconstruction as a method of literary and social critique; they deploy in key ways psychoanalytic categories and perspectives; they favor a de-centering or deconstructive strategy that retreats from positive programmatic social and political proposals; they imagine the social as a text to be interpreted and criticized towards the aim of contesting dominant knowledges and social hierarchies' (p.125).

10 Parallel to the post-structuralist formulation of identity, queer theory advocates the notion of an unstable 'queer identity'. As opposed to the more fixed meanings of terms such as homosexual (medical inclination) or gay/lesbian (white and middle class), queer is an identity that is always under construction. It is a site of permanent becoming which has grown out of a history of changing responses to economic, political and cultural forces, and it is almost always in opposition to other identities (Jagose 1996: Ch. 7–8). As Edelman (1995: 346) argued, '[U]topic in its negativity, queer theory curves endlessly towards a realization that its realization remains impossible, that only as a force of derealization, of dissolution into the fluxions of a subjectless desire, can it ever be itself.'

11 For example, Lancaster's idea of the Nicaraguan *machistas* who have sex with other men but do not consider themselves homosexuals (Lancester 1988); Herdt's idea of 'ritualized homosexuality', in which 'semen transaction' between boys and young men is a common practice that is supported by the whole social order in Papua New Guinea (Herdt 1994); the 'third' gender such as Thai *kathoey*, the Filipino *bakla*, the Indonesian *waria*, the Polynesian *fa'afafine*, and India's *Hijra* – all of which by and large indicate the polymorphous nature of sexuality across traditional Asian and Pacific societies. Thus, studies of gender, sex and sexuality in non-Western countries tend to show a picture that does not necessarily reflect Western knowledge. See other examples suggested by Weston (1993), Herdt (1997), Johnson *et al.* (2000) and Boellstorff (2007a: Ch. 6).

12 Williams and Chrisman (1993) argue that colonialism refers to a particular phase in the history of imperialism that is now best understood as including 'the globalisation of the capitalist mode of production, its penetration of previously non-capitalist regions of the world, and destruction of pre- or non-capitalist forms of social organisation' (p. 2). As argued by Mongia (1996: 1–3), post-colonialism is a newly emerging school of thought, which tackles the issue of 'post-coloniality' on at least two levels. On the first level, post-colonialists view post-colonialism as an historical marker, signifying the era after the official de-colonialization of the once-colonized Third World. They study those unequal and uneven processes of exploitation and domination by which the historical, social and political experiences of those countries have come to be framed in the West. On the second level, post-colonialists argue that Western power has enabled the production of a wealth of knowledge about other cultures that in turn has permitted the deployment of Western power in those other countries both before and after official de-colonization. They urge a methodological revisionism that offers a wholesale critique of Western structures of knowledge and power and examines the very process of the production of knowledge about the other.

13 There is a new debate to discuss colonialism within non-Western societies and cultures. As noted by Appadurai (1996: 32), 'for the people of Irian Jaya, Indonesianization may be more worrisome than Americanization, as Japanization may be for Koreans, Indianization for Sri Lankans, Vietnamization for the Cambodians, and Russianization for the people of Soviet Armenia and the Baltic republics'.

14 See, for example, the early works that brought race and sexuality together, especially in the Asian American context: Takagi (1996); articles in the special issue 'Circuits of desire' in *positions*, edited by Yukiko Hanawa (1994: 2(1)); and collected works in Leong (1996).

15 See also Stoler (1995), articles in anthologies such as Lancaster and di Leonardo (1997), and Manderson and Jolly (1997).

16 Since the British came to rule Hong Kong in 1842, no convicted sodomist was ever hanged. The death penalty for sodomy was abolished in 1861 in England and Hong Kong followed suit in 1865; very few cases were reported (Lethbridge 1976: 306; see also Chapter 2).

17 In his second edition, Samshasha (1997) argued that homophobia in Chinese culture functioned implicitly through a 'fuzzy-transgender-transsexual pansexualism' (p. 12). His shift of argument can be interpreted, as argued by Leung (2007: 562–65) in her careful and meticulous reading of Samshasha's works, as a shift of the discursive relationships between homophobia, coloniality and nationalism during 1997 – 'a very recent history of homophobia appropriated as a form of anti-colonial discourse, the advent of Chinese nationalism replacing colonial ideology as the new hegemony, and the rise of a global homosexual identity that threatens to subsume all sexual variance in its monolithic image' (p. 564). By making this shift, Samshasha attempted to advance an argument for the uniqueness of Chinese homosexuality while refraining from celebrating it as a solely positive tradition.

18 Leung (2007: 560–61, 2008: 6) points out one more intellectual force that offers theoretical insights into Hong Kong queer culture. This is that of cultural workers/artists who mainly publish works in Chinese that appear in newspapers, magazine articles and other multi-media productions. She gives Yau Ching and Anson Mak as examples. Due to the colonial legacy and the corporate university's drive towards internationalization, scholars tend to write in English, as English publications 'weigh' more significantly towards promotion and tenure. As a result, these local Chinese-writings are often largely ignored even though they offer sophisticated theoretical insights into specific problems in Hong Kong. This imbalance reflects the power of academic, global and English-writing 'theory' over non- or quasi-academic and local Chinese-writings (see also Chan's (2002) similar discussion of the case of cultural studies in Hong Kong). Leung thus calls for a weaving between theoretical works in English and local Chinese-language writings that would yield fruitful interventions for creative and (queerer) ways of localizing the global phenomenon of queer theory.

19 I agree with Manalansan (2003: 5–9) that new queer theorists, those who come from a rather marginalized terrain within the American academy such as ethnic studies, post-colonial studies, women's studies, and gay and lesbian studies, have critically located themselves and their works within the discourse of an 'international' lesbian and gay movement that examines the meanings of queerness in the local/global transnational nexus. See Manalansan 2003: Ch. 1 note 3 for a list of important works which he identifies as 'new queer studies'. See also Cruz-Malave and Manalansan 2002: 1–10; Eng *et al.* 2005.

20 By deconstruction, I mainly refer to Jacques Derrida, Ernesto Laclau, Chantal Mouffe and Stuart Hall. For example, Derrida (1976) offers a strong critique of the logocentrism of Western metaphysics in philosophy. In terms of identity, as argued by Fuss (1989: 102–3), '(D)econstruction dislocates the understanding of identity as self-presence and offers, instead, a view of identity as difference. To the extent that identity always contains the spector of non-identity within it, the subject is always divided and identity is always purchased at the price of the exclusion of the Other, the repression or repudiation of non-identity.' Identity is always implicated in its opposite. The logic of identity is a logic of boundary, defining that which, necessarily, produces a subordinated other. Derrida's deconstructive critique of an essentialist notion of identity, or any concept, thus puts identity or any concept 'under erasure'. This approach has been largely employed by other scholars in fashioning a politics of difference – for example,

Mouffe's (1995) critique of an essentialist notion of woman in order to advance a non-identity-based radical democratic movement, and Hall's (1996a, 1996b) formulation that cultural identity, based on similarity and continuity as well as difference and rupture, is always a politics of positioning and repositioning. Their works inspire my critique of the essentialist notion of Chinese (gay) identity.

21 As noted by Yuval-Davis (2008: 162), the term 'intersectionality' was first used by Kimberlé Crenshaw in discussing American Black women and work in 1987, even though she, among others (e.g., hooks (1981), Anthias and Yuval-Davis (1983, 1992)), has been working on intersectional analysis for a long time.

22 I draw insights from Mouffe's (1995) critique of an essential category of 'woman' – that there is no 'woman' in general, but only women who occupy different subject positions simultaneously along the line of race, class, etc., which cannot be reduced to one single position.

23 Hall (1996a) argues that identity, or cultural identity, can be thought of in at least two ways. On the one hand, cultural identity is defined in terms of 'one shared culture, a sort of collective "one true self" . . . which people with a shared history and ancestry hold in common' (p.110). On the other hand, cultural identities, rather than identity, are a matter of 'becoming', 'unstable points of identification or suture, which are made, within the discourses of history and culture' (p. 113). So identities are always 'subject to the continuous "play" of history, culture and power' (p. 112), and do not have an essence, but a positioning. That's why there is 'always a politics of identity, a politics of position, which has no absolute guarantee in an unproblematic, transcendental "law of origin"' (p. 133). See Hall (1996b: 1–17) for a theoretical discussion of the notion of identity from a deconstructionist approach.

24 As argued by Grewal and Kaplan (2001), there are at least two ways of looking at the complexity of identity. One is the 'intersectionality' theory I have just described, which is mainly drawn from Black feminist thought (e.g., Kimberlé Crenshaw, bell hooks, Patricia Hill Collins, Floya Anthias and Nira Yuval-Davis). For example, Collins (1991, 1998) argues that relations of domination for Black women should not merely describe the similarities and differences of systems of race, class, and gender oppression as if they were three separate systems; rather we should look at the intersections and interconnectedness, i.e., the 'intersectionality', of how these three interlocking systems of oppression structure Black women's experiences at any given socio-historical context. The other is articulation theory, as proposed by postmodernists such as Gilles Deleuze, Félix Guattari and Stuart Hall. For example, Stuart Hall, in an interview with Lawrence Grossberg, argues that articulation is a form of connection that makes a unity of two or more different elements under certain conditions that are 'not necessary, determined, absolute and essential for all time' (Grossberg 1986: 53). Thus a unified notion of identity is only possible in a certain articulation of discourse. A theory of articulation, as argued by Hall, is thereby 'both a way of understanding how ideological elements come, under certain conditions, to cohere together within a discourse, and a way of asking how they do or do not become articulated, at specific conjunctures, to certain political subjects' (p. 53).

25 Foucault (1982) argues that human beings are made subjects through three modes of objectification: the first is the mode of inquiry, which tries to give itself the status of science; the second is the study of 'dividing practices', in which a subject is either divided inside himself or divided from others (e.g., the mad and the sane, the sick and the healthy, the criminals and the 'good boys'); and the third is the way a human being turns him- or herself into a subject – i.e., how one has learnt to recognize him/herself as a subject of 'sexuality'. The second and third processes are relevant to my study of identity formation, by which we engage in a dual process of 'subject-ification' (to borrow Ong's (1996) term, in her discussion of the

making of cultural citizenship). See also Foucault's notions of 'governmentality' (1991) and 'technologies of the self' (1988).

26 For example, Adrienne Rich's term 'compulsory heterosexuality' is a social system such as capitalism or racism, in which sexual preference has never been a 'free choice', but 'something that has had to be imposed, managed, organized, propagandized, and maintained by force' (1980: 648). Judith Butler (1990) offers a strong critique of the system of compulsory heterosexuality, which normalizes a bipolar sex/gender system. Summarizing her (1990) work, Butler (1995: 31) argues that the very notion that gender originates from sex should be contested. Gender is produced by a ritualized repetition of conventions, and that this ritual is socially compelled, in part, by the force of compulsory heterosexuality. The performance of gender is produced retroactively by the illusion that there is an inner gender core or natural sex, the effect of some true or abiding sexual essence or disposition: 'the "unity" of gender is the effect of a regulatory practice that seeks to render gender identity uniform through a compulsory heterosexuality' (Butler 1990: 31). Women and men are forced to conform to a binary men/women or masculine/feminine opposition (what she calls the 'heterosexual matrix', p. 5, see also Ch. 1 note 6) that appears to be natural. Ken Plummer (1992) defines 'heterosexism' as '*a diverse set of social practices* – from the linguistic to the physical, in the public sphere and the private sphere, covert and overt – *in an array of social arenas* (e.g., work, home, school, media, church, courts, streets, etc.), *in which the homo/hetero binary distinction is at work whereby heterosexuality is privileged*' (p. 19, emphases in the original).

27 See Ahmed's (2004: 146–55) discussion of the power of the everydayness of heteronormativity that produces a public form of heterosexual comfort at the expense of discomfort to the queer feelings of queer subjects.

28 As argued by Rubin (1993), a hierarchical sexual value system is expressed as including the 'charmed circle' and the 'outer limits'. Sexuality inside the 'charmed circle' is seen as 'good', 'normal', 'natural' and a 'blessing', and should ideally be 'heterosexual, marital, monogamous, reproductive, and non-commercial. It should be coupled, relational, within the same generation, and occur at home. It should not involve pornography, fetish objects, sex toys of any sort, or roles other than male and female' (pp. 13–14). Any sex that violates these rules is considered 'bad', 'abnormal' and 'unnatural', and thus falls into the 'outer limits'. This 'bad sex' may be 'homosexual, unmarried, promiscuous, non-procreative, or commercial'. Such sex 'may be masturbatory or take place at orgies, may be casual, may cross generational lines, and may take place in "public", or at least in the bushes or the baths. It may involve the use of pornography, fetish objects, sex toys, or unusual roles' (p.14). Rubin argues that these hierarchies of sexual value function in much the same way as other ideological systems such as racism, ethnocentrism and religious chauvinism.

29 See also Duncombe's (2002) *Cultural Resistance Reader* Part 3, which includes articles that discuss 'politics that doesn't look like politics', and Moore's (2005) *Global Resistance Reader* Part 4, which also contains texts that explore the expression of resistance through music, poetry, images and artwork.

30 In contrast with the idea of 'public spheres' in the conceptualization of civil society (e.g., Jeffrey Alexander, Jürgen Habermas), scholars have been increasingly discussing the 'differences' inside civil society and the creation of 'counterpublics' especially by subordinated groups such as women, ethnic minorities and queers. For example, Fraser (1992) defines 'subaltern counterpublics' as 'parallel discursive arenas where members of subordinated social groups invent and circulate counterdiscourses to formulate oppositional interpretations of their identities, interests, and needs' (p. 123). Warner (2002) defines a counterpublic as 'a scene

where a dominated group aspires to re-create itself as a public and in doing so finds itself in conflict not only with the dominant social group but with the norms that constitute the dominant culture as a public' (p.112). See also Meeks' (2001) discussion of civil society and the sexual politics of difference.

31 Berlant and Warner (1998: 562–64) argue that the 'sleazy' public sexual culture, like that in bars, sex clubs, bookshops and porn shops around Christopher Street in New York in the 1990s, had been nurturing a critical mass which later became 'a political base from which to pressure politicians with a gay voting bloc' (p. 563). However, they criticized gay politicians for being what they called 'respectable gays' who did not acknowledge the sexual subcultures as part of the basis of their political success, as they thought these subcultures were sleazy.

32 Bourdieu (1986) classifies four types of capital – economic capital (e.g., income); cultural capital (e.g., long-lasting dispositions of the mind and body in the embodied state, cultural goods in the objectified state and educational qualifications in the institutionalized state); social capital (which is made up of social connections); and symbolic capital (when these three types of capital are being represented and perceived as legitimated). See also Bourdieu (1989, 1984); and Moi (1991) and Skeggs (1997) in their appropriation of Bourdieu's notion of class in gender relations.

33 Marshall (1950: 8) defines citizenship according to three components. Civil or legal rights consist of rights necessary for individual freedom – e.g., freedom of speech, property rights, etc. as well as the right to justice. The institutions mostly associated with civil (legal) rights are those of the courts of justice. Political rights involve the right to participate in the exercise of political power – e.g., the right to vote and the right to be elected to political authority – and corresponding institutions are parliament and councils of local government. Social rights refer to a range of rights, including the right to economic welfare, to employment and social security; and the institutions connected to social rights involve education and social services.

34 See Richardson (2000, 2004, 2005). Bell and Binnie (2000: Ch. 1) gives a good summary of key thinkers who theorize the notion of sexual citizenship. See also Plummer (2003: Ch. 4).

35 In a similar line, Bawer (1993) argues that most gay men in America are 'mainstream gays', who, as contrasted with 'subculture-oriented gays', exhibit no difference from heterosexuals and choose to live a conventional life similar to that of most heterosexuals.

36 Dangerous Bedfellows (1996) includes a collection of articles whose intentions are to rethink the working definitions of public sex, AIDS activism and queer politics and fashion a new politics that goes beyond 'liberal reformist (calls for inclusion of gays in the military) or radical performative (kiss-ins at the mall)' (p. ix). The book serves as a good example of the radicalness of certain 'dangerous' queers who 'play with the dividing line between public and private, screw with the notion of a totalizing queer leadership class or gay "community", and fuck with the false binary between regulation and education' (p. 14).

37 Butler (1993) argues that identity politics, usually crystallized in terms of universal coming out, must become subject to a critique of the exclusionary operations of their own production: 'For whom is outness a historically available and affordable option? Is there an unmarked class character to the demand for universal "outness"? Who is represented by *which* use of the term, and who is excluded? For whom does the term present an impossible conflict between racial, ethnic, or religious affiliation and sexual politics?' (p. 227).

38 For example, Nardi (1999) argues that friendship is the crucial feature of gay men's lives and that by looking at gay men's friendship we have come to a new insight that blurs our conventional understanding of what constitutes the family, the

romantic relationship, the friendship and masculinity. See Weeks *et al.*'s (2001) discussion of families of choice and other 'life experiments' among gay men and lesbians, and the special issue on the notion of polyamory in *Sexualities* 9 (5), edited by Haritaworn, Lin and Klesse (2006). See Chapter 4 for fuller discussion.

39 See Kivisto and Faist's (2007: 2) and Plummer's (2003: 61) long list of newly emerged citizenships.

40 See also Boellstorff's (2005: 25–30) critique of the globalization of homosexuality and his call for a third way to conceptualize non-Western non-normative sexualities that would be sensitive to both the impact of globalization and the continuing existence of traditions.

Part I: Hong Kong

1 See the Introduction to Part III (p. 143) for a brief discussion of citizenship in mainland China.

2 See various articles collected by Ku and Pun (2004), especially So (2004) and Ho (2004); see also Ku (2002); Lo (2001).

3 Except a few who were elected members of Urban Council, a municipal body of the colonial government that provided municipal services to the population. It was dissolved in 1999.

4 See Chapter 4 for further discussion of Lau's model.

5 See Ho (2004: 29–30) for an interpretation of Turner's (1995) analysis.

6 Led mainly by students and intellectuals, the 1989 June Fourth Incident refers to a series of demonstrations in and around Tiananmen Square during 1989, which was ended by the government's clearing of the square, which resulted in hundreds of deaths on June Fourth. It is commonly called the 1989 Tiananmen Square massacre. In Hong Kong, it is usually referred to in the shorthand '64', read 'six four'.

7 As argued by So (2004: 242), the SAR government was ready to cut social welfare, civil sector jobs, and salaries, and was also prepared to cut back civil rights, such as by carrying out the Public Order Ordinance (which granted the police the power to interfere and prohibit any public procession and social gathering from being held, for the sake of 'national security') and by pushing through the controversial Article 23 of the Basic Law (basically, a bill to prohibit subversion of the PRC government that has been seen as a drastic curtailment of freedom of speech by many Hong Kong people). See also So's (2002) discussion of how the first Chief Executive, Tung Chee-hwa, had tried for a 'soft authoritarianism' in the HKSAR to deal with a legitimacy crisis and social protests.

8 As argued by Sautman (2004: 125–26), new Mainland migrants occupy a notch lower in the SAR ethnic hierarchy. They are generally disadvantaged in terms of socio-economic rights due to their temporary lack of full political citizenship. However, they can anticipate being included in the dominant group after residing in Hong Kong for seven years. They thus represent a denizen/margizen hybrid.

9 The July 1 March in 2003 is believed to have been the largest demonstration in Hong Kong since 1997. An estimated 500,000 people protested the proposed legislation of the Hong Kong Basic Law Article 23 (see note 7) in particular but also the poor governance of the HKSAR in general. Since then, the July 1 March (in shorthand, the 7.1 March) has been held annually, and serves as a platform from which to voice various political, economic, social and cultural discontents of society which seems to transform the political landscape of Hong Kong (see Sing (2009)).

10 See, for example, Mathews (1997) conception of Hong Kong identity as being both 'apart from China' and 'a part of China'; various articles collected in Pun and Yee's (2003) *Narrating Hong Kong Culture and Identity* and in Cheung and Chu's (2004) *Between Home and World: A Reader in Hong Kong and Cinema*,

especially Leung's (2004) cinematic analysis of Hong Kong cultural identity from the 1950s to the 1990s. See also Lui's (2007) book on Hong Kong people of four generations.

11 See especially Introduction and Chapters 1–2 of Sing's (2009) edited volume *Politics and Government in Hong Kong*. See also articles published (on politics, social movement, freedom of speech) by the newly emerged alternative media group Inmedia (www.inmediahk.net), which offers strong critiques to various issues of Hong Kong society.

12 See Introduction note 4, and Chapter 4 for my appropriation of Aihwa Ong's family politics on Chinese gay men.

Chapter 2: Queers are ready!?: sexual citizenship and tongzhi movement

1 As pointed out by Liang (1987: 4–6), although the British assumed sovereignty over Hong Kong in 1842, Hong Kong, with a few exceptions, continued to follow the pre-existing Qing code until 1844. In that year, the law of England was said to be in full force in Hong Kong except for where it was 'inapplicable to the local circumstances of the said Colony, or of its inhabitants' (Ordinance No. 15 (3) of 1844). One of such exceptions was the acceptance of non-monogamous marriage (men might have concubines), which was abolished by the Marriage Reform Ordinance of 1971. Thus, from 1844 to 1997, Hong Kong closely followed British laws.

2 As argued by Lethbridge (1976: 300–306), in English law buggery is a generic term for both sodomy (between two men or between a man and a woman) and bestiality (between a man and an animal or between a woman and an animal). Thus, three types of sexual behaviour – with a man, a woman and a beast – are covered. The first is a homosexual act that may entail affection, while the second was considered an unconventional heterosexual act, believed to be engaged in by working-class people in England as a convenient and cheap method of birth control; and the third is generally associated with youth and immature behaviour. To conflate these diverse sexual acts under the single term 'buggery' not only reinforces the stigma of homosexuality but also renders it more difficult to abolish the law.

3 The term 'gross indecency' is also arbitrary in meaning. There was no need to show evidence of physical contact for a person to be convicted of 'gross indecency'; if two men were seen to be behaving in a 'grossly indecent' manner, they could be convicted. It is, however, uncertain when 'indecency' becomes 'gross indecency'.

4 As Lethbridge (1976: 309) argues, European *esprit de corps* to some degree protected middle-class European homosexuals. Those who were too outrageous were usually sent back home, with their contracts unrenewed; or they would be encouraged to resign by their employers.

5 John MacLennan was a Scottish Inspector of the Royal Hong Kong Police Force. In 1980, he was charged with gross indecency by the Special Investigation Unit (SIU), which had been set up by the government in 1978 to track down homosexual civil and uniformed officers. When the police went to arrest him at his living quarters, he was found dead, with five gunshot wounds. Although he was judged to have committed suicide, the Hong Kong media cast doubt on this conclusion. Questions were raised about how a person could have remained conscious long enough to shoot himself four times after the first shot. The public was more shocked when it was revealed that MacLennan had been under investigation by the SIU. Since he had worked in the Vetting Section of the Special Branch in 1977, he had had access to a file that contained the names of officials who were suspected of homosexual activities, and other information about them. His death was thus alleged to have been a murder and a police cover-up because MacLennan knew too much about other homosexual senior members of the police force. The justice and integrity of the colonial government was brought into question (Ho 1997: Ch. 1;

see the Commissioner of Inquiry, the Hon. Mr Justice T. L. Yang (1981), for Yang's comprehensive report on the case; see also Chan (2007: 38–45) for his discussion of the legal development concerning laws governing homosexuality in Hong Kong.

6 See Klesse (2007: Ch. 1) for his discussions of the effect of decriminalization acts in the UK.

7 In Hong Kong, the Legislative Council does *not* have the power to establish laws as, for instance, Parliament does in the UK, and the Congress in the US, but only to recommend and debate them.

8 This is similar to queer politics in the West, where internal schisms have always been part of the movement. Seidman (1993) argues, in the case of the US since the 1970s, that internal schisms have always existed. The queer community has been dominated by white and middle-class lesbians and gay men, and this has been contested by queers who are not white or middle class, as well as by bisexuals, paedophiles, transvestites, transsexuals and those who engage in non-conventional sexual or gender practices such as SM. Similarly, Plummer (1999) points out that, in the case of Britain, there had been three internal schisms since the 1970s: one between assimilationists and transgressors, which constituted a basic tension between liberal and radical gay activists; one centred on a debate about gender, which manifested itself as a split between radical feminists and gay men (lesbians split away from the Gay Liberation Front in 1972); and a class-based schism involving an antagonism between those advocating left-wing politics and those who celebrated capitalism and gay consumerism.

9 They argued that the Hong Kong Red Cross statement in its 'guidelines for prospective donors' that 'You should NEVER give blood if you are a man who has had sex with another man' is discriminatory, as this draws up a rather simple formula that equates gay men with unprotected sex (Chen 2001).

10 Please see Wong (2004: 208–12) for a detailed description of this action.

11 BDSM is a short term for 'bondage and discipline' (BD), 'domination and submission' (DS) and 'sadism and masochism' (SM). The BDSM couple, Brenda and Laurence Scofield (together with the manager of their shop 'Fetish Fashion'), were charged with keeping a 'disorderly house' by the police in 2001. However, they won the case in 2001.

12 In 2005, the government announced that it would conduct an opinion survey of the population and would enact an ordinance against discrimination based on sexual orientation if the result favoured legislation. In protest, Hong Kong Alliance for Family, an anti-gay Christian front with a group of religious people posted a declaration consisting of four full pages in a local newspaper, *Ming Pao*, with the headlines 'Tolerating homosexuals ≠ encouraging homosexual acts' and 'Being against discrimination against homosexuals ≠ supporting legislation against discrimination based on sexual orientation'. By detailing the 'danger' of homosexuality, they called for Hong Kong people to oppose the proposed antidiscrimination legislation as they worried that passing the law would promote an 'unhealthy' lifestyle and erode the heterosexual monogamous family ideal (Ho 2008: 465–66). This backlash against tongzhi triggered the launch of the first IDAHO in Hong Kong.

13 In 2008, the IDAHO committee consisted of 16 NGOs: Womens' Coalition of the HKSAR, The Association for the Advancement of Feminism, Amnesty International Hong Kong Section, AIDS Concern, Social Movement Resource Centre (SMRC Autonomous 8A), Rainbow of Hong Kong, Rainbow Action, Horizons, Blessed Minority Christian Fellowship, Hong Kong Christian Institute, Christ Loves Homosexuals Campaign, Spiritual Seekers Society, Transgender Resource Centre, Civil Human Right Front, HK 10% Club and Les Peches. Supporting partners include F' union, Queer Sisters, Justice and Peace Commission of the Hong Kong Catholic Diocese, Church of Christ in China Sham Qi Church Social Concern Fellowship, Nutongxueshe, Society for the Study of Sexualities and Sex-pol, Gay Radio and Dim Sum.

14 There was a section where participants were asked to lay down on the floor for one minute to memorialize sexual minorities who had been murdered or attacked with homophobic violence.

15 One day before IDAHO (18 May 2008), there was another 'gay-straight alliance' rally called 'Straights Back Up Gays' (*jikyan caang tungzi* 直人撐同志 Cant.), for which the route was changed from Hong Kong Island to the Kowloon side, from Sham Shui Po to Mongkok, where an open forum was held afterwards.

16 As articulated by Yee (1989: 226–28) who, following his participant observation in some universities in Hong Kong in the mid 1980s, argued that readings and assignments could be characterized as 'anti-intellectual', that student-teachers assumed a 'spoon-feeding' role, and that lectures were 'rapid-fire and authoritative'.

17 According to Louie (2002), traditional Chinese masculinities have been conceptualized as *wen* 文 and *wu* 武 in Chinese literature. The *wen* and *wu* ideals formed the opposing poles by which Chinese masculine identity was constructed. See Chapter 6 for further elaboration.

18 Samshasha was a public figure, and also one of my respondents. He has since passed away.

19 Clarke (1993) discusses the new trend in advertisers' strategies in the 1980s, which targeted lesbian (along with gay) fashion consumers without offending heterosexual consumers. In the section 'When dykes go shopping', Clarke urges us to rethink the newly delicate relationship between lesbian identity politics and capitalism, which seems to move away from the earlier feminist's anti-fashion critique of consumer culture, femininity and resistance. See also Chang's (1998: 294–96) discussion of the homophobia/homophilia popular culture in Taiwan.

20 Representations of gay men in movies can be classified according to several types. The first type may represent various forms of transgenderism: transsexuals (e.g., Dongfang Bubai in *Swordsman II*, dir. Ching Siu-tung, 1992), male actors who play *dan* characters in traditional Peking Opera (e.g., Cheng Dieyi in *Farewell My Concubine*, dir. Chen Kaige, China, 1993), modern men in drag and glamorous drag queens (e.g., Joey in *Boy's?* dir. Hau Wing-choi, 1996), and 'temporary transvestites' – characters cross-dressed temporarily out of a necessity for sexual disguise (Straayer 1996: Ch.3) (e.g., Lam Chi-wing in *He's a Woman, She's a Man?* dir. Peter Chan, 1994). The second type is that of the pervert, psychopath or villain (e.g., Hu Jin-gwan in *Crazy*, dir. Hau Wing-choi, 1999) or AIDS patient (e.g., Kam Wing-lit in *A Queer Story*, dir. Shu Kei, 1997). The third, dominant type is the campy, bitchy man or sissy, who is usually an 'out', educated and fashionable gay man (e.g., Chau Chau in *Lavender*, dir. Yip Kam-hung, 2000). The fourth type is the straight-acting gay man (e.g., Lai Yiu-fai in *Happy Together*, dir. Wong Kar-wai, 1997), usually closeted (Law Ka-sing in *A Queer Story*, dir. Shu Kei, 1997), or the man who may convert to straight at the end (e.g., Ching Yu-hoi in *Oh! My Three Guys*, dir. Derek Chiu, 1994), or the *gamgong Barbie* (Cant.) – a well-built, usually gym-trained muscular gay man. Finally, there are the 'homosocial' men (e.g., the killer-cop couplet in *The Killer*, dir. John Woo, 1989), who exhibit an intense same-sex friendship.

In a similar vein, Yau (2005: 135–39) classifies the representation of lesbianism according to five categories of characters: (1) lesbians converted to heterosexuality (*Full Moon in New York*, dir. Stanley Kwan, 1989); (2) women with 'frozen' lesbian desires, set in historical times and/or in the martial arts genre (e.g., *Intimate Confessions of a Chinese Courtesan*, dir. Chor Yuen, 1972; *Intimates*, dir. Cheung Chi-leung, 1997; *Peony Pavilion*, dir. Yonfan, 2001); (3) perverts and criminals in gangster films (e.g., *Portland Street Blues*, dir. Raymond Yip, 1998); (4) lesbian lovers in soft pornography directed by heterosexual male directors (e.g., *Sex and Zen II*, dir. Chin Man-kei, 1996); and (5) the 'temporary transvestites' (Straayer 1996: Ch.3) (e.g., *Who's the Woman, Who's the Man*, dir. Peter Chan, 1996).

21 Lan Kwai Fong is the name of a small street in Central, the business district of Hong Kong, but Hong Kong people use it to refer to the surrounding area as well. The area is characterized by new, bright and trendy cosmopolitan-style bars, restaurants, cafés, saloons and other entertainment venues. It thus signifies an 'uptown' atmosphere and the glorification of values of hedonism and consumption. It is also alleged to be a 'gay ghetto'.

22 Please see the newly emerged alternative media group, In-media, that combines cultural critique with social activism (www.inmediahk.net).

23 Leung (2008: Ch. 4) suggested that it may not have been his transgression or pride in the tongzhi community but his extreme ambivalence about gender embodiment, sexual identity and queer kinship that still rendered him (he died in 2003) the queerest of the queer icons in Hong Kong.

24 However, as noted by scholars, this mainstreaming of queers has produced two seemingly contradictory effects. On the one hand, there is the increasing integration of the dual moments of 'queering the straights and straightening the queers' (Emig 2000; McNair 2002: Ch. 7). The most well-known phenomenon of 'queering the straights' is represented by the US TV series *Queer Eye for the Straight Guy*, which features five gay men ('the Fab Five') who have expertise in fashion, style, grooming, interior design and culture, and thus can coach and advise other, usually straight, men on lifestyle, taste and consumption; and the parallel, and perhaps partially resultant, creation of 'metrosexuals' (who first appeared in Mark Simpson's 'Here comes the mirror men' in *The Independent* 15 November 1994), who are usually straight urban men who have a strong aesthetic sense, are into fashion and grooming, spend a great deal of time and money on appearance and are not ashamed to show their vanity (see also www.marksimpson.com). Then there is the trend of 'straightening the queers', as gay men increasingly become more and more like straight men. However, it is the 'good homosexual', different from the 'dangerous queer', who is able to make him- or herself indistinguishable from heterosexuals (Smith 1994: 204–16; Sinfield 1998: 168). It is through these dual moments that sexualities are commodified and sexual difference is 'dissolved'. The good thing about this is that the visibility brings the issue of homosexuality before the public and partially circulates discourses to counter heterosexism, which may enhance tolerance in society and even serve as a basis for growing recognition of demands for civil rights for queers.

On the other hand, however, as noted by Kellner (1995), 'Difference sells. Capitalism must constantly multiply markets, styles, fads, and artefacts to keep absorbing consumers into its practices and lifestyles' (p. 40). hooks (1999) is right to point out that the commodification of difference functions to silence resistance and to transform subversive potential into consumption. Like tourists, a straight audience views a gay character in a film as if they were 'visiting' queer communities without necessarily changing their straight minds. As Emig (2000) asks, 'If the intriguing solidarity between "straight" and "gay" men brought about by commodity culture signals a new hegemony, then it must produce its own exclusion and fringes. What are they?' (p. 223). Cultural citizenship operates as inclusion and exclusion. Those who cannot afford the glamorous gay lifestyle, who fail to perform the hegemonic cult masculinity (e.g., straight-acting, middle class, young, full body, etc.) and who are marginal in the male-dominated gay world (e.g., lesbians) are usually seen as 'second class' queer citizens (see Chapter 3).

25 Chan (2008) can be seen as the first comprehensive and systematic study of the development of Hong Kong cultural policy.

26 See Richardson (2005) for her discussion of this form of neo-liberal governance of queer organizations in the UK.

27 See www.leslovestudy.com for a detailed archive on the issue.

28 According to Nutong Xueshe (2007), the Obscene Article Tribunal classified a piece of artwork simply because of the four words *zyut wat si cyu* (啜核私處 Cant.)

[witty private parts] of the title. The four words have been frequently used in the media, and they argued that the possible explanation was that the artwork suggested oral sex between two girls that rendered it 'indecent' under the arbitrary and subjective obscenity law. Following its usual practice, the Tribunal makes interim classifications in closed-door meetings and bears no legal obligation to disclose the reasons for its decision.

Chapter 3: Memba only: consumer citizenship and cult gay masculinity

1 Rice Bar was closed in 2008.
2 Ong (1999) uses the notion of 'flexible citizenship' to discuss transnational Chinese professionals and entrepreneurs who have the capacity to move around and get benefits from different nation-states for investment, work and family relocation. I borrow her concept and apply it to the case of Hong Kong memba, who also manoeuvre among different straight and gay spaces in order to create their own sense of gay citizenship.
3 For example, see reviews of literature in Featherstone (1987), Bocock (1992) and Miles (1998: Ch.2).
4 See, for example, Ma's (2001) discussion of the hierarchy of drinks among Hong Kong people and Cheng's (2001) ethnographic study of the highly Westernized consumption area of Lan Kwok Fong in Mathews and Lui's (2001) anthology of Hong Kong consumption cultures.
5 As argued by Mort (1980) and Evans (1993: Ch. 2–5) in the UK, the decriminalization of homosexuality might also contribute to the apolitical and consumer gay subculture. See Chapter 2.
6 A comprehensive and updated list of venues can be found in the free monthly gay paper *Dim Sum Magazine*.
7 The PRC implements an even more stringent (in principle) drug policy, but a space for drug use still exists due to its slacker enforcement of drug laws.
8 See Tang's (2008) meticulous discussion of the relationship between lesbian identities and Hong Kong urban space, esp. Ch. 7.
9 For example, Altman (1996a, 1996b); for a critique of 'global' queering, see Manalansan (1993, 2003).
10 See Connell and Messerschmidt's (2005) summary of the various uses of the concept 'hegemonic masculinity' since its appearance in the 1990s, especially those which came into being after Connell (1995), and their call to rethink its theoretical and empirical significance.
11 An historical analysis of gay images in Euro/American societies shows a series of changes from 'camp' to 'gay' to 'super macho' (Forrest 1994; Segal 1990: Ch. 6; Gough 1989; Humphries 1985). It is argued that masculinity has been claimed, asserted, or re-appropriated by male homosexuals. This 'super macho' look seems to focus entirely on the body, and the athletic male, masculine body in particular is glorified. I agree with Gough (1989: 120) – that this super-macho look is more pronounced among those gay men who are young, in-the-scene and living in large cities.
12 See also Lin's (2006) witty and eloquent discussion of anti-sissy gay male culture in Taiwan.
13 The term *gwailo* (or *gweilo* 鬼佬 Cant.) literally means 'ghost man/men', but is often translated as 'foreign devil(s)'. The term has been used widely in Hong Kong with a long history of racial derogatory sense of insult and condemnation, but nowadays, it has a much less negative connotation and may even be a neutral term as used by local Chinese and even by Caucasians – although some Caucasians might still feel uncomfortable with it.
14 *Caufui* (湊魁 Cant.) literally means 'taking care of a ghost'. *Fui* (魁 Cant.) usually means 'chief' or 'gigantic body or figure', but here it can also mean 'ghost'

(*gwai* 鬼 Cant.). 'Taking care of a ghost' is read by memba as 'going out with a ghost', i.e., 'going out with a *gwailo*, a Westerner'.

15 In this article, Ho and Tsang argue that the change of political sovereignty has impacted on the interracial relationship between Chinese gay men and their Westerner partners, using their sexual practices (mainly focus on anal intercourse) as the site of investigation.

16 See, for example, Ku and Pun 2004, Part II: 'Migration, belonging and exclusion'.

17 Bluetooth is a wireless protocol that creates personal area networks by exchanging data over short distances from fixed and mobile devices such as cellphones.

18 Many respondents, including some of my memba friends, have had bad experiences hanging out in gay venues in mainland China. See Chapter 7 for my discussion of similar bad experiences of my Guangdong respondents with money boys in China.

19 See articles in Bell and Valentine (1995); and Ingram *et al.* (1997).

Chapter 4: All about family: intimate citizenship and family biopolitics

1 This framework has been rigorously criticized, as it simplifies the process of modernization by regarding only industrialization and utilitarianism; overemphasizes the size, structure and (especially) the materialistic functions of family; and neglects the non-material and affective aspects of the family and the dynamics among family members in the current post-colonial Hong Kong context (e.g., Shae and Ho 2001; Ng 1994, 1995). Recent studies have tended to be situated in the specific socio-political, economic and colonial conditions that shape and have shaped family life in Hong Kong, and to treat family not as a 'thing' but as a series of everyday life practices through which different family members 'do family' (see *Social Transformation in Chinese Societies*, 2009, Vol. 4 Special Focus on 'Doing Families in Hong Kong').

2 See Law's (2009) later work, in which he coins the term 'collaborative colonialism' to represent the (post-)colonial power shared by both colonizers and Chinese in making Hong Kong Chineseness.

3 His story of his coming out to the gay world has been told in the previous chapter.

4 Lui (2007) discusses four generations alive in Hong Kong today. The first generation were born in the 1920s and 1930s, mainly in mainland China, and came to Hong Kong in the 1940s–1950s. The second generation is the post-war baby generation (1946–1965). The third generation were born between 1966 and 1975. The fourth generation are the offspring of the second generation, born between 1976 and 1990.

5 Salaff (1981) calls the Hong Kong family unit the 'modified centripetal family', as it focuses on 'economic cooperation and pooling of members' earnings to advance the family economy' (p. 258), and emphasizes 'the pride of place of all sons who continue the religious–cultural focus on the patriliny as well as the hallmark of the ancestral tradition' (p. 258). As a result of this focus, the son is the main recipient of family benefits while the daughter abides by the strictures of this family system, which demand her loyalty to her family of origin before marriage and devotion to her husband's family thereafter.

6 Please see Chapter 6 for a detailed description of the face issue in Chinese society.

7 See similar experiences reported by Adam (2006: 13) in his study of 70 gay male couples in Toronto who drew their blueprints for successful relationships from heterosexual models and viewed the commercial bar-and-bath scene as antithesis to couple relationships.

8 Seidman (2002) is a study of contemporary gay life in the US over the previous few decades. It traces gay life from the formation of the closet in post-war America to the present movement for equal rights sexual citizenship.

9 This was noted by Taiwanese scholar Ni Jia-chen in a conference about tongzhi politics in Taiwan. See Chu (2008 note 10).

10 As argued elsewhere (Kong 2000: Ch. 4), it is not easy for Hong Kong gay men to come out in social institutions such as at schools, workplaces and churches. Some are bullied at school, some need to remain in the closet due to the nature of their jobs (e.g., the disciplinary forces), and some have extreme difficulty in integrating homosexuality into religion (especially Christianity). However, it seems that the family has been the dominant institution, and that no one can escape it completely in the particular post-colonial situation and under the physical constraints of Hong Kong. See Chao (2002) for her critique of how Chinese patrilineal household and heterosexual marriage institutions incorporated within the state policy and housing arrangement constrain and limit lesbians in claiming a legitimate (cultural) citizenship in Taiwan.
11 This section is derived from Kong (2009b).
12 See Chapter 5 for my London respondents, some of whom had.
13 See also Bech's (1997: 141–48) discussion of the fluidity of sex, love and friendship in gay relationships and his link between the 'homosexual form of existence' and modernity.
14 For example, this is vividly depicted by Nardi (1999) in his discussion of the role of friendship among gay men in America.
15 Beck and Beck-Gensheim (1995) argue that individuals in the West (using Germany as the major example) are compelled to 'search for the right way to live' (p. 2) under the rigorous process of individualization in modern times. This has resulted in a greater autonomy in forming intimate relationships, experimenting with sexual lives and structuring family forms, with all sorts of possibilities as well as dangers, in a 'new era' – what they call the 'normal chaos of love'. See Lewis' (2001) examination of the debate about family change and anxieties about the growth of individualism. See also articles collected in edited volumes such as those of Mason *et al.* (2003) and Scott *et al.* (2004) to examine the rapid changes in family and marital lives in contemporary times.
16 As argued by Jamieson (2004), Giddens (1992) acknowledges that sexual relationship tends to be dyadic, but he draws on the psychoanalytic explanation that the feeling of exclusivity may stem from the unconscious desire to recapture that which 'the infant enjoys with its mother'. Moreover, the dyadic character of sexual relationships tends to be enforced by the nature of trust, which should not be treated as having the capacity for indefinite expansion, as 'the disclosure of emotions and actions is unlikely to hold up to a public gaze' (Giddens 1992: 138). Jamieson (2004) points out that the concept 'does not envisage any challenge to being-a-couple as the most sought after type of relationship in adult life' (p. 41).
17 Woods (1998: 344–58) argues that the family has always been a key major theme in Western gay literature. He refers to: (1) the story of how lesbians and gay men actually come from within families; (2) the story of how gay men and lesbians try to accommodate with, or distance themselves from, their (parent) families, or how families reject or eject them; and (3) the story of how lesbians and gay men create their own families, a new configuration of relationship which might be called 'alternative families' or 'alternatives to the family'.
18 For the debate over same-sex marriage, see, for example, Sullivan (1995: Ch. 5), Bawer (1993: 145–46), Warner (1999: Ch. 3); Meeks and Stein (2006); see also Bell and Binnie (2000: 53–61, Ch. 8).
19 For example, for Britain, see Yip (1997); Weeks *et al.* (2001, 2004); Heaphy *et al.* (2004); for Canada, see Adam (2006); for the States, see Mutchler (2000).
20 This can also be seen in the sex education in Hong Kong. See Ng (1998), Ng and Ma (2004: 491–92), Ho and Tsang (2004b: 704–5), see also Chapter 2.
21 Cases of remarriage were calculated by adding the figures of 'first marriage of bridegroom and remarriage of bride', 'first marriage of bride and remarriage of bridegroom' and 'remarriage of both parties', excluding registration of couples

who had either customarily married in Hong Kong before the Marriage Reform Ordinance enacted in 1971 or had married outside Hong Kong (Census and Statistics Department, HKSAR: Women and Men in Hong Kong: Key Statistics, 2008).

22 'Cottaging' is a British term for cruising at public toilets. This is called a 'beat' in Australia and 'fishing' in Hong Kong. Other unique sexual practices in gay cultures include sex in dark rooms (i.e., rooms inside gay bars or clubs for sex, common in most European countries) and in gay saunas or bathhouses, where there are many private cubicles and public halls for sexual possibilities.

23 Illouz (1997) argues how a culture of romantic (heterosexual) love plays a central role in defining the self in modern society and how this culture, intertwined with capitalism, particularly the culture of consumption, has become a utopia. See also an interview with Illouz (2007).

24 Mutchler (2000) presents four dominant scripts (romantic love, erotic adventures, safer sex and sexual coercion) that seem to frame the sexual experiences of his 30 young gay male respondents, whom he interviewed in California.

25 Swidler (1980) argues that there are four distinguishable oppositions within the love mythology in contemporary American culture: the tension between choice and commitment, that between rebellion against social obligation versus attachment to the social world, that between self-realization and self-sacrifice, and that between libidinal expression through love and libidinal restraint. I found the first and the third tensions (i.e., choice versus commitment and self-realization versus self-sacrifice) the most relevant to explain my respondents' responses to the Mr Right script, especially that of Aron.

26 My findings of factors leading to sexual non-exclusivity are similar to those in Yip's (1997) study of gay male Christian couples in Britain (n = 30).

27 For example, in Yip's (1997) study of gay male Christian couples in Britain (n = 30), no couples were in the category 'couples who expect the partnership to be sexually non-exclusive, but are so far behaviourally exclusive'.

28 I gained insight from Adam's (2006) discussion of 70 gay men who were in coupled relationships in Toronto and experimented with alternative relationships within the monogamy script. See also Heaphy *et al.* (2004), and Weeks *et al.* (2001).

29 As noted by others (e.g., Adam 2006), gay men have been able to separate sex-as-love from sex-as-play. In a similar vein, sex workers are also able to separate work sex and personal sex (see my discussions of male sex workers in Chapter 7 and of female sex workers in Kong (2006c)).

30 His story continues in Chapter 5.

31 I have argued that de Certeau's (1984: xi–xxiv) discussion of the tactics of the weak – e.g., 'ambivalence', 'camouflage', 'clever tricks', 'knowing how to get away with things' – can apply to my respondents' tactics in handling the coming out issue.

32 See also Plummer (1995: Ch. 6); Weeks *et al.* (2001); Weston (1991).

33 More alternative 'ways of life' are in the making: for example, solo living or singlehood; 'living apart together', i.e., committed long-term couples that are not co-resident (Levin and Trost 1999); polyamory, 'a form of relationship where it is possible, valid and worthwhile to maintain (usually long-term) intimate and sexual relationships with multiple partners simultaneously' (Haritaworn *et al.* 2006: 515); see Easton and Liszt's (1997) classic *Ethical Slut*; also Haritaworn *et al.*'s (2006) special issue on polyamory in *Sexualities*; and Barker (2005).

Chapter 5: Queer diaspora: Hong Kong migrant gay men in London

1 Informed by post-Althusserian Marxism and deconstructionism, both of which view identity as an entity of operating along the axes of similarity and difference, Hall

(1996c) urges a new conception of ethnicity that struggles between the nation, 'race' and Englishness, on the one hand; and the margins, the periphery, the 'Blackness', on the other. His formulation of Black cultural politics involves 'a new cultural politics which engages rather than suppresses difference and which depends, in part, on the cultural construction of new ethnic identities' (p. 169). I borrow his idea to examine Chinese gay migrant men's struggle of identity, among discourses of Britishness, Chineseness and gayness in Britain, in order to fashion a new queer cultural politics.

2 In the British context, 'Asian' and 'Asian British' usually refer to South Asians – people from the Indian subcontinent and Sri Lanka and their later generations born in the UK; while in the North American context, 'Asian' and 'Asian American' usually refer to people from East and Southeast Asia, including places such as China, Hong Kong, Taiwan, the Philippines, Thailand, Indonesia, etc. and their later generations born in North America. My London respondents, when talking about East and Southeast Asians, used the term 'Asian', even though in British society the term refers to South Asians.

In the 2001 census in the UK, all non-whites constituted 7.9 per cent (n = 4,635, 296) of the total population (58,789,194). Asian or Asian British (i.e., people whose origin is from South Asia such as India, Pakistan, Bangladesh) was the largest non-white group, consisting of 2,331,423 persons and representing 4 per cent of the total population and 50.3 per cent of the non-white population. Black or Black British (i.e., Black Caribbean and African) was the second largest non-white group, numbering 1,148,738, and representing 2 per cent of the total population and 24.8 per cent of the non-white population. See www.statistics.gov.uk.

3 For North America, see, for example, Leong (1996), Eng and Hom (1998), Eng (2001); for Australasia, see Jackson and Sullivan (1999) and Martin *et al.* (2008).

4 I mainly draw from Baker (1994), Parker (1998), and Skeldon (1994a). See also Skeldon (1994b), Cheng (1996), Benton and Gomez (2008).

5 Canada removed racial restrictions in its immigration policies in 1962, the United States in 1965, Australia in 1973 and New Zealand in 1978 (see Skeldon 1994a: 26–27).

6 In this article, Tam criticizes the essentialized framework that always stresses the voluntary 'separateness' of the Chinese community and renders it a culturally deprived 'problem'. She argues that this not only underscores the complexity of Chinese social and cultural organization but also ignores the structural inequalities that shape Chinese people's lives in Britain.

7 See Klesse's (2007: Ch.1) writing of the history of UK legal practice and the role of political discourses in policing queer identities and practices according to the public/private distinction. See also Waites' (2003) comprehensive and vivid discussion of the debate over the age of consent in the UK.

8 Informed by Foucault's conception of power and resistance, Cooper (2002: Ch. 6) directs our attention to the complicated relationship between the state and sexuality – in particular, to how lesbians and gay men struggle to shape state form and practice, and how the state enables and limits lesbian and gay equality initiatives. See also Cooper (1995). In a similar vein, Stychin (2003: Ch. 2) argues that law operates in both enabling and restrictive ways in governing (homo)sexuality.

9 Drawing insights from Mort (1980) and Evans (1993), Klesse (2007: 25–26) argues that this legal confinement is believed to be responsible for the growth of the apolitical and pleasure-seeking gay subculture. See Chapter 2.

10 Please see Keogh *et al.* (2004b) for their research on the living experiences of two ethnic minority groups of gay men in the London gay community – namely, British-born Black Caribbean men and White Irish immigrants.

11 *Farewell My Concubine* is a film adaptation (dir. Cheng Kaige, 1993) of a novel by Lee Bik-wa (Li Bihua) (1992) that tells the sad story of a gay Beijing opera actor who always plays the feminine role on stage and falls in love with his lifelong stage partner, a straight man. *M. Butterfly* is a film adaptation (dir. David Cronenberg, 1993) of a play by David Henry Hwang (1988) which is based on the true story of the French diplomat Bernard Boursicot, who 'mistakenly' fell in love with opera singer Shi Peipu, who was actually both a Chinese spy and a *man*. The film actors in these two films, Leslie Cheung and John Lone respectively, might have gained some 'sexual currency' for Chinese males. They were praised for dragging as women, as they passed the test of behaving like women with their elegant performances and delicate sensitivities. See my discussion of Asian male bodies in the Western context (Kong 2007).

12 In traditional Chinese culture, *jin tong* 金童 ('golden boy') and *yunu* 玉女 ('jade maiden') referred to a young virgin boy and a girl, respectively, who were innocent, young, and pure.

13 See also Hoang's (2004) discussion of a new Asian American porn star, Brandon Lee, who assumes the top position only through being constructed as an assimilated American masculine top; while Asian men in general again relegated the same position of sexual submission, abjection and bottomhood.

14 See Manalansan's (1993, 2003) similar discussions of Filipino gay migrants in New York City.

15 'Potato queen' refers to non-white (usually East and Southeast Asian) men who are solely interested in Caucasian men. 'Size queen' refers to those gay men who adore men with large sexual organs.

16 Madam JoJo's is a club in Soho, London, which caters mainly to drag queens and their admirers.

17 See similar discussion of UK-born Black Caribbean gay men in Keogh *et al.* (2004b).

18 See Luibhéid and Cantú's (2005) edited volume, which brings migration and sexuality scholarship together to examine the lives of queer migrants in the US context.

Part III: China

1 See Goodman and Perry (2002: 1–19); Keane (2001); Li and Wu (1999); and Harris (2002), for their discussions of the changing meanings of citizenship in contemporary China. As the literature points out, in the PRC lexicon of citizenship, there are a few terms referring to 'citizen', such as *renmin* (人民 'people'), which is the official term used by the PRC and implies national, meta-ethnic identity (e.g., *Zhongguo renmin* (中國人民 'Chinese people'); *guomin* (國民 'national people') (more a Taiwanese term and seldom used in China); *gongmin* (公民 'public people' – i.e., 'the public'), which seems to bear the meanings closest to the Western definition of citizenship, and whose use is often avoided due to its connotation of implying various 'rights', although it is believed to be increasingly used at present due to the development of economic and cultural citizenship since the 1990s; and *shimin* (市民 'town/city-people'), which is widely used in Hong Kong and in China to refer to citizens of a particular municipality or district (e.g., Beijing *shimin*).

Chapter 6: *New* new China, *new* new tongzhi

1 His story will be given in more detail later.

2 The idea of active fashioning is borrowed from Keane's (2001) discussion of Chinese citizenship since the 1990s, which in turn has been drawn from Hartley's

(1999: 154–65) notion of DIY (i.e., 'do-it-yourself') citizenship and Foucault's (1988) notion of 'technology of the self'.

3 Sommer (1997) argues that sexual relations between men in the late imperial era should not be seen as having been characterized by a prohibition of consensual sex between men after the introduction of 'the new Manchu morality', but as having been increasingly stigmatized by the penetrated male in Qing society.

4 Using non-literary publications produced by official, semi-official and popular agencies since 1949, Evans (1997) shows how Chinese women have become gendered and sexualized subjects within the broad parameters of dominant discourses and practices, both in the constrained ideological atmosphere from the 1950s to the early 1970s and in the more consumer-oriented context of the 1990s.

5 It seemed that homosexuality was increasingly handled as a case of hooliganism from 1949 to 1997. It is interesting to note that no criminal laws were ever formulated between 1949 and 1979, so that *no* law, technically speaking, outlawed or applied to homosexuality. Hooliganism was first introduced in Article 106 of the Criminal Law in 1979 to refer to a wide range of social misbehaviours such as 'group fighting, provoking trouble, humiliating women, or engaging in other hooligan activities, thus disrupting public order, under aggravated circumstances' (Gao 1995: 66; Liu 1995). Thus homosexuality was not even on the list, though it might be considered one of the 'other hooligan activities' referred to (Gao 1995: 75). However, from 1949 to 1997 (the year when the revised Criminal Law deleted specific reference to the crime of hooliganism), homosexuality had always been associated with (and thus penalized as) 'hooliganism'.

6 Pan (2006: 24–28) argues that the 'sexual revolution' of contemporary China is a result of a complex change of sexual culture throughout the life cycle, seen as the total sum of functions of the most fundamental aspects of human activity, and relations between them. As noted, five salient features of China's sexual revolution are: 'the increasing separation of sex from reproduction; the challenge posed to traditional conceptions of marriage by the more recent concept of love; the increasing recognition of the significance of sex in marriage; the growing detachment of sexual desire from romantic commitment; and the changed nature of life for women in China today' (p. 24). Pan argues that the government initiatives on reproduction, fertility, marriage, etc., whether intended or unintended, have played a key role in shaping the new meanings of sexual culture in contemporary China. See also Y. X. Yan's (2003) anthropological study of Xiajia village in Heilongjiang, which discusses the changing culture in terms of spouse selection, post-marital residence, conjugal power and fertility choices among the younger generations since 1949.

7 See, for example, Farrer's (2002) discussion of vibrant youth sexual cultures in Shanghai; Erwin's (2000) discussion of the open discussion of sexuality fostered by telephone hotlines; and Rofel's (2007) observations of a plethora of public discussion of people's desires, aspirations, longings and passions in public culture. See also Hershatter 1996: 88–93.

8 See note 5.

9 Indigenous writings have been published, though mainly by heterosexual academics who wrote in a traditional objective and scientific sociological manner – for example, *Their World – Perspectives of Male Homosexual Groups in Mainland China* (Li Yinhe and Wang Xiaobo, 1992) and *Same-Sex Love* (Zhang Beichuan, 1994). Wu (2003: 125–33) noted a few other publications, such as the monthly newsletter *Friends* (1998–) and a biweekly bilingual webzine, *taohong man tianxia* [Pink Dollar All over the World], from 1997 to 2001.

10 See also Hershatter (1996); Evans (1997); Sigley (1998); Honig (2003).
11 I had the opportunity to participate in part of the 4th Beijing Queer Film Festival, chairing a post-screening discussion one evening. I learnt that the organizers, mainly artists, had huge problems in organizing the festival without getting troubled by the government.
12 Permanent residents, *changzhu renkou* 常住人口, are defined as consisting of those people who live in a city for more than six months.
13 Interviewees spoke in Cantonese or Mandarin, depending on where they were from. In this chapter, I specify all Cantonese quotes; those without specification were spoken in Mandarin.
14 *Ng gwong coi* 唔光彩 literally means 'not bright', and usually refers to behaviours or relationships that are disgraceful (e.g., shoplifting, extra-marital affairs) and thus bring shame to the doer, making him or her 'disgraceful' or 'unrespectable'. In conversations with my respondents, most of them referred to homosexuality as an example of *ng gwong coi*.
15 See, for example, interviews reported in Li (2006); Gil (2002), Chou (1996a: Ch. 6).
16 The controlling mechanisms in the countryside used to be the production brigades and production teams, but these were eradicated by Dengist reforms.
17 See Bray's (2005) study of *danwei* 單位 as a distinctive form of socialist governmentality in urban China.
18 Hu followed the Giles system of Romanization, so the Chinese term 丟臉 was translated in the article as Tiulien, instead of Diulian.
19 *Taibuqitou* 抬不起頭, literally meaning 'cannot lift up one's head', usually refers to moral shamefulness with respect to someone else.
20 See Solinger's (1999) seminal study of rural-to-urban migrants in relation to citizenship in urban China. See also Zhang's (2001) ethnographic study of the migrant settlement in Zhejiang village in Beijing.
21 There is a debate as to whether the *danwei* has lost its impact on urban citizens. See Bray (2005), Yu and Liu (2004), Li (2008).
22 See Cho's (2009) critique of 'contract marriage' between Korean gays and lesbians.
23 See similar findings and discussions in Li (2006: 94–99).
24 See a similar discussion of Indonesian gay men in Boellstorff (2007b).
25 Lei Feng 雷鋒 was a soldier of the People's Liberation Army in the 1950s. He died in 1962 at the age of 21 while he was performing his duty. After his death, he was treated as an icon of a model citizen who was selfless, noble and willing to sacrifice to the nation. The youth of the whole country were indoctrinated with the so-called 'Lei Feng spirit' in the 'Learn from Comrade Lei Feng' campaign, which paralleled the Great Leap Forward campaign during the early 1960s. Lei Feng has periodically been revived since, whenever the ruling Party has wished to slow and control the growth of individualism (e.g., after the 1989 June Fourth Incident).

Chapter 7: Sex and work in a queer time and place

1 This chapter is a different version of Kong (2010).
2 Most literature about prostitution comes from the public health perspective, which focuses on the relationship between female prostitution and STDs and HIV/AIDS transmission. See, for example, Cohen *et al.* (1996); Gil *et al.* (1996); Hong and Li (2007).
3 See also Dikötter (1995: 133–35).
4 See also Jeffreys (2004: Ch. 4).
5 As compared with female prostitution, study of male prostitution is relatively rare and most of the studies of male prostitution focus on men who serve men as the majority clients are men; studies of men who serve women are even fewer.

6 As argued by Biddulph (2007: Ch. 1 note 46), 'yanda' is a short term of 'yanli daji yanzhong xingshi fanzui' (嚴厲打擊嚴重刑事犯罪) translated as 'the hard strike against serious crime'. The term 'hard strike' is also translated as 'stern blows' or 'severe blows' by other scholars (e.g., Bakken 2000: 391–98). The police have launched an ongoing series of hard strikes against 'serious crimes', including (mainly) female prostitution, since 1983. *Yanda* 嚴打 on commercial sexual practices is also called *Saohuang* (掃黃). See also Biddulph (2007: 153–76), Jeffreys (2004: Ch. 4).

7 See Jeffreys' (2007) detailed and meticulous discussion of Li Ning's case and its subsequent broader legal debate in the PRC media.

8 Drawn from a continuing research project on the male sex industry in greater China (major sites: Hong Kong, Beijing, Shanghai, Dali, Guangzhou and Shenzhen) since 2003, this chapter is based on field visits made in Beijing and Shanghai from 2004 to 2005. Participants were all Chinese in origin, at least 18 years old, who reported having had sex with at least one other man in exchange for money over the previous six months. During the period I conducted 30 in-depth face-to-face interviews with Chinese male sex workers in Beijing (n = 14) and Shanghai (n = 16), the two cities believed to have high numbers of homosexuals (or MSM) and men who sell sex.

9 See Tong (2007: Ch. 2) for a list of slang and terms used in the male sex industry in China.

10 See Aggleton's (1999) collection of articles about men who sell sex in different places such as France, Canada, the US, Mexico City, Santo Domingo, Costa Rica, Brazil, Lima, Thailand and the Philippines. See also West and de Villiers (1993) study in west London.

11 In my sample, nine respondents belonged to the first type; eight to the second type; 11 to the third and two to the fourth.

12 In China, there are four special municipalities, or *zhixiashi* (直轄市) – Beijing, Shanghai, Chongqing and Tianjin – special self-governing municipalities independent of provincial rule.

13 In my sample, all respondents were ethnic Han Chinese, the dominant ethnicity in China. They ranged in age from 19 to 32, but clustered in their early twenties. Three identified themselves as heterosexual. Seven were ambivalent about their sexuality (but showed interest in men), while the rest identified themselves as homosexual (self-labelled 'tongzhi', 'gay' or '*quanneiren*' 圈內人). All but one were single; four claimed to have steady non-paying affective relationships with men, and three had such with women. More than half had attained average or higher levels of education (three had primary education, eight had attended junior middle school, 13 had attended senior middle school, and six had post-secondary or university education). All were born in mainland China, in different regions but they mainly came from rural or semi-rural villages. See the Appendix.

14 I borrow Rofel's (2007: 3) argument that Chinese people since the reform era have increasingly become desiring subjects who operate through sexual, material and affective self-interest to satisfy a wide range of inspirations, needs and longings.

15 For a detailed discussion of the development of the *hukou* 户口 system, see Chan and Zhang (1999) and Wang (2004); for discrimination and stigmatization experienced by rural-to-urban migrants, see Li *et al.*(2007); Goodkind and West (2002); and Amnesty International (2007).

16 In his study of Fujian province, Zhu (2007) argues that most of his migrant respondents did not ask for permanent settlement in cities. The problem is not just the difficulty of obtaining an urban *hukou* (which has been lessened recently by *hukou* reform), but a combination of factors that limits the temporary nature of the floating population: the demand for temporary migrants from the labour market (e.g., even if they stay permanently in cities they cannot find jobs); the household

strategies of migrants to diversify and maximize economic opportunities (e.g., an urban *hukou* would not be attractive if they had to give up the land in their hometowns for 'complete' migration) and minimize risk (e.g., their dependence on resources in their hometowns, especially land, for livelihood in adverse circumstances). Moving away from a *hukou*-centred approach, Zhu (2007) argues that structural (e.g., *hukou*, labour market) and personal (migrants' conscious rational strategies in migration) factors both contribute to the temporary nature of the floating population in China.

17 'People of three withouts' are people 'without a fixed residence, without a regular job, and without a regular income' (Guang 2003: 621).

18 For example, for England, see Davies and Feldman (1997); for the States, Calhoun and Weaver (1996); for Australia, Browne and Minichiello (1995); see also Prestage (1994) and Vanwesenbeeck (2001: 258–71).

19 See my discussion of Chinese male sex workers in the Hong Kong sex industry (Kong 2009a).

20 See Browne and Minichiello's (1995: 606–11) classification of client types.

21 See also Kipnis' (2006) 'keyword' approach in the semiotic politics of the *suzhi* discourse in contemporary China's governance, culture and society.

22 See my discussion of male sex workers in Hong Kong, Kong (2005c: 32–45); Browne and Minichiello's (1995) discussion of Australian male sex workers. For similar discussions of female sex workers, see, Kong (2006c); Sanders (2005: Ch.8); and O'Connell Davidson (1996). For a review of the labour process of modern Western prostitution, see Brewis and Linstead's (2000a, 2000b) excellent literature review, drawn mainly from UK and Australian experiences.

23 For example, Joffe and Dockrell (1995: 341–42); Browne and Minichiello (1995: 602–6); see also Vanwesenbeeck (2001: 251–58).

24 See Kong (2009a: 718–19) for a brief review of literature.

25 Ho (2000) mainly discusses the context of female sex workers in Taiwan, but I think the idea can also be applied to money boys in China.

26 See also Delany's (1999) discussion of the subcultural lives of sex workers in New York City's Time Square.

27 See O'Neil's (1996: 21) discussion of female sex workers, quoted in Brewis and Linstead (2000a: 92).

Conclusion: transnational Chinese male homosexualities and citizenship

1 There are some exceptions. For example, symbolic interactionists acknowledge the constant flux and flexibility of the self in their notion of a multiplicity of social roles (Plummer 1996: 223–4).

2 I have gained insight from Sautman's (2004) discussion that Hong Kong has developed into a semi-ethnocracy, in which a hierarchy of citizens (citizen–denizen–margizen) has been created. See Part I Hong Kong.

3 As noted by Ho (2008), East Asia's new liberal states, although claiming respect for diversity, sometimes work closely with the pastoral power of Protestant Christian- or Catholic-based NGOs to institute and maintain a 'reign of civility and respectability' that regulates sexual acts and information exchanges.

4 Please see similar discussions of how non-Western gay men respond to the ostensibly Western queer identity within the constellation of global queer culture – e.g., Boellstorff's (2005) discussion of Indonesian gay men and Manalansan's (2003) discussion of Filipino gay migrants living in New York City.

5 I draw insight from Deleuze and Guattari (1986: Ch.3), who talk about the politics of minor literature as a genre of resistance.

Appendix

1 See various articles collected in Strauss and Corbin (1997), and Parts IV and V in Denzin and Lincoln (2000).

2 Plummer (1995), after interviewing a man who was a foot fetishist, asked a series of thoughtful questions: 'What brought me to seek out a man who wanted to talk about his "unusual" sexual life? Why should I, or anyone else, want to coax anyone to tell me about their sexual lives in the name of Holy Social Science? . . . How could he produce such stories, and how did my "tolerant" responses to him actively encourage him to tell a certain sort of story . . . How much of his story was a performance of a dress rehearsal he had practised many times in solitude before? What, then, was the relationship of my transcribed interview to his actual life? And how was I to write this? In his voice, or in my voice, or in his voice through my voice, or even in my voice through his voice? And then, once read by others – including me and him – what multiple interpretations would it be open to? Would there perhaps be a correct reading which would finally get us all to the truth of such foot fetishists? Or would it be used as an occasion for condemnation, or curiosity, or simply titillation, or as a guide for someone else to locate their sexual nature?' (pp. 11–12).

3 Studying a lesbian community in Midwest America using participant observation and in-depth interviews, Krieger (1985) is a very good self-reflection of the problem of representation in the (inter-)relationship between observer and observed.

4 Even by having research subjects as 'authors', this problem cannot be completely solved, because the institutional constraints under which they became authors and the historical limitations within which they speak or write need to be considered (Clifford 1986: 13). So, although the idea of 'speaking for' others is rejected and the voices of both the author/researcher and research subjects can be heard in the text/field, the problem is whether the singular authorial voice has denied the claims of the other multiple voices.

5 Seale *et al.* (2004) point out that new concepts have been proposed which emphasize quality and credibility instead of the traditional sense of reliability, validity and generalizability for legitimatization, such as '*completeness* of descriptions . . . *saturation* of categories . . . *authenticity* as certification of the researcher's presence in the setting; *ecological validity* . . . *consistency*, "with which instances are assigned to the same category by different observers or by the same observer on different occasions" . . . *credibility* as a bridge between a researcher's interpretation and "reality" . . . and *plausibility* as the consistency between the researcher's findings and theories accepted by the scientific community.' (p. 407, emphasis original).

References

English-language sources

Abbas, A. (1992) 'Introduction: The last emporium: verse and cultural space', in Leung Ping-kwan, *City at the End of Time*, trans. G.T. Osing and the author, Hong Kong: Twilight Books in association with the Department of Comparative Literature, University of Hong Kong, pp. 3–19.

—— (1997) *Hong Kong: Culture and the Politics of Disappearance*, Hong Kong: Hong Kong University Press.

Abbas, A. and Erni, J.N. (eds) (2005) *Internationalizing Cultural Studies: An Anthology*, Malden, Mass.: Blackwell Publishing: 'Introduction', pp. 1–12.

Adam, B.D. (1985) 'Structural foundations of the gay world', *Society for Comparative Study of Society and History*, 27(4): 658–71.

—— (2006) 'Relationship innovation in male couples', *Sexualities*, 9(1): 5–26.

Adam, B.D., Duyvendak, J.W. and Krouwel, A. (eds) (1999) *The Global Emergence of Gay and Lesbian Politics: National Imprints of a Worldwide Movement*, Philadelphia, PA: Temple University Press.

Agamben, G. (1995) *Homo Sacer: Sovereign Power and Bare Life*, trans. D. Heller-Roazen, Stanford, CA: Stanford University Press.

Aggleton, P. (ed.) (1999) *Men Who Sell Sex: International Perspectives on Male Prostitution and AIDS*, London: UCL Press.

Ahmed, S. (2004) *The Cultural Politics of Emotion*, New York: Routledge.

Altman, D. (1982) *The Homosexualization of America, the Americanization of the Homosexual*, New York: St Martin's Press.

—— (1995) 'The new world of "gay Asia"', in S. Perera (ed.) *Asian & Pacific Inscriptions: Identities, Ethnicities, Nationalities*, Melbourne: Meridian, pp. 121–38.

—— (1996a) 'On global queering', *Australian Humanities Review*. Online. Available at: www.australianhumanitiesreview.org/archive/Issue-July-1996/altman.html (accessed 30 Sept 2008).

—— (1996b) 'Rupture or continuity? The internationalization of gay identity', *Social Text*, 48: 77–94.

—— (1997) 'Global gaze/global gays', *GLQ: A Journal of Lesbian and Gay Studies*, 3: 417–36.

—— (2001) *Global Sex*, Chicago: The University of Chicago Press.

Amnesty International. (2007) *China: Internal Migrants: Discrimination and Abuse. The Human Cost of an Economic 'Miracle'*. Online. Available at: www.amnesty.org/en/library/info/ASA17/008/2007 (accessed 30 Sept 2008).

Anagnost, A. (2004) 'The corporeal politics of quality (suzhi)', *Public Culture*, 16(2): 189–208.

Anthias, F. and Yuval-Davis, N. (1983) 'Contextualizing feminism: gender, ethnic and class divisions', *Feminist Review*, 15: 62–75.

—— and —— (1992) *Racialized Boundaries: Race, Nation, Gender, Colour and Class and the Anti-racist Struggle*, London: Routledge.

Appadurai, A. (1996) *Modernity at Large: Cultural Dimensions of Globalization*, Minneapolis, MN: University of Minnesota Press.

Appiah, K. A. (2006) *Cosmopolitanism: Ethics in a World of Strangers*, New York: W. W. Norton.

Au Yeung, S. (2006) 'Hong Kong's Alternative Film and Video Movement as an Agent for Social Change', unpublished MPhil thesis, The University of Hong Kong.

Baker, H.D.R. (1994) 'Branches all over: the Hong Kong Chinese in the United Kingdom', in R. Skeldon (ed.) *Reluctant Exiles? Migration from Hong Kong and the New Overseas Chinese*, Hong Kong: Hong Kong University Press, pp. 291–307.

Bakken, B. (2000) *The Exemplary Society: Human Improvement, Social Control, and the Dangers of Modernity in China*, Oxford: Oxford University Press.

Barker, M. (2005) 'This is my partner, and this is my . . . partner's partner: constructing a polyamorous identity in a monogamous world', *Journal of Constructivist Psychology*, 18: 75–88.

Barmé, G. (1994) 'Soft porn, packaged dissent, and nationalism: notes on Chinese culture in the 1990s', *Current History*, 93(584): 270–75.

Baudrillard, J. (1988) *Jean Baudrillard: Selected Writings*, edited and introduction by M. Poster, Stanford, CA: Stanford University Press.

Bawer, B. (1993) *A Place at the Table: The Gay Individual in American Society*, New York: Touchstone.

Bech, H. (1997) *When Men Meet: Homosexuality and Modernity*, trans. T. Mesquit and T. Davies, Chicago, IL: University of Chicago Press.

Beck, U. (2006) *The Cosmopolitan Vision*, trans. Ciaran Cronin, Cambridge, UK: Polity.

—— and Beck-Gernsheim, E. (1995) *The Normal Chaos of Love*, trans. T. Mesquit and T. Davies, Cambridge: Polity Press.

Bell, D. (1995) 'Pleasure and danger: the paradoxical spaces of sexual citizenship', *Political Geography*, 14(2): 139–53.

Bell, D. and Binnie, J. (2000) *The Sexual Citizen: Queer Politics and Beyond*, Cambridge: Polity.

Bell, D. and Valentine, G. (1995) *Mapping Desire: Geographies of Sexualities*, London and New York: Routledge.

Benton, G. and Gomez, E.T. (2008) *The Chinese in Britain, 1800-Present: Economy, Transnationalism, Identity*, Basingstoke: Palgrave Macmillan.

Berlant, L. and Warner, M. (1998) 'Sex in public', *Critical Enquiry*, 24: 547–66.

Berry, C. (2001) 'Asian values, family values: film, video, and lesbian and gay identities', *Journal of Homosexuality*, 40(3/4): 211–31.

Berry, C., Martin, F. and Yue, A. (eds) (2003) *Mobile Cultures: New Media in Queer Asia*, Durham, NC and London: Duke University Press.

Biddulph, S. (2007) *Legal Reform and Administrative Detention Powers in China*, Cambridge: Cambridge University Press.

Binnie, J. (1995) 'Trading places: consumption, sexuality and the production of queer space', in D. Bell and G. Valentine (eds) *Mapping Desire: Geographies of Sexualities*, London and New York: Routledge, pp. 182–99.

—— (2004) *The Globalization of Sexuality*, London: Sage.

Binnie, J., and Skeggs, B. (2004) 'Cosmopolitan knowledge and the production and consumption of sexualized space: Manchester's gay village', *The Sociological Review*, 52 (1): 39–61.

Blackwood, E. (2005) 'Transnational sexualities in one place: Indonesian readings', *Gender and Society*, 19(2): 221–42.

Blackwood, E. and Wieringa, S.E. (2007) 'Globalization, sexuality, and silences: women's sexualities and masculinities in an Asian context', in S.E. Wieringa, E. Blackwood, and A. Bhaiya (ed.) *Women's Sexualities and Masculinities in a Globalizing Asia*, New York: Palgrave Macmillan, pp. 1–20.

Blum, S.D. and Jensen, L.M. (eds) (2002) *China Off Center: Mapping the Margins of the Middle Kingdom*, Honolulu: University of Hawai'i Press.

Bocock, R. (1992) 'Consumption and lifestyles' in R. Bocock and K. Thompson (eds) *Social and Cultural Forms of Modernity*, Cambridge: Polity in association with Open University, pp. 119–67.

Boellstorff, T. (2005) *The Gay Archipelago: Sexuality and Nation in Indonesia*, Princeton, NJ and Oxford: Princeton University Press.

—— (2007a) *A Coincidence of Desire: Anthropology, Queer Studies, Indonesia*, Durham, NC and London: Duke University Press.

—— (2007b) 'When marriage falls: queer coincidences in straight time', *GLQ: A Journal of Lesbian and Gay Studies*, 13(2–3): 227–48.

Bourdieu, P. (1984) *Distinction: A Social Critique of the Judgement of Taste*, trans. R. Nice, Cambridge, MA: Harvard University Press.

—— (1986) 'The forms of capital', in J. Richardson (ed.) *Handbook of Theory and Research for the Sociology of Education*, New York: Greenwood, pp. 241–58.

—— (1989) 'Social space and symbolic power', *Sociological Theory*, 7: 14–25.

—— (1992) *An Invitation to Reflexive Sociology*, Chicago: University of Chicago Press.

Bray, A. (1988) *Homosexuality in Renaissance England*, London: Gay Men's Press.

Bray, D. (2005) *Social Space and Governance in Urban China*, Stanford, CA: Stanford University Press.

Brewis, J. and Linstead, S. (2000a) '"The worst thing is the screwing" (1): consumption, and the management of identity in sex work', *Gender, Work and Organization*, 7(2): 84–97.

—— (2000b) '"The worst thing is the screwing" (2): context and career in sex work', *Gender, Work and Organization*, 7(3): 168–80.

Browne, J. and Minichiello, V. (1995) 'The social meanings behind male sex work: implications for sexual interaction', *The British Journal of Sociology*, 46(4): 598–622.

—— (1996a) 'Research directions in male sex work', *Journal of Homosexuality*, 31(4): 29–36.

—— (1996b) 'The social and work context of commercial sex between men: a research note', *Australian and New Zealand Journal of Sociology*, 32(1): 86–92.

Bullough, V.L. (1976) *Sexual Variance in Society and History*, New York: Wiley.

Butler, J. (1990) *Gender Trouble: Feminism and the Subversion of Identity*, London: Routledge.

—— (1993) *Bodies that Matter: On the Discursive Limits of 'Sex'*, New York and London: Routledge.

—— (1995) 'Melancholy gender/refused identification', in M. Berger, B. Wallis, and S. Watson (eds) *Constructing Masculinity*, New York and London: Routledge, pp. 21–36.

Calhoun, T.C. and Weaver, G. (1996) 'Rational decision making among male street prostitutes', *Deviant Behavior*, 17: 209–27.

Campbell, C. (1987) *The Romantic Ethic and the Spirit of Modern Consumerism*, Oxford: Blackwell.

Cass, V.C. (1979) 'Homosexual identity formation: a theoretical model', *Journal of Homosexuality*, 4(3): 219–35.

—— (1984) 'Homosexual identity formation: testing a theoretical mode', *Journal of Sex Research*, 20(2): 143–67.

Census and Statistics Department, HKSAR (2008) *Women and Men in Hong Kong: Key Statistics 2008*, Hong Kong: The Government of the HKSAR. Online. Available at: www.censtatd.gov.hk/products_and_services/products/publications/index.jsp (accessed 8 Dec 2008).

Chan, K.W. and Zhang, L. (1999) 'The *hukou* system and rural-urban migration in China: processes and changes', *The China Quarterly*, 160: 818–55.

Chan, P.C.W. (2007) 'Same-sex marriage/constitutionalism and their centrality to equality rights in Hong Kong: a comparative-socio-legal appraisal', *The International Journal of Human Rights*, 11(1): 33–84.

—— (2008) 'Male/male sex in Hong Kong: privacy, please?' *Sexuality and Culture* 12(2): 88–115.

Chan, S.C.K. (2002) 'Building cultural studies for postcolonial Hong Kong: aspects of the postmodern ruins in between disciplines,' in S. Herbrechter (ed.) *Cultural Studies, Interdisciplinarity, and Translation*, Amsterdam: Rodopi, pp. 217–37.

Chang, H.H. (1998) 'Taiwan queer valentines', in K.H. Chen (ed.) *Trajectories: Inter-Asia Cultural Studies*, London: Routledge, pp. 283–98.

Chao, A. (2002) 'How come I can't stand guarantee of my life?' Taiwan citizenship and the cultural logic of queer identity', *Inter-Asian Cultural Studies*, 3(3): 369–81.

Chasin, A. (2000) *Selling Out: The Gay and Lesbian Movement Goes to Market*, New York: St Martin's Press.

Chauncey, G. (1994) *Gay New York: Gender, Urban Culture, and the Making of the Gay Male World, 1890–1940*, New York: Basic Books.

Cheng, S.L. (2001) 'Consuming places in Hong Kong: experiencing Lan Kwan Fong', in G. Mathews and T.L. Lui (eds) *Consuming Hong Kong*, Hong Kong: Hong Kong University Press, pp. 237–62.

Cheng, Y. (1996) 'The Chinese: upwardly mobile', in C. Peach (ed.) *The Ethnic Minority Population of Great Britain: Ethnicity in the 1991 Census*, vol. 2, London: HMSO, pp. 161–79.

Cheung, E.M.K. and Chu, Y.W. (eds) (2004) *Between Home and World: A Reader in Hong Kong Cinema*, Hong Kong: Oxford University Press.

China Ministry of Health, Joint United Nations Program on HIV/AIDS, and World Health Organization (2006) *2005 Update on the HIV/AIDS Epidemic and Response in China*, Beijing, China: National Center for AIDS/STD Prevention and Control, China CDC.

Chiu, S.W.K. and Lui, T.L. (eds) (2000) *The Dynamics of Social Movement in Hong Kong*, Hong Kong: Hong Kong University Press.

Cho, J. S.P. (2009) 'The Wedding Banquet revisited: "contract marriages" between Korean gays and lesbians', *Anthropological Quarterly*, 82 (2): 401–22.

Choi, K.H., Diehl, E., Yaqi, G., Qu, S., and Mandel, J. (2002) 'High HIV risk but inadequate prevention services for men in China who have sex with men: an ethnographic study', *AIDS and Behavior*, 6(3): 255–66.

Chou, E. (1971) *The Dragon and the Phoenix*, New York: Bantam Books.

Chou, W.S. (2000) *Tongzhi: Politics of Same-sex Eroticism in Chinese Societies*, New York: Haworth Press.

Chow, R. (1998) *Ethics After Idealism: Theory-Culture-Ethnicity-Reading*, Bloomington, IN: Indiana University Press.

Chu, W.C. and Martin, F. (2007) 'Editorial introduction: global queer, local theories', *Inter-Asia Cultural Studies*, 8 (4): 483–84.

Clarke, D. (1993) 'Commodity lesbianism' in H. Abelove, M.A. Barale and D.M. Halperin (eds) *The Lesbian and Gay Studies Reader*, London: Routledge: pp. 186–201.

Clifford, J. (1986) 'Introduction: partial truths', in J. Clifford and G.E. Marcus (eds) *Writing Culture: The Poetics and Politics of Ethnography*, Berkeley, CA: University of California Press, pp.1–26.

Cohen, M.S., Henderson, G.E., Aiello, P. and Zheng, H. (1996) 'Successful eradication of sexually transmitted disease in the People's Republic of China: implications for the 21st century', *Journal of Infectious Diseases*, 174: S223–S229.

Collins, P.H. (1991) *Black Feminist Thought: Knowledge, Consciousness, and the Politics of Empowerment*, London: Routledge.

—— (1998) 'Towards a new vision: race, class, and gender as categories of analysis and connection', in R.F. Levine (ed.) *Social Class and Stratification: Classic Statements and Theoretical Debates*, Lanham, MD: Rowman & Littlefield Publishers, pp. 231–48.

Connell, R.W. (1995) *Masculinities*, Cambridge: Polity Press.

Connell, R.W. and Messerschmidt, J.W. (2005) 'Hegemonic masculinity: rethinking the concept', *Gender & Society*, 19(6): 829–59.

Coombs, N.R. (1974) 'Male prostitution: a psychosocial view of behaviour', *American Journal of Orthopsychiatry*, 55(5): 782–89.

Cooper, D. (1995) *Power in Struggle: Feminism, Sexuality and the State*, Buckingham: Open University Press.

—— (2002) 'Imagining the place of the state: where governance and social power meet', in D. Richardson, and S. Seidman (eds) *Handbook of Lesbian and Gay Studies*, London: Sage, pp. 231–52.

Corber, R.J. and Valocchi, S. (eds) (2003) *Queer Studies: An Interdisciplinary Reader*, Malden, Mass.: Blackwell Publishing: 'Introduction', pp. 1–17.

Crenshaw, K. (1989) *Demarginalizing the Intersection of Race and Sex*, Chicago: University of Chicago Press.

Cruz-Malavé, A. and Manalansan IV, M. (eds) (2002) *Queer Globalizations: Citizenship and the Afterlife of Colonialism*, New York and London: New York University Press.

Currie, J., Petersen, C.J. and Mok, K.H. (2006) *Academic Freedom in Hong Kong*, Lanham, MD: Lexington Books.

Cvetkovich, A. (2003) *An Archive of Feelings*, Durham, NC and London: Duke University Press.

Dangerous Bedfellows (eds) (1996) *Policing Public Sex: Queer Politics and the Future of AIDS Activism*, Boston, MA.: South End Press.

Davies, P. and Feldman, R. (1997) 'Prostitute men now', in G. Scambler and A. Scambler (eds) *Rethinking Prostitution: Purchasing Sex in the 1990s*, London: Routledge, pp. 29–53.

de Certeau, M. (1984) *The Practice of Everyday Life*, trans. S. Rendall, Berkeley, CA: University of California Press.

D'Emilio, J. (1983) 'Capitalism and gay identity', in A. Snitow, C. Stansell and S. Thompson (eds) *Powers of Desire*, New York: Monthly Review Press, pp. 100–113.

de Kloet, J. (2008) 'Gendering China studies: peripheral perspectives, central questions', *China Information*, 22(2): 195–219.

de Lauretis, T. (1991) 'Queer theory: lesbian and gay sexualities', *differences: a journal of feminist cultural studies*, 3: iii–xviii.

Delanty, G. (2007) 'Theorising citizenship in a global age', in W. Hudson and S. Slaughter (eds) *Globalization and Citizenship: The Transnational Challenge*, London and New York: Routledge, pp. 15–42.

Delany, S.R. (1999) *Times Square Red, Times Square Blue*, New York and London: New York University Press.

Deleuze, G. and Guattari, F. (1986) *Kafka: Toward a Minor Literature*, trans. D. Polan, Minneapolis, MN: University of Minnesota Press.

Denzin, N.K. and Lincoln, Y.S. (1994) 'The fifth moment', in N.K. Denzin and Y.S. Lincoln (eds) *Handbook of Qualitative Research*, London: Sage, pp. 575–86.

—— (eds) (2000) *Handbook of Qualitative Research*, Thousand Oaks, CA: Sage.

Derrida, J. (1976) *Of Grammatology*, translated by Gayatri Chakravorty Spivak, Baltimore, MD: John Hopkins University Press.

Dikötter, F. (1995) *Sex, Culture and Modernity in China: Medical Science and the Construction of Sexual Identities in the Early Republican Era*, Hong Kong: Hong Kong University Press.

Duncombe, S. (ed.) (2002) *Cultural Resistance Reader*, London and New York: Verso.

Easton, D. and Liszt, C.A. (1997) *The Ethical Slut: A Guide to Infinite Sexual Possibilities*, San Francisco, CA: Greenery Press.

Edelman, L. (1995) 'Queer theory: unstating desire', *GLQ: A Journal of Lesbian and Gay Studies*, 2(4): 343–46.

Emig, R. (2000) 'Queering the straights: straightening the queers: commodified sexualities and hegemonic masculinity', in R. West and F. Lay (eds) *Subverting Masculinity: Hegemonic and Alternative Versions of Masculinity in Contemporary Culture*, Amsterdam: Rodopi, pp. 207–26.

Eng, D.L., Halberstam, J. and Munoz, J.E. (2005) 'What's queer about queer studies now?' *Social Text*, 23(3–4): 1–17.

Eng, D.L. (2001) *Racial Castration: Managing Masculinity in Asian America*, Durham, NC and London: Duke University Press.

Eng, D.L. and Hom, A.Y. (eds) (1998) *Q & A: Queer in Asian America*, Philadelphia, PA: Temple University Press.

Epstein, S. (1987) 'Gay politics, ethnic identity: the limits of social constructionism', *Socialist Review*, 17(3–4): 9–50.

Erni, N.J. (2003) 'Run queer Asia run', *Journal of Homosexuality*, 45 (2/3/4): 381–84.

Erni, N.J. and Spires, A.J. (2001) 'Glossy subjects: G & L magazine and "tongzhi" cultural visibility in Taiwan', *Sexualities*, 4(1): 25–49.

Erwin, K. (2000) 'Heart-to-heart, phone-to-phone: family values, sexuality, and the politics of Shanghai's advice hotlines', in D.S. Davies (ed.) *The Consumer Revolution in Urban China*, Berkeley, CA: University of California Press: pp. 145–70.

Escoffier, J. (1998) *American Homo: Community and Perversity*, Berkeley, CA: University of California Press.

Evans, C. and Gamman, L. (1995) 'The gaze revisited, or revisiting queer viewing', in P. Burston and C. Richardson (eds) *A Queer Romance: Lesbians, Gay Men and Popular Culture*, London: Routledge, pp. 13–56.

Evans, D. (1993) *Sexual Citizenship: The Material Construction of Sexualities*, London: Routledge.

Evans, H. (1997) *Women and Sexuality in China: Dominant Discourses of Female Sexuality and Gender since 1949*, Cambridge: Polity Press.

Faist, T. (2000) *The Volume and Dynamics of International Migration and Transnational Social Spaces*, Oxford: Oxford University Press.

Farr, K. (2007) 'Globalization and sexuality', in G. Ritzer (ed.) *The Blackwell Companion to Globalization*. Malden, MA and Oxford: Blackwell. Online. Available at: www.blackwellreference.com/subscriber/tocnode?id=g9781405132749_chunk_g978140513274935 (accessed 1 Aug 2008).

Farrer, J. (2002) *Opening Up: Youth Sex Culture and Market Reform in Shanghai*, Chicago and London: University of Chicago Press.

—— (2006) 'Sexual citizenship and the politics of sexual storytelling among Chinese youth', in E. Jeffreys (ed.) *Sex and Sexuality in China*, New York: Routledge, pp. 102–23.

Featherstone, M. (1987) 'Lifestyle and consumer culture', *Theory, Culture and Society*, 4(1): 55–70.

Ferguson, J. (2006) *Global Shadows: Africa in the Neoliberal World Order*, Durham, NC: Duke University Press.

Fiske, J. (1989) *Reading the Popular*, London: Routledge.

Fong, V.L. and Murphy, R. (eds) (2006) *Chinese Citizenship: Views from the Margins*, London and New York: Routledge.

Forrest, D. (1994) 'We're here, we're queer, and we're not going shopping: changing gay male identities in contemporary Britain', in A. Cornwall and N. Lindisfarne (eds) *Dislocating Masculinity: Comparative Ethnographies*, London: Routledge, pp. 97–110.

Foucault, M. (1977) 'Nietzsche, genealogy, history', in D.F. Bouchard (ed.) *Language, Counter-memory, Practice: Selected Essays and Interviews by Michel Foucault*, New York: Cornell University Press, pp. 139–64.

—— (1980) *The History of Sexuality, Volume One: An Introduction*, trans. Robert Hurley, New York: Vintage; first American edition published by Pantheon Books (1978).

—— (1982) 'The subject and power', in H.L. Dreyfus and P. Rabinow (eds) *Michel Foucault: Beyond Structuralism and Hermeneutics*, Chicago: The University of Chicago Press, pp. 208–26.

—— (1984a) 'On the genealogy of ethics: An overview of work in progress', in P. Rabinow (ed.) *The Foucault Reader*. Chicago: University of Chicago Press, pp. 40–372.

—— (1984b). 'What is enlightenment?' in P. Rabinow (ed.) *The Foucault Reader*, New York: Pantheon Books, pp.32–50.

—— (1988) 'Technologies of the self', in L.H. Matin, H. Gutman and P.H. Hutton (eds) *Technologies of the Self: A Seminar with Michel Foucault*, London: Tavistock, pp. 16–49.

—— (1991) 'Governmentality', in G. Burchell, C. Gordon and P. Miller (eds) *The Foucault Effect: Studies in Governmentality*, London: Harvester Wheatsheaf, pp. 87–104.

—— (1996; 1st edn 1989) 'Friendship as a way of life', in S. Lotringer (ed.), trans. L. Hochroth and J. Johnston, *Foucault Live (Interviews, 1961–1984)*, New York: Semiotext (e), pp. 308–12.

Fraser, N. (1992) 'Rethinking the public sphere: a contribution to the critique of actually existing democracy', in C. Calhoun (ed.) *Habermas and the Public Sphere*, Cambridge, MA: MIT Press, pp. 109–42.

Fung, R. (1995) 'Burdens of representation, burdens of responsibility', in M. Berger, B. Wallis, and S. Watson (eds) *Constructing Masculinity*, London: Routledge, pp. 291–98.

—— (1996) 'Looking for my penis: The eroticised Asian in gay video porn', in R. Leong (ed.) *Asian American Sexualities: Dimensions of the Gay and Lesbian Experience*, London: Routledge, pp. 181–98.

Fuss, D. (1989) *Essentially Speaking: Feminism, Nature and Difference*, London: Routledge.

Fuss, D. (ed.) (1991) *Inside/Out: Lesbian Theories, Gay Theories*, London: Routledge.

Gagnon, J. (1977) *Human Sexualities*, Glenview, IL: Scott, Foresman.

Gagnon, J., and Simon, W. (1974) *Sexual Conduct: The Social Sources of Human Sexuality*, London: Hutchison.

Gao, G. (1995) 'Comparative research on hooliganism', *Chinese Sociology and Anthropology*, 27(3): 64–78.

Giddens, A. (1991) *Modernity and Self-Identity: Self and Society in the Late Modern Age*, Cambridge: Polity.

—— (1992) *The Transformation of Intimacy: Sexuality, Love and Eroticism in Modern Societies*, Cambridge: Polity Press.

Gil, V.E. (2002) 'The cut sleeves revisited: A contemporary account of male homosexuality', in S.D. Blum, and L.M. Jensen (eds) *China Off Center: Mapping the Margins of the Middle Kingdom*, Honolulu: University of Hawai'i Press, pp. 238–48.

Gil, V.E., Wang, M.S., Anderson, A.F., Lin, G.M. and Wu, Z.O. (1996) 'Prostitutes, prostitution and STD/HIV transmission in Mainland China', *Social Science & Medicine*, 42: 141–52.

Glaser, B.G. and Strauss, A.L. (1967) *The Discovery of Grounded Theory: Strategies for Qualitative Research*, New York: Aldine de Gruyter.

Goodkind, D. and West, L.A. (2002) 'China's floating population: definitions, data and recent findings', *Urban Studies*, 39(12): 2237–50.

Goodman, M. and Perry, E.J. (eds.) (2002) *Changing Meanings of Citizenship in Modern China*, Cambridge, MA: Harvard University Press.

Gopinath, G. (2005) *Impossible Desires: Queer Disaporas and South Asian Public Cultures*, Durham, NC: Duke University Press.

Gough, J. (1989) 'Theories of sexual identity and the masculinization of the gay man', in S. Stepherd and M. Wallis (eds) *Coming on Strong: Gay Politics and Culture*, London: Unwin Hyman, pp. 119–36.

Greenberg, D.F. and Bystryn, M.H. (1984) 'Capitalism, bureaucracy, and male homosexuality', *Contemporary Crimes: Crime, Law and Social Policy*, 8: 33–56.

Grewal, I. and Kaplan, C. (2001) 'Global identities: theorizing transnational studies of sexuality', *GLQ: A Journal of Lesbian and Gay Studies*, 7(4): 663–79.

—— (eds) (1994) *Scattered Hegemonies: Postmodernity and Transnational Feminist Practices*, Minneapolis, MN: University of Minnesota.

Grossberg, L. (1986) 'On postmodernism and articulation: an interview with Stuart Hall', *Journal of Communication Inquiry*, 10(2): 45–60.

Guang, L. (2003) 'Rural taste, urban fashion: the cultural politics of rural/urban difference in contemporary China', *positions: east asia cultures critique*, 11(3): 613–46.

Halberstam, J. (2005) *In a Queer Time & Place: Transgendered Bodies, Subcultural Lives*, New York: New York University Press.

Hall, S. (1977) 'Culture, media, and the "ideological effect"', in J. Curran, M. Gurevitch and J. Woollacott (eds) *Mass Communication and Society*, London: Edward Arnold, pp. 315–48.

—— (1991) 'Ethnicity: Identity and Difference', *Radical America*, 23: 9–20.

—— (1996a) 'Cultural identity and diaspora', in P. Mongia (ed.) *Contemporary Postcolonial Theory: A Reader*, London: Arnold, pp.110–21.

—— (1996b) 'Introduction: who needs identity?', in S. Hall and P. Gay (eds) *Questions of Cultural Identity*, London: Sage, pp. 1–17.

—— (1996c) 'New ethnicities', in H.A. Baker, M. Diawara and R.H. Lindeborg (eds) *Black British Cultural Studies: A Reader*, Chicago: Chicago University Press, pp. 163–72.

Hanawa, Y. (ed) (1994) Special Issue: Circuits of Desire. *positions: east asia culture critique*, 2(1) spring issue.

Hannerz, U. (1996) *Transnational Connections: Culture, People, Places*, London and New York: Routledge.

Haraway, D. (1991) *Simians, Cyborgs, and Women: The Reinvention of Nature*, London: Free Association.

Haritaworn, J., Lin, C.J. and Klesse, C. (eds) (2006) Special Issue on Polyamory, *Sexualities*, 9(5).

Harris, P. (2002) 'The origins of modern citizenship in China', *Asia Pacific Viewpoint*, 43(2): 181–203.

Hartley, J. (1999) *The Uses of Television*, London: Routledge.

He, N. and Detels, R. (2005) 'The HIV epidemic in China: history, response, challenge', *Cell Research*, 15(11–12): 825–32.

He, N., Wong, F.Y., Huang, Z.J., Thompson, E.E. and Fu, C. (2007) 'Substance use and HIV risks among male heterosexual and "money boy" migrants in Shanghai, China', *AIDS Care*, 19(1): 109–15.

Healey, E. and Mason, A. (eds) (1994) *Stonewall 25: The Making of the Lesbian and Gay Community in Britain*, London: Virago Press.

Heaphy, B., Donovan, C. and Weeks, J. (2004) 'A different affair? Openness and nonmonogamy in same sex relationships', in J. Duncombe, K. Harrison, G. Allan and D. Marsden (eds) *The State of Affairs: Explorations in Infidelity and Commitment*, London: Lawrence Erlbaum Associates: pp. 167–86.

Heater, D. (2002) *World Citizenship: Cosmopolitan Thinking and Its Opponents*, London: Continuum.

Hennessy, R. (1995) 'Queer visibility in commodity culture', in L. Nicholson and S. Seidman (eds) *Social Postmodernism: Beyond Identity Politics*, Cambridge: Cambridge University Press, pp. 142–83.

—— (2000) *Profit and Pleasure: Sexual Identities in Late Capitalism*, London and New York: Routledge.

Herdt, G. (1994; 1st edn 1981) *Guardians of the Flutes: Volume 1 Idioms of Masculinity*, Chicago: The University of Chicago Press.

—— (1997) *Same Sex, Different Cultures: Exploring Gay and Lesbian Lives*, Boulder, CO: Westview Press.

Herdt, G. and Howe, C. (eds.) (2007) *21st Century Sexualities: Contemporary Issues in Health, Education, and Rights*, London: Routledge.

Hershatter, G. (1996) 'Sexing modern China', in G. Hershatter, E. Honig, J.N. Lipman and R. Stross (eds) *Remapping China: Fissures in Historical Terrain*, Stanford, CA: Stanford University Press, pp. 77–93.

—— (1997) *Dangerous Pleasure: Prostitution and Modernity in Twentieth-century Shanghai*, Berkeley, CA: University of California Press.

Hinsch, B. (1990) *Passions of the Cut Sleeve: The Male Homosexual Tradition in China*, Berkeley, CA: University of California Press.

Ho, D.K.L. (2004) 'Citizenship as a form of governance: a historical overview', in A.S. Ku and P. Ngai (eds) *Remaking Citizenship in Hong Kong*, Oxford: RoutledgeCurzon, pp. 19–36.

Ho, J. (2000) 'Self-empowerment and "professionalism": conservations with Taiwanese sex workers', *Inter-Asia Cultural Studies*, 1(2): 283–99.

—— (2008) 'Is global governance bad for east asian queers?' *GLQ: A Journal of Lesbian and Gay Studies*, 14(4): 457–79.

Ho, P.S.Y. (1995) 'Male homosexual identity in Hong Kong: a social construction', *Journal of Homosexuality*, *29*(1), 71–88.

—— (1997) 'Politicising Identity: Decriminalisation of Homosexuality and the Emergence of Gay Identity in Hong Kong', unpublished PhD thesis, University of Essex.

—— (1999) 'Developing a social constructionist therapy approach for gay men and their families in Hong Kong', *Journal of Gay & Lesbian Social Services*, 9 (4): 69–97.

—— (2006) 'The (charmed) circle game: reflections on sexual hierarchy through multiple sexual relationships', *Sexualities*, 9 (5): 549–66.

Ho, P.S.Y. and Tsang, A.K.T. (2000) 'Negotiating anal intercourse in inter-racial gay relationships in Hong Kong', *Sexualities*, 3 (3): 299–323.

—— (2004a) 'Beyond being gay: the proliferation of political identities in colonial Hong Kong', in A.K.W. Chan and W.L. Wong (eds) *Gendering Hong Kong*, Hong Kong: Oxford University Press, pp. 667–89; first published in D. Howarth, A.J. Norval and Y. Stavrakakis (eds) (2000) *Discourse Theory and Political Analysis: Identities, Hegemonies and Social Change*, Manchester, New York: Manchester University Press, pp. 134–50.

—— (2004b) 'The things girls shouldn't see: relocating the penis in sex education in Hong Kong,' in A.K.W. Chan and W.L. Wong (eds) *Gendering Hong Kong*, Hong Kong: Oxford University Press, pp. 690–708; first published in (2002) *Sex Education*, 2 (1): 61–73.

—— (2007) 'Lost in translation: sex and sexuality in elite discourse and everyday language', *Sexualities*, 10 (5): 623–44.

Hoang, N.T. (2004) 'The resurrection of Brandon Lee: the making of a gay Asian American porn star', in L. Williams (ed.) *Porn Studies*, Durham, NC: Duke University Press: pp. 223–70.

Holton, R.J. (2009) *Cosmopolitanisms: New Thinking and New Directions*, Basingstoke, NY: Palgrave Macmillan.

Hong Kong Cultural Policy Studies (1995) *Hong Kong Film Forum 1994 – Final Report*, Hong Kong: Zuni Icosahedron.

Hong Kong Government (1996) *Equal Opportunities: A Study of Discrimination on the Grounds of Sexual Orientation, A Consultation Paper*, Hong Kong: The Government Printer.

Hong Kong Government (Law Reform Commission of Hong Kong) (1983) *Report On Laws Governing Homosexual Conduct (Topic 2)*, Hong Kong: The Government Printer.

—— (1988) *Homosexual Offences: Should the Law be Changed? A Consultative Paper*, Hong Kong: The Government Printer.

Hong, Y. and Li, X. (2007) 'Behavioral studies of female sex workers in China: a literature review and recommendation for future research', *AIDS and Behavior*, 12(4): 623–36.

Honig, E. (2003) 'Socialist sex: the cultural revolution revisited', *Modern China*, 29(2): 143–75.

hooks, b. (1981) *Ain't I a Woman: Black Women and Feminism*, London: South End Press.

—— (1999) 'Eating the other,' in S. Hesse-Biber, C. Gilmartin and R. Lydenberg (eds) *Feminist Approaches to Theory and Methodology*, New York: Oxford University Press, pp. 179–94.

Hu, H.C. (1944) 'The Chinese concepts of "face"', *American Anthropologist*, 46(1): 45–64.

Hubbard, T.K. (ed.) (2003) *Homosexuality in Greece and Rome: A Sourcebook of Basic Documents*, Berkeley, CA: University of California Press.

Hudson, W. and Slaughter, S. (eds) (2007) *Globalisation and Citizenship: The Transnational Challenge*, London and New York: Routledge, 'Introduction', pp. 1–12.

Humphries, M. (1985) 'Gay Machismo', in A. Metcalf and M. Humphries (eds) *The Sexuality of Men*, London: Pluto Press, pp. 70–85.

Illouz, E. (1997) *Consuming the Romantic Utopia: Love and the Cultural Contradictions of Capitalism*, Berkeley, CA: University of California Press.

—— (2007) 'Romantic love: interview with Eva Illouz', in S. Seidman, N. Fischer and C. Meeks (eds) *Introducing the New Sexuality Studies*, London and New York: Routledge, pp. 36–44.

Inda, J.X. and Rosaldo, R. (eds) (2002) *The Anthropology of Globalization: A Reader*. Malden, MA and Oxford: Blackwell, 'Introduction: A world in motion', pp. 1–33.

—— and —— (2008) *The Anthropology of Globalization: A Reader*. Malden, MA and Oxford: Blackwell, 'Tracking global flows', pp. 3–46.

Ingram, G.B., Bouthillette, A.M. and Retter, Y. (eds) (1997) *Queers in Space: Communities, Public Spaces, Sites of Resistance*, Washington, DC: Bay Press.

Isin, E.F. and Wood, P.K. (1999) *Citizenship and Identity*, London: Sage.

Jackson, P.A. and Cook, N.M. (eds) (1999) *Genders and Sexualities in Modern Thailand*, Silkworm, Chiang Mai.

Jackson, P.A. and Sullivan, G. (eds) (1999) Special Double Issue 'Multicultural queer: Australian narratives', *Journal of Homosexuality*, 36(3–4).

Jackson, S, and Scott, S. (2004) 'The personal is still political: heterosexuality, feminism and monogamy', *Feminism and Psychology*, 14(1): 151–57.

Jagose, A.R. (1996) *Queer Theory: An Introduction*, New York: New York University Press.

Jamieson, L. (2004) 'Intimacy, negotiated nonmonogamy, and the limits of the couple', in J. Duncombe, K. Harrison, G. Allan and D. Marsden (eds) *The State of Affairs: Explorations in Infidelity and Commitment*, London: Lawrence Erlbaum Associates, pp. 35–57.

Janoski, T. (1998) *Citizenship and Civil Society: A Framework of Rights and Obligations in Liberal, Traditional and Social Democratic Regime*, Cambridge: Cambridge University Press.

Jeffreys, E. (2004) *China, Sex and Prostitution*, London: RoutledgeCurzon.

—— (2007) 'Querying queer theory: debating male–male prostitution in the Chinese media', *Critical Asian Studies*, 39(1): 151–75.

—— (ed.) (2006) *Sex and Sexuality in China*, New York: Routledge, 'Introduction', pp. 1–12.

Joffe, H. and Dockrell, J.E. (1995) 'Safer sex: lessons from the male sex industry', *Journal of Community and Applied Social Psychology*, 5: 333–46.

Johnson, M., Jackson, P. and Herdt, G. (2000) 'Critical regionalities and the study of gender and sexual diversity in South East and East Asia', *Culture, Health & Sexuality*, 2(4): 361–75.

Jones, R. (2005) 'Identity, community, and social practice among men who have sex with men in China', in M.M. Tam, H.B. Ku and T. Kong (eds) *Rethinking and Recasting Citizenship: Social Exclusion and Marginality in Chinese Societies*, Hong Kong: Centre for Social Policy Studies, The Hong Kong Polytechnic University, pp. 149–66.

Jones, R. (2007) 'Imagined comrades and imaginary protections: identity, community and sexual risk among men who have sex with men in China', *Journal of Homosexuality*, 53(3): 83–115.

Kam, L.Y.L. (2003) 'Negotiating Gender: Masculine Women in Hong Kong', unpublished MPhil thesis, The Chinese University of Hong Kong.

—— (2008) 'Recognition through mis-recognition: masculine women in Hong Kong', in F. Martin, P.A. Jackson, M. McLelland and A. Yue (eds) (2008) *AsiapacifiQueer: Rethinking Genders and Sexualities*, Urbana, IL and Chicago: University of Illinois Press, pp. 99–116.

Kang, W.Q. (2009) *Obsession: Male Same-Sex Relations in China, 1900–1950*, Hong Kong: Hong Kong University Press (Queer Asia Series).

Keane, M. (2001) 'Redefining Chinese citizenship', *Economy and Society*, 30(1): 1–17.

Kellner, D. (1989) 'Commodities, needs and consumption in the consumer society', in D. Kellner (ed.) *Jean Baudrillard: From Marxism to Postmodernism and Beyond*, Stanford, CA: Stanford University Press, pp. 7–32.

Kellner, D. (1995) *Media Culture: Cultural Studies, Identity and Politics between the Modern and the Postmodern*, London: Routledge.

Keogh, P., Dodds, C. and Henderson, L. (2004a) *Migrant Gay Men: Redefining Community, Restoring Identity*, London: Stigma Research. Online. Available at: www.sigmaresearch.org.uk/files/report2004b.pdf (assessed 26 November 2008).

Keogh, P., Henderson, L. and Dodds, C. (2004b) *Ethnic Minority Gay Men: Redefining Community, Restoring Identity*, London: Stigma Research. Online. Available at: www.sigmaresearch.org.uk/files/report2004c.pdf (assessed 26 November 2008).

Khong, T.K. (2008) 'Chinese representation in British politics', Viewpoints, The British Chinese Community Website. Online. Available at: www.dimsum.co.uk/viewpoints/chinese-representation-in-british-politics.html (assessed 26 November 2008).

Kibria, N. (2002) *Becoming Asian American: Second-Generation Chinese and Korean American Identities*, Baltimore, MD: The John Hopkins University Press.

Kipnis, A. (2006) 'Suzhi: a keyword approach', *The China Quarterly*, 186: 295–313.

Kivisto, P. and Faist, T. (2007) *Citizenship: Discourse, Theory, and Transnational Prospects*, Malden, MA: Blackwell Publishing.

Klesse, C. (2007) *The Spectre of Promiscuity: Gay Men and Bisexual Non-monogamies and Polyamories*, Aldershot: Ashgate.

Kong, T.S.K. (1993) 'Self-identity and Love of the Hong Kong People', unpublished MA thesis, University of Essex.

—— (2000) 'The Voices In-Between: The Body Politics of Hong Kong Gay Men', unpublished PhD thesis, University of Essex.

—— (2002) 'The seduction of the golden boy: the body politics of Hong Kong gay men', *Body & Society*, 8(1): 29–48.

—— (2004) 'Queer at your own risk: marginality, community and Hong Kong gay male bodies', *Sexualities*, 7(1): 5–30.

—— (2005a) *HIV/AIDS Prevention Programme on Male Sex Workers in Mainland China (In-depth Interviews).* [Unpublished internal report submitted to UNAIDS on behalf of Chi Heng Foundation]

—— (2005b) 'Queering masculinity in Hong Kong movies', in L.K. Pang and D. Wong (eds) *Masculinities and Hong Kong Cinema*. Hong Kong: Hong Kong University Press, pp. 57–80.

—— (2005c) *The Hidden Voice: The Sexual Politics of Chinese Male Sex Workers*. Hong Kong: Centre for Social Policy Studies, Department of Applied Social Sciences, the Hong Kong Polytechnic University.

—— (2006a) 'Asian sexual cultures', in G. Ritzer (ed.) *The Blackwell Encyclopedia of Sociology*. London: Blackwell, pp. 4213–18.

—— (2006b) 'Repositioning the Asian diasporic male bodies', paper presented at *Asia Reconstructed: From Critique of Development to Postcolonial Studies, the 16th Biennial Conference of the Asian Studies Association of Australia*, University of Wollongong, Australia, 26–29 June 2006.

—— (2006c) 'What it feels like for a whore: the body politics of women performing erotic labour in Hong Kong', *Gender, Work and Organization*, 13 (5): 409–34.

—— (2007) 'Asian male bodies', in S. Seidman, N. Fischer, and C. Meeks (eds) *Introducing the New Sexuality Studies*, London and new York: Routledge, pp. 90–95.

—— (2008) 'Risk factors affecting condom use among male sex workers who serve men in China: a qualitative study', *Sexually Transmitted Infections*, 84: 444–48.

—— (2009a) 'More than a sex machine: accomplishing masculinity among Chinese male sex workers in the Hong Kong sex industry', *Deviant Behaviour*, 30: 715–45.

—— (2009b) 'Where is my Brokeback Mountain?' *Social Transformations in Chinese Societies* 4: 135–59.

—— (2010) 'Outcast bodies: money, sex and desire of money boys in Mainland China', in C. Yau (ed.) *As Normal as Possible: Negotiating Sexualities in Hong Kong and China*, Hong Kong: Hong Kong University Press (in press).

Kong, T.S.K., Laidler, K.A., Lau, G.L. and Cheung, Y.W. (2009) *Final Report on Understanding Drug Use and Its Associated Risk for HIV Infection among MSM in Hong Kong* [Unpublished internal report submitted to Council for AIDS Trust Fund].

Kong, T.S.K., Plummer, K. and Mahoney, D. (2002) 'Queer(y)ing the interview: from criminalised homosexuals to post-modern queers', in J. Gubrium and J. Holstein (eds) *The Handbook of Interviewing*, London: Sage, pp. 239–58.

Krieger, S. (1985) 'Beyond "subjectivity": the use the self in social science', *Qualitative Sociology*, 8: 309–24.

—— (1991) *Social Science and the Self: Personal Essays on an Art Form*, New Brunswick, NJ: Rutgers University Press.

Ku, A.S. (2002) 'Postcolonial cultural trends in Hong Kong: imagining the local, the national, and the global', in M. Chan and A. So (eds) *Crisis and Transformation in China's Hong Kong*, Armonk, NY: M.E. Sharpe, and Hong Kong: Hong Kong University Press, pp. 343–62.

Ku, A.S. and Pun, N. (eds) (2004) *Remaking Citizenship in Hong Kong*, Oxford: RoutledgeCurzon.

Kulick, D. (1998) *Travesti: Sex, Gender, and Culture Among Brazilian Transgendered Prostitutes*, Chicago: University of Chicago Press.

Lai, Y.K. (2004) 'Lesbian Masculinities: Identity and Body Construction among Tomboys in Hong Kong', unpublished MPhil thesis, The Chinese University of Hong Kong.

Lam, C.W., Lam, W.M. and Leung, T.Y.K. (2005) 'The changing nature and ideology of marriage in Hong Kong', in K.P.H. Young and A.Y.L. Fok (eds) *Marriage, Divorce and Remarriage: Professional Practice in the Hong Kong Cultural Context*, Hong Kong: HKU Press, pp. 243–66.

Lam, W.M. (2004) *Understanding the Political Culture of Hong Kong: The Paradox of Activism and Depoliticization*, Armonk, NY; London: M.W. Sharpe.

—— (2005) 'Depoliticization, citizenship, and the politics of community in Hong Kong', *Citizenship Studies*, 9(3): 309–22.

Lancaster, R.N. and di Leonardo, M. (eds) (1997) *The Gender Sexuality Reader*, London: Routledge.

Lancester, Roger N. (1988) 'Subject honour and object shame: the construction of male homosexuality and stigma in Nicaragua', *Ethnology*, 27(2): 111–25.

Lau, H.L. (2004) 'Gay Specificity: The Reworking of Heteronormative Discourse in the Hong Kong Gay Community', unpublished MPhil thesis, The Chinese University of Hong Kong.

Lau, S.K. (1978) 'From traditional familism to utilitarianistic familism: the metamorphosis of familial ethos among the Hong Kong Chinese', *Hong Kong: Occasional Paper No. 78*, Social Research Centre, the Chinese University of Hong Kong.

—— (1982) *Society and Politics in Hong Kong*, Hong Kong: The Chinese University Press.

—— (2002) 'Tung Chee-hwa's governing strategy: the shortfall in politics', in S.K. Lau (ed.). *The First Tung Chee-hwa Administration: The First Five Years of the Hong Kong Special Administration Region*, Hong Kong: The Chinese University Press, pp.1–40.

Law, W.S. (1998) 'Managerializing colonialism', in Chen, K.H. (ed.) *Trajectories: Inter-Asia Cultural Studies*, London: Routledge, pp.109–21.

—— (2009) *Collaborative Colonial Power: The Making of the Hong Kong Chinese*, Hong Kong: Hong Kong University Press.

Lee, M., Chan, A., Hannah, B. and Green, G. (2002) 'Chinese migrant women and families in Britain', *Women's Studies International Forum*, 25(6): 607–18.

Lee, Q. (1994) 'Delineating Asian (Hong Kong) intellectuals: speculations on intellectual problematics and post/coloniality', *Third Text*, 26: 11–23.

Leong, R. (ed.) (1996) *Asian American Sexualities: Dimensions of the Gay and Lesbian Experience*, London: Routledge.

Lethbridge, H.J. (1976) 'The quare fellow: homosexuality and the law in Hong Kong', *Hong Kong Law Journal*, 6(3): 292–326.

Leung, H.C. and Lee, K.M. (2005) 'Immigration controls, life-course coordination, and livelihood strategies: a study of families living across the mainland-Hong Kong border', *Journal of Family and Economic Issues*, 26(4): 487–507.

Leung, H.H.S. (2007) 'Archiving queer feelings in Hong Kong', *Inter-Asia Cultural Studies*, 8(4): 559–71.

—— (2008) *Undercurrents: Queer Culture and Postcolonial Hong Kong*, Hong Kong: Hong Kong University Press.

Leung, P.K. (2004) 'Urban cinema and the cultural identity of Hong Kong', in E.M.K. Cheung and Y.W. Chu (eds) *Between Home and World: A Reader in Hong Kong Cinema*, Hong Kong: Oxford University Press, pp. 369–98.

Levin, I. and Trost, J. (1999) 'Living apart together', *Community, Work and Family*, 2: 279–94.

Lewis, J. (2001) *The End of Marriage: Individualism and Intimate Relations*, Cheltenham: Edward Elgar Publishing.

Li, B. and Piachaud, D. (2006) 'Urbanization and social policy in China', *Asia-Pacific Development Journal* 13(1): 1–26.

Li, B.Y. and Wu, Y.H. (1999) 'The concept of citizenship in the People's Republic of China', in A. Davidson and K. Weekley (eds) *Globalization and Citizenship in the Asia-Pacific*, Basingstoke: Macmillan, pp. 157–68.

Li, C. (1996) 'Surplus rural laborers and internal migration in China: current status and future prospects', *Asian Survey*, 36 (11): 1122–45.

Li, S.L. (2003) *Cross-dressing in Chinese Opera*, Hong Kong: Hong Kong University Press.

Li, X.M., Zhang, L.Y., Fang, X.Y., Xiong, Q., Chen, X.G., Lin, D.H., Mathur, A. and Stanton, B. (2007) 'Stigmatization experienced by rural-to-urban migrant workers in China: findings from a qualitative study', *World Health & Population*, 9(4): 29–43.

Li, Y.H. (2006) 'Regulating male same-sex relationships in the People's Republic of China', in E. Jeffreys (ed.) *Sex and Sexuality in China*, London: Routledge, pp. 82–101.

Lim, S.H. (2006) *Celluloid Comrade: Representations of Male Homosexuality in Contemporary Chinese Cinemas*, Honolulu: University of Hawai'i Press.

Lin, D. (2006) 'Sissies online: Taiwanese male queers performing sissinesses in cyberspaces', *Inter-Asia Cultural Studies*, 7 (2): 270–88.

Liu, H. (1995) 'Hooliganism', *Chinese Sociology and Anthropology*, 27(3): 57–63.

Liu, H., Yang, H.M., Li, X.M., Wang, N., Liu, H.J., Wang, B., Zhang, L., Wang, Q.Q. and Stanton, B. (2006) 'Men who have sex with men and human immunodeficiency virus/sexually transmitted disease control in China', *Sexually Transmitted Diseases*, 33(2): 68–76.

Lo, S.H. (2001) 'Citizenship and participation in Hong Kong', *Citizenship Studies*, 5(2): 127–42.

Louie, K. (2002) *Theorising Chinese Masculinity: Society and Gender in China*, Cambridge: Cambridge University Press.

—— (2003) 'Chinese, Japanese and global masculine identities', in K. Louie and M. Low (eds) *Asian Masculinities: The Meaning and Practice of Manhood in China and Japan*, London and New York: RoutledgeCurzon, pp. 1–15.

Luibhéid, E. and Cantú, L. (eds) (2005) *Queer Migrations: Sexuality, U.S. Citizenship, and Border Crossings*, Minneapolis, MN: University of Minnesota Press.

Ma, E.K.W. (2001) 'The hierarchy of drinks: alcohol and social class in Hong Kong', in G. Mathews and T.L. Lui (eds) *Consuming Hong Kong*, Hong Kong: Hong Kong University Press, pp. 117–40.

Mackenzie, P.W. (2002) 'Strangers in the city: the *hukou* and urban citizenship in China', *Journal of International Affairs*, 56 (1): 305–19.

Mak, A. (2000) 'Bi All Means: The Trouble with Tong Zhi Discourse: Beyond Queer Looks in the East is Red and Swordsman II', unpublished M Phil thesis, University of Hong Kong.

Mak, A. and King, M.A. (1997) 'Hong Kong's tongzhi movement: through the eyes of Queer Sisters', in S. Woodman (ed.) *Hong Kong's Social Movements: Forces from the Margin*, Hong Kong: 1 July Link and Hong Kong Women Christian Council, pp. 100–8.

Malinowski, B. (1922) *Argonauts of the Western Pacific: An Account of Native Enterprise and Adventure in the Archipelagoes of Melanesian New Guinea*, London: Routledge & Kegan Paul.

Manalansan IV, M.F. (1993) '(Re)locating the gay Filipino: resistance, postcolonialism, and identity', *Journal of Homosexuality*, 26(2/3): 53–72.

—— (2003) *Global Divas: Filipino Gay Men in the Diaspora*, Durham and London: Duke University Press.

Manderson, L. and Jolly, M. (eds) (1997) *Sites of Desire/Economies of Pleasure: Sexualities in Asia and the Pacific*, London: University of Chicago Press.

Marcuse, H. (1964) *One Dimensional Man: Studies in the Ideology of Advanced Industrial Society*, London: Routledge & Kegan Paul.

Marshall, T.H. (1950) *Citizenship and Social Class and Other Essays*, Cambridge: Cambridge University Press.

Martin, F., Jackson, P.A., McLelland, M. and Yue, A. (eds.) (2008) *AsiapacifiQueer: Rethinking Genders and Sexualities*, Urbana and Chicago: University of Illinois Press.

Mason, M.A., Skolnick, A. and Sugarman, S.D. (eds) (2003) *All Our Families: New Policies for a New Century: A Report of the Berkeley Family Forum*, New York: Oxford University Press.

Massey, D. (1994) *Space, Place, and Gender*, Minneapolis: University of Minnesota Press.

Mathews, G. (1997) 'Heunggongyahn: on the past, present, and future of Hong Kong identity', *Bulletin of Concerned Asian Scholars*, 29(3): 3–13.

Mathews, G. and Lui, T.L. (2001) (eds) *Consuming Hong Kong*, Hong Kong: Hong Kong University Press, 'Introduction'.

McIntosh, M. (1968) 'The homosexual role', *Social Problems*, 16: 182–92.

McNair, B. (2002) *Striptease Culture: Sex, Media and the Democratisation of Desire*, London, New York: Routledge.

Mead, M. (1952) *Sex and Temperament in Three Primitive Societies*, London: Routledge & Kegan Paul; first published by William Morrow & Co., New York (1935).

Medhurst, A. and Munt, S.R. (eds.) (1997) *Lesbian and Gay Studies: A Critical Introduction*, London: Cassell.

Meeks, C. (2001) 'Civil society and the sexual politics of difference', *Sociological Theory*, 19(3): 325–43.

Meeks, C. and Stein, A. (2006) 'Refiguring the family: towards a post-queer politics of gay and lesbian marriage', in D. Richardson, J. McLaughlin, and M.E. Casey (eds) *Intersections between Feminist and Queer Theory*, Basingstoke: Palgrave Macmillan, pp. 136–55.

Miles, S. (1998) *Consumerism: As a Way of Life*, London: Sage.

Mills, C.W. (1959) *The Sociological Imagination*, Oxford: Oxford University Press.

Minichiello, V., Marino, R. and Browne, J. (2002) 'Knowledge, risk perceptions and condom usage in male sex workers from three Australian cities', *AIDS Care*, 13(3): 387–402.

Moi, T. (1991) 'Appropriating Bourdieu: feminist theory and Pierre Bourdieu's sociology of culture', *New Literary History*, 22: 1017–49.

Mongia, P. (ed.) (1996) *Contemporary Postcolonial Theory: A Reader*, London: Arnold.

Moore, L. (ed.) (2005) *Global Resistance Reader*, London and New York: Routledge.

Mort, F. (1980) 'Sexuality: regulation and contestation', in Gay Left Collective (ed.) *Homosexuality: Power and Politics*, London: Allison & Busby, pp. 38–51.

—— (1988a) 'Boy's own? Masculinity, style and popular culture', in R. Chapman and J. Rutherford (eds) *Male Order: Unwrapping Masculinity*, London: Lawrence & Wishart.

—— (1988b) *Cultures of Consumption: Masculinities and Social Space in Late-Twentieth Century Britain*, London: Routledge.

Mouffe, C. (1995) 'Feminism, citizenship, and radical democratic politics', in L. Nicholson and S. Seidman (eds) *Social Postmodernism: Beyond Identity Politics*, Cambridge: Cambridge University Press, pp. 315–31.

Mulvey, T.J. (2005) 'Hong Kong families in the twenty-first century', in R.J. Estes (ed.) *Social Development in Hong Kong: The Unfinished Agenda*, Hong Kong: Oxford University Press, pp. 225–35.

Mutchler, M.G. (2000) 'Young gay men's stories in the states: scripts, sex, and safety in the time of AIDS', *Sexualities*, 3(1): 31–54.

Nardi, P. (1999) *Gay Men's Friendships: Invincible Communities*, Chicago: University of Chicago Press.

Nardi, P.M. and Schneider, B.E. (eds) (1998) *Social Perspectives in Lesbian and Gay Studies: A Reader*, London: Routledge.

Nee, V. (1996). 'The emergence of a market society: changing mechanisms of stratification in China', *American Journal of Sociology* 101 (4): 908–49.

Nederveen Pieterse, J. (2004) *Globalization and Culture: Global Mélange*, Lanham: Rowman & Littlefield Publishers.

Ng, C.H. (1994) 'Power, identity, and economic change – 25 years of family studies in Hong Kong', in B.K.P. Leung and T.Y.C. Wong (eds) *25 Years of Social and Economic Development in Hong Kong*, Hong Kong: Center of Asian Studies, University of Hong Kong, pp. 94–110.

—— (1995) 'Bringing women back in: family change in Hong Kong', in V. Pearson and B.K.P. Leung (eds) *Women in Hong Kong*, Hong Kong: Oxford University Press, pp. 74–100.

Ng, M.L. (1998) 'School and public sexuality education in Hong Kong', *Journal of Asian Sexuality*, 1: 32–35.

Ng, M.L. and Ma, J.C. (updated by Lau, M.P. and Francoeur, R.T.) (2004) 'Hong Kong', in R.R. Francoeur and R. Noonan. (eds) *Continuum Complete International Encyclopedia of Sexuality*, New York: Continuum, pp. 489–502.

Ng, V. (1987) 'Ideology and sexuality: rape laws in Qing China', *Journal of Asian Studies*, 46(1): 57–70.

—— (1989) 'Homosexuality and the state in late imperial China,' in M. B. Duberman, M. Vicinus and G. Chauncey (eds) *Hidden from History: Reclaiming the Gay and Lesbian Past*, New York: Nal Books.

Ngo, T.W. (2000) 'Social values and consensual politics in colonial Hong Kong', in H. Antlov and T.W. Ngo (eds) *The Cultural Construction of Politics in Asia*, Surrey: Curzon Press, pp. 131–53.

Nutong Xueshe (2007) ‘In/Out: Hong Kong tongzhi creative workshop and exhibition’, *Inter-Asia Cultural Studies*, 8(4): 589–99.
O’Connell Davidson, J. (1996) ‘Prostitution and the contours of control’, in J. Weeks and J. Holland (eds) *Sexual Cultures: Communities, Values and Intimacy*, London: Macmillan, pp. 180–98.
O’Neil, M. (1996) ‘The aestheticization of the whore in contemporary society: desire, the body, self and society’, paper presented to the Body and Organization Workshop, Keele, September 1996.
Ong, A. (1993) ‘On the edge of empires: flexible citizenship among Chinese in diaspora’, *positions: east asia culture critiques*, 1(3): 745–78.
—— (1996) ‘Cultural citizenship as subject making: immigrants negotiate racial and cultural boundaries in the United States’, *Current Anthropology* 37(5): 737–62.
—— (1998) ‘Flexible citizenship among Chinese cosmopolitans’, in C. Pheng and B. Robbins (eds) *Cosmopolitics: Thinking and Feelings Beyond the Nation*, Minneapolis, MN: University of Minnesota Press, pp. 134–62.
—— (1999) *Flexible Citizenship: The Cultural Logics of Transnationality*, Durham, NC and London: Duke University Press.
—— (2007) *Neoliberalism As Exception: Mutations in Citizenship and Sovereignty*, Durham, NC and London: Duke University Press.
Ooi, V. (1997) ‘The best cultural policy is no cultural policy: cultural policy in Hong Kong’, *Cultural Perspective Hong Kong 1997*, complied by Hong Kong Cultural Sector Joint Conference, International Association of Theatre Critics (Hong Kong), Zuni Icosahedron, Hong Kong, pp. 31–43.
Padilla, M. (2007) *Caribbean Pleasure Industry: Tourism, Sexuality, and AIDS in the Dominican Republic*, Chicago: University of Chicago Press.
Padilla, M., Hirsch, J.S., Munoz-Laboy, M., Sember, R.E. and Parker, R.G. (eds) (2007) *Love and Globalization: Transformations of Intimacy in the Contemporary World*, Nashville, TN: Vanderbilt University Press.
Pakulski, J. (1997) ‘Cultural citizenship’, *Citizenship Studies*, 1(1): 73–86.
Pan, S.M. (2006) ‘Transformation in the primary life cycle: the origins and nature of China’s sexual revolution’, in E. Jeffreys (ed.) *Sex and Sexuality in China*, New York: Routledge, pp. 21–42.
Pang, M. (1996) ‘Barriers perceived by young Chinese adults to their employment in companies in the UK’, *International Journal of Human Resource Management*, vol. 7, London: Routledge.
—— (1999) ‘Employment situation of young Chinese adults in the British labour market’, *Personnel Review*, 28(1/2): 41–57.
Parker, D. (1998) ‘Chinese people in Britain: Histories, futures and identities’, in G. Benton and F.N. Pieke (eds) *The Chinese in Europe*, New York: St Martin’s Press, pp. 67–95.
Parker, Richard G. (1999) *Beneath the Equator: Cultures of Desire, Male Homosexuality, and Emerging Gay Communities in Brazil*, London: Routledge.
Perry, E.J. and Selden, M. (eds) (2000) *Chinese Society: Change, Conflict and Resistance*, London and New York: Routledge.
Phelan, S. (2001) *Sexual Strangers: Gays, Lesbians, and Dilemmas of Citizenship*, Philadelphia, PA: Temple University Press.
Plummer, K. (1975) *Sexual Stigma: An Interactionist Approach*, London: Routledge & Kegal Paul.
—— (1983) *Documents of Life: An Introduction to the Problems and Literature of a Humanistic Method*, London: Unwin Hyman.

—— (1992) 'Speaking its name: inventing a lesbian and gay studies', in K. Plummer (ed.) *Modern Homosexualities: Fragments of Lesbian and Gay Experience*, London: Routledge, pp.3–25.

—— (1995) *Telling Sexual Stories: Power, Change and Social Worlds*, London and New York: Routledge.

—— (1996) 'Symbolic interactionism in the twentieth century: the rise of empirical social theory', in B. Turner (ed.) *The Blackwell Companion to Social Theory*, Oxford: Blackwell Publishers, pp. 223–51.

—— (1998) 'Afterword: the past, present, and futures of the sociology of same-sex relations', in P.M. Nardi and B.E. Schneider (eds) *Social Perspectives in Lesbian and Gay Studies: A Reader*, London and New York: Routledge, pp. 605–14.

—— (1999) 'The lesbian and gay movement in Britain: Schisms, solidarities, and social worlds', in B.D. Adam, J.W. Duyvendak and A. Krouwel (eds) *The Global Emergence of Gay and Lesbian Politics: National Imprints of a Worldwide Movement*, Philadelphia, PA: Temple University Press, pp. 133–57.

—— (2001) 'The square of intimate citizenship: some preliminary proposals', *Citizenship Studies*, 5(3): 237–53.

—— (2003) *Intimate Citizenship: Private Decisions and Public Dialogues*, Montreal; Kingston: McGill-Queen's University Press.

—— (2008) 'Foreword', in P. L. Hammack and B. J. Cohler (eds) *The Story of Sexual Identity: Narrative Perspectives on the Gay and Lesbian Life Course*, Oxford: Oxford University Press.

Podmore, D. and Chaney, D. (1974) 'Family norms in a rapidly industrializing society: Hong Kong', *Journal of Marriage and the Family*, 36(2): 400–407.

Prestage, G. (1994) 'Male and transsexual prostitution', in R. Perkins, G. Prestage, R. Sharp and F. Lovejoy (eds) *Sex Work and Sex Workers in Australia*, Sydney: University of New South Wales Press Ltd, pp. 174–90.

Pun, N. (2003) 'Subsumption or consumption? The phantom of consumer revolution in "globalizing" China', *Cultural Anthropology*, 18(4): 469–92.

—— (2005) *Made in China: Women Factory Workers in a Global Workplace*, Durham, NC and London: Duke University Press.

Pun, N. and Wu, K.M. (2004) 'Lived citizenship and lower-class Chinese migrant women: a global city without its people', in A.S. Ku and N. Pun (eds) *Remaking Citizenship in Hong Kong: Community, Nation and the Global City*, Oxford: RoutledgeCurzon, pp. 139–54.

Pun, N. and Yee, L.M. (eds) (2003) *Narrating Hong Kong Culture and Identity*, Hong Kong: Oxford University Press.

Rassool, N. (1999) 'Flexible identities: exploring race and gender issues among a group of immigrant pupils in an inner-city comprehensive school', *British Journal of Sociology and Education*, 20(1): 23–36.

Reibstein, J. and Richards, M. (1993) *Sexual Arrangements: Marriage and the Temptation of Infidelity*, New York: Scribner.

Reiss, A.J. (1961) 'The social integration of queers and peers', *Social Problems*, 9: 102–19.

Rich, A. (1980) 'Compulsory heterosexuality and lesbian existence', *Signs*, 5: 631–60.

Richardson, D. (1998) 'Sexuality and citizenship', *Sociology*, 32(1): 83–100.

—— (2000) 'Constructing sexual citizenship: theorizing sexual rights', *Critical Social Policy*, 20(1): 105–35.

—— (2001) 'Extending citizenship: cultural citizenship and sexuality', in N. Stevenson (ed.) *Culture and Citizenship*, London: Sage, pp. 153–66.

—— (2004) 'Locating sexualities: from here to normality', *Sexualities*, 7(4): 391–411.

—— (2005) 'Desiring sameness? The rise of a neo-liberal politics of normalization', *Antipode*, pp. 514–35.
Richardson, D. and Seidman, S. (2002) *Handbook of Lesbian and Gay Studies*, London: Sage.
Robinson, W.I. (2007) 'Theories of globalization', in G. Ritzer (ed.) *The Blackwell Companion to Globalization*, Malden, MA and Oxford: Blackwell. Online. Available at: www.blackwellreference.com/subscriber/tocnode?id=g9781405132749_chunk_g97814051327498 (accessed 1 Aug 2008).
Rofel, L. (2007) *Desiring China: Experiments in Neoliberalism, Sexuality, and Public Culture*, Durham, NC and London: Duke University Press.
—— (2010) 'The traffic in money boys', *Positions: East Asian Cultures Critique*.
Rose, N. (1996) 'Governing "advanced" liberal democracies', in A. Barry, T. Osborne and N. Rose (eds) *Foucault and Political Reason*, Chicago: University of Chicago Press, pp. 37–64.
Ruan, F. and Bullough, V. (1989) 'Sex repression in contemporary China', in P. Kurtz (ed.) *Building a World Community: Humanism in the Twenty-First Century*, Buffalo, New York: Prometheus Books, pp. 198–201.
Ruan, F.F. (1991) *Sex in China*, New York: Plenum Press.
—— (1997) 'China', in D.J. West and R. Green (eds) *Sociolegal Control of Homosexuality: A Multi-nation Comparison*, New York: Plenum Press, pp. 57–66.
Ruan, F.F. and Tsai, Y.M. (1987) 'Male homosexuality in the traditional Chinese literature', *Journal of Homosexuality*, 14: 21–33.
—— and —— (1988) 'Male homosexuality in contemporary mainland China', *Archives of Sexual Behavior*, 17(2): 189–99.
Rubin, G.S. (1993) 'Thinking sex: notes for a radical theory of the politics of sexuality', in H. Abelove, M.A. Barale and D.M. Halperin (eds) *The Lesbian and Gay Studies Reader*, London: Routledge: pp. 3–44; first published in C. S. Vance (ed.) (1984) *Pleasure and Danger: Exploring Female Sexuality*, Routledge and Kegan Paul.
Russo, V. (1981) *The Celluloid Closet: Homosexuality in the Movies*, New York: Harper & Row.
Ryan, G.W. and Bernard, H.R. (2000) 'Data management and analysis methods', in N.K. Denzin and Y.S. Lincoln (eds) *Handbook of Qualitative Research*, 2nd edn, Thousand Oaks, CA: Sage, pp. 769–802.
Said, E.W. (1978) *Orientalism: Western Conceptions of the Orient*, London: Routledge & Kegan Paul.
Salaff, J. (1976) 'Working daughters in the Hong Kong Chinese family: female filial piety or a transformation in the family power structure?', *Journal of Social History*, 9: 439–65.
—— (1981) *Working Daughters of Hong Kong: Filial Piety or Power in the Family?* Cambridge: Cambridge University Press.
Salaff, J., Shik, A. and Greve, A. (2009) 'Like sons and daughters of Hong Kong: the 1.5 generation returns', in *Social Transformation in Chinese Societies 'Doing Families'* (in press).
Sanders, T. (2005) *Sex Work: A Risky Business*, Devon: Willan.
Sang, T.L.D. (1999) 'Translating homosexuality: the discourse of tongxing'ai in republican China', in L.H. Liu (ed.) *Tokens of Exchange: The Problem of Translation in Global Circulation*, Durham, NC and London: Duke University Press, pp. 276–304.

—— (2003) *The Emerging Lesbian: Female Same-sex Desire in Modern China*, Chicago and London: The University of Chicago Press.

Sautman, B. (2004) 'Hong Kong as a semi-ethnocracy: "race," migration and citizenship in a globalized region', in A.S. Ku and N. Pun (eds) *Remaking Citizenship in Hong Kong: Community, Nation and the Global City*, Oxford: RoutledgeCurzon, pp. 115–38.

Scott, J. (1985) *Weapon of the Weak: Everyday Forms of Peasant Resistance*, New Haven, CT.: Yale University Press.

Scott, J., Treas, J. and Richards, M. (eds) (2004) *The Blackwell Companion to the Sociology of Families*, London: Blackwell.

Seale, C., Giampietro, G., Jaber, F. and Silverman, D. (eds) (2004) *Qualitative Research Practice*, London: Sage.

Sedgwick, E.K. (1990) *Epistemology of the Closet*, Berkeley, CA: University of California Press.

Segal, L. (1990) *Slow Motion: Changing Masculinities, Changing Men*, London: Virago.

Seidman, S. (1993) 'Identity and politics in a "postmodern" gay culture: some historical and conceptual notes', in M. Warner (ed.) *Fear of a Queer Planet: Queer Politics and Social Theory*, Minneapolis, MN: University of Minnesota Press, pp.105–42.

—— (1995) 'Deconstructing queer theory or the under-theorization of the social and the ethical', in L. Nicholson and S. Seidman (eds) *Social Postmodernism: Beyond Identity Politics*, Cambridge: Cambridge University Press, pp.116–41.

—— (1998) 'Are we all in the closet? Notes towards a sociological and cultural turn in queer theory', *European Journal of Cultural Studies*, 1: 177–92.

—— (2002) *Beyond the Closet: The Transformation of Gay and Lesbian Life*, New York and London: Routledge.

—— (2005) 'From outsider to citizen', in E. Bernstein and L. Schaffner (eds) *Regulating Sex: The Politics of Intimacy and Identity*, New York and London: Routledge, pp. 225–46.

Seidman, S. (ed.) (1996) *Queer Theory/Sociology*, Oxford: Basil Blackwell.

Seidman, S., Meeks, C. and Traschen, F. (1999) 'Beyond the closet? The changing social meaning of homosexuality in the United States', *Sexualities*, 2(1): 9–34.

Sheller, M. and Urry, J. (2006) 'The new mobilities paradigm', *Environment and Planning A*, 38: 207–26.

Sigley, G. (1998) 'Guest editor's introduction', *Chinese Sociology and Anthropology*, 31(1): 3–13.

Sinfield, A. (1998) *Gay and After*, London: Serpent's Tail.

Sing, M. (ed.) *Politics and Government in Hong Kong: Crisis Under Chinese Sovereignty*, London: Routledge.

Skeggs, B. (1997). *Formations of Class and Gender*, London: Sage.

Skeldon, R. (1994a) 'Hong Kong in an international migration system', in R. Skeldon (ed.) *Reluctant Exiles? Migration from Hong Kong and the New Overseas Chinese*, Hong Kong: Hong Kong University Press, pp. 21–51.

—— (1994b) 'Reluctant exiles or bold pioneers: an introduction to migration from Hong Kong', in R. Skeldon (ed.) *Reluctant Exiles? Migration from Hong Kong and the New Overseas Chinese*, Hong Kong: Hong Kong University Press, pp. 3–18.

Skeldon, R. (ed.) (1994) *Reluctant Exiles? Migration from Hong Kong and the New Overseas Chinese*, Hong Kong: Hong Kong University Press.

Smith, A.M. (1994) *New Right Discourse on Race and Sexuality: Britain, 1968–1990*, Cambridge: Cambridge University Press.

So, A.Y. (2002) 'Social protests, legitimacy crisis, and the impetus toward soft authoritarianism in the Hong Kong SAR', in S.K. Lau (ed.) *The First Tung Chee-hwa Administration: The First Five Years of the Hong Kong Special Administration Region*, Hong Kong: The Chinese University Press, pp. 399–418.

—— (2003) 'Cross-border families in Hong Kong: the role of social class and politics', *Critical Asian Studies*, 35 (4): 515–34.

—— (2004) 'One country, three systems? State, nation, and civil society in the making of citizenship in the Chinese triangle of Mainland-Taiwan-Hong Kong', in A.S. Ku and N. Pun (eds) *Remaking Citizenship in Hong Kong: Community, Nation and the Global City*, Oxon: RoutledgeCurzon, pp. 235–53.

Solinger, D. (1999) *Contesting Citizenship in Urban China: Peasant, Migrants, the State, and the Logic of the Market*, Berkeley, CA: University of California Press.

Sommer, M.H. (1997) 'The penetrated male in late imperial China: judicial constructions and social stigma', *Modern China*, 23(2): 140–80.

Song, G. (2004) *The Fragile Scholar: Power and Masculinity in Chinese Culture*, Hong Kong: Hong Kong University Press.

Spivak, G.C. (1988) 'Can the subaltern speak?' in C. Nelson and L. Grossberg (eds) *Marxism and the Interpretation of Culture*, Urbana, IL: University of Illinois Press, pp. 271–313.

Stacey, J. (2003) 'Gay and lesbian families: queer like us', in M.M. Mason, A. Skolnick, S.D. Sugerman (eds) *All Our Families: New Policies for a New Century: A Report of the Berkeley Family Forum*, Oxford: Oxford University Press, pp. 144–69.

Stein, A. (1997) *Sex and Sensibility: Stories of a Lesbian Generation*, Berkeley, CA: University of California Press.

Stoler, A.L. (1995) *Race and the Education of Desire: Foucault's History of Sexuality and the Colonial Order of Things*, Durham, NC: Duke University Press.

Straayer, C. (1996) *Deviant Eyes, Deviant Bodies: Sexual Re-orientations in Film and Video*, New York: Columbia University Press.

Strathern, M. (1987) 'Out of context: the persuasive fictions of anthropology', *Current Anthropology*, 28(3): 251–81.

Strauss, A.L. and Corbin, J.M. (eds) (1997) *Grounded Theory in Practice*. Thousand Oaks, CA: Sage.

Stychin, C. (2003) *Governing Sexuality: The Changing Politics of Citizenship and Law Reform*, Oxford: Hart.

Sullivan, A. (1995) *Virtually Normal: An Argument about Homosexuality*, London: Picador.

Sun, Z.X., Farrer, J. and Choi K.H. (2006) 'Sexual identity among men who have sex with men in Shanghai', *China Perspectives*. Online. Available at: http://chinaperspectives.revues.org/document598.html (accessed 18 August 2007).

Swidler, A. (1980) 'Love and adulthood in American culture', in N.J. Smelser, and E.H. Erikson (eds) *Themes of Work and Love in Adulthood*, Cambridge, MA: Harvard University Press, pp. 120–47.

Szeto, M.M. (2004) 'The Radical Itch: Rethinking Radicalism in Contemporary Chinese Societies', unpublished PhD Thesis, University of California, Berkeley, CA.

Takagi, D.Y. (1996) 'Maiden voyage: excursion into sexuality and identity politics in Asian America', in S. Seidman (ed.) *Queer Theory/Sociology*, Oxford: Basil Blackwell, pp. 243–58.

Tam, M.S.M. (2005) 'We-women and they-women: imagining mistresses across the Hong Kong-China border', in M. Tam, H.B. Ku and T.S.K. Kong (eds) *Rethinking and Recasting Citizenship: Social Exclusion and Marginality in Chinese Societies*, Hong Kong: Centre for Social Policy Studies, the Hong Kong Polytechnic University, pp. 107–30.

Tam, S.T. (1998) 'Representation of "the Chinese" and "ethnicity" in British racial discourse', in E. Sinn (ed.) *The Last Half Century of Chinese Overseas*, Hong Kong: Hong Kong University Press, pp. 81–90.

Tang, D.T.S. (2008) 'Conditional Spaces and Infinite Possibilities: Hong Kong Lesbians and Urban Spatialities', unpublished PhD thesis, The Hong Kong Polytechnic University.

Thompson, P. (1988; 1st edn 1978) *The Voice of the Past: Oral History*, Oxford: Oxford University Press.

Tong, C.K.M. (2008) 'Being a young tomboy in Hong Kong: the life and identity construction of lesbian schoolgirls', in F. Martin, P.A. Jackson, M. McLelland and A. Yue (eds.) (2008) *AsiapacifiQueer: Rethinking Genders and Sexualities*, Urbana, IL and Chicago: University of Illinois Press, pp. 117–30.

Trinh, M.H. (1987) 'Of other peoples: beyond the "salvage" paradigm', in Foster, H. (ed.) *Discussions in Contemporary Culture*, Seattle: Bay Press.

Troiden, R. (1979) 'Becoming homosexual: a model of gay identity acquisition', *Psychiatry*, 42(4): 362–73.

—— (1988) *Gay and Lesbian Identity: A Sociological Analysis*, New York: General Hall.

Trouillot, M.R. (2001) 'The anthropology of the state in the age of globalization: close encounters of the deceptive kind', *Current Anthropology*, 42(1): 125–38.

—— (2003) *Global Transformations: Anthropology and the Modern World*, New York: Palgrave Macmillan.

Tsang, A.K.T. (1987) 'Sexuality: the Chinese and the Judeo-Christian traditions in Hong Kong', *Bulletin of the Hong Kong Psychological Society*, 19/20:19–28.

Tsang, D.Y.K. (2005) *2005–2006 Policy Address: Strong Governance for the People*, Hong Kong: The Government of the HKSAR. Online. Available at: www.policyaddress.gov.hk/09–10/eng/archives.html (accessed 8 Dec 2008).

—— (2006) *2006–2007 Policy Address: Proactive, Pragmatic, Always People First*, Hong Kong: The Government of the HKSAR. Online. Available at: www.policyaddress.gov.hk/09–10/eng/archives.html (accessed 8 Dec 2008).

Tung, C.H. (2001) *2001 Policy Address: Building on Our Strengths, Investing in Our Future*, Hong Kong: The Government of the HKSAR. Online. Available at: www.policyaddress.gov.hk/09–10/eng/archives.html (accessed 8 Dec 2008).

Turner, B. (2001) 'Outline of a general theory of cultural citizenship', in N. Stevenson (ed.) *Culture and Citizenship*, London: Sage, pp. 11–32.

Turner, M. (1995) 'Hong Kong sixties/nineties: dissolving the people' in Turner, M., and I. Ngan (eds) *Hong Kong Sixties: Designing Identity*, Hong Kong: Hong Kong Arts Centre, pp. 13–34.

Turner, M. and I. Ngan (eds) (1995) *Hong Kong Sixties: Designing Identity*, Hong Kong: Hong Kong Arts Centre.

Turner, N. (1994) 'Out of the closet and into the fire', *Eastern Express* 23 April: 17.

Urry, J. (2007) *Mobilities*, Cambridge: Polity.

Van Gulik, R.H. (1961) *Sexual Life in Ancient China: A Preliminary Survey of Chinese Sex and Society from ca. 1500 B.C. till 1644 A.D.*, Leiden, Netherlands: E.J. Brill.

Vanwesenbeeck, I. (2001) 'Another decade of social scientific work on sex work: a review of research 1990–2000', *Annual Review of Sex Research*, 12: 242–89.

Waites, M. (2003) 'Equality at last? Homosexuality, heterosexuality and the age of consent in the United Kingdom', *Sociology*, 37 (4): 637–55.

Walby, S. (1994) 'Is citizenship engendered?', *Sociology*, 28(2): 379–95.

Wang, F.L. (2004) 'Reformed migration control and new targeted people: China's *hukou* system in the 2000s', *The China Quarterly*, 177: 115–32.

Warner, M. (1999) *The Trouble with Normal: Sex, Politics, and the Ethics of Queer Life*, New York: Free Press.

—— (2002) *Publics and Counterpublics*, New York: Zone Books.

Warner, M. (ed.) (1993) *Fear of A Queer Planet: Queer Politics and Social Theory*, Minneapolis, MN: University of Minnesota Press.

Warren, C. (1974) *Identity and Community in the Gay World*, New York: Wiley.

Weeks, J. (1981) *Sex, Politics and Society: The Regulation of Sexuality Since 1800*, Harlow: Longman.

—— (1985) *Sexuality and Its Discontents: Meanings, Myths and Modern Sexualities*, London: Routledge.

—— (1990 [1977]) *Coming Out: Homosexual Politics in Britain from the Nineteenth Century to the Present*, London: Quartet Books.

—— (1998) 'The sexual citizen', *Theory, Culture & Society*, 15(3–4): 35–52.

—— (2003 [1986]) *Sexuality*, London and New York: Routledge.

—— (2007) *The World We Have Won: The Remaking of Erotic and Intimate Life*, London and New York: Routledge.

Weeks, J., Heaphy, B. and Donovan, C. (2001) *Same-Sex Intimacies: Families of Choice and Other Life Experiments*, London: Routledge.

Weeks, J., Heaphy, B. and Donavan, C. (2004) 'The lesbian and gay family', in J. Scott, J. Treas and M. Richards (eds) *The Blackwell Companion to the Sociology of Families*, London: Blackwell, pp. 340–55.

Wei, W. (2007) '"Wandering men" no longer wander around: the production and transformation of local homosexual identities in contemporary Chengdu, China', *Inter-Asia Cultural Studies*, 8(4): 572–88.

West, C. (1987) 'The dilemma of the black intellectual', *Critical Quarterly*, 29(14): 39–52.

West, D.J. and de Villiers, B. (1993) *Male Prostitution*, London and New York: The Haworth Press.

Weston, K. (1991) *Families We Choose: Lesbians, Gays, Kinship*, New York: Columbia University Press.

—— (1993) 'Lesbian/gay studies in the house of anthropology', *Annual Review of Anthropology*, 22: 339–67.

Wieringa, S.E., Blackwood, E. and Bhaiya, A. (eds) (2007) *Women's Sexualities and Masculinities in a Globalizing Asia*, New York: Palgrave Macmillan.

Williams, P. and Chrisman, L. (eds) (1993) *Colonial Discourse and Post-colonial Theory: A Reader*, London: Harvester Wheatsheaf.

Wilson, A. (2006) 'Queering Asia', *Intersections: Gender, History and Culture in the Asian Context*. Issue 14. Online. Available at: http://intersections.anu.ed.au/issue14/wilson.html (accessed 24 Aug 2008).

Wong, D. (2004) '(Post-)identity politics and anti-normalization: (homo)sexual rights movement', in A.S. Ku and P. Ngai (eds) *Remaking Citizenship in Hong Kong*, Oxon: RoutledgeCurzon: pp. 195–214.

—— 'Hong Kong lesbian partners actively create their own families', paper presented at *Doing Families in Hong Kong Workshop*, organized by the Department of Sociology, The University of Hong Kong, 11 November 2006.

—— (2007) 'Rethinking the coming home alternative: hybridization and coming out politics in Hong Kong's anti-homophobia parades', *Inter-Asia Cultural Studies*, 8(4): 600–616.

Wong, F.M. (1972) 'Modern ideology, industrialization, and conjugalism: the case of Hong Kong', *International Journal of Sociology of the Family*, 2: 139–50.

—— (1975) 'Industrialization and family structure in Hong Kong', *Journal of Marriage and the Family*, 27(4): 985–1000.

Wong, F.Y., Huang, Z.J., He, N., Smith, B.D., Gin, Y., Fu, C. and Young, D. (2008) 'HIV risks among gay- and non-gay-identified migrant boys in Shanghai, China', *AIDS Care*, 20(2): 170–80.

Wong, T.W.P. (1998) 'Colonial governance and the Hong Kong story', *Occasional Paper No.7*, Hong Kong: Hong Kong Institute of Asia-Pacific Studies, The Chinese University of Hong Kong.

Wong, W.C.W. and Kong, T.S.K. (2007) 'To determine factors in an initiation of a same-sex relationship in rural China: using ethnographic decision model', *AIDS Care*, 19(7): 850–57.

Wong, W.C.W., Zhang, J., Wu, S.C., Kong, T.S.K. and Ling, D.C.Y. (2006) 'The HIV Related risks among men having sex with men in rural Yunnan, China: A Qualitative Study', *Sexually Transmitted Infections*, 82: 127–30.

Woo, M.Y.K. (2006) 'Contesting citizenship: marriage and divorce in the People's Republic of China', in E. Jeffreys (ed.) *Sex and Sexuality in China*, New York: Routledge, pp. 62–81.

Woodhead, D. (1995) '"Surveillant gays": HIV, space and the constitution of identities', in D. Bell and G. Valentine (eds) *Mapping Desire: Geographies of Sexualities*, London: Routledge, pp. 231–44.

Woods, G. (1998) *A History of Gay Male Literature: The Male Tradition*, New Haven, CT: Yale University Press.

Wu, C.C. (2004) *Homoerotic Sensibilities in Late Imperial China*, London and New York: RoutledgeCurzon.

Wu, J. (2003) 'From "long yang" and "dui shi" to tongzhi: homosexuality in China', *Journal of Gay & Lesbian Psychotherapy*, 7(1/2): 117–43.

Wu, Y.H., Bai, L.S., Liu, Y.C. and Zhao, Z.H. (2004) 'Men who have sex with men and HIV/AIDS prevention in China', in Y. Lu and M. Essex (eds) *AIDS in Asia*, New York: Kluwer Academic/Plenum Publishers, pp.365–77.

Yan, H.R. (2003a) 'Neoliberal governmentality and neo-humanism: organizing suzhi/value flow through labor recruitment networks', *Cultural Anthropology*, 18(4): 493–523.

—— (2003b) 'Spectralization of the rural: reinterpreting the labor mobility of rural young women in post-Mao China', *American Ethnologist*, 30(4): 578–96.

Yan, Y.X. (1996) *The Flow of Gifts: Reciprocity and Social Networks in a Chinese Village*, Stanford, Calif.: Stanford University Press.

—— (2003) *Private Life Under Socialism: Love, Intimacy, and Family Change in a Chinese Village, 1949–1999*, Stanford, CA: Stanford University Press.

Yang, M.M.H. (2002) 'Mass media and transnational subjectivity in Shanghai: Notes on (re-)cosmopolitanism in a Chinese metropolis', in J.X. Inda and R. Rosaldo (eds) *The Anthropology of Globalization: A Reader*, Malden, MA and Oxford: Blackwell, pp. 325–49; first published in A. Ong and D. M. Nonini (eds) (1997) *Ungrounded*

Empires: The Cultural Politics of Modern Chinese Transnationalism, New York: Routledge, pp. 287–319.

Yang, T.L. (1981) *Report of Inquiry into Inspector MacLennan's Case*, Hong Kong: The Government Printer.

Yee, A.H. (1989) 'Cross-cultural perspectives on higher education in East Asia: psychological effects upon Asian students', *Journal of Multilingual and Multicultural Development*, 10(3): 213–45.

Yip, A K.T. (1997) 'Gay male Christian couples and sexual exclusivity', *Sociology*, 31(2): 289–306.

Yung, D. (1997a) 'In Search of Cultural Policy 93', in *Cultural Perspective Hong Kong 1997*, complied by Hong Kong Cultural Sector Joint Conference, International Association of Theatre Critics (Hong Kong), Zuni Icosahedron, Hong Kong, pp. 51–53.

Yuval-Davis, N. (2008) 'Intersectionality, citizenship and contemporary politics of belonging', in B. Siim and J. Squires (eds) *Contesting Citizenship*, London and New York: Routledge, pp. 159–72.

Zhang, B.C. and Chu, Q.S. (2005) 'MSM and HIV/AIDS in China', *Cell Research*, 15(11–12): 858–64.

Zhang, B.C., Liu, D.C., Li, X.F. and Hu, T.Z. (2000) 'A survey of men who have sex with men: mainland China', *American Journal of Public Health*, 90(12), 1949–50.

Zhang, B.C., Wu, S.W., Li, X.F., Zhu, M.Q. and Yang, L.G. (2004) 'Study on high risk behaviours among male sex workers related to STI/HIV', *Chin J STD/AIDS*, 10: 329–31.

Zhang, L. (2001) *Strangers in the City: Reconfigurations of Space, Power, and Social Networks within China's Floating Population*, Stanford, CA: Stanford University Press.

Zhu, Y. (2007) 'China's floating population and their settlement in the cities: beyond the *hukou* reform', *Habitat International*, 31(1): 65–76.

Zito, A. (1994) 'Silk and skin: significant boundaries', in A. Zito and T.E. Barlow (eds) *Body, Subject & Power in China*, Chicago and London: The University of Chicago Press, pp. 103–30.

Chinese-language sources

Ah Qiang 阿強 (ed.) (2008) *Fengyu hou de caihung* 風雨後的彩虹 [Rainbow after Rain], Hong Kong: Chi Heng Foundation.

Chan, Natalia 洛楓 (2005) *Nansheng nuxiang, cihong tongti: Zhang Gurong de geshan wuying yu meijie lunshe* 男生女相, 雄雌同體: 張國榮的歌衫舞影與媒介論述 [Queering body and sexuality: Leslie Cheung's gender representation in Hong Kong popular music], Meijie yixiang 媒介擬想 [Envisage: Journal of Chinese Media Studies], 3: 134–46.

Chan, Wan 陳雲 (2008) *Xianggang you wenhua: Xianggang de wenhua zhengce (shang juan)* 香港有文化: 香港的文化政策 (上卷) [Hong Kong has Culture: Hong Kong's Cultural Policy (Part 1)], Hong Kong: Arcadiapress.

Chen, Noel 陳諾爾 (ed.) (2001) *Qishi gean zhuanti yantao: Xianggang hongshizihui juanxiezhe xuzhi* 歧視個案專題研討: 香港紅十字會<<捐血者須知>> [A Special Study on a Discrimination Case: Hong Kong Red Cross (Guidelines for Prospective Donors)], Hong Kong: Rainbow of Hong Kong, Rainbow Action and Phenomena Study Centre.

Chou Wah-shan 周華山 (1995) *Tongzhi lun* 同志論 [The Discourse of Tongzhi], Hong Kong: Hong Kong Tongzhi Research Centre.

—— (1996a) *Beijing tongzhi gushi* 香港同志故事 [Stories of Tongzhi in Beijing], Hong Kong: Hong Kong Tongzhi Study Press.

—— (1996b) *Xianggang tongzhi gushi* 北京同志故事 [Stories of Hong Kong Tongzhi], Hong Kong: Hong Kong Tongzhi Press.

Chou, Wah-shan 周華山 and Chiu Man-chung 趙文宗 (1995) *Yigui xingshi: Xianggang ji Yingmei tongzhi yundong* 衣櫃性史: 香港及英美同志運動 [The Closeted Sexual History: Hong Kong, British and American Tongzhi Movements], Hong Kong: Hong Kong Tongzhi Research Centre.

Chou, Wah-shan 周華山, Anson Mak 麥海珊 and Kong Kin-bong 江建邦 (eds.) (1995) *Xianggang tongzhi zhan chu lai* 香港同志站出來 [Coming Out Stories of Hong Kong Tongzhi], Hong Kong: Hong Kong Tongzhi Study Press.

Chu, Wei-cheng 朱偉誠 (2008) *Taiwan tongzhi yundong de hou zhimin sikao: lun xianshen wenti* 台灣同志運動的後殖民思考: 論現身問題 [Coming out or not: postcolonial autonomy and /gay/activism in Taiwan] in Chu, W.C. (ed.) *pipan de xing shengzhi: taishe xingbie yu tongzhi duben* 批判的性政治: 台社性/別與同志讀本 [Critical Sexual Politics: Taishe Reader in Gender/Sexuality and Queer], Taiwan: Tonsan: pp. 191–213.

Kam, Yip Lo Lucetta 金曄路 (ed.) (2001) *Yueliang de saodong: ta ta de chulian gushi – women de zishu* 月亮的騷動：她她的初戀故事－我們的自述 [Lunar Desires: Her Same-sex Love, In Her Own Words], Hong Kong: Cultural Act Up.

Lam, Edward 林奕華 (1997) *27.01.97–30.09.97*, Hong Kong: Chen Mi Ji.

—— (1996) *Taiduo nanren, taishao shijian* 太多男人，太少時間 [Too Many Men Too Little Time], Hong Kong: Bo Yi.

Lee, Bono 李照興 (2008) *Chaobao Zhongguo* 潮爆中國 [Chic China Chic], Hong Kong: Enrich Publishing Ltd.

Lee, Chi-chiu, Julian 李志超 (2001) *Ranshao yuwang ditu* 燃燒慾望地圖 [The Map of Burning Desire], Hong Kong: Top Art Color Separation & Publishing Company Ltd.

Lee, Ming-kwan 李明堃 (1987) *Bianqian zhong de Xianggang zhengzhi he shehui* 變遷中的香港政治和社會 [Hong Kong Politics and Society in Transition], Hong Kong: The Commercial Press: '*Xianggang jiating de zuzhi he bianqian*' 香港家庭的組織和變遷 [The Hong Kong family: organization and change], pp. 152–78.

Li Hanlin 李漢林 (2008) *Bianqian zhong de Zhongguo danwei zhidu: huigu zhong de sikao* 變遷中的中國單位制度：回顧中的思考 [The changing Chinese work unit system: thinking in retrospective] *Shehui* 社會 [Society] 28 (3): 3–40.

Li, Lulu 李路路 (2002) *Lun danwei yanjiu* 論單位研究 [Discuss the studies of *danwei*] *Shehuixue yanjiu di wu qi* 社會學研究: 第五期 [Sociology Research Vol. 5]: 23–32.

Li, Yinhe and Wang, Xiaobo 李銀河、王小波 (1992) *Tamen de shijie: Zhongguo nan tongxinglian qunluo toushi* 他們的世界: 中國男同性戀群落透視 [Their World: The Male Homosexual Community in China in Perspective], Taiyuan, China: Xhanxi People's Press.

Li, Yinhe 李銀河 (1998) *Tongxinglian yawenhua* 同性戀亞文化 [Homosexual Subculture]. Beijing: Jinri Zhongguo chubanshe.

Liang, Ding-bong 梁定邦 (1987) 'Xianggang fazhi jianjie' 香港法制簡介 [Introduction to Hong Kong's legal system], in Hong Kong People's Association (ed.) *Xianggang falu shihpa jiang* 香港法律＋八講 [Eighteen Lectures in the Laws of Hong Kong], Hong Kong: Commercial Press, pp. 1–35.

Lui Tai-lok 呂大樂 (1997) *Wugai, maidan!: yige shehui xuejia de Xianggang biji* 唔該, 埋單: 一個社會學家的香港筆記 [Check, Please!: A Sociologist's Notes on Hong Kong], Hong Kong: Xian Ren Hang Publisher.
Lui, Tai-lok 呂大樂 (2007) *Xianggang si dai ren* 香港四代人 [Hong Kong's Four Generations], Hong Kong: Stepforward Multimedia.
Maike 邁克 (1993a) *Jia xing jing* 假性經 [Fake Sexual Bible], Hong Kong: Da ben ying.
—— (1993b) *Ying yin ben* 影印本 [Photocopies], Hong Kong: Da ben ying.
—— (1994) *Nan jie* 男界 [The Male Boundary], Hong Kong: Da ben ying.
—— (2000) *Xing wenben* 性文本 [Sex Text], Hong Kong: Oxford University Press.
—— (2003) *Hu chui bu ru dan da* 互吹不如單打 [Single-minded, double-entendre], Hong Kong: Oxford University Press.
—— (2005) *Mi hun zhen* 迷魂陣 [Spellbound], Hong Kong: Oxford University Press.
Ng, Chun-hung 吳俊雄 (2001) 'Xunzhou Xianggang bentu yishi' 尋找香港本土意識 [In search of the local consciousness], in Ng Chun-hung 吳俊雄 and Cheung Chi Wai 張志偉 (eds) *Yuedu Xianggang puji wenhua, 1970–2000* 閱讀香港普及文化, 1970–2000 [Reading Hong Kong Popular Culture 1970–2000], Hong Kong: Oxford University Press, pp. 86–95.
People's Radio Hong Kong 1 (2005–2008) *Gaau mat gwai tungzi wandung* 搞乜鬼同志運動 [What the Hell Kind of Tongzhi Movement], http://prhk2004.sinacool.com/hsu/000.html.
Samshasha 小明雄 (1989) *Tongxingai wenti 30 jiang* 同性愛問題30講 [30 Questions about Homosexuality], Hong Kong: You he zhi zuo shi wu suo.
—— (1997; 1st edn 1984) *Zhongguo tongxinglian shilu* 中國同性愛史錄 [History of Homosexuality in China], Hong Kong: Rosa Winkel Press.
Shae, Wan-chor 佘雲楚 and Ho, Kwok-leung 何國良 (2001) Xianggong jiating ji jiating yanjiu hequhecong: cong chuan tong, jing xian dai dao hou xian dai? 香港家庭及家庭研究何去何從: 從傳統, 經現代, 到後現代? ['W(h)ither Hong Kong families and family studies: from the traditional via the modern to the postmodern?'], *Hong Kong Journal of Sociology*, 2: 85–122.
The Hong Kong Christian Institute 基督徒學會, Blessed Minority Christian Fellowship 基恩之家, Civil Rights for Sexual Diversities 性權會, and f'union (2006) *Kandejian de zhenxiang: Xianggang tongzhi pingquan baogao* 看得見的真相: 香港同志平權報告 [Naked Truth: Report on Equal Rights of Hong Kong Tongzhi], Hong Kong: The Hong Kong Christian Institute, Blessed Minority Christian Fellowship, Civil Rights for Sexual Diversities, and F'union.
Tong, Ge 童戈 (2005) *Zhongguoren de nannan xingxingwei: xing yu ziwo rentong zhuangtai diaocha* 中國人的男男性行為：性與自我認同狀態調查 [Male Homosexuality in China: A Survey on the State of Sexual Self-acceptance]. Beijing, China: Beijing Gender Health Education Institute.
—— (2007) *Zhongguo nannan xingjiaoyi zhuangtai diaocha* 中國男男性交易狀態調查 [An Inquiry to Commercial Sex in MSM Community in China]. Beijing, China: Beijing Gender Health Education Institute.
Women's Coalition of Hong Kong (2004) *Tamen de nüqing yinji: Xianggang hui aishang nüren de nüren koushu lishi* 她們的女情印記：香港會愛上女人的女人口述歷史 [In The Tracks of Their Love: Oral History of Women Who Could Fall in Love with Women in Hong Kong], Hong Kong: Women Coalition of HKSAR.
Yau, Ching 游靜 (2005) *Xingbie guangying: Xianggang dianying zhong de xing yu xingbie wenhua yanjiu* 性／別光影：香港光影中的性與性別文化研究 [Sexing Shadows: Genders and Sexualities in Hong Kong Cinema], Hong Kong: Hong Kong Film Critics Society.

Yip Chi-wai 葉志偉 (2003) *Turan dushen* 突然獨身 [Suddenly Single], Hong Kong: Friendmily Business.

—— (2004) *Buneng* 不能 [Almost Perfect], Hong Kong: Kubrick.

Yu Hong 余紅 and Liu Xin 劉欣 (2004) *Danwei yu daiji diwei liugong: danwei zhi zai shualuo ma?* 單位與代際地位流動：單位制在衰落嗎？ [The work unit and intergenerational mobility: Is the work unit system declining?] *Shehuixu Yanjiu* 社會學研究 [Sociological Studies] 6: 52–63.

Yung, Danny [Rong Nianceng 榮念曾] (1997b). *Xianggang˙bianyuan˙yishu* 香港˙邊緣˙藝術 [Hong Kong˙marginality˙art], in *Xianggang juiqi wenhua shiye wenjian ji* 香港九七文化視野文件 [Cultural Perspective Hong Kong 1997], complied by Hong Kong Cultural Sector Joint Conference, International Association of Theatre Critics (Hong Kong), Zuni Icosahedron, Hong Kong, pp. 29–30.

Zhang, Beichuang 張北川 (1994) *Tongxingai* 同性愛 [Homosexual Love], Jinan, China: Shangdong Province Science and Technology Press.

Dictionaries

Lin, Yutang 林語堂 (1972) *Dangdai Han Ying Cidian* 當代漢英詞典 [Chinese-English Dictionary of Modern Usage], Hong Kong: The Chinese University of Hong Kong.

Wong, S.L. [Huang Xi-ling 黃錫凌] (1980) *Yue Yin Yun Hui: Guangzhou Biaozhunyin Zhi Yanjiu* 粵音韻彙：廣州標準音之研究 [A Chinese Syllabary Pronounced According to the Dialect of Canton], Hong Kong: Chung Wa Book Co.

Websites

http://intersections.anu.edu.au
http://news.cnfol.com
www.amnesty.org
www.australianhumanitiesreview.org
www.blackwellreference.com
www.censtatd.gov.hk
www.dimsum.co.uk
www.fridae.com
www.gayhk.com
www.inmediahk.net
www.leslovestudy.com
www.marksimpson.com
www.policyaddress.gov.hk
www.sigmaresearch.org.uk
www.statistics.gov.uk
www.stats.gov.cn
www.stonewall.org.uk
www.tt1069.com
www.utopia-asia.com

Filmography

English-language sources

Beautiful Thing, dir. Hettie MacDonald, 1996.
Celluloid Closet, dir. Rob Epstein and Jeffrey Friedman, 1995.
Clapham Junction, Channel 4, 2007. [TV series]
Cut Sleeve Boys, dir. Raymond Yeung, 2006.
Gaytime TV, BBC, 1995–1999. [TV series]
Little Britain, BBC, 2003–. [TV series]
M. Butterfly, dir. David Cronenberg, 1993.
Midnight Cowboy, dir. John Schlesinger, 1969.
My Beautiful Laundrette, dir. Stephen Frears, 1986.
Out on Tuesday, Channel 4, 1989–1990. [TV series]
Paris is Burning, dir. Jennie Livingston, 1990.
Queer as Folk, Channel 4, 1999–2000. [TV series]
Queer Eye for the Straight Guy, Bravo Cable Television Network, 2003–2007.
Victim, dir. Basil Dearden, 1961.
Yang ± Yin: Gender in Chinese Cinema, dir. Stanley Kwan, 1996.
Yellow Fever, dir. Raymond Yeung, 1998.

Chinese-language sources

A House is Not a Home (家變), TVB, 1977. [TV series]
A Queer Story (基佬四十 40), dir. Shu Kei (舒琪), 1997.
Boy's? (假男假女), dir. Hau Wing-choi (侯永財), 1996.
Crazy (四級殺人狂2 瘋男), dir. Hau Wing-choi (侯永財), 1999.
Farewell My Concubine (霸王別姬), dir. Chen Kaige (陳凱歌), 1993.
Full Moon in New York (人在紐約), dir. Stanley Kwan (關錦鵬), 1989.
Gay Lover (同志・戀人) [Hong Kong Connection (鏗鏘集) RTHK], dir. Li Junping, 9 July, 2006. [TV series]
Happy Together (春光乍洩), dir. Wong Kar-wai (王家衛), 1997.
He's a Woman, She's a Man (金枝玉葉), dir. Peter Chan (陳可辛), 1994.
Intimate Confessions of a Chinese Courtesan (愛奴), dir. Chor Yuen (楚原), 1972.
Intimates (自梳), dir. Cheung Chi-leung (張之亮), 1997.
Lavender (薰衣草), dir. Yip Kam-hung (葉錦鴻), 2000.
Let's Love Hong Kong (好郁), dir. Yau Ching (游靜), 2005.
Oh! My Three Guys (三個相愛的少年), dir. Derek Chiu (趙崇基), 1994.
Peony Pavilion (遊園驚夢), dir. Yonfan (楊凡), 2001.

Portland Street Blues (古惑仔情義篇之洪興十三妹), dir. Raymond Yip (葉偉文), 1998.
Queer China (誌同志), dir. Cui Zi'en (崔子恩), 2009.
Sex and Zen II (玉蒲團二之玉女心經), dir. Chin Man-kei (錢文琦), 1996.
Sex for Sale (面具), dir. Chang Tseng-chai (張曾澤), 1972.
Songs of the Goddess (似是故人來), dir. Ellen Pau (鮑藹倫), 1993. [Video]
Swordsman II (笑傲江湖之東方不敗), dir. Ching Siu-tung (程小東), 1992.
The Accident (心猿意馬), dir. Julian Lee Chi-chiu (李志超), 1999.
The Killer (喋血雙雄), dir. John Woo (吳宇森), 1989.
The Night Corridor (妖夜迴廊), dir. Julian Lee Chi-chiu (李志超), 2003.
Who's the Woman, Who's the Man? (金枝玉葉 2), dir. Peter Chan (陳可辛), 1996.

Theatre plays [Chinese-language sources]

Best Memories in My Life (馴情記), dir. Wong Chi-lung (黃智龍) and Leung Cho-yiu (梁祖堯), 2003.
How to Love a Man Who Doesn't Love Me (教我如何愛四個不愛我的男人), dir. Edward Lam (林奕華), 1989.
Mr. Snow White and Mr. Cinderella (白雪先生灰先生), dir. Wong Chi-lung (黃智龍) and Leung Cho-yiu (梁祖堯), 2008.
Once a Princess, Always a Princess (男裝帝女花), dir. Edward Lam (林奕華), 1995.
Queer Show (攣到爆), dir. Wong Chi Lung (黃智龍) and Leung Cho Yiu (梁祖堯), 2004, 2006, 2008.
Scenes from Men's Changing Room (男更衣室的四種風景), dir. Edward Lam (林奕華), 1991.
Water Margins (水滸傳), dir. Edward Lam (林奕華), 2006.

Subject index

Page numbers in *italics* indicate illustrations

Author index

Interviewees